PANDORA AND OCCAM

Advances in Semiotics

Thomas A. Sebeok, General Editor

PANDORA AND OCCAM

On the Limits of Language
and Literature

HORST RUTHROF

INDIANA UNIVERSITY PRESS

Bloomington and Indianapolis

The paper used in this publication meets the minimum requirements of American
National Standard for Information Sciences—Permanence of Paper for Printed
Library Materials, ANSI Z39.48-1984.
⊗™

Manufactured in the United States of America

Library of Congress Cataloging-in-Publication Data

Ruthrof, Horst.
    Pandora and Occam : on the limits of language and literature /
Horst Ruthrof.
        p.   cm. — (Advances in semiotics)
    Includes bibliographical references and index.
    ISBN 0-253-34995-8 (cloth : alk. paper)
    1. Semiotics and literature.   2. Criticism.   3. Discourse
analysis, Literary.   I. Title.   II. Series.
PN98.S46R88   1992
801′.4—dc20   91-26539

1 2 3 4 5   96 95 94 93 92

For Kai and Katinka

... there is no such thing as a language, not if language is anything like many philosophers and linguists have supposed.

Donald Davidson,
"A Nice Derangement of Epitaphs"

CONTENTS

PREFACE

Pandora and Occam presents a directional theory of meaning according to which meaning is regarded as a relation of linkage between different sign systems. Meaning, it is proposed, occurs when one sign system activates one or more other forms of signification. This is argued not analytically but by way of a mixture of discursive forms to allow for an appropriate description of discourses ranging from the literary to the digital. I will not enter the debate about *where* meanings are located, except to say that they are neither 'objects in the world' nor purely mental states (as Hilary Putnam puts it, "meanings ain't in the head"); meanings are seen as tied to *instantiations* or semiosis *in actu*. Meaning is argued to operate pragmatically within the constraints of two axes—meaning as directional process and meaning as negotiation. The former refers to the material coding of signification, for instance, as in linguistic expressions; the latter draws our attention to the ways in which a semiotic community typically activates signifiers. This view will be elaborated in chapter 1.

The position advocated here no doubt creates many more problems than it eliminates. But I believe that the shift from considering meanings as entities toward describing meaning as process is unavoidable if we wish to describe what is actually going on in communication by means of language. This book looks at several of the consequences of this perspective, such as: the collapse of language into discourse and of semantics into semiotics; the schematic nature of linguistic expressions; the underdetermination as well as indeterminacy of propositions and speech acts; the reincorporation of reference into meaning, whereby reference is viewed in a textualist manner; the restriction of the validity of meaning as sense to a small number of discursive operations; the pragmatic-political rather than logical termination of the process of signification; and the constitution of reality as the corroboration of one sign system by at least one other.

Above all, I argue that language as a self-contained set of operations does not exist, and that theories which stipulate it as such are construing possible analytical worlds but are literally out of touch with the social semiotic of which language is an intricate part. Recent moves in analytical philosophy suggest that the problem is being recognized by casting the net of semantic inquiry wider and wider to include belief systems and desire (Donald Davidson) and intentionality and background (John R. Searle) without, however, being prepared to abandon the notion of meaning as strict sense, which I believe is at the hub of this misorientation.

It is difficult to try to claim the fundamental heterogeneity of discursive strategies which make up the social while at the same time attempt to anonymize and so idealize the important relationships between specific discourses. The proposal of a ladder of discourses in chapter 8, for example, is intended above all as a heuristic device for presenting an argument rather than a mirroring of discursive reality. Yet to concede that argument relies on idealization does not imply that the kind of idealization present in the definition of meaning as minimal sense can act as an appropriate umbrella for all discursive practices.

In a broad sense, *Pandora and Occam* belongs to the critique of assumed stability in signification initiated by Kurt Gödel and renewed in a very different vein by Jacques Derrida. Where the book differs is that it offers a discussion of specific *opacities* in the production of meaning without either arguing the case in mathematical fashion, as does Gödel, or creating a new philosophical rhetoric, as does Derrida. The book is sympathetic also to the kind of argument presented by Nelson Goodman in *Ways of Worldmaking*[1] and the more recent *Fictional Worlds* by Thomas G. Pavel,[2] except that the latter favors the ontic, propositional, or representational side of fictions, where I would grant equal emphasis to the epistemic, modal, or deictic aspects of sign systems. *Pandora and Occam* continues the shift from the abstraction of linguistic norms toward verbal utterance as social event instigated by V. N. Voloshinov in *Marxism and the Philosophy of Language*, without the Marxist commitment and, more importantly, with an insistence on the nonverbal background of all linguistic transactions.[3]

I have taught in the English and Comparative Literature Program at Murdoch University since its inception in 1974. It is here that most of the ideas in this book have been generated through lively exchanges with colleagues and students. I wish to express my appreciation to all of them, in particular to John Frow, with whom I was able to lay down the foundations of a theoretically oriented Literature Program, which is now flourishing.

Special thanks goes to John de Reuck for his meticulous critical reading and discussion of the draft manuscript. Readings by Veronica Brady and John Frow are likewise gratefully acknowledged. I also thank Cynthia Baker and Diana Clegg for helping to feed the book into the word processor and Dorle Ruthrof for putting ideas down that were no good as well as putting up with the inconvenience of a husband who spent much of his time attending to a monitor instead of the family. Finally, my thanks to Murdoch University for granting me research leave in 1989 without which this book would not have been possible.

Portions of chapters in this study have appeared elsewhere. An earlier, short version of chapter 3 was published in *Not the Whole Story*, edited by Ian Reid and Sneja Gunew (Sydney: Local Consumption, 1984), pp. 117–24; parts of chapter 5 appeared as "From Frege to Derrida: The Destabilization of Meaning" in the *Australian Journal of Cultural Studies* 4 (1986), 77–92; a brief section of chapter 7 forms part of "Critical Manoeuvres: Three Phases in Australian Literature" in *Kunstgriffe: Auskünfte zur Reichweite von Literaturtheorie und Literaturkritik, Festschrift für Herbert Mainusch*, edited by Ulrich Horstmann and Wolfgang Zach (Frankfurt: Peter Lang, 1989), pp. 365–77; and parts of chapter 8 can be found in "Literature and the Ladder of Discourse" in *Analecta Husserliana* 29 (1985), 413–31. I am grateful to the editors for permission to include the published material in this book.

Pandora and Occam: Two Stories

Pandora

At the command of Zeus and with the assistance of Haephaistos and Aphrodite, Prometheus "makes an evil thing for mankind" for having relinquished fire to the mortals. He molds earth into the likeness of a "modest young girl," endows her with a voice and names her Pandora. Thus equipped with captivating and dangerous gifts she is taken down to the world. In spite of warnings from his brother Prometheus, the foolish Epimetheus offers shelter to the bewitching stranger. But no sooner is she made welcome than she opens one of her jars, releasing every evil and plague which now infests the world. Only hope is left inside as Pandora replaces the lid. So much for the official version.

But few readers are taken in by this tale. For one thing, Pandora's name tells a very different story, one of generosity and "all-gifts" (*pan dora*). Her name also tells of the violations the goddess has suffered at Hesiod's pen. Pandora, the all-giver, has been diminished to a merely all-gifted; the material reality of the earth's fertility aestheticized into a decoy of "sheer delusion" (*Theogony*); her life-bringing presents (*dora*) turned into deadly poisons (*toxa*) and de-moralized to strike us as evil.

Nor is Pandora alone in this narrative of demotion. There are Peruvian, Ca-nadian-Indian and Polynesian goddesses who share her fate. The biblical Eve or Havvah, meaning life, is her best known cousin. Both endure the ignominy of being dispatched to mate with simple-minded mortals (Epimetheus and Adam). Pandora and Eve mark the transition from earth worship to the abstrac-tion of the divine, from the celebration of material fertility to the picturesque follies of Greek deities and the monotheistic wrath of an imageless Jehovah—from Elysian bliss to the plight of the present.

Not just her name, but a number of sources predating Hesiod also nudge us into telling her tale in this way. Ancient vases depict her as a goddess emerging from the earth as farmers hoe the ground; there are texts which tell of Zeus's mating with Pandora, who gives birth to Graikos and Hellen. Pandora, mother of Greek culture, appears as a *chthonic* deity, a goddess from the underworld, or is identified with Ge or Demeter, goddess of fertility and protector of women. Aeschylus transforms her into Gaia or Themis, to present her once more as mother of the earth as well as guardian of justice.

During the Renaissance Pandora suffered her most recent wrong when Eras-mus Rotterdamus, confusing *pithos* with *pyxis*, reduced her jar to a box. In this pathetic state, carrying a box, we find Pandora today in the phrase of standard

English. Perhaps it is time to restore Pandora to her full glory as mother goddess of the fertile earth, creator of society and the rich materiality of its culture: the provider of *all* gifts, the goddess of ecology.

Occam

Somehow we expect William of Ockham's tale to be more laconic. And so it is, except that his writings have had an enormous influence on modern thought. Born sometime in the late thirteenth century, William grew up to become a Franciscan minor. Though he studied for his magisterium he never made it to *magister regens*. In 1324 while teaching at Oxford as a *venerabilis inceptor* (a junior lecturer), he was dobbed in by his Chancellor, John Lutterell, and cited to appear before a papal inquiry at Avignon. Occam was accused of heresy on account of his commentary in the *Sentences*, from which 51 propositions had been taken to be scrutinized. In Avignon brother Wilhelm was persuaded by the Franciscan General Michael de Cesena to contribute to a debate on evangelical poverty. Needless to say, the real dispute turned out to be about ecclesiastical versus secular power. Unhappily, William felt that he had a scholarly reputation to protect and so argued his case too well; as a result he was excommunicated in June 1328. Fearing for his life, he followed his protector Ludwig of Bavaria to Munich where he continued his work until he was struck down by the Black Death in 1349.

Curiously, the things for which Occam has become famous, a philosophical razor and the principle of logical economy, are apocryphal. The razor, "*le rasoir des nominaux*" (Condillac), is a fairly recent attribution, while the rule that "entities are not to be multiplied beyond necessity" goes back to one Odo Rigaldus a century earlier: "*frustra fit per plura quod potest fieri per unum.*"

But even if Occam did not invent the "*entia non sunt multiplicanda praeter necessitate,*" he made use of the idea whenever he found an opportunity. And he did so quite often:

Pluritas non est ponenda sine necessitate (Sent., prol., q. 1; d. 1; q. 3)

...frustra fit per plura quod potest fieri per pauciora. (*Summa Logicae* I, 12)

...sufficient singularia, et ita tales res universales omnio frustra ponuntur. (*Sent.,* d. 2, q. 4)

Nihil debet poni sine ratione assignata nisi sit per se notum vel per experientiam scitum vel per auctoritatem Scripturae Sacrae probatum. (*Sent.,* d. 30, q. 1)

Much later Immanuel Kant generalized the logical precept to entail an "*inneres Gesetz der Natur*" (1781); Ernst Mach applied it to his *Denkökonomie* to mean "*möglichst vollständig die Tatsachen mit dem geringsten Gedankenaufwand darzustellen*" (1910); and Bertrand Russell, in "Logical Atomism" (1924), rephrased the principle to read "whenever possible, substitute constructions of known entities for inferences to unknown entities."

Above all, Occam is remembered for having launched the *via moderna*, a protoempiricism whose nominalist rejection of medieval realism paved the way for the scientific empiricism of the seventeenth century. His strict separation of matters of faith from those of logic can be rightly said to anticipate Hume and Kant. But Occam's most eminent contribution remains a radical evidential empiricism which found its way into the logical analysis of language. This is what Karl-Otto Apel is referring to when he says that empiricist language philosophy starts with Occam, and for this reason Wittgenstein wrote: *"Wird ein Zeichen nicht gebraucht, so ist es bedeutungslos. Das ist der Sinn der Devise Ockham's"* (*Tractatus*, 3.328).

PANDORA AND OCCAM

INTRODUCTION

I. Starting in Reverse

> To deconstruct the opposition is above all, at
> a particular moment, to reverse the hierarchy.
>
> Jacques Derrida, *Positions*

Pandora and Occam are invoked to act as metaphoric cornerstones in an argument about language as discourse. If this strategy signals a structural homogeneity it needs to be emphasized that throughout this study there will be a bias toward the heterogeneity of discursive operations and their semantic-semiotic background. In this sense Pandora stands for culturally and socially saturated speech, the language of everyday life, the discourse of humor as well as the paroles of the political text. "Pandoric" reading, likewise, characterizes the kind of reading which activates rich rather than minimal meanings, the richest of which I shall argue is a certain kind of literary reading.

William of Occam (Ockham), too, is known for something he is unlikely to have supplied himself: a philosophical razor. But he is rightly associated with the principle of parsimony and parsimonious discourse. Occam, then, lends himself conveniently to the characterization of language in its reduced form, a discourse from which the penumbra of meaning has been excised to reveal a strictly circumscribed sense. "Parsimonious" reading, then, is understood as an act of meaning making in which language expressions are treated as ruled by definitions proper rather than as directional schemata to be filled with the cultural saturations shared by a semiotic community. Such forms of reading, I shall argue, are appropriate for certain kinds of discourse, but illegitimately reductive if applied to natural language and in particular, the literary text.

Occam's legacy was to yield impressive results in the schools of the positivist Vienna circle and British atomistic language philosophy. Their parsimonious shrinking of the range of issues to be handled philosophically and the ensuing curtailment of language lead to an extraordinary degree of accuracy within strictly defined laboratory conditions. However, when the methods and goals of this enterprise began to spill over into the study of general discourse, as was bound to happen, the narrowness of the focus and the limitations of the method became apparent.

In retrospect, the startling lucidity of a good many works by as diverse a group of philosophers as the early Russell, Moritz Schlick, Ryle, or even Strawson (whatever their philosophical differences) now also radiates an astonishing tenor of arrogance. As the blind spots and errors of this philosophical period of roughly the first three quarters of the twentieth century became targets in the crossfire between the movement's heirs and scholars dedicated to other strands of inquiry, the immodesty of the style of positivist theorizing began to look odd. Now the assumed superiority of the language philosophy not only of logical positivism but analytical philosophy in general, including the work of 'ordinary language philosophers,' can be viewed as part of the process of an empire's decline, a process in which philosophy reveals itself as one of the last dominant codes still asserting a rule which the quicker thinking politicians had already abandoned as an anachronism.

But there are other, and from the viewpoint of the Humanities more deplorable, consequences of this kind of analytical philosophizing. Never in the history of philosophy and literature have these two hermeneutic disciplines been as far apart and indeed opposed to one another as during the first six decades of this century. To put the blame at the doorstep of philosophy alone is of course unfair, and there is ample material to testify to the hostility of literary critics toward matters philosophical. Nonetheless, philosophers have always been in a privileged position to rationalize their field of inquiry and could have staked out their domain in such a way as to be able to discuss broad definitions of meaning, definitions which are more akin to what goes on in actual language use and so also have a relation to the most complex forms of signification, the meanings generated in literary readings. Unfortunately, leading philosophers of language failed to do so. Their interest in such things as truth and falsity could at best inspire theories of strict literality, from the perspective of which metaphoric and other complex discursive strategies must appear deviant. On the other hand, whatever one may think of the style of Heidegger's theorizing, it is impossible to remove from it the discussion of Trakl's and Hölderlin's poetry or Tolstoy's narrative, "The Death of Ivan Ilych," without falsification. Nor can it be regarded as a mere coincidence that the work of Jacques Derrida, straddling as it does philosophical and literary concerns, has had such a powerful impact on the Humanities.

In the absence of a similar interpenetration of hermeneutic thought in England and the United States, both disciplines have been hampered. Though Ludwig Wittgenstein, John L. Austin, and Nelson Goodman have tried to find ways out of the impasse, there is no powerful successor to the spirit of the later Wittgenstein; nor does the theory of speech acts now look as liberating as it promised at its inception. Worse could be said for literary studies. Methodologically tenuous, except for bits and pieces of philological and historiographic techniques and only a smattering of current linguistics and other theories, English literature departments appeared doomed to operate within the boundaries of critical commonplaces on literary content and a stuffy, self-congratulatory rhetoric.

But since the mid-sixties, both philosophy and literary studies around the globe have been rocked by a series of detonations: the controversies in linguistics, by generative grammar and deep structure analysis, the revival of Saussurean linguistics, Halliday's approach to language as a social semiotic, the semiological explosion in the broader sense, the arrival of Marxist literary theory in the United Kingdom and the States, the revival of Hegel, the rediscovery of Bakhtin, the rewriting of Freudian analysis by Lacan, the emergence of Feminist theories, the dissemination of Existentialist thought and phenomenological description, and the transformation of Heidegger's *Destruktion* into deconstruction by Derrida. The debate is certainly on, but it can be sustained only if philosophy turns hermeneutic in the full sense of the term and if literary study takes theorizing seriously as one of its indispensable tools. There are promising signs in both camps.

On the analytical side, the work of Donald Davidson can be construed as one of the most serious attempts at negotiating between truth conditional semantics and a Heideggerian horizon of truth as hermeneutic unconcealment. If the writings of Richard Rorty are seen from his own camp as more than simply those of a philosophical turncoat, a more radical shift toward critical-speculative and deconstructive thought has already been achieved. From the discipline of literary studies such respectable inroads into philosophical inquiry as *The Contest of Faculties: Philosophy and Theory after Deconstruction* by Christopher Norris, or Reed Way Dasenbrock's *Redrawing the Lines: Analytic Philosophy, Deconstruction, and Literary Theory* suggest indeed that the dialogue between the two broad paradigms is beginning to gather momentum.[1]

Analytical definitions of meaning take as their starting point such minimal languages as formal logic, mathematics and formal semantics. The assumption here is that minimal discourse contains the necessary and sufficient conditions of all language and that natural languages therefore operate principally like formalized systems. What is believed then to be required for their description is the separation of those fundamental conditions from the "warped slip of wilderness" of language, those murky and unnecessary features which are part of social discourse. This is a forceful procedure capable of yielding grammars of elegant homogeneity. And yet it should not come as a surprise that we can discover the existence of formal relations in natural languages for the very reason that the former have been derived from the latter. Logico-mathematical discourse and other purely formal speech systems are after all upstarts in the society of sign systems. On the other hand, one must not expect this procedure to yield a full account of what goes on in the discourse of everyday life.

To complement analytical approaches to the description of meaning in socially saturated and literary discourse I am proposing a procedure 'in reverse.' Instead of building the inquiry up from the clarity of formal logic and trying by degrees to account for the increasing murkiness of socially more and more highly saturated speech forms, the present strategy takes as its starting point what I regard as the richest discourse of all, the literary text and concomitant forms of reading.

The broad assumption is that I should be able to account for a significant number of salient features of complex languages if I describe the habitual acts of conventional performance.

But there is also an assumption of an epistemological kind, namely that language is not graspable as an empirical object but is what it is only by virtue of the acts which we must perform when we *do* it. Language in this view is wholly dependent on *instantiations*, i. e., particular acts of uttering, a position which favors the specificity of *parole* over *langue* as abstractable system. But I am not arguing the wholesale dismissal of *langue* as much as the foregrounding of instantiation as a dynamic system at a lower level. *Langues* can always be abstracted from discursive events, but we need to determine whether such formalizations are useful or misleading in a specific theory. Instantiations on this view are both *paroles* and a kind of grammar at a low level of abstraction. Instantiation is seen as a necessary part of all discourses, from logico-mathematical language to the socially fully saturated speech of everyday life. And even if it is not possible to alter the propositional sense of mathematical expressions by a variant intonation, they too have to be performed to constitute mathematics as a sign system. Less controversially, in everyday speech the prosodic contour which we impose on words and expressions can modify dramatically what is 'meant.' In this view, language does not exist outside instantiations nor independently of social semiosis at large. Therefore I have on the whole collapsed the concepts of 'language' and 'speech' into discourse.

Another obstacle to regarding the meanings of words, expressions, and sentences as stable entities is the observation that expressions do not only have to be instantiated, but that they can be instantiated only within certain conventions. No matter whether we read a literary text in a literary manner or as if it were a pragmatic text, such as an instruction sheet, in either case we have consciously, unconsciously, or nonconsciously 'opted' for a certain kind of reading convention. Such conventions or, more generally, frames or horizons, govern all utterances from formal logic to the speech of commerce and fiction. To violate these conventions in earnest, etiolatorily or in error, is to generate startling shifts in the production of meaning.

To demonstrate my claim of the instability of meaning as semiotic linking process I want to introduce three kinds of vagueness which any theory of meaning must address and account for: *modal opacity, propositional opacity*, and *semiotic opacity*.

These, as I shall argue, render deficient all descriptions of meaning which rest on what one might call a 'semantic foundationalism;' that is to say, descriptions which assume that there is something like a semantic ground level or core meaning which generates literality and in relation to which other meanings are derivative or deviant.[2]

Part of my argument will be to show that instead of regarding propositions as autotelic we can account for meaning processes by recognizing the dependency of propositional content on ways of uttering. Such a description leads us to notice a fundamental vagueness in linguistic communication, which I shall call *modal opacity*. But the modification of word or sentence meanings by the utterance situation and their framing conventions are not the only reasons why we should be skeptical of suggestions that language is stable. There is yet another fundamental feature of natural languages which renders any stability of propositional sense highly implausible. This is the fact that dictionary definitions of words are not actually definitions in any strict sense at all, but on the contrary are merely strings of signifiers of random length. They will therefore be regarded throughout this study as directional schemata which merely guide but never entirely control the processes of meaning. Words and expressions, then, act as recipes for linking linguistic operations with those of non-verbal systems. As a result of the schematic nature of linguistic signifiers, there arises in all natural languages of necessity a second fundamental fuzziness which I shall call *propositional opacity*.

Modal opacity, the instability of meaning arising from necessary inferences about an utterance situation, and propositional opacity undermine attempts at getting at the heart of natural language by providing it with an analytical lucidity which is merely one of its formalizable possibilities but not its 'essence.' Together with *semiotic opacity*, a vagueness resulting from the relative incommensurability of different sign systems (another claim to be substantiated later), they could be called the 'uncertainty principle' of discourse. Examples commonly adduced to shore up the notion of meaning as strict sense and thus the possibility of full meaning exchange deny this principle at a cost. 'The cat on the mat' or 'Close the window' are laboratory examples which conceal a significant portion of what characterizes natural languages. To make the thesis of the reliability of linguistic meaning stick one would have to show that the same lucidity pertains to discursive formations containing words such as "honor" or "trust" or "ratbag" or "freedom." Yet, as I shall show in chapter 1, even as apparently simple a word as 'open' must be associated with very different meaning processes in different discursive formations. The literal meaning of 'open' which John R. Searle, for example, argues for dissolves into very different semioses.

Perhaps it is impossible in the final analysis to come to grips with the shadowy sides of linguistic communication, for to make sense of discourse in the face of modal and propositional intransigence means not only to disambiguate syntactic structures but also to negotiate semantics, a terrain which as I shall maintain cannot be mapped satisfactorily by linguistics on its own. Engaging in meanings I shall say is to relate language to other sign systems, i.e., to saturate its underdetermined schemata by means of the non-verbal semioses of a community.

But here we face another impasse: the relative incommensurabilty of different sign systems. This third impediment I have called *semiotic opacity*. Perhaps it is the combined difficulties which accrue from these three opacities—modal, propositional, and semiotic—which make it attractive for semantics to restrict itself to the security of linguistic meaning. Yet such a focus creates its own difficulties. For if it is true that, as Donald Davidson says, "the point of the concept of linguistic meaning is to explain what can be done with words," then a narrow view of meaning as sense is a self-defeating procedure.[3] As I shall try to show, language cannot mean by itself but can do so only semiotically, i.e., in relation to and through corroboration by non-verbal systems. Hence, from the perspective chosen here there is no such thing as "linguistic meaning." However, the claim of semiotic 'corroboration' must seem paradoxical when we speak at the same time of the 'relative incommensurability' of sign systems. All I want to say about this at this point is that we cannot assume any congruence between, for example, tactile and linguistic grasp, and yet the two kinds of signification are able to 'inform' us about the 'same' terrain.

In spite of all these difficulties I do believe that inroads can be made into this thicket by describing what we habitually and typically do when we engage in language acts and especially in acts of reading. I shall be asking not only "how does meaning arise from the reader's encounter with just these words on the page?" as does J. Hillis Miller in *Fiction and Repetition*, but also the question of "what degree of stability is attached to the meanings so produced?"[4] We can either opt for an artificial but unwarranted stability by embracing formal explanations or address a broad spectrum of not so stable semantic-semiotic processes by including extra-linguistic phenomena. As Julia Kristeva puts it in "The System and the Speaking Subject,"

> The theory of meaning now stands at a cross-road: either it will remain an attempt at formalizing meaning-systems by increasing sophistication of the logico-mathematical tools which enable it to formulate models on the basis of a conception (already rather dated) of meaning as an act of a transcendental ego, cut off from its body, its unconscious, and also its history; or else it will attune itself to the theory of the speaking subject as a divided subject (conscious/unconscious) and go on to attempt to specify the types of operations characteristic of the two sides of this split; thereby exposing them to those forces extraneous to the logic of the systematic; exposing them, that is to say, on the one hand to bio-physiological processes (themselves already inescapably part of signifying processes; what Freud labelled "drives", and, on the other hand, to social constraints (family structures, modes of production, etc.).[5]

The procedure proposed here is to focus on what Kristeva calls the "social constraints" of meaning by idealizing typical acts of meaning making from the habitual performance of discourse. This should lead to insights into the mechanisms of both partial understanding and misunderstandings, in short the instabilities in the production of the meanings by which we live. But is not such a procedure bound to reaffirm the very "presence" which Derrida has so persuasively attacked? What Derrida rightly denies is the certitude of the "given" and the stability of the "now" of what is "thought;" he denies the neomatic presence of Husserl's "geometry of experiences." That other presence, albeit a less secure kind, the presence of 'uttering,' its noetic counterpart, remains forever unavoidable. In this sense Derrida's own noetic or modal presence 'merely' replaces Husserl's propositional/noematic variety. Whether Derrida's own master tropes "differance," "iterability," and "arche-writing" are in the end able to escape metaphysical foundationalism and thus presence is a moot point, as I have tried to show elsewhere and as Habermas notes in *The Philosophical Discourse of Modernity*. "With the tools of a negative foundationalism," writes Habermas, "Derrida returns to the historical locale where mysticism once turned into enlightenment."[6]

As an attempt to resolve the dilemma of meaning instability and pragmatic demands, Geoffrey Hartman suggests that "what is happening" at present "is that the reader is in fact taking back some of his authority and struggling with the problems this poses." Part of the problematic, as I see it, is that the reader cannot be content alone with exploring "how books or habits of reading penetrate our lives," but must also be aware of the reasons why that penetration is so heterogeneous and affects us so differently; how it is possible, in other words, that the construction of meaning from linguistic signals is so slippery and yet so effective a mechanism.[7]

The approach to language by formal semantics tends to begin by seeing opacity as an enemy to be sought, identified, and exterminated. However, our inability to pin down the meanings of ordinary and literary discourse can be seen from quite the opposite position: as an indication of an emancipatory potential which needs to be recognized. In very different ways both Jürgen Habermas and Harold Bloom have responded to this phenomenon. Habermas sees ordinary language aiming at consensus as opposed to language directed at domination and in contrast with disambiguated structures of technical speech. Where the second form of discourse is used by its speaker to accomplish a position of power in relation to its recipient and technical language is designed *per se* to achieve and maintain control, everyday speech oriented toward understanding for Habermas holds the promise of emancipation.[8] This I think needs to be supported by way of a description of meaning which establishes the space where such a potential can be realized. Habermas's communicative competence as argued in "What is Universal Pragmatics?" does not provide a sufficient basis for his emancipatory claim.

From a very different perspective, Harold Bloom, passionately in opposition to the language of theory and far less optimistic about social reason, sees emancipation to be accomplishable only as the result of a struggling imagination: "There is always and only bias, inclination, prejudgment, swerve; only and always the verbal agon for freedom, and the agon is carried on not by truth-telling, but by words lying against time."[9] Unfortunately Bloom's account is very much a celebration of a romantic, creative individualism in which social semiosis plays a subordinate role. In this sort of worldview notions such as "freedom" cannot be coherently argued.

I do not wish to cajole the reader into accepting political recipes for sorting out specific instances, but I do want to propose a basis on which such distinctions as between "words lying against time" and those that do not can be reasonably made. My modest proposal will take the shape of a defense of socially saturated discourse and in particular of literary speech. In these, I will argue, various kinds of opacities are strongly present and require special interpretive attention;

their study therefore is likely to produce a reader attuned to the complexities of the interpenetration between statements, their inferrable modalities, and their various possible discourse frames. Hence literary reading, which I regard as the most comprehensive form of meaning construction, is being privileged as a profoundly political and, in the literal sense of the word, radical activity.

II. Toward a Realist Textualism

It remains now to describe the position I am adopting, in order to make the sort of case sketched so far. The answer may sound paradoxical: the position of a *realist textualist*. To define briefly what a realist textualist would look like we need an even briefer characterization of philosophical realism and radical textualism. First, a few perspectives on realism. For Thomas Nagel to be a realist is to believe that "the world is in a strong sense independent of our possible representations, and may well extend beyond them."[10] Likewise, Michael Devitt understands realism as the position according to which "common-sense physical entities exist independently of the mind."[11] This independence thesis of realism goes with the distinction drawn by Michael Dummett in "Realism" between a realist who holds that statements are true or false against the background of an independent reality and an anti-realist who ties truth conditions for statements to human knowledge. Dummett finds both convictions unsatisfactory because "it is unclear whether the realist's defence . . . can be made convincing" and "whether the anti-realist's position can be made coherent."[12] In Dummett's sense both the radical textualist and my realist textualist would be anti-realists, leaving the arena of realism to hard-headed empiricists.

This sort of realism is termed "metaphysical realism" by Hilary Putnam because it stipulates a "fixed totality of mind-independent objects" of which we could have "exactly one true and complete description . . . some sort of correspondence relation between words or thought-signs and external things and sets of things."[13] As Jeff Malpas has pointed out, the metaphysical realism that Putnam sketches entails three separate theses: an independence thesis (mental acts and world are independent of one another); a uniqueness thesis (there is only one true account of the world); and a truth by correspondence thesis (the relation between language and world).[14]

If ideology and discursive formations did not play such a fundamental role in Michel Pêcheux's *Language, Semantics, and Ideology*, one might be tempted to read what he says of thought and the real as a realist position: "The real exists necessarily independently of thought and outside it, but thought necessarily depends on the real, i.e., it does not exist outside the real." But we need to construe Pêcheux's "real" as the real of history and social practice, that is, as a semiotic textualist real rather than a positivist real.[15] Pêcheux's position highlights the sort of difficulties we encounter in this debate.

The critique of correspondence theories of truth (where language matches the world) has a long history. According to Frege, to support it "we should have to inquire whether it is true that an idea and a reality, say, correspond in a specified respect. And then we should be confronted by a question of the same kind and the game could begin again."[16] The circularity to which Frege points here affects not only the notion of realism but that of truth itself. Following Frege, for whom "the word 'true' is *sui generis* and indefinable," Donald Davidson regards it as "primitive."[17] It underlies the "semantic realism" of the latter according to which "the applicability of the truth predicate to a sentence is determined by extra-linguistic reality."[18]

Another variant of realism is "internal realism," characterized by Hilary Putnam as the view that "signs do not correspond to objects, independently of how those signs are employed and by whom." Accordingly "*we* cut up the world into objects when we introduce one or other scheme of description."[19] This is the point where correspondence turns into coherence. Signs correspond to objects, both being part of one and the same scheme. One could therefore argue that realism has now been transformed into anti-realism, a position we could also call a form of textualism.

The special case of the romantic realist is argued by David Novitz in *Knowledge, Fiction and Imagination* which, he says, allows him to avoid the trap of an entirely significatory reality and yet to make a case for the fundamental role of imaginary processes in cognition and learning. I believe that he succeeds in persuading the reader on the role of the imagination, but does so by becoming a reluctant textualist himself. For the route by which he tries to avoid textualism already entails its tenets: he separates perception and other "non-mediated" forms of cognition from sign systems. But what his argument fails to address is that even though we do not *design* such 'primary' experiences we nevertheless *read* them. Reading requires the construing of a sign system, and without our readings perceptions could not signify: we would not be aware of them as significatory structures.[20]

There is a realist position, however, which avoids textualism, except that there is no way of showing whether the position is true or false. This is the "anthropic thesis" formulated by physicists. In its most condensed form it states that if the universe were radically different from what it is we would not be here to observe it.[21] In this view our descriptions of the world are a function of brute reality, which is the obverse of a radical textualism in which the world is entirely a function of human signification. One such radical textualist is Friedrich Nietzsche.

Notwithstanding post-structuralism, Friedrich Nietzsche is yet to be surpassed in textualist rigor. Our descriptions of nature and its laws are available to us only "as sums of relations" whereby "relations refer only to one another and are absolutely incomprehensible to us in their essence." The regularity which we so admire in the so-called laws of nature is not part of nature at all but of the "mathematical rigour and the inviolability of the conceptions of time and space. These however," says Nietzsche, "we produce within ourselves and throw them forth with the necessity with which the spider spins." To argue otherwise is to pretend that we have access to "the standard of right perception...a standard which does not exist."[22]

If no right standard exists, the particular language with which we are engaged at a specific cultural moment nevertheless admits alternatives. Though all "language contains a hidden philosophical mythology," other "grammars" direct us to construe a different world.[23] As Nietzsche writes in "Of the Prejudices of Philosophers" (1886), "Philosophers within the domain of the Ural-Altaic languages (in which the concept of the subject is least developed) will in all probability look 'into the world' differently."[24] Moreover, Nietzsche, contrary to popular belief, does not celebrate our textualist dependence on the linguistic.

> Language and the prejudices upon which language is based very often act as obstacles in our paths when we proceed to explore inner phenomena and impulses.... Wrath, hatred, love, pity, desire, recognition, joy, pain: all these are names indicating extreme conditions; the milder and middle stages, and even more particularly the ever active lower stages, escape our attention, and yet it is they which weave the warp and woof of our character and destiny.[25]

A more recent textualist is Martin Heidegger who develops a critique of science and its experimental methods on the basis of our deployment of specific discursive practices: "Because physics, already as pure theory, requests nature to manifest itself in terms of predictable forces, it sets up experiments precisely for the sole purpose of asking whether and how nature follows the scheme preconceived by science."[26]

In Heidegger this attitude is a metaphysics gone wrong rather than the only way of responding to Being. Less radical a textualist than Nietzsche, Heidegger allows for different significatory worlds or beings as responses to the "call" of Being. Rephrasing Heidegger, we could say that the ontic-ontological difference is the unbridgeable gap between sign systems and their directional goal. We shall discuss later the kind of textualism offered by Jacques Derrida and his attempt to transcend Heidegger's position via *differance*. Whether Derrida's textualist stance is as radical as Nietzsche's or more akin to Heidegger's is a moot point. The clarification of this question hinges on the status we are prepared to grant his statement that there is nothing outside the text.[27] Put differently, textualist theories can be distinguished by the way they address the question of constraints. This, as we shall see much later, is of crucial importance to our assessment of the work of Derrida.

Whatever its special way of presenting the world, any such textualist theory commits what David Novitz has called the "occlusive fallacy," which assumes

> that our experience of X, where X is the world and its objects, can be explained in terms of a favoured entity or process Y. From this it is inferred that we *really* experience only Y, and that X is no more than an inference from, or a construction out of, Y. Ys are believed to form a 'veil,' a 'barrier,' between experiencing subjects

and the Xs that were previously considered to be the *bona fide* objects of their experience; and sometimes the Ys even come to be regarded as the ultimate constituents of reality.[28]

I suggest that a *realist textualism* escapes this fallacy by first insisting, in opposition to Novitz, that what is called "experience" is in need of theorization, which reveals that experience can be known only once it is a differentiated structure of signs. Only when it is describable in terms of boundaries, contrasts, parallels, asymmetries, texture, and hence as a collection of individuated items is it available as an explanatory tool. To this extent, there is no escape from texts. Second, a realist textualist does not deny either the possibility of a nou-menal something or what Jean-François Lyotard calls an "extra-linguistic per-manence," toward which our significations point, while insisting that we cannot know either the nature or the extent of the constraint such a permanence has on our conceptions. Physicists in Niels Bohr's tradition support a realist tex-tualism by adhering to the view that we cannot separate neatly our observations from our measuring, i.e., significatory, equipment. At the same time, to *deny* a nonsignificatory permanence would be to commit a kind of atheistic leap of faith which assumes a position outside both the noumenal and the world of conceptualized appearances. And yet to *affirm* such a permanence would be committing the "ontological fallacy," which applies to all statements asserting brute reality: nothing can be said about it that does not already assume its existence.[29]

What remains valid of realism in a realist textualism is the non-denial of non-textual constraints which our texts respect willy-nilly: that death surely will be the result if I restrict my diet to mercury, a brute fact which cannot be altered by any sign system. But even this constraint is available to us only in the form of textualization. What remains of a coherence thesis is that social semiosis in general is always cohesive, even where it is in competition with other such systems. The cohesiveness of a social semiotic guarantees that individual signs are meaningful, i.e., have meaning. And yet meaning is not necessarily linked with truth. What is jettisoned from both coherence and correspondence realism is the very privileged notion of truth. In the realist textualist view advocated here truth belongs to specialized discursive practices where it fulfills specific tasks.

The kind of realist textualism suggested here goes further than what Steven Lukes defines as a "strong form of perspectivism" according to which "there can be no perspective-neutral interpretation and explanation" but without rel-ativist implications. For as Lukes sees it, "interests, background assumptions and value judgments enter not into the accounts themselves, but into their justifi-cation." Yet how would we be able to draw a clear distinction between accounts and their justification?[30] Nor does it make sense from a realist textualist per-spective to speak without qualification, as does W. Newton-Smith in "Relativism and the Possibility of Interpretation," of "the phenomenon of increasing pre-dictive power of scientific theories" which are in the process of "capturing more and more theoretical truth about the world."[31] Perhaps it would be better to say that this is true relative to the scientific frames in use at any given time.

As Nelson Goodman puts it, "we are confined to ways of describing whatever is described. Our universe, so to speak, consists of these ways rather than of a world or of worlds." Typical ways of "worldmaking" in Goodman's terms are such processes as ordering, supplementation, deletion, division, composition, deformation, or weighting. In this way we constitute our reality textually. Acceptance of multiple alternative world-versions does not, however, promote a policy of "everything goes." Apart from constraints which we can infer from our versions of the world, drift is textually controlled. In Goodman's words, "where otherwise equally well-qualified hypotheses conflict, the decision normally goes to the one with the better entrenched predicates."[32]

Lastly, a realist textualism cannot be merely linguistic; it needs to be broadly and dynamically semiotic, with languages as subordinate structures, however efficient. We need to acknowledge the roles that pictorial, kinetic, proxemic, tactile, aural, photic, electrical, chemical, thermal, and other forms of non-linguistic grasp must play in the way we shape reality. This encompasses our semiotic relations with both the animate and inanimate environment, or "exteroception."[33] Yet it is the principal manner in which non-linguistic forms of understanding interact with linguistic expressions in constituting meanings which is at issue here, rather than the pursuit of specialized behavioristic research.[34] Ultimately, such a semiotic perspective of realist textualism would also require a review of the theory of judgment, a project beyond the confines of this study. It would involve, as Goodman rightly notes, a new concept of "judgment," one which is "freed of exclusive association with statements;" it would include also "apprehension of design, and the decisions a pool-player takes in aiming his shots."[35]

Given this scope and those boundaries, the apparent paradox of a *realist textualism* becomes both attractive and useful. It better explains, I suggest, than do more formally semantic studies why meanings are meaningful and allows us to form a holistic view of a broad spectrum of discursive practices. Such a hermeneutics, as Richard Rorty views it, "sees the relations between various discourses as those of strands in a possible conversation, a conversation which presupposes no disciplinary matrix which unites the speakers, but where the hope of agreement is never lost so long as the conversation lasts."[36] Perhaps Rorty is too much a textualist and too little a realist here, for there are certain hard boundaries to which all our texts appear to respond, limits which may furnish the negative ground for that "hope of agreement." A realist textualism allows for this possibility. In any case, as Ian Hacking assures us, we cannot possibly doubt the value of a realist textualist position which has been historically confirmed by President Nixon who "chose to end his career rather than burn his tapes."[37]

Far from being an exhaustive treatment of the subject my defense of the relative vagueness of language as discourse against the background of a textualist realism unfolds as a series of perspectives on how meanings are generated by means of linguistic expressions in interaction with other signs. What links these perspectives is the thesis developed progressively in this book that the complexity and relative indeterminacy of language have their source in the inextricable way in which verbal expressions and discursive formations are woven into the network of non-verbal sign systems. This point of departure has a great many consequences, only a few of which are addressed in this book. I am content with raising questions and encouraging debate rather than offering solutions. Instead of presenting a tightly argued case aiming at a complete theory I have restricted myself to a few issues which recur throughout the theory of meaning.

Chapter 1 opposes the idea that meanings are ruled by definitions and instead offers a rudimentary theory in which sense acts as a directional schema for meaning to occur. Accordingly, different discursive formations are shown to operate with fundamentally different schemata. Such a theory also provides a new view of so-called figurative langage and especially metaphor.

Chapter 2 is one of two literary chapters which poses the question of propositional vagueness and the limits of interpretive exploration. In so doing it demonstrates typical interpretive strategies permitted in a specific discourse, strategies which however need not be confined to the literary; they are also available in the language games of everyday life.

Chapter 3 addresses an interpretive vagueness which stems from the framing conventions of a particular genre. In the artist's novel this modal opacity, as I have called it, produces a high degree of tentativeness of narrative construction. Though this genre has its own set of constraints its world remains peculiarly underdetermined, such that the kind of art and the sort of artist we are guided to construe in each of the novels chosen are characterized by a high degree of indeterminacy.

Chapter 4 challenges current readings of Husserl's work as "subjectivist" on the grounds of a confusion between his epistemological and ontological strategies. Though epistemically (as to the way in which we can know the world) he is a 'subjectivist,' ontically (as to the way he thinks the world is) Husserl, I argue, grounds all acts in the *Lebenswelt*. The main part of the chapter offers a critique of eidetically informed noematic meaning in favor of a highly noetic theory, a critique which rejects the transfer of formal meanings to the discourse of everyday life as illegitimate and suggests that Husserl's own theory of noesis can be adduced to support this view.

Chapter 5 provides a selective overview of descriptions of meaning as strict, propositional sense from Frege to Davidson, followed by Derrida's contribution to the debate. While traditional notions of meaning are shown to be too restrictive to satisfy the requirements of language in diverse discursive practices, Derrida's theory of significatory dissemination is questioned as to its absence of constraints on semantic drift.

Chapter 6 argues against the simple distinction between a phenomenal and a theoretical level of language description, between language in action and its theorization. Grammatics, though unavoidable, can operate at many different levels of formalization, at that of a highly abstract *langue* or at the level of the system of its *instantiations*. It is the latter, not the former, which reveals the inextricable relation of linguistic signs with general semiosis. This chapter concludes with a brief exploration of what I call the semiotic corroboration thesis, according to which linguistic signs receive their meanings in interaction with their non-linguistic counterparts and so constitute our reality.

Chapter 7 is a critique of Jean-François Lyotard's theory of discourse from the perspective of *Lebensformen* and non-linguistic signs. A textualism of considerable depth, Lyotard's theory is shown to rest on a strong linguistic bias which cannot be fully rescued by the introduction of quasi-phrases, a flaw which likewise mars the otherwise convincing critique of Lyotard's work by Geoffrey Bennington.

Chapter 8 sketches a number of discourses: literary, mythical, historiographic, juridical, everyday, technical, scientific, formal logical, and digital. Recent publications have foregrounded the figurative commonality in a range of discourses, thus supporting the heuristic tool of a ladder. In this chapter the emphasis is on the heterogeneity of the acts which we habitually perform as we engage in distinct signifying practices. This suggests that it is unproductive to insist on a unifying principle of explanation for all discourses and that the description of meaning must pay attention to these differences.

Chapter 9 suggests that all meaning generated from linguistic expressions is of necessity a function of hypocrisis, a substitutionary act by which readers feign subject positions not normally their own. Usually concealed, hypocrisis becomes foregrounded when our meaning endowing acts run into difficulties. This requires that we look anew at the way language is instantiated in utterance and review available theories of subjectivity.

Chapter 10 looks at the double fiction of the political text, the fiction of what is said, and the hidden but inferrable fiction of the world of its speaker. From this angle literary reading can be shown to have its own political strength, not so much on grounds of content as for formal reasons. The chapter concludes with a critical list of different recent critical politics and the kinds of constraints they impose on reading.

The Conclusion presents the 'subject' as an irretrievable textual event in which the instantiation of a particular reading stands in a largely (but never fully) determined relation to the system of dominant instantiations. This allows for reading as a creative bridge between linguistic expressions and general semiosis and a critical intervention in established linkages which need to be challenged from the perspective of a chosen social vision.

I

THE DIRECTIONALITY OF MEANING

> There is no limit to what a metaphor draws to our attention.
>
> Donald Davidson, "What Metaphors Mean"

It is the aim of this chapter to offer a *directional theory of meaning* in opposition to semantic descriptions of meaning as strict sense. Different discursive practices are shown to exhibit typically different constructions of meanings as a result of the convergence of linguistic guiding principles and processes of meaning negotiation which are not themselves linguistic. In presenting this directional approach to meaning this chapter addresses such issues as metaphor, reference, and the notion of literal meaning.

Donald Davidson's assertion above looks attractive not only for what it appears to say about metaphors but also because it seems to hint at a generous directional description of language. In one sense it does, yet in another it does not, for Davidson does not quite mean what he says, at least from the perspective of an ordinary use of language. The generosity of his description applies only to the *use* of metaphor which he distinguishes from the level of its literal meaning, as we shall see later. But even if his apparently liberal stance remains in the end opposed to the argument pursued here, the sharpness of the distinction which he maintains between pragmatic use and semantic meaning is instructive. Perhaps it is important to stress at this point that the view asserted here does not question the achievements of analytical philosophy in the sphere of formal logic, but does so quite vehemently where it claims to be able to extend its analysis with equal cogency to natural languages and fictional discourse.

Certainly, for the purposes of disentangling muddled logic Occam's razor is not to be sneered at. Yet this cannot mean that disambiguating procedures can ever eradicate the fundamental imprecision of language. I am not referring here to the unbridgeable abyss which exists between the noumenal universe (whatever that may be) and its textual mastery, which sets the realist against the textualist. The only way of escaping this sort of dualism, as we have seen, is by a realist textualist compromise according to which there is no neutral outside against which we could objectively check the texts constituting our world. Nor is it possible to deny noumenal constraints, a denial which would be committing the ontological fallacy in reverse. This has become painfully clear to post-Einsteinian physics in pursuit of a unified theory whose descriptions are forever shifted by the semioses of their measurements.[1]

What I am referring to as an insurmountable imprecision is the double vagueness within language itself, the lack of certitude which attaches to semantic definitions—in short, propositional opacity—and the semantic modifications introduced by our necessary inferences about the world of the speakers of utterances—modal opacity. No matter how well we form our sentences, no matter how precisely we formulate what we want to say, this twin source of indeterminacy remains beyond the cutting edge of Occam's blade. But if meanings are always already unstable in principle, how is it possible for speech communities to function at all? The short answer is 'by negotiation against the background of non-verbal semiosis' rather than by an inherent identity of meaning.

Traditionally, the theory of meaning requires the notion of full identity to constitute its operations from basic predication (S is p) to the most complex logical relations. As long as predication is applied to formal logic or mathematics the univocality of definition for its three elements can be said, at least for simplicity's sake, to be guaranteed; but in ordinary discourse the same three elements S, is, and p can be demonstrated to 'leak' or 'shimmer.' For S and p to be unequivocal requires definitions proper for both. But as I shall argue, such definitions do not exist in any strict sense for the vocabulary of most of everyday language. Nor is the copula 'is' as unproblematic as an equal sign, as Peirce, Heidegger, and more recently Derrida have shown. Apart from its meanings of existence and identity, assertion or denial, the copula usually stands for 'is the same,' 'means roughly,' or 'has more or less the following features,' each of which generates *more* text rather than indicating what Heidegger called 'the *merely* identical.' Modifying Heidegger's phrasing, we could say that instead of pinning down sense, language 'calls' things into our world of general semiosis. In this sense language hints at rather than fixes meanings. The main reason that Heidegger argues this way is due to his holistic approach to language within which the copula has its many functions. Accordingly, every linguistic item invokes in its special fashion the horizon of human understanding as a whole. Heidegger is usually the philosopher who is quoted on this view, so it may come as a bit of a surprise that a very similar position was advocated much earlier by the logician Charles Sanders Peirce.

> *Copula* is often defined as that which expresses the relation between the subject-term and the predicate-term of a proposition. . . . The essential office of the copula is to express a relation of a general term or terms to the universe. The universe must be well known and mutually known to be known and agreed to exist, in some sense, between speaker and hearer, between the mind as appealing to its own further consideration and the mind as so appealed to, or there can be no communication, or "common ground," at all. The universe is, thus, not a mere

concept, but is the most real of experiences. Hence, to put a concept into relation
to it . . . is to use a most peculiar sort of sign. . . . This, then, is what the copula
essentially does. . . . My universe is the momentary experience as a whole. . . . The
universe is that of determinate states of things that are admissable hypothetically.[2]

If the copula, one of the minimal ways of linking subjects to predicates, can
be shown to be less univocal than formal semantics would like us believe it is,
perhaps there are other equally fundamental components of language which
are likewise vulnerable to rigorous inquiry. One recent critique which has a
special bearing on what I have called propositional opacity is Derrida's broad
attack on the notion of the concept itself. In this, Derrida is not saying that
concepts are impossible fictions but that they belong to a special realm of writing,
constructs whose clarity is achieved at the expense of repressing other language
features. In order to establish this critique from different perspectives he developed a range of tools, 'infrastructures,' each of which chips away at the armor
of univocality. 'Differance' has the task of unmasking the hidden fiction of the
'now,' the timelessness of conceptuality; 'supplementarity' reminds us of the
ignored but nevertheless active shadow meanings of concepts; 'hymen,' 'pharmakon,' and others draw our attention to the fact that the either/or (*tertium
nor datum*) of univocality requires the denial of the in-between; and 'metaphoricity' suggests that not only are all concepts metaphoric but that language
as a whole stands in a metaphoric relation to what we try to signify: there is
always one last metaphor.[3]

To cope with Heidegger's, Derrida's, and other similar critiques, the theory
of meaning must abandon the absolutist claims of its linear model of logical
relations. This should not mean that the linearity of logical sense and the notions
of definitions proper and univocality are to be jettisoned. Even if they too can
be shown to 'leak,' as we shall see in chapter 8, we cannot do without them.
What is required is a much broader model within which strict predication and
its more complex formal relations occupy a special position. I propose such a
model under the provisional title of the 'directionality of meaning.'

In the schematization below, the left column lists five discursive possibilities
selected from a large range of actual communication: (1) pragmatic, (2) ludic
or playful, (3) analytic, (4) so-called metaphoric meaning, and (5) the breakdown
of meaning. The right-hand column sums up the kind of meaning process associated with each of these discursive options. The chart is framed by two axes,
the axis of meaning as directed process (horizontal) and the axis of meaning
negotiation (vertical). At the center of the chart is the utterance as social event,
with our constructions of its modalities on the left side and its propositions on
the right. This illustrates the claim that the construction of meaning requires
the inferential construal of tentative modal and propositional possibilities of
utterance. In pragmatic discourse (1) these inferences are controlled by the
constraints of social semiosis, marked by narrow angles; playful discourse (2)
is characterized by a wide-angle directionality; analytic meaning (3) is the special
case of discourse in which the axis of meaning negotiation collapses into that

TABLE 1 **The Directionality of Meaning**

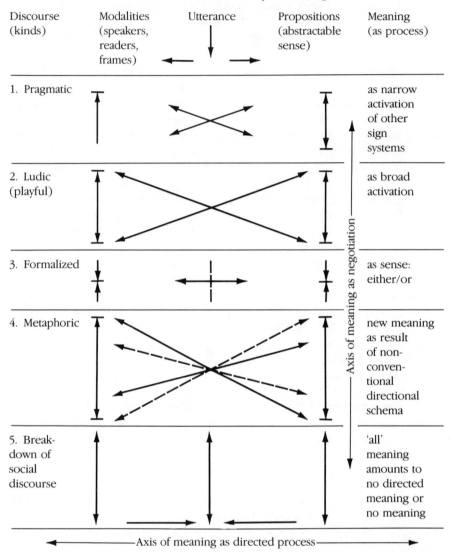

Discourse (kinds)	Modalities (speakers, readers, frames)	Utterance	Propositions (abstractable sense)	Meaning (as process)
1. Pragmatic				as narrow activation of other sign systems
2. Ludic (playful)				as broad activation
3. Formalized				as sense: either/or
4. Metaphoric				new meaning as result of non-conventional directional schema
5. Breakdown of social discourse				'all' meaning amounts to no directed meaning or no meaning

Axis of meaning as negotiation

————Axis of meaning as directed process————

of directionality to allow for univocality; so-called metaphor (4) is one version of linguistic innovation combining a number of established schemata; and 'discourse' (5) marks the opposite of analytic discourse and univocality by the collapse of the axis of directionality into that of negotiation: undirected meaning is 'all' meaning and therefore no meaning; no specific linkage can be established between linguistic signs and non-linguistic semiosis.

(Please also note that the relation between the axis of meaning as directed process and that of meaning as negotiation is not congruent with Saussure's between paradigmatic and syntagmatic or Jakobson's metaphoric/metonymic schema.)

Discourse 1, e.g., "Open the window," generates the kind of meanings which can be pragmatically resolved by negotiation, be it verbal or gestural. But it would be quite wrong to think therefore that univocality in an analytic sense is being accomplished or that identity of meaning is even a necessary condition for this form of communication. Part of the negotiation of meaning is the determination of whether an unproblematic, technical meaning is to be construed or a more political one, one which foregrounds the possible reasons for the utterance. In this case, what are at stake are such questions as domination by way of speech, so that the semantic fields of "opening" and "window" shift to become functions of the semantic field "manipulation." This is not to confuse the propositional and modal sides of an utterance, but rather to argue for the unavoidable feed-back interaction between the two. Each always contaminates the other.

If we choose as an example "Thank you for helping," the infectious relationship between modality and proposition becomes obvious, for it is crucial to the semantic field of "helping" whether or not its modality is construed as sincere. If it is not, the semantics of "helping" is disseminated over a broad range of alternative meanings, including some at the opposite side of the semantic terrain. This directional vagueness is the key to the ludic, i.e., playful, possibilities of Discourse 2.

Discourse 3 typifies the special case of analyticity. Here, modal and proportional inferences are reduced to the linear sequence of unequivocally defined signifiers. (I leave aside for the time being the kind of critique of formal systems which we find in Kurt Gödel's work.) Viewed simply then, the directional schema collapses into the linearity of sense, the relative neatness of which has seduced us into assuming that analyticity provides the master patterns for semantics in general. A directional theory of meaning must reject this position. Instead, it sees analyticity as the result of multiple reductions performed on the semiotic complexity of social discourse which cannot be theorized satisfactorily by its derivative and reduced relation.[4]

Discourse 4, metaphoric expressions, is somewhat more difficult to sketch in that two or more directional schemata appear to be superimposed on one another, at various angles. In the view of language advocated here it would be preferable not to talk about metaphors at all, but instead simply of different ways of activating directional schemata. However, since metaphor plays such a prevalent role in language theory I refer to it as if it was a special case. If we take as an example "kicking the bucket," the standard meanings of neither "kicking" nor "bucket" provide any clues as to the size of semantic overlays. Unless we are aware of the function of buckets in the historical context of hanging the new combination is simply endowed with an altogether different meaning, that of dying, albeit with a special modal flavor. Specific historic and social circumstances can sometimes be isolated as having generated such new formations without, however, allowing the abstraction of a general rule. The drift of meaning of the phrase "out for lunch" from a description of actuality to the indication of a state of mind such as "not with it" or even "nuts" cannot be reconstructed from so-called literal meanings. Reconstruction is simply an unsatisfactory way of dealing with the historical dynamics of discourse. To understand the new discursive formation is to learn the new way in which a novel linguistic combination gears into non-verbal sign systems. That there are, on the other hand, metaphors which can be 'reconstructed' should only remind us of the structural heterogeneity of metaphoric expressions and so caution us against a uniform theory.

Semantic overlap is what characterizes some but not all metaphoric discourse, a heterogeneous set of structures which plays a much larger role in everyday discourse than linguistics has led us to believe. Exceptions are such approaches as George Lakoff's and Mark Johnson's in "Conceptual Metaphor in Everyday Language," or the account offered by Michael Halliday in *An Introduction to Functional Grammar*. Halliday rejects the strict separation of literal from figurative meanings and sees "no clear line to be drawn between what is congruent and what is incongruent." Instead of assuming the literal, or the congruent, as the basis on which language evolves its incongruent variants, he suggests that "much of the history of every language is a history of demetaphorizing: of expressions which began as metaphors gradually losing their metaphoric character." At the same time Halliday shifts the emphasis of description from the lexical to the systemic "lexicogrammatical" plane on the grounds that "there is a strong grammatical element in rhetorical transference." Lexical selection is subsumed under lexicogrammatical selection or, extending Halliday's view, under discursive formations.[5]

From the double perspective of instantiation and directionality of meaning metaphor looks quite different if compared with its Aristotelian and analytical descriptions. The reader may therefore wonder why metaphor has not been placed at the center of a study exploring the complexities of saturated discourses. The reason, quite simply, is that I wish to argue first that language which looks quite straightforward is not really straightforward at all and, second, that metaphor is a typical rather than an atypical kind of instantiation. The first argument will unfold in the following chapters, the second I now wish to present as briefly as possible.

I am suggesting that the traditional Aristotelian explanation of metaphor either as substitution or as double condensation of a comparison is unsatisfactory. The substitution theory sees metaphor as "the application of the name of a thing to something else" whereby we proceed either from "genus to species" or from "species to genus" or from "species to species" or, lastly, "by proportion" when "the second term is related to the first in the same way as the fourth to the third or vice versa."[6] Aristotle's comparison theory of metaphor rests on the assumption of condension or ellipsis. Accordingly, the comparison 'the moon is like an orange' and its simile an 'orange-like moon,' are condensed to the metaphoric 'orange-moon.' This, however, is not a very fruitful way of looking at the trope. In the condensation theory the explanatory motivation comes from the logic of 'identity out of difference' or that of 'synthesis out of antithetic elements.' It is an immanent approach in the sense that all the materials and structural relations necessary for description are 'inside' the merging linguistic elements. The theory also suggests that the new expression presents a new semantic identity, an assumption which denies any 'leakage' of meaning. The condensation theory finds incidental support in the Germanic terms for poetry and poet, e.g., German *Dichtung* (poetry) which literally means a tightening of language. But *Dichtung* also means gasket, something which allows us to combine flanges and pipes in such a way that they do not leak. Because of the absence of leakage the immanent theory of metaphor leads us to reconstruct the trope from its initial parts; it assumes that the new identity is made up of two old identities. This is why most theories of metaphor explain the new (metaphoric) meaning in terms of the literal meanings of its components. According to John R. Searle's reformulation of the Aristotelian view, metaphor can be understood "as a shortened version of the literal simile."[7] Applied to relatively 'tame' expressions this procedure appears to deliver the goods. But when we are dealing with highly creative metaphors the immanent theory and the explanatory move from literal to transferred meaning fails. Neither "jumping the twig" nor even "falling out of the tree" can be constructed as alternatives for "dying" and "going insane" in this way. What we need here is an entirely new description.

From the perspective of a directional theory of meaning metaphors are combinations of expressions whose area of semantic overlap either creates a new semiotic relation or settles inside established parameters. In the case of "jumping the twig" associations with 'jumping' and 'twig' are combined into a schema context or use (and not literal meaning) tells us is closely associated with the schema for "dying." It is in this way that metaphor acts as one of the indicators that language is always on the move, always evolving its combinatory potential. This much is allowed for in Paul Ricoeur's *The Rule of Metaphor*, which goes beyond metaphor as a foundation of a "new semantic pertinence" to its "power to 'redescribe' reality."[8] But neither new metaphors nor other new expressions take their cues primarily from *langue* or even, as Ricoeur urges, from discourse, but from the larger semiotic from which they emerge: the ghetto, digital technology, experimental writing, the Australian outback, or computer commerce. It is here, in the semiosis which exists between social action and discursive formations, that we must look for meaning. *Use* is never purely linguistic, nor just discursive.

What happens then to the custom of distinguishing 'dead' from 'living' metaphors? Again, I suggest, that the distinction is misleading if phrased in this way. Why do we not call all language dead, with the exception of its latest neologisms? This is roughly Heidegger's intention when he calls ordinary language a "used-up and forgotten poem." But Heidegger posits a specific goal, our realization of language as a thoughtful creative and philosophical potential against its degradation to a merely technical device of notational identification. So-called dead metaphors indicate simply standardized use of expression which are not merely to be found here and there, but everywhere. New metaphors are rebellious instantiations which draw our attention to the creative and evolutionary side of verbal sign systems. It is this side which tends to be played down by our structuralist bias toward the control mechanism of an abstracted grammar. At the same time we need to acknowledge that much as we may disdain the authority of grammar we cannot do without schematic explanations altogether. I shall address the inevitability of a minimum of grammatical projection by offering a textualized version of Kant's schematism at the beginning of chapter 6.

A directional theory of meaning which ties metaphor (and all other expressions) to non-verbal signification is bound to clash with analytical semantics. Donald Davidson, for example, argues in "What Metaphors Mean" that "a metaphor doesn't say anything beyond its literal use meaning."[9] This literal meaning is distinguished from a pragmatic meaning which caters to the kinds of effects a metaphor produces in discourse. It is this pragmatic effect of metaphor which "makes us attend to some likeness" and "nudges us into noting" all kinds of things.[10] As strict is Davidson's delimitation of the trope's literal meaning, so liberal is his view of its pragmatic extensions; he sees "no limit to what a metaphor draws to our attention."[11] Indeed, we must ask, what is the "literal" meaning of "the lascivious pleasing of a lute?" (Richard III, I, i, 1.13)

Phrases such as "draws our attention to," "makes us attend to," or "nudges us into noting" are all directional and should go well with the theory offered here rather than with Davidson's. And so they do, except in reverse; i.e., what Davidson regards as the pragmatics of metaphor is its "meaning" here. It is really surprising to see that any philosopher could so stubbornly hang on to conceptions of sense meaning and literality when they achieve nothing except at best the display of a non-contradictory game of logic. If semantics insists, as in Davidson's version, that metaphor "does not say anything beyond its literal meaning," this means that it cannot address discourse at all, but only the ahistoricity of the dictionary. Accordingly, "amber fluid" means a liquid of a light brown color but never "beer;" "nudging the turps" means giving a bottle of turpentine a slight push, but not "drinking an alcoholic beverage;" "throttling pit" could mean anything but a "powder room." The way I am therefore inclined to read Davidson's account is as a radical attack on strict semantic meaning itself.

Nor can any of these 'metaphoric' meanings be derived from the congruent meanings of their constituent parts. Only acquaintance with cultural semiosis or at least its summary directives supplied by the context of written statements are reliable guides to the construction of meaning. This even throws a wrench in the works of as attractive an explanation as Max Black's interaction theory of metaphor.[12] What I am suggesting quite bluntly is that semantics without pragmatics, discourse analysis, and a broad notion of semiotic is a sterile and self-consuming artifact.

Umberto Eco has consistently offered a much broader approach to the description of metaphor. In "The Semantics of Metaphor" he rightly links metaphor with the creativity of language which we encounter whenever language "must invent combinatory possibilities or semantic couplings not anticipated by the code." In this process metaphors testify to the "internal disturbance of semiosis" but at the same time act as "metasemiotic judgments." By forcefully merging unassociated significations metaphors increase the density of information "in the most proper sense of the term: an excess of disorder in respect to existing codes." When metaphors are incorporated into standard discourse they become "catachreses;" the linguistic "field has been restructured, semiosis rearranged, and metaphor (from the invention which it was) turned into culture."[13] In his more recent *Semiotics and the Philosophy of Language* Eco drives home the point that metaphor is the touchstone for the study of language: "When closely studied in connection with verbal language, metaphor becomes a source of scandal in a merely linguistic framework, because it is in fact a *semiotic* phenomenon."

According to Eco, the internal structure of metaphor is responsible for "a shifting of the linguistic explanation onto semiotic mechanisms that are not peculiar to languages." Other sign systems, such as oneiric images, likewise display the work of metaphor. Vice versa, "verbal metaphor itself often elicits references to visual, aural, tactile, and olfactory experiences." From the point of view of language use this suggests that there is perhaps a functional link between metaphoric structure and the format of a "subject's encyclopedia." As Eco puts it, "metaphors are produced solely on the basis of a rich cultural framework."[14] A directional theory of meaning welcomes this kind of analysis because it draws our attention to the question of the linking procedures which we are forced to assume exist between verbal and non-verbal signification.

Discourse 5 marks the possibility of no discursive operations being performed at all. This means that the speech community (or the program) is not in a position to construct either modalities or propositions as a result of all linguistic rules being violated. If only some rules have been violated, meaning negotiation is still possible, then discourse types (1) and (2) are applicable. Certainly, for a speech community to be functional Occam's prescriptions are not required. A logically clumsy communication is still communication. Indeed, for a directional theory of meaning the notion of identity is not necessary, certainly not in its full form and not at the level of expressions. In most cases of social discourse, i.e., communication, 'identity' can be replaced by similarity or the partial overlap of semantic fields. In other words, what is required for communication is *orientation*, rough directions so that we can find our way about, rather than fully determinate sense meanings. This applies to both 'rich' and 'poor' meanings, that is, to meanings which are culturally highly as against minimally charged. Only in formal and highly technical discourse does it make sense to speak of the identity of meaning.

There are also a number of other issues in traditional descriptions of meaning which are affected by a directional theory. They will reappear throughout this book but need to be mentioned briefly here. In socially saturated discourses the strict separation of meaning and significance becomes untenable. Speaker's meaning and sentence meaning collapse, as do such pairs as semantics and semiotics, language and discourse, and semantics and pragmatics. The main reason for this fusion is that sentence meanings do not exist outside utterance, so that the artificial constructions of what a sentence means by itself and what a speaker means apart from an expression are misleading abstractions. Misleading, that is, because the grammarian's or logician's language games which produced the abstraction have furnished new utterance situations, which should not be disregarded. Likewise, the very notion of semantics is a misleading theorization of language as a system isolated from other sign systems. Semantics separated from semiotics leads to self-referential explanations of meaning on the one hand and, on the other, to an empiricist dualism between language and the objects of our world, characteristic of much of linguistics and most of language philosophy.

Special mention must be made here of reference which is detached from meaning in formal logical accounts, but plays a central role in a directional description. One of the theorists of reference whose work is compatible to a certain degree with the position presented here is Gareth Evans in *The Varieties of Reference*. Evans suggests that "the notion of the intended referent is rather like the notion of a *target*" in the sense that "the speaker's *linguistic* target when he utters the sentence 'That man over there is F' . . . is directing . . . his audience's attention." This approach would go well with what I am offering here were it not for the fact that Evans at the same time upholds the empiricist split between language and the objects of the world.

> The conventions governing referring expressions are such that, as uttered in a context of utterance, they are associated with a property which an object must satisfy if it is to be the referent of the fully conventional use of that expression in that context; I call such property '*the referential feature* which the expression conventionally has in that context.'[15]

What remains untheorized is this: (1) how we can know "a property;" (2) what kind of signification "satisfaction" is; and (3) in what sort of sign system a "referential feature" appears to a speech community. From the position sketched here the answers seem to be: (1) "properties" are identifiable portions of semiotic overlap (parts of reality); (2) "satisfaction" is an act of corroboration between at least two sign systems; and (3) "referential features" can be realized by a great variety of sign systems; without phrasing it in this way, the important point that Evans is making is that they are sign structures about which there exists special social agreement, i.e., they are semiotically overdetermined and so more stable than less conventional references.

Evans repeatedly employs the term "information" when he describes linkages between language and objects. For instance, he says that "in order to understand an utterance containing a referring expression . . . the hearer must link up the utterance with some information in his possession."[16] Again, "information" is taken for granted but should be understood as some non-verbal and yet significatory acquaintance with the referent. In short, if we semiotize the empiricist features in Evans his account can be used as a powerful backup for a directional, *textual* theory of meaning.

The directional position canvassed here allows more readily for traditional phenomenological explanations according to which such concepts as 'outer and inner horizon' refer to different aspects of states of affairs. The outer horizon of items of consciousness constitutes their delimiting identification, but by virtue of this horizonality "a given object also anticipates the other co-objects of the same *field.*" Identity and differential relation, however, are distinct phenomena within different discourse frames. As to its inner horizon we can say that "every object of experience not only is capable of further determination, but *points to* the possibilities of such determination."[17] Again, we should add that both interior structuring and the possibilities of more detailed determination are dependent on the rung of the "ladder of discourse" we have before us. As we shall see, in the language of formal logic, for example, the inner and outer horizons collapse into the hard line of a definition proper (itself open to further critique), while in referentially and modally saturated discourse neither the inner nor outer horizon is as stable as the analogy would have us believe.

It does not compromise a directional theory to describe acts of meaning making as processes of 'identification' as long as it refers to the relative matching of a linguistic schema with our multiple semiotic grasp of a relevant portion of the world, and as long as this sort of matching is not equated with closure. But there are two kinds of matching: one, which could be characterized as a "this-there" act, or an act of numerical identification which relies on the principle of exclusive difference; the other, as an ascriptive act or an act of differential qualitative identification. The difference is brought out by C. M. Meyers in "The Determinate and Determinable Modes of Appearing" where he proposes that an item of perception "is apprehended incompletely but is not apprehended as incomplete."[18] What holds for perceptual typification I believe applies also to meaning making in language. The external horizonal identification of our world through propositional sense is accompanied by our concretizing acts of filling the linguistic schema with semiotic typfications of various kinds and to differing degrees, concretizations which, however, never thereby accomplish any final saturation of meaning.

In spite of common practice and with particular reference to metaphor, we should not speak of meanings as rich or poor, for strictly speaking there is no such thing as "a meaning." And we should not be misled by semantics or entries in the dictionary to assume otherwise, a point to which I shall return later. What we should say about meanings instead is that we never deal with a discrete unit, an entity, but always with processes of meaning making that, assuming a certain perspective, operate between two poles, authoritarian control and anarchic free-play. Between these extremes full or curtailed meaning operations are performed. Nor are the various positions on this scale isolated and accidental, but rather they are intricately tied into the political life-world so that the typical modes of meaning production can be regarded as institutions in a broad sense. I will try to show how these processes of meaning making function and argue

that the dream of secure and literal meanings rests on a number of false assumptions about language. Thus, a view of language evolves along a broad
spectrum from culturally highly saturated signification endowed with all (*pan*)
of the goddess's gifts (*dora*), to William of Occam's ideal of a radically reduced
philosophical speech, to Gottlob Frege's *Begriffsschrift* as realized in fully analytical sign systems. It is the confusion between what is happening when we
use such formally empty discourse and the speech events in ordinary and literary
language that is responsible for the fallacy of the univocality of meaning rooted
in an untheorized *semantic foundationalism*.[19]

What is being attacked throughout this book is the notion of *literality*, which
acts as a base for propositional meaning as stipulated in socially saturated discourse. As viewed from several perspectives *literality* reveals itself as a political
fiction rather than as a logical ground. This has consequences not only for the
meaning of isolated expressions but also for all semantic, hierarchical constructs,
such as high-level summary interpretive propositions. And the more highly
saturated a discursive operation the greater its various opacities. This implies
that the construction of meaning in any discourse relies on the performance of
a hermeneutic helix by means of which we work toward relative clarity, with
the qualification that in socially rich discourse this performance is elaborate,
while it needs to be stunted in technical and formal sign systems.

Much has been achieved in the critique of analytical descriptions of meaning
by recent theory. But it is important to remember that, for example, Derrida's
denial of meaning as presence as argued against the early Husserl in *Speech
and Phenomena* questions neither the process of meaning constitution itself
nor the fact of intentionality, but merely their assumed role of origin and stability.[20] On the other hand, Derrida's attempt at strengthening the case of writing
over speaking has led to the popular notion of a signifying chain emptied of
signifieds, as if the mere iterability of the vehicle would guarantee meaning
constitution. Not that Derrida did not make a justified assault. But the attack
seems rightly directed at the claim that the speaking voice is capable of granting
the written word any security of meaning. The case for *graphe* should certainly
not mean that language exists outside its performance. On the contrary, as I am
going to argue here, without enunciation there is no language. In Derrida's
terms any such instantiation would be once more a case of *écriture* in a broad
sense.[21]

The observation that the manner of speaking is often a more powerful message than its propositional content reminds us of the case of Socrates who—as
constructed through Plato's dialogues—was executed neither on grounds of
impiety nor for the untruth of his statements, but for a rhetorical stance which
was bound to offend a large and democratic jury, a jury that would very likely
have preferred to avoid the political embarrassment of his execution. The claim
that he was infallibly protected from wrongdoing by a divine inner voice must
have irked his more enlightened contemporaries, but it was probably the rhetorical intensity of his arrogance rather than the content of his speech which
insulted the jury. They must have rightly felt that such oratorical talent and

technique were pedagogically undesirable and certainly politically dangerous.[22] But Socrates is merely the *locus classicus* of the argument for language as speech. Neither "pure" enunciation, nor materiality, nor indeed any purely formal abstraction of language into *langue* are in themselves sufficient for a description of what happens in the process of meaning making. The event of meaning making is both individual, in that it requires an enunciating and re-enunciating medium, a consciousness or a high-powered 'machine' of the future, and social in that this very medium is always already woven into the semiotic fabric of a speech community.[23]

To reduce this dialectic to the static logic of a chicken-and-egg causality misses entirely the point of the denting of the system by certain instantiations and the subject's response to the system by which it is constituted in ever new ways. But we must not forget that all attempts at exhausting the definition of the 'subject' as an intersection of forces within frames of discursive formations have no logical barrier other than the abyss of infinite regress. How then can we take sound decisions in pinpointing the relevant and crucial forces at work in the constitution of the subject? The early answer seems to be that this is precisely what all reading is bound to be: a process of meaning making within politically limited and limiting constraints. Put differently, reading in its broad sense defines the 'subject' as the event of semiotic intersubjectivity.

In this scenario, the subject or the moment when meaning making crystallizes is by no means absent but is as crude or as sophisticated an entity as the network of explanatory systems which we bring to bear on it. This amounts to adopting at least the principle of Foucault's stance that we cannot legitimately provide a single subject and so a unified meaning for any discursive formation, but only a number of possible subject positions suitable to statements as part of systems of discursive regularity.[24] Even though there is no reliable way of constructing, let alone reconstructing, a unitary subject and its meanings, it is one of Foucault's major achievements to have resolved the problem of linguistic chaos at the higher level of discourse, or "the group of statements that belong to a single system of formation." One might wish to add here the even broader perspective of Wittgenstein who saw such a higher level regularity in what he termed *Lebensformen*, or forms of life.[25] Meaning making then becomes a function of the discursive formations which actual readers 'choose' as the frames for linguistic instantiation. As I shall argue later, it is this sort of activity which constitutes the subject as irretrievable event. At the same time, the act of 'choosing' itself is yet another case of operating within and against the constraints of a discursive domain.[26]

The combination of Derrida's destabilization of meaning as presence and Foucault's reassurance at the level of discourse that semantic chaos can be held at bay provides a highly persuasive and powerful set of tools for interpretation. But if their arguments on meaning and the subject hold, then we may wish to know whether there are indeed aspects of language which make cogent the argument for the instability of meaning and its necessary resolution at a level of greater generality. In what follows I will try to show from various perspectives, and in opposition to the established view, those features of language-in-action which in my view undermine the very possibility of univocal meanings.

We can now return to propositional and modal opacity mentioned earlier and the reasons why I think that the meanings which speakers of everyday language and readers of literary texts generate display a fuzziness which defies strict formalization, as Tarski maintained half a century ago. I have suggested that there are two fundamental sources for this vagueness. The one I have called *propositional opacity*, or a semantic opaqueness inherent in the way in which the meanings of words and their combinations in expressions and sentences are circumscribed. Since this opacity, it appears, cannot be fully removed from language except by a violent procedure of formalization, the term does precisely the work it needs to do. The second and perhaps even more important source of the fuzziness and semantic instability which we find in ordinary speech and more pointedly in literary texts I have called *modal opacity*, or the opaqueness introduced into language by enunciation. *Modal opacity* thus refers to the various framing devices which impinge on any utterance situation and in particular to the manner in which a speaker (or a machine) instantiates linguistic expressions. In the written text, with which I shall be mainly concerned, we construct the marked and the hidden modalities of speaking in conjunction with our construction of propositional contents. As a result, the two opacities are always deceptively intertwined and so further resist the clarity of meaning which formal semanticians and their less rigorous disciples wish to discover.

Modal opacity is above all the consequence of the absence of speakers from written texts. In filling their vacant subject positions the actual reader imaginatively posits likely aspects of probable speech situations. These aspects include the logical relations of speaking, the spatial locus of speech, the temporal locus of speech, acts of speaking, the personality of the speaker, the social position of the speaker, the speaker's system of values, and the speaker's—or in the case of a machine, the program's—abstractable ideological motivation. *Inferable modality*, then, could be regarded as the *modal shadow* of the propositional content of sentences.[27] Both opacities in other words can always partially, but never fully, be 'cleared up' by the activation of the vast apparatus of the semiotic relations which define a community. This implies of course that we cannot strictly separate sentence meanings from utterance meanings.

There is no such thing, then, as a sentence by itself or a propositional content in pure form without the performance of utterance. Words, statements, and texts, in this theory, do not exist unless they are uttered, i.e., unless they are provided with an actual or silent "prosodic contour."[28] Without such habitual acts as supplying an intonation, stress, and rhythmical pattern, sentences would not exist as signs but merely as material entities, as marks on paper, their iterability a mere potential. And the looser the framing conditions the greater the range of and need for modal inference on the part of the reader.

On the one hand, all utterances of texts always take place within the constraints of speech act formations and the flexible boundaries of language use as circumscribed by a dynamic speech community; on the other hand, uttering is also always an individual historical event, an instantiation. No matter how far a theory may wish to argue down the importance of the speaking subject, whenever a text is uttered, whenever in other words language takes place or a text finds a tongue (or a membrane), the inscription undergoes a complex process by which its content is profoundly affected. This effect is not exhausted in my view by the *hic et nunc* of utterance, the spatial and temporal co-ordinates of speaking, nor by such acts as have been described by speech act and indirect speech act theory.[29] What I will attempt to show is that the acts of uttering as they occur in a good deal of everyday speech and in all literary reading result in a significant bending of the propositional contents which can be abstracted from sentences and texts.

As to propositional opacity, we should not be surprised to discover that it is active not only in texts and sentences, but also in single words. The rhetoric of examples employed in formal semantics from its mathematical beginnings in Frege to Grice and Searle tend to support the opposite view, namely, that if we only look hard enough and express ourselves with sufficient care, the vagueness of natural language will disappear. And indeed it almost does in illustrations which range from the evidential "morning star" and "evening star" to the fictitious "the present King of France is bald."[30] However, it is also not surprising to see that under pressure the logician often retreats to the safer, i.e., referentially and enunciatively empty, examples of mathematics.[31]

I want to postpone the argument about the undecidability of certain propositions in logical systems advanced by Kurt Gödel until later (see chapter 8). In the meantime, I suggest that for pragmatic purposes propositional and modal opacity are absent from formal logic precisely because it is a referentially and deictically neutralized sign system, but powerfully present in such sentences as "Parliamentary debate is chaotic in Australia," "Parliamentary debate used to be well ordered in East Germany," "The mock-medieval architecture of Yale University blends well with New Haven," or in an exchange such as " 'He's a ratbag, isn't he?' 'Isn't he ever!' " To press the point a little further, let us consider the following definitions.

> *Ratbag*:
> "an odd or disagreeable person"
> "a plain-clothes detective"
> "an ill-disposed person . . . an eccentric"
> "a worthless person, especially if young and with near criminal tendencies and habits . . . "
> "a thoroughly objectionable person"
> "eccentric or unpleasant person, troublemaker, unruly horse"
> "an Australian enthusiast"

Or compare the way Barry Humphries describes a ratbag: a man who "writes letters to Raquel Welch enclosing his photograph and a stamped addressed envelope," someone who "takes correspondence lessons in ballroom dancing" or who is "always lending you books you don't read, and giving advice you don't need." In this parodic version the concept includes people who "believe in the Divine Right of Kings, The Flat Earth Society, flying saucers and the Book of Revelations." Ratbags also typically have "their ancestries traced, their faces lifted and eat Chinese food with chopsticks when they are at home when no-one is watching."[32]

I would like to reassure those readers who firmly believe in the sanctity of empirical data that I have supplemented this library work on "ratbags" with interviews to get at the heart of the matter. But I do not wish to belabor with lengthy statistics a point which can be summarized in a few lines: in spite of some superficial agreements, the majority of speakers consulted could not fully accept any of these definitions, not even the generally negative judgment implied in most of them. To some, like the comedian Barry Humphries (who is of course describing himself) the term evidently has a positively endearing ring. Nor should it come as a surprise that any extended description of a "ratbag" is bound to take on a parodic flavor. This merely drives home the point that we are in the habit of using linguistic expressions the semantic identity of which is by no means clear. And as soon as we attempt to scrape away the murkiness to get to an assumed semantic core the ludicrousness of our undertaking becomes apparent.

The reader may wish to rule my example out as an unusual and extreme case. Ratbaggish no doubt it is, but it is by no means an illustration which falsifies the issues at hand. It serves to indicate that there is another pole to the lucidity assumed and aimed at in semantics. What I do wish to insist on is the observation that words as well as their combinations in expressions, sentences, and entire texts, function at best as intersubjective, more or less shared directional schemata, a concept which underlines the differences that exist between the terms of natural languages and those of their logico-mathematical cousins.

But if there is such a degree of vagueness, how is it possible that as Ludwig Wittgenstein observes, we "*understand* the meaning of a word when we hear or say it . . . in a flash"?[33] What, when I read "ratbag," do I spontaneously grasp? What, when I read "Season of mists and mellow fruitfulness, Close bosom-friend of the maturing sun" do I realize? The sense in which Wittgenstein uses the phrase "the meaning of a word" shifts as we know throughout his work towards an increasingly complex and intuitively attractive definition of meaning as "use" in its total linguistic as well as non-verbal semiotic sense. What I grasp initially then cannot be a definition but only a way of being guided toward meaning construction, toward an "appresentation" or "concretization" of the schematic matrix of the linguistic items from the position which I occupy by virtue of my biographical situation and my position in a fluid network of social relations and language games, in short, as a member of a semiotic community.[34] In the view advocated here, meaning conferment is never complete but continuously changing along the irreversible arrow of historical time. In turn, meaning endowment affects the very 'starting point,' the schematic sense definitions which are shared *cum grano salis* by a community of speakers. In this view the limits of 'semantic drift' are not set by linguistic meanings but by a broader semiotic dynamic.

The notion of *literal meaning* on which hinges much of the semantic argument presented by the powerful lobby of analytical language theory is untenable from the perspective of a directional theory of meaning. Let me take as an example the position of John R. Searle, whose interest in the performance of speech acts against a "preintentional" background should, one might expect, lead him to doubt the stability of meaning. But as recently as in *Intentionality* he steadfastly holds to the existence and usefulness of "literal meaning."[35]

In Searle's view, " 'The cat is on the mat' only determines a definite set of truth conditions against a Background of preintentional assumptions that are not part of the literal meaning of the sentence." This is so, he says, because if we change the background "the same sentence with the same literal meaning will determine different truth conditions, different conditions of satisfaction, even though there is no change in the literal meaning of the sentence." But how can the meanings not change? Imagine that Searle's example remains a standard expression in radically different circumstances where 'cat' refers to an animal that cannot sit, but only fly, and that 'carpets' signify hanging items of some sort; then the meaning of 'sitting' is radically different. In fact, none of these items have strictly literal meanings; they are directional schemata referring us to the very semiotic background Searle alerts us to, even though he does not textualize non-linguistic phenomena in this manner. In my account, so-called literal meanings are habitual illusory entities which have evolved for pragmatic convenience. As I have argued, meanings would be more usefully and more accurately described as processes of linkage between linguistic expressions and other sign systems.

Searle thinks he clinches the argument by asserting that in the following list "the word 'open' has the same literal meaning."

> Tom opened the door
> Sally opened her eyes
> The carpenter opened the wall
> Sam opened his book to page 37
> The surgeon opened the wound

To be able to question this view we need only to visualize acts of 'opening doors' and those involved in 'opening a wound.' The ensuing visual significations could in no way be said to be congruent. Or, to dramatize this intersemiotic test, imagine a tactile, but 'blind,' encounter with those events. Our realizations of an opening door and an opening wound would differ drastically. Yet we could not say that it is merely the circumstances which have changed while what we refer to as 'opening' has remained the same. A directional theory offers a more satisfactory explanation: the directional schema of 'open' changes as a result of the discursive formations in which it occurs, regularities which themselves are functions of social semiosis at large. There is no *literal* meaning of 'open,' but rather a spectrum of possibilities for meaning activation.

If we did not accept the literal equivalence of 'open' in these examples, Searle says, we would be "forced to hold the view that the word 'open' is indefinitely or perhaps even infinitely ambiguous." But, he insists, "indefinite ambiguity seems an absurd result." Searle then presents another set of examples for which he concedes that the "semantic content" which we grasp changes. "In each case the truth conditions marked by the word 'open' are different, even though the semantic content is the same."

> The chairman opened the meeting
> The artillery opened fire
> Bill opened a restaurant.

What is peculiar is that Searle notes that "what constitutes opening a wound is quite different from what constitutes opening a book, and understanding these sentences literally requires understanding each differently" and yet he insists that the word 'open' still "has the same literal meaning in each case."

Searle's account of literality is supported by a large number of linguists and philosophers of language, with Dieter Wunderlich providing perhaps the most succinct definition. "The meaning of an utterance of a sentence s of language L is literal iff [if and only if] the context used to determine the meaning is neutral with respect to s."[36] Yet we must ask what such a "neutral" context would look like. The interaction between different semiotic systems negates the very possibility of neutrality just as it negates the construal of the condition of *no* context. And since there is no such thing as a neutral context, there is no such beast as a literal meaning either.

Both Searle's and Wunderlich's are unsatisfactory explanations. Instead we should say that 'open,' like any other word or expression, receives meaning in the specific process of linking discursive formations with non-verbal sign systems. The minimal dynamic activated by the isolated 'open' as against 'closed' produces a wide directional schema of 'openness' as against 'closedness' which we can vary imaginatively to suit all kinds of circumstances. We know *roughly* what is meant, but this knowledge does not amount to a literal meaning, for it lacks the completeness of definition and the stability of an entity. Meaning is better described as something on the move, a dynamic which at times is deceptively slow but never comes to rest in social discourse.

His very own examples lead Searle to concede that "there is more to understanding than grasping meanings because, to put it crudely, *what one understands goes beyond meaning*." If one stays with literal meanings, this is certainly the logical consequence. But why separate *meaning* from *understanding*? What is it that we understand, meanings or meanings plus something else? Other meanings? Or additional non-meanings? A directional theory of meaning, even if it still has Wittgenstein's eggshells about its ears, avoids this sort of absurdity.[37]

The fundamental fuzziness of word meanings and the propositional opacity of sentences become a worry only to the analyst.[38] In practice I do not appear to be bothered by such problems. After all, communication appears to be possible. But how? Provisionally we could say that when I engage in the discourse of everyday life, I supply intuitively and spontaneously what is not given. I appresent, or concretize, or fill in the schemata of words in their context within broad intersubjective, semantic-semiotic strategies and so feel at home in the world of my language and the language which projects my world.

But to regard the relative fuzziness of lexemes as a weakness of natural languages would be a highly prejudiced view. It is a stance which overemphasizes language as an abstracted *langue* and must therefore be bothered by features which threaten its fiction of homogeneity. The view of language as a fully systemic or even closed structure no doubt yields impressive grammars, but it also makes natural language into something which it is not. It is silly to deplore the fact that natural language is not a formal logic with definitional certitude. After all, in natural languages certainty is as Wittgenstein says of Moore's 'knowing' "*as it were* a tone of voice."[39] As a literary theorist I take the view that we should celebrate the complex, material heterogeneity and relative fuzziness of language as its fundamental potential for new social visions and practices. Less optimistically, there is no point in seeking stability where there is none, for expressions and words, as T. S. Eliot tells us in "Burnt Norton," "slip, slide, perish, Decay with imprecision, will not stay in place, Will not stay still."

II

THE RAPE OF AUTUMN OR
THE RICH AND FUZZY LIFE
OF MEANINGS

Now golden fruits on loaded branches shine,
And grateful clusters swell with floods of wine.

Alexander Pope, "Pastoral III: Autumn"

The teeming autumn rich with big increase

William Shakespeare, Sonnet 97

This chapter illustrates that propositional opacity or, roughly, the relative vague-ness of linguistic expressions is a strength rather than a weakness, if we are prepared to extend liberally the limits of interpretive exploration. But no matter how radical our readings may claim to be, they are determined to a great degree by the hermeneutical frames we bring to bear on texts. This chapter also suggests that interpretive strategies accepted in the discourses of the literary are by no means confined to this particular practice but also play a considerable role in the language games of everyday life.

Granted, the type of directional theory of meaning proposed here is more easily demonstrated by way of literature than by other discursive structures. Nevertheless, in the literary as in other language uses the limits of meaning are not logically embedded in linguistic expressions but are the consequence of certain reading strategies and a specific semiotic practice. This may sound trivial, but it has serious implications for the theory of meaning, consequences which we must address later. Suffice it to say, it is deplorable that the discursive for-mations typically available for writing as a practice of 'demonstration' are not easily related to those associated with the strategies involved in the practice of 'argument.' This bears out the fundamental observation made by Jean-François Lyotard that conflict is not an anthropomorphic ingredient but a *sine qua non* of "genres of discourse."[1] With this apology I turn to my central example, Keats's ode "To Autumn."

Season of mists and mellow fruitfulness,
Close bosom-friend of the maturing sun;
Conspiring with him how to load and bless
With fruit the vines that round the thatch-eves run;
To bend with apples the moss'd cottage trees,
And fill all fruit with ripeness to the core;
To swell the gourd, and plump the hazel shells
With a sweet kernel; to set budding more,
And still more, later flowers for the bees,
Until they think warm days will never cease,
For Summer has o'er-brimm'd their clammy cells.

We must accept as a *primitivum* that a given reading can never start from a position of neutrality. All readings are always already burdened with ways of reading. Let us also assume that I do not read this stanza primarily as an intonation exercise or as an example in a purely formal argument, but against a broad background of literary convention. In that case, then, I tend to perform at least the following acts of meaning construction, though not necessarily in this order.

I lend the signifiers prosodic contour, an activity which already involves complex semantic operations; I re-read certain passages, aloud or silently, which I judge to have been supplied with an inappropriate intonation, rhythmical balance, or stress. Thus the paradigms of sound which I activate from non-linguistic semiosis are differentially related to semantic fields.

This means at the same time that I have made tentative 'sense' of the text against the background of two systems: the structure of language (linguistic operations) and the structure of general semiosis in which the signifiers of language play a powerful role but are not the only kind of signifiers activated (semantic-semiotic operations). For contrary to common belief, language does *not* function as a self-contained system. Its meanings cannot be realized within its own linguistic frame without the involvement of a broad "social semiotic."[2]

I abstract, compare, discard, select, hold available, and settle tentatively for a number of propositional meanings. These I qualify by similar acts concerning the poem's speech modalities.

I return to the textual surface with the meanings generated so far and so realize the poem's euphonic aspects as well as its syntactic and semantic patterns.

I relate parts of this discourse intertextually to other poems which add further chains of signification. In this way I instigate discursive conflicts and their always only partial resolutions by the reader.

I relate the text intersemiotically to other artistic discourses which I find add further thematic adumbrations.

I concretize the text in terms of the double matrix of semiotic grasp by way of my typifications of the presented world and my understanding of possible speakers and their worlds.

I review the text for coherent semantic, macrostructural patterns which I have already intuited, with a view toward constructing a web of values.

I abstract portions of both the ideological position of speaker and presented world and synthesize the results into an overall work ideology— a statement as to what the work says at a specific historical moment by way of a certain kind of reading.

These procedures tend to be fragmentary in casual reading and totalizing, or deliberately selective in different kinds of critical practice.

Such interpretive moves I believe play a role in the seemingly trivial ways in which literary texts are read. Moreover, they inform otherwise radically opposed critical strategies, from New Criticism to deconstruction. Reading procedures ranging from the phonic to macro-structural semantic-semiotic signification are part of even minimally goal-oriented and to that extent teleological interpretive enterprise. If fully developed they form institutionalized bodies of knowledge which from the outset look over the reader's shoulder and predetermine interpretive bias.

Genre theory, literary history, reception theory, philology, New Criticism, psychoanalysis, Marxist theories, phenomenology, hermeneutics, structuralism, post-structuralist stances, and competing feminist theories entail different premises and methods and so produce different and often conflicting readings. Yet the assumption that the actual reader can choose not to use any such systemic arrangement of critical tools and instead *merely read* is quite wrong. Attempts of this sort do no more than to conceal and deny their own theoretical foundations.

Yet it is here that we face an instructive paradox. In spite of those constraints, and in whatever manner we theorize responses to literary discourse, a fundamental openness confronts us which can be handled adequately only by engaging with a project of radical reading. From the perspective of such a reading, *literal meanings* and other strategies of stunting the processes of signification can be shown to lack any logical grounding.

The difficulty is in reconciling this *logical* openness with the finite pragmatics of actual interpretation. All interpretative practice of particular works and passages, and not only New Critical readings, tend to furnish if not the closure of totalization, at least a high degree of hermeneutical coherence. This is as true of the kind of "critical linguistics" recently proposed by David Birch in the tradition of Roger Fowler's work as it is of the interpretive moves in Marie Maclean's *Narrative Performance*.[3] Ironically perhaps, it even applies to the most radically challenging reading strategies of Marxist criticism and decon-struction. Terry Eagleton's *The Rape of Clarissa*, for example, is disruptive not so much of reading a novel in terms of a functionally structuring process as of a dominant because scholarship-sanctioned reading tradition.[4] More surprisingly perhaps, Jacques Derrida's reading of Foucault's analysis of a passage of Des-cartes' *Meditations* cannot hide that its interpretive fulcrum is noetic, i.e., the insistent questioning of propositional content from the basis of speech/writing processes. Once we occupy this vantage point of reading Derrida, deconstruction reveals itself likewise to be in collusion with a cohesion-producing herme-neutical strategy.[5] This, however, is less a failure of critical method as a byproduct of the pragmatic limits of discursivity (cf. chart, chapter 1). It is indeed ques-tionable whether even the most radically intentioned reading strategies with their creatively disruptive local tactics are able to escape the kinds of constraints somewhat conservatively sketched in the writings of Hans Robert Jauss. A suc-cinct formulation of his views can be found in his recent *Question and Answer: Forms of Dialogic Understanding* where he contrasts "the open horizon of a first reading with the retrospective horizon of a second reading."

> Thus, in the first phase of an analysis, one can trace the formation of aesthetic perception *in actu*. It can be described in terms of poetic structure and still-undefined expectations about the meaning of the text. In the second phase of the analysis, when one circles back from the end of the poem and the whole that has been established to the beginning, the aesthetic experience of the first reading can become the horizon of interpretive understanding, an understanding that elaborates a context of meaning from the conjecture and unanswered ques-tions that were part of that experience. Since this interpretation leaves unclear which of its elements have been engendered by the text and which have been imposed by the interpreter, the third phase of the analysis must delineate the earlier horizon in order to bring into play the temporal distance that was at first ignored. In addition, the meaning intended by the author must be reconstructed as a historical countervoice, and the interpreter's own understanding must be elucidated on the basis of the reception history that defines his horizon of inter-pretation.[6]

However difficult it may be to circumvent such conventions, they are, of course, not logical but *hermeneutical* constraints, i.e., limits laid down by a particular politics of reading. To return to the *logical* openness of reading, we are reminded of the liberality of Donald Davidson's schema for "radical inter-pretation." And indeed there are a number of agreements between his position and the kind of argument advanced here. However, there are also pivotal dif-ferences. Where we do concur is on his statement that any methodology of interpretation is "nothing but epistemology seen in the mirror of meaning." Except, of course, that meaning in Davidson is an *entity* to be backed up by recourse to the background of beliefs and desire, in short the social, while I regard meaning as the very *process* which activates portions of that semiotic. In his theory of radical interpretation Davidson draws substantially on two thinkers,

Tarski and Quine. From Tarski he adopts the theory of truth, even though he insists that in its application to natural languages it "differs widely in both aim and interest," and that the Tarskian "sharpness of application is lost."[7] In chapter 8 I shall briefly address the *aporia* which results from Davidson's pursuit of meaning via the route of Tarskian truth. Here we need to point out how Davidson reworks certain Quinean concepts to formulate his holistic theory of interpretation.

Davidson's "radical interpretation" is developed out of Quine's "radical translation" which ultimately yields no full guarantee of agreement between source and target language. There always remains what Quine has called an "indeterminacy of translation," the equivalent to Davidson's "indeterminacy of interpretation." To overcome this vagueness and so link utterances and the backgrounds of speaker/writer and listener/reader we need to "deliver simultaneously a theory of belief and a theory of meaning" in which "meanings and beliefs are interrelated constructs." Davidson's account promises to go a long way toward elucidating hermeneutic problems because he casts his net much wider than traditional theorists of meaning. "Both belief and desire," he states, "are related to meaning and knowledge," a linkage which necessitates the abandonment of strictly logical closure in favor of some broad assumptions and approximating explanations of meaning.[8]

The most general assumption is the Quinean "principle of charity" which stipulates basic similarities between an alien language and our own or, in Davidson's theory, between speaker and listener, writer and reader. In this sense Davidson speaks of an assumed "agreement between speaker and interpreter," but qualifies that it is "uncertain to what extent these principles can be made definite." Although the principle of charity assumes a certain level of agreement, the "*aim* of interpretation is not agreement but *understanding*."[9] By leaving aside his tying verbal signification to its backgrounds by means of truth we can read Davidson as loosening the traditional constraints of the meaning equation in favor of 'reading' as hermeneutical exploration.[10] This allows for the kind of radical reading I am proposing here.

This chapter, then, is meant as a demonstration of the stubborn plurality of paths to signification. If we accept the radical principle of semiosis, which is nothing but the possibility of differentially related signs, we are relieved forever of the illusion of a logical or otherwise binding barrier to meaning making. Instead of viewing the world in terms of language as opposed to objects, which sets limits to meaning, semiosis subsumes everything under the umbrella of significatory exchange. This principle of semiosis or, as Wlad Godzich has termed it, the "substance-effect," is no more than a "differentialist concept that marks the location where an inscription can take place."[11] My specific interpretive examples are meant merely to indicate such possible locations.

Why then choose a text as firmly entrenched in the syllabus as Keats's ode? The answer is simply to write against an embarrassment shared by many critics who fear that theorizing within the canon might destroy the very enterprise of theorizing in the institution of literature. Yet handing the 'canon' over to the anti-theoretical critic may frustrate the very attempt at re-embedding the literary text in the broader field of cultural studies.[12] Both the canon and its shifting margins provide us with a vast discursive, experimental playground, a language laboratory *par excellence*. This not only points to the complexity of the literary; it also says that almost all non-literary, discursive techniques are structurally prefigured in the intricacies of the literary text and its speech processes. Re-enter Keats, or any other similar discursive formation.

As I read the first lines of "To Autumn" my meaning making faculties are assaulted by a multitude of semiotic associations. If I choose to concentrate on the level of language itself, I may be fascinated by such simple alliterative euphonies as "mist" and "mellow," "round" and "run," and the rhythmic flow of "Until they think warm days will never cease." Or the semantic crescendo of "load," "bless with fruit," "bend with apples," "fill all fruit," "swell," "plump," and "set budding more, and still more" may draw on the paradigm of other techniques of accelerando, semantically quite unrelated to Keats's lines. If the substance-effect as a mere structural point of semiosis has at all a role to play it is to facilitate at this point my recalling the power of anaphora in Shakespeare's Sonnet 66:

> *And* needy nothing trimmed to jollity,
> *And* purest faith unhappily foresworn,
> *And* guilded honour . . . ,
> *And* maiden virtue . . . ,
> *And* right perfection . . . ,
> *And* strength by limping sway disabled,
> *And* art made tongue-tied by authority,
> *And* folly . . .
> *And* Simple truth miscalled simplicity,
> *And* captive good attending captain ill.[13]

There are actually two kinds of linguistic self-referentiality, a fact highlighted by literary discourse. Whenever I am referred back to the surface properties of language, I can perform acts without semantic-semiotic grasp, such as the musicality of words and their arrangements. The recognition of structural relations such as the repetition of letters and words does not depend on full meaning-giving acts. On the other hand, there are self-referential acts which depend on full semantic-semiotic exploration, as for example the crescendo of Nature's pregnancy in the first stanza.

The ninth month of the year, the pregnant season, affects all aspects of the opening of Keats's ode. As Harold Bloom puts it, "the fullness of nature's own grace, her free and overwhelming gift of herself, unfallen, is the burden of this ripe stanza."[14] Where "the teeming autumn big with rich increase" in Shakespeare's Sonnet 97 is placed in the gloomier picture of "mute" birds and leaves "dreading the winter's near," the world here is gloriously blessed. Having said this, does it make sense to claim a iiteral meaning or individual poetic achievement with which we should stay content? Obviously not. The notion of a limit to Keats's 'meanings' dissolves before a literary history to which he was tied, however inscrutably.

Autumnal ripeness and the abundance of lavish gifts is an ubiquitous poetic topos. Keats's sources could have included, for example, the works of Ovid, Virgil, Horace, Spenser, Pope, Blake, or Wordsworth. In Ovid's *Metamorphoses* and *Fasti* I find a male Autumnus, "stained with the trodden grapes (*calcatis sordidus uvis*);"[15] the speaker of Virgil's *Georgics* welcomes Dionysos: "Approach, Leneaen Father: here all things Are brimming with your gifts, for you the farmlands Flourish, large with Autumn's trailing vine, The vintage foams in swelling vats;"[16] and in Horace, "fruitful autumn has poured forth its harvest (*pomifer autumn fruges effuderit*)" or rears his head "crowned with ripened fruits" and "delights to pluck the grafted pears and grapes that with the purple vie."[17] Spenser's "Mutabilitie" in *The Faerie Queene* contains the following passage depicting personified Autumn who cheerfully surveys and reaps his harvest.

> Then came the Autumne all in yellow clad,
> As though he ioyed in his plentious store,
> Laden with fruits that made him laugh, full glad
> That he had banisht hunger, which to-fore
> Had by the belly oft him pinched sore.
> With eares of corne, of every sort he bore:
> And in his hand a sickle he did hold,
> To reape the ripened fruits the which the earth had yold.[18]

To Pope, the "pastoral is an image of what they call the Golden Age" and his autumn vision is tuned mellower by the transformation of Autumnus into the fair Pomona, whose task it is "the ripening fruits to tend, And see the boughs with happy burdens bend." As in Ovid's *Metamorphoses*, Pomona bears a pruning hook "To lop the growth of the luxurient year" (*qua modo luxuriem premit*), and so guards a vision in which the trees are crowned "with Autumn's Bounty."[19]

A sense of happy ripeness is associated with autumn also by Blake, who writes that "grapes and figs burst their covering to the joyful air" and asks Autumn, once more *sordidus uvis*, to stay for a while and sing:[20]

> To Autumn
>
> Autumn, laden with fruit, and stained
> With the blood of the grape, pass not, but sit
> Beneath my shady roof, there thou may'st rest,
> And tune thy jolly voice to my fresh pipe;
> And all the daughters of the year shall dance!
> Sing now the lusty song of fruits and flowers.

Keats's first stanza also appears to recast the joining of mellowness and pregnant abundance which I discover in Wordsworth's "Excursion": "And mellow

Autumn, charged with bounteous fruit, Where is she imagined? . . . Her lavish pomp and ripe magnificence?"[21]

While it is within the rules of the institution of literary criticism to root "To Autumn" in older discursive conventions beyond the author's conscious grasp, it is less acceptable to allow for the modern reader's post-Keatsian horizon of expectations. And yet the reader's whole poetic, linguistic-semiotic grasp functions as an ever present enabling fabric of meaning differentiation.

The risks involved in breaking the historical frame of 'influence' and so violating the 'arrow of time' are real, for once we accept this broader view we can no longer say that the later poetry of Hölderlin, Rilke, Trakl, or Baudelaire do not affect, legitimately qualify, or unavoidably bend the process of meaning making. Rilke's *"Befiehl den letzten Früchten voll zu sein; gib ihnen noch zwei südlichere Tage . . . und jage die letzte Süsse in den schweren Wein"* hovers over our reading, as do Hölderlin's *"Mit gelben Birnen hänget Und voll mit wilden Rosen Das Land in den See,"* or Trakl's *"Gewaltig endet so das Jahr Mit goldnem Wein und Frucht der Gärten."*[22]

The simple fact that the modern reader cannot free himself without considerable mental distortions from a set of semioses different from those available to Keats and his contemporaries renders problematic the question of historical meanings, not to mention its univocality. What applies to the whole of a text applies also, even if in a weaker fashion, to single expressions. There simply is no logical point at which propositional opacity may be segregated from propositional clarity—neither in the domain of literary speech, nor, as I shall argue, in the language of everyday life.

Although we are aware of the arrow of time in literary history, in the practice of reading we tend to move forward and backward without any great restraint and so activate discursive formations and specific topoi in a liberal manner. This is why Keats's opening question of the third stanza, "Where are the songs of Spring? Ay, where are they?" now cannot be read altogether outside such contexts as Hölderlin's *"Weh mir, wo nehm ich, wenn Es Winter ist, die Blumen, und wo Den Sonnenschein Und Schatten der Erde?"* or Baudelaire's sentiment in *"Chant d'Automne,"*: *"Bientôt nous plongerons dans les froides ténèbres; Adieu vive clarté de nos étés trop courts."*[23] The topos of melancholy farewell to the ending year is a generic convention which encourages semantic differential relations beyond the strictures of philological causality. It would be silly to say that Yeats's "Among what rushes will they build, By what lake's edge or pool Delight men's eyes when I awake some day To find they have flown away?" played a part in the genesis of "To Autumn," but it would be equally silly to claim that now that "The Wild Swans at Coole" is a facet of our reading conventions we could altogether escape the semiotic directionality of its lines and so produce pure, historical meanings out of Keats's ode. Yeats adds a new ambiance to the discourse of autumn.[24]

The argument for historically specific and other 'pure' (*a posteriori*) sense meanings ruled by a dictionary is bound to exaggerate semantic independence and undermine the contaminating linkages between discursive formations across time and their tenuous ties with other sign systems. It also assumes that dictionaries contain actual definitions, a view as incorrect as it is widespread. All that can be claimed for lexemes is that they act as directional schemata which facilitate meaning making within certain pragmatic constraints but without markers to terminate that process. Nor is it entirely satisfactory to argue as does Derrida that the subject is "a 'function' of language" and "becomes a speaking subject only by conforming his speech . . . to the system of linguistic prescriptions."[25] Although this goes a long way toward explaining what occurs in routine discourse, it fails to account for that substantial portion of social speech which violates this assumption. A more heterogeneous explanation is needed, for speakers can refuse to comply with linguistic prescriptions and so bend or dent them. It is in the possibility of such deviation that part of the vitality of language lies, as Derrida has himself demonstrated. Otherwise, one would have to describe language as a closed system into which speakers are forever and fully inscribed, a description which would relegate the necessary notion of dynamic change to the very metaphysic Derrida rightly attacks.

Such is the paradox of discourse, that a speech community and indeed any of its members is always in a position to alter its linguistic system by speaking against the rules which define both that system and the community itself. Paradoxically, the very discourse introduced by Jacques Derrida to philosophy and the humanities in general is both a demonstration of a counterdiscourse and a substantive critique of conceptuality and its limits. We shall return to this point in a later chapter.

Neither the summary descriptions of the lexicon nor the chess rule metaphor can supply an adequate description of language as speech event.[26] Nor is it cogent to argue that the meanings of expressions, literary or otherwise, can be isolated in any propositional form without doing violence to language as it actually occurs. Put in Austinean terms, there are no locutions per se, independent from illocutionary and perlocutionary acts. When I read, i.e., re-speak, the lines of "To Autumn" I cannot access its locutions without at the same time performing speech intentions as well as acts of affective concretizations, the fictional equivalent of perlocutions. And only if I were able to crystallize pure locutions out of Keats's poem could I be said to have achieved pure sense and literal meanings.[27]

If this is not possible, the unavoidable conclusion is that any reading involves as much 'extraneous' linguistic and semiotic material as is manageable in a given reading situation. Yet have we not now moved from the domain of meaning to that of significance? E. D. Hirsch has developed a strong argument along those lines.[28] My main objection to his strict separation of meaning and significance is that it confuses the sense of formal logic and that of the lexemes of natural language, a conflation he has inherited from the eidetic convictions in Husserl. This problem will recur as we look at discourse from various perspectives.

Suffice it here to reiterate that only the former is defined by a definition proper, and the latter can only metaphorically be said to be ruled in this way. Only in signification systems without reference and deixis, such as formal logic, can we argue cogently that significance has been split off from meaning. In culturally saturated discourses this distillation is not possible without violating meaning; what is meaningful, what has meaning as opposed to a lack of meaning, for a member of a semiotic community is always also at the same time significant. What something means to me cannot be fully severed from its significance in my holistic grasp of communal understanding of the world.

What is perhaps more in need of enquiry is the fact that those seemingly random additional interpretive moves illustrated so far with respect to Keats's ode are never purely subjective but are constrained by the multiple matrices of intersubjective typifications or typical ways of constituting semiosis. This is why I think John Lyons unnecessarily weakens his position at the end of *Language, Meaning and Context* when he suggests that

> The terms "subjectivity" and "subjectivism" have rather a bad name in the social sciences. It is my conviction, however, that any theory of meaning which fails to account for the subjectivity of reference, deixis and modality, in the sense which "subjectivity" has been explained in this chapter, is condemned to sterility.[29]

As I argue throughout, instead of stressing the subject we would be better served by talking about the necessity of instantiation. For even if the dissolution of the subject into networks of social forces means facing a description of infinite regress, we cannot leave it simply there, a last remnant of an untheorized metaphysic. Rather, we should address the rationale by which one determines the point where that *regressus infinitus* is to be terminated, a rationale linked to a specific reading practice.

To return to Keats and extend our hermeneutic helix, consider the teacher who brings into the classroom copies of van Gogh's *Wheatfield behind the Hôpital Saint Paul, The Siesta, The Reaper*, and one of his various *Sunflowers* in order to conduct a seminar in the "mutual illumination of the arts." He may be accused of a multiplicity of sins: that he or she is content oriented, that Keats could not have possibly been influenced by van Gogh, that van Gogh was definitely not influenced by Keats, that the landscapes the two artists thematize are profoundly different, that Keats's work is serene while van Gogh's never is, and so forth. Yet apart from the rules of a compartmentalizing convention, is there really a good reason for barring us from reading Keats through van Gogh or vice versa? In reading poems and paintings aren't we merely combining linguistic-semiotic and visual-semiotic explorations?

There is nothing in van Gogh's letters to suggest that those paintings could have taken their cue from Keats. And yet, the middle stanza of "To Autumn" as well as the poet's own commentary mark a point of entry into a broader interpretive field. "Somehow, a stubble-field looks warm—in the same way that some pictures look warm."[30] Do we, however, need such legitimating signatures in the first place? I suggest we do not, other than as political, not logical, backups for continuing our acts of reading.

The extension of reading a linguistic code by way of visual semiosis again enriches by virtue of relational differences. The combination of language and image makes us place verbal discourse consciously into a semiotic context of being always in some respects related and at the same time differing typifications of experiential grasp. This sort of procedure, I suggest, merely makes conscious an activity which occurs all the time between not just two but numerous, distinct sign systems.

To van Gogh, "the burnt-up grass takes on lovely tones of gold," and "the sun sheds a radiance of pale sulphur."[31] And yet there is a violence in the glow of these pictures which is much more closely related to Baudelaire than to Keats. In "Le Soleil" in *Les Fleurs du Mal* we read, "*Quand le soleil cruel frappe à traits redoublés Sur la ville et les champs, sur les toits et les blés.*"[32] The Keats text is thus juxtaposed to and freshly read against the darker brightness of van Gogh's perspective: "There. The Reaper is finished . . . it is an image of death as the great book speaks about it—but what I have sought is the 'almost smiling.' It is yellow except a line of violet hills, a pale fair yellow. . . . "[33] At the same time we are also being referred back to other poems. The meaning chain which we could hitch to the signifier "yellow" alone could sustain an exercise in comparative reading. Spenser sees autumn "in yellow clad," in Shakespeare's Sonnet 104 spring and youth decline to "yellow autumn," and Hopkins marks the season in the line, "And scarcely does appear the autumn yellow feather in the boughs."[34]

Reading in this broad sense is by no means bound to the content of a yellow season. Perhaps more interesting is a reading of the ways of seeing which we can posit in the literary text. This again may remain confined to a merely technical discussion of point of view, presentational processes and perspective. On the other hand, a more committed investigation of the speaker's gaze as construable in Keats's "To Autumn" may well yield altogether different results.

The middle stanza is characterized by acts of seeing and discovery. "Who hath not seen thee . . . may find thee . . . ," a situation of viewing and being viewed. But who does the gazing and who is being looked at? In the poems of classical antiquity, autumn is a male *autumnus* who visits the vineyards and orchards to partake in harvest feasts. Gradually *autumnus* is replaced by Pomona, and with this transformation of gender occurs also a change in the speaker's gaze. Ovid's *Metamorphoses* must be regarded as one of the founding celebratory texts presenting a desirable and pursued Pomona, a figure which informs later versions of female personifications of autumn. In Keats this voyeuristic tradition takes on a special form.

We can observe a peculiar symmetry in "To Autumn," in that the first and last stanzas are framing devices for a personified female in the middle. At the center of that middle stanza we are directed to stare at a woman "on a half-reap'd furrow sound asleep, Drowsed with the fume of poppies." She is presented as drugged and helpless, as vulnerable to the gaze of the reader as she is passive to the fantasies of her creator. It is probably with unconscious irony that Keats writes about the occasion of his artistic inspiration, "How fine the air—a temperate sharpness about it . . . without joking, chaste weather. . . . "[35]

If one were to press the point of sexual representation and gazing further, one could develop a quite cogent argument for a reading of "To Autumn" under the heading "The Rape of Autumn." What has hitherto been read as a statement about the pregnant autumnal season can now be viewed from the perspective of the author's slip of the pen on "chastity." A reading in terms of negation and repression transforms images of swelling and ripening into those of unacknowledged but irrepressible arousal. At the level of poetic fantasy, then, the autumn landscape turns into a patient object of desire. This would make sense also macrostructurally in that the bursting aggression of the first stanza leads to the rape of a female autumn, while the lingering oozings of the cider press give way to the postcoital melancholy of the poem's finale.

Yet this framing of the female in Keats's ode is strangely absent in the critical literature, especially in the New Critical literature, the defenders of which are so fond of charging literary theory with having lost sight of the details of the text. Whichever way we look at the words, the detail of the voyeuristic gaze is now present, even in the flawed sense of a literal reading. Why then was it not seen before? The answer, I suggest, has two sides. Even where it can be shown at a given moment in literary criticism that a certain signification is 'present' it cannot be seen unless the appropriate system of reading is available. Feminist and psychoanalytic theory have prepared the ground and, suddenly, obvious meanings, not so obvious a short while ago, spring from the text, or rather, they constitute a new text. This is the other side of the answer, namely that meaning is not present in the words at all but is always the result of a particular reading practice, a practice which is both a function of a critical vocabulary and the producer of deviations from that norm.

The propositional opacity of Keats's poem—as of all culturally saturated language—has turned out not to be a defect, but on the contrary, a rich resource. From the perspective of radical reading as a permissive activity in search of signification this should not be surprising. Far from being an obstacle to discovery the relative vagueness of expressions permits and even demands the production of ever new statements, in Foucault's sense of the term. Perhaps we should recall here the point which Godzich makes with respect to substance-effect, or the principle, not the specific instance of differential relations as the logical basis on which signification can take place. Propositional opacity is likewise a principle, a condition without which words and their combinations cannot be read. It adheres to all culturally saturated language. As such it must be distinguished from the specific opaqueness of a particular expression which that principle leads us to explore. Furthermore, as we have seen from our cursory readings, statements about literary texts never emerge fortuitously or in isolation; rather, they are part of horizontally arranged webs of concepts which act as their hermeneutic frame.

But is our reading of necessity restricted to the purview of poetic and semiotic intertextuality, or schools of literary theory? What about the domains of philosophy? Again, we must insist, there is no logical marker in "To Autumn" (or for that matter any other literary discourse) to declare its readings through the philosophical text a deviant procedure. The only guidance we can admit is the distinction, not self-evident to be sure, between philosophical discourses which spawn rich and interesting readings and those which do not.

As a heterogeneous speech act the poem is of course not to be identified with an ordinary assertion. Otherwise we might be tempted to secure its meaning by construing Tarskian truth sentences, as does Davidson with natural language expressions. Truth notions aside, there are nevertheless fields of propositional content, however opaque, with which communities of readers respond to literary discourse. And even if we were to insist that all poetic texts and their literary readings be prefaced by a general modal such as "Poetically speaking . . . " semiosis can take place only in terms of their differential relations to other texts and alternative propositional contents.

In this sense our readings always say something; they assert a certain propositional certitude, or what has so variedly and unhappily been referred to as a 'truth.' Here the term will be used not in its own right, but merely as a quotation. In a totalizing kind of reading truth could be said to be a subsummation of central ideas, such as the tranquil and pure (or tranquillized and puritanical) vision of autumn. The work of art, such as "Grecian Urn," or the vista depicted on that Attic shape, or the poetic vision of the autumnal season are to the Romantic writer "a friend to man" advising us that "Beauty is truth, truth beauty," the ultimate knowledge which we can know and need to know.[36] European Romanticism is in part characterized by the fusion of the aesthetic with the epistemic and moral and thus by a peculiar aestheticization of the notion of truth. It is for this reason that any reading of Romantic poetry which wishes to go beyond New Critical, autobiographical or narrowly political constrictions is bound to address the question of how the assertion of this identity relates to other discourses on "truth."

Again, the choice is not entailed in the 'literal' meaning of "To Autumn." But then, there was no sign-post to tell us where literal meanings ended and other forms of significations took their place. For such is the propositional opacity of the literary text that we can cogently argue the absence of logical barriers for further discursive exploration, but not the rules for the specifics which we must bring to bear on that text. The choice is always political, as, for example, in Nietzsche and Heidegger. Perhaps the most devastating attacks on truth concepts ever launched are those by Nietzsche, especially in his late work *The Will to Power* and in the paper "On Truth and Falsity in Their Ultramoral Sense." In its Cartesian as well as moral and religious forms "truth" is hounded as the projection of "our oldest faith . . . our habit of believing this to be true or false." Nietzsche rests his critique on questioning the unclarified assumptions underlying notions of truth. "Logical accuracy, transparency, considered as the criterion of truth (*'omne illud verum est, quod clare et distincte percipitur.'*— Descartes); by this means the mechanical hypothesis of the world becomes desirable and credible." Before he offers a summary dismissal of all claims to truth Nietzsche divides the concept "true" into three categories: "True—from the standpoint of sentiment—is that which most provokes sentiment ('I'); from the standpoint of thought—is that which gives thought the greatest sensation of strength; from the standpoint of touch, sight, and hearing—is that which calls forth the greatest resistance."

It is not any inherent truth value, then, but rather "the highest degrees of activity which awaken belief in regard to the object, in regard to its reality." Anticipating Freud's new basis of conjecture, Nietzsche psychologizes the various truth criteria: "What is truth?—Inertia; that hypothesis which brings satisfaction." And it is a radically anti-empiricist stance which results in the assertion that "the criterion of truth lies in the enhancement of the feeling of power."[37] The question receives a well known answer in a likewise psychological explanation in "On Truth and Falsity in Their Ultramoral Sense:" "What therefore is truth? A mobile army of metaphors, metonymies, anthropomorphisms: in short a sum of human relations which become poetically and rhetorically intensified, metamorphosed, adorned . . . truths are illusions of which one has forgotten that they *are* illusions."[38]

In one sense the assertion of a "valid" vision of Autumn as of any 'representation' or the visual and verbal mastery of a Greek vase support Nietzsche's psychologization of truth as a rationalization of satisfaction, which stems from being in charge, from having and holding control, from having imposed a special order on things. At the same time the institution of reading Romantic poetry has tended to deny those hidden features of the Keatsean text which guarantee the return of the repressed: the darker beautiful "truth" of a transformed *autumnus*. Yet the authorial emphasis on the innocent vista of the autumnal scene with its "fine air," "Dian skies," and "chaste weather" is bound to be replaced at a certain point in the history of reading by the focus on the meticulous voyeur-phenomenologist who feasts and entices the reader to feast likewise on the adumbrational picture sequence of an Attic shape or the tranquillized female of "To Autumn."

Nietzsche is probably right not merely in a polemical sense in substituting notions of satisfaction and power for those of truth. To pinpoint in the poetic text and even more so in its institutionalized readings where precisely the assertion of a 'truthful and beautiful vision' conceals those unacknowledged significations probably yields insights not so much into 'truth' as into the mechanics of composition and the reception of texts.

Because it seems best to postpone until later the discussion of the principle of truth, falsity and verification in relation to the description of meaning, I would like to restrict myself at this point to a brief introduction to another non-analytic treatment of the notion of truth: Heidegger's view of truth as "unconcealment." In "The Origin of the Work of Art" Heidegger talks about van Gogh's *Peasant Shoes*: "a pair of peasant shoes and nothing more. And yet—"

> From the dark opening of the worn insides of the shoes the toilsome tread of the worker stares forth. In the stiffly rugged heaviness of the shoes there is the

accumulated tenacity of her slow trudge through the far-spreading and ever-uniform furrows of the field swept by a raw wind. On the leather lie the dampness and richness of the soil. Under the soles slides the loneliness of the field-path as evening falls. In the shoes vibrates the silent call of the earth, its quiet gift of the ripening grain and its unexplained self-refusal in the fallow desolation of the wintry field. This equipment is pervaded by uncomplaining anxiety as to the certainty of bread, the wordless joy of having once more withstood want, the trembling before the impending childbed and shivering at the surrounding menace of death. This equipment belongs to the earth, and it is protected in the world of the peasant woman. From out of this protected belonging the equipment itself rises to its resting-within-itself.[39]

In arguing for his notion of truth as it reveals itself through the work of art Heidegger has actually pleaded for a rich form of meaning constitution. Vastly different as Heidegger's truth conception may be from those in the analytic tradition, it too is an unwarranted ingredient in a theory of meaning which tries to address discursive actualities rather than thought experiments. So we leave the issue of truth once more to one side and salvage instead those aspects of the argument which contribute to the question of meaning conferment. My reasons for this evasion are thus: first, I believe that Heidegger's etymological procedure of reviving buried meanings in order to enrich an impoverished present cannot be accomplished by way of his hermeneutic helix, even if it makes for excitingly rich readings. Present significations loom far too large for the past to reveal itself in its being. Second and more seriously, I think that his attempt at replacing the empty truth notions of rival philosophers was a dangerous intellectual move. Heidegger's stipulation of truth as the "unconcealment of that which is as something that is" abandons responsible social vision and so holds no guarantees as to the particular nature of what "slouches towards Bethlehem to be born." It was precisely this unreason which misled him deplorably in his own political sympathies.[40]

If truth notions are misplaced in literary discourse, so is the assumption of the possibility of any neutral sort of meaning endowment. All meaning making is colored by interest in its referential and self-referential senses, which always amounts to a politics, and Heidegger's reading of van Gogh's painting is no exception. There is the philosopher's interest in finding an interpretation which best unconceals the hidden truth of his own theory of unconcealment. I recognize this modality in a certain animation of detail: "from the opening . . . stares forth . . . in the shoes vibrates the silent call of the earth." At the same time we cannot help but concretize the more sinister aspects of a political unconscious which made Heidegger ground van Gogh's work in a mythology of the soil and blood.

In the act of viewing a painting I move from one ontological region, the social semiotic, to another, that of the imaginative projection of possible worlds, of what is pictured and its modal shadow, an inferrable painter/viewer. For both worlds the picture acts as indispensable point of departure, as visual directional schema. With the aid of this visual guide we 'transport' ourselves, or in Heidegger's more passive formulation, "in the vicinity of the work we were suddenly somewhere else than we usually tend to be."[41] As I have argued that verbal expressions act as schemata with a beginning and multiple targets, so too would I wish, beyond Heidegger, to understand pictures as doubly directional signs which launch and guide my imaginative acts of propositional and modal meaning constitution.

Those who believe in the stability of a given sense must reject this account. They must present the altogether different view that I look at a painting, understand or fail to understand its basic message, enjoy it or otherwise, and decide to act upon it or abstain from any pragmatic response. To be sure, minimal meaning making is always a possible choice, but I would suggest that in the case of paintings or poetic discourse this would be a reading not just against conventional frames but against the ladder of discourse (cf. chapter 8). Heidegger rightly supports this view. "If anything is questionable here," he says about his interpretation of van Gogh's painting, "it is rather that we experience too little in the neighbourhood of the work and that we expressed the experience too crudely and too literally."[42]

Indeed. And why should we not explore broader and richer fields of signification and so violate Gadamer's fusion of the "horizons" of past and present?[43] If we feel that reading the 'canon' from intertextual, intersemiotic, and a range of theoretical perspectives is to commit a dastardly version of the affective fallacy, we need to remind ourselves that it is an illusion to assume that we ever read without such admixtures. To insist that affective and intentional, or perlocutionary and illocutionary, materials lie outside literary meaning requires a positivist legitimation procedure which is no more than a political act.

In spite of my shelving the definitional task, a description of sorts of what happens when we engage in meaning making will eventually emerge from my quirky use of the hermeneutic helix in which I must do the round again and again without ever reoccupying my starting position in any identical sense. It would no doubt be less cumbersome to propose a tight definition of meaning and then demonstrate its applicability by way of example. But the formal ideal of a definition in its very tautness contradicts in principle that which it wishes to codify. What is worse, the task would not really be that much simpler, since once I have fixed discourse in this manner I would need to spend the rest of my effort on widening the Spanish boots of the definition in order to accommodate forever wider feet, higher insteps, and bigger toes. This is precisely what has happened throughout the history of the description of meaning in ordinary language philosophy, formal logic, modal logic, speech act theory, and indirect speech act theory from Frege to Davidson and Searle.

The methodological linearity of arguing from an atomistic starting point toward ever more complex data requires as its dialectical counterpart an analysis which begins with the description of the acts which I am bound to perform in the processes of actual speech, or discourse. In this, the *process* of literary meaning plays a crucial role since literarity is the experimental crucible for all discourse. Propositional opacity in literature, the fact that one cannot pin down the meaning content of literary expressions seems disadvantageous only from the perspective of full-scale formalization. From the viewpoint of imaginative meaning making literary discourse, for the very same reasons, holds great promise. It encourages acts of concretization far beyond sense definition and in so doing reveals itself as the ludic extension of everyday speech.

Literary discourse and the speech performance of everyday life, however, are more closely related than theories of language tend to acknowledge. To foreshadow a thesis which will be posited from various perspectives throughout this book, all signification can be shown to produce meaning only in relationship to at least one other sign system. As far as language is concerned, this means that linguistic expressions mean by way of intersemiotic linkage, by being activated by non-verbal sign systems. Propositional opacity, then, has its roots in the depth of the non-linguistic, semiotic background to which language refers. Therefore there is strictly no such thing as a linguistic semantics without a broad semiotics.[44]

Inferrable modality, the Siamese twin of propositional vagueness, further undermines the possibility of any stable propositional content in literary discourse and, more controversially, also in everyday speech. Because inferrable modality is always a dynamic construction, it too escapes any precise fixing and so adds to the fuzziness and rich interpretability of natural language. One way of giving a generalized demonstration of the effects of inferrable modalities on meaning is to look at a systemic example rather than at individual speech instantiation: the analysis of a genre. Modal opacity, as it functions in a special literary genre, the *Künstlerroman*, will be the focus of the following chapter.

III

THE MODALITIES OF THE "KÜNSTLERROMAN"

> All of them moments which remain inklings
> rather than confirmations.
>
> Patrick White, *Flaws in the Glass*[1]

I have described inferrable modality as the modal shadow of all propositional content. This implies that every reading must construct propositional meanings against the backdrop of the parallel construction of a speech stance and an utterance motivation. Yet the concept of inferrable modality implies more. It says also that my reading does not innocently start with the word on the page but sets in motion at the same time my own set of literary and non-literary typifications, discursive as well as non-discursive formations, and linguistic as well as non-linguistic orders of semiosis as a massive background into which my acts of meaning making are embedded. In turn this thematized background knowledge acts upon my reading as an all-pervasive modal force.

Why, however, choose the *Künstlerroman* as an illustration? Do not its discursive formations and macrostructural design attempt to revive the Romantic notion of genius which literary theory is at pains to deconstruct? Possibly. What is of primary interest here is that the *Künstlerroman* mediates what it projects more radically than other genres. Its polymodal discourse of 'art' constitutes meanings in an instructively indirect manner. Here interpretive inferences are realized above all as intertextual generic and intersemiotic *deferred* modalities. To highlight this special kind of opacity is the aim of this chapter.

The indefinite article in the title of *A Portrait of the Artist as a Young Man*, the search for something as unpromising as time in *A la recherche du temps perdu*, the distancing by naming in *Doctor Faustus*, the irony in *My Brilliant Career*, the expression "I am listening" as a likely filler for the ellipsis in Nabokov's *Speak Memory*, or the polysemic acts launched by Boris Pasternak's title *Okhrannaya Gramata* (*Secret Record*, or is it *Intimate Document* or perhaps *Grammar of my Heart?*) impart vectoriality of signification rather than propositional certitude.[2]

All signs can be understood as typified recipes for meaning endowment.

Phenomenologically speaking, they invite us to reconstitute our intersubjective stock-of-knowledge-at-hand into ever new structures of themes and horizons. This vectorial definition of meaning reminds us of the classical definition of intentionality as directional activity of consciousness. In this sense, language is a subset of signs which encodes semiotic instructions, a process of which literary discourse makes special use. Whereas in artificial language meaning endowment amounts to the strict sense of fully sharable noematic formalization (the fixing of meaning units and formal abstraction or emptying of material content), in literary discourse and its forms of reading much of the construction of meaning relies on acts of noetic deformalization, i.e., imaginative realization of deixis and appresentation, or on processes of concretization.[3]

I have chosen the *Künstlerroman* as a paradigm for all texts most appropriately read by stressing reading expansion and ongoing interpretive processes versus texts favoring stability of meaning and subsuming abstraction. On the double coordinates of noema-noesis, the meant and the process of meaning, and of formalization-deformalization, the *Künstlerroman* is situated on the side of the noetic and deformalizing or concretizing acts. This means that the reader must oppose the "Linnean lust to define and categorize"[4] just as he must question the positivist lunacy of tracing the word *Dreck* and its synonyms through the verbal organism of *The Vivisector* in order to arrive at an interpretative crotch and half-Nelson hold.[5] Instead, this chapter attempts to demonstrate the technical appropriateness and by implication the social value of interpretation in favor of meaning instability and thus a high rate of semantic drift as a necessary consequence of the expansive process of meaning construction from multiple perspectives. What keeps the semantic drift of different discourses within the boundaries of communication is a question which will be dealt with in later chapters.

One of the tasks in reading the *Künstlerroman* is to engage the hermeneutic code which hides the kinds of art the protagonists strive for and confront, to unravel how, as Shakespeare puts it, "we are mock'd with art." (*The Winter's Tale*, V, 3, 1.60) Much as we would like to be able to actualize whatever art is 'embedded' in *The Moon and Sixpence, Sons and Lovers,* Hesse's *Peter Camenzind,* or Theodore Dreiser's *The Genius* we tend to perform considerable hermeneutic labor and often manage little more than a glimpse of the arcanum of artistic vision. The *Künstlerroman* is a genre which systemically supports the claim that meaning is a linking procedure between linguistic schemata and non-verbal sign systems, with language to language reference as a special instance. In this the *Künstlerroman* highlights two related phenomena, intersemiotic processes and the opaque and largely unclarified nature of such linkages.[6]

When Gauguin says that "people accuse me of being incomprehensible only because they look for an explicative side to my pictures which is not there,"[7] he points to a general desire in interpretation to jump to propositional conclusions instead of savoring the instability of meaning exploration. This inclination is particularly problematic when we project possible art works through semiotic translation. Or, through Hurtle Duffield's double transformation, "If you could put it in words, I wouldn't want to paint" (*The Vivisector*, 196). When we do get descriptions of artworks within the presented world, our actualizations often remain more schematic than we would perhaps have expected:

> There his Doppelganger was leering at him out of a distorting mirror. He took a brush and extenuated the rather too desirable mouth into a straight line. He was right. The eyes agreed. The shoulders sank into place. For the rest of daylight he hung about, dabbing and wiping, tidying his paint, unexpectedly meticulous in attending to unimportant details. He realized his physical mouth was hanging open, his breath snoring in a solid stream from between his lips, as though he had just woken from a demanding sleep (239).

White's authorial narrator knows, as does his artist, that even if he attempted to present a true "representation of reality he couldn't achieve it." "He had never been altogether dishonest; nor yet entirely honest because that isn't possible" (235). The shift to the present tense transforms the statement from Hurtle's speech to a more confessional discourse. But even photography is realized as a process of destabilization: "Now he was appalled by his own dirty, horny feet. In the snapshot they looked deformed. Or was it distorted?" (229). Much clearer than a propositional vision of any artwork in Patrick White's novel is Hurtle's will to conceive art again and again as if with the power of a monstrous eja-culation with which "to shoot at an enormous naked canvas a whole radiant chandelier awaiting in his mind and balls" (207).

Although Elstir's paintings in *A la recherche du temps perdu* "are described with the detail necessary to attach Marcel's thoughts to an actual experience of specific works of art,"[8] the reader is not really guided to visualize his world with any precision. Rather, they function as signs directing us to imagine me-taphoric, intentional image combinations, especially fusions of discrete universes of imagery. Here our reading should also perhaps rest substantially on processes of artistic imagining and their possible functions as aspects of the presented world, aspects of Marcel's development as experiencing persona, Marcel as nar-rating self, and certain tentatively inferrable authorial insights.

Likewise, La Berma's "complete identification with her roles," Bergotte's lit-erary "harmony of image and idea," or Vinteuil's sonata lend themselves far less to any fixing of their form or content than to their realization as vectors toward artistic possibilities which we may wish to entertain.[9] Of the four artists, Elstir's way of seeing probably comes closest to what the reader might construct as Marcel's vision and, at a further remove, Proust's own. Incidentally, in Elstir Proust pursues certain phenomenological principles of cognition and meaning endowment, as for example the imaginative, eidetic variation of experience through acts of forgetting, faulty vision, and incorrect identification, with the result of producing imaginative extensions, reversals of experience and other acts of defamiliarization. Elstir's paintings "virtually recreate" the world by ex-tracting, "*du chaos que sont toutes choses que nous voyons.*"[10]

On the beach in the foreground the painter had contrived that the eye should discover no fixed boundary, no absolute line of demarcation between land and sea. The men who were pushing down their boats into the sea were running as much through the waves as along the sand, which, being wet, reflected the hulls as if they were already in the water. The sea itself did not come up in an even line but followed the irregularities of the shore, which the perspective of the picture increased still further, so that a ship actually at sea, half-hidden by the projecting works of the arsenal, seemed to be sailing through the middle of the town; women gathering shrimps among the rocks had the appearance, because they were sur- rounded by water and because of the depression which, beyond the circular barrier of rock, brought the beach (on the two sides nearest the land) down to sea-level, of being in a marine grotto overhung by ships and waves, open yet protected in the midst of miraculously parted waters. (*Recherche I*, 894f.)

Understood primarily as static visual representations, Elstir's work, like that of the other fictitious Proustian artists, produces merely "an appreciation in a void," and so "Marcel's impressions often seem abstract and unconvincing."[11] Viewed modally, or as a manner of seeing, we arrive at a more generative response. Not only can we imaginatively apply Elstir's methodological insights to vary our own habitual way of viewing, but we also find that his art links much more richly with Marcel's artistic philosophical vision at the end of the novel if read noetically rather than noematically.

If the art of painting is particularly reticent to translation into linguistic signs, perhaps musical compositions are more readily grasped through their linguistic masks. Even though we are given the most detailed discussions of music in Thomas Mann's *Doctor Faustus*, the tunes of Adrian Leverkühn's "Apocalypsis cum figuris" or "The Lamentation of Doctor Faustus" remain as shadowy as the paintings of Hurtle Duffield or Paul Morel. Even if the expert assistance of Theodor Adorno as recorded in *The Genesis of a Novel* points to accuracy, it is not an accuracy in the sense of noematic reproduction of music as an art: " ' . . . if you will allow me—this is important; this is something we want to be quite accurate about.' And in a few words he briefed me on the technical aspects of the opus (Leverkühn's violin concerto), the parody of being carried away."[12] Nor does Mann's diary enlighten us as to specific sounds. "Drawing on the scrapbook for ideas for the Faust oratorio. The whole thing to be chronic his- torically linked to the *lamento* of the seventeenth-century breakthrough from formal construction to expression."[13] Nor, moreover, does it help to know that the novel draws on some seventy composers and presents a variant of Schön- berg's twelve-tone scale, even if the analyses given are often so detailed that one is led to assume Mann had a "clear musical image before him."[14] In the absence of a tape or record as part of the material of the novel, the reader must remain content with a high degree of tonal indeterminacy. We know the kind of music but not what music it is.

Just as Elstir's painting may serve as an illustration of a Proustian method, or Hurtle Duffield's paintings as a metaphor for White's way, perhaps, of excising reality, so musical descriptions in *Doctor Faustus* can serve as "a cipher concealing the element of personal confession in the novel, as a symbol-language whereby he (Mann) gains perspective on his own preoccupations and manages to work them into the biography of his fictitious musician."[15] Yet far beyond autobiographical implications, the musical ciphers point also to the parallel of an excess in formalist art and political reaction. As George Lukács observed in his *Essays on Thomas Mann*, "inevitably, then, this desire for order and synthesis, which springs from the modern disintegration of individuality and so remains purely subjective, continually verges on those tendencies which feed into imperialist reaction and ultimately fascism. What comes out here is the essential bond between the formal synthesis of modern art and the reactionary ideologies of the age."[16] Not only does behind Leverkühn's music—even though we have only a vague notion of its sounds—"lurk the deepest despair, the despair of a real artist for the social function of art,"[17] but his music, in "startling its own humanity for the sake of art,"[18] also hints at that "monstrous flowering of the German soul,"—Fascism.[19] We may sense something like this in Adrian's proposal of what he calls "strict style":

> words of twelve letters, certain combinations and interrelations of the twelve semitones, series of notes from which a piece and all the movements of a work must strictly derive. Every note of the whole composition, both melody and harmony, would have to show its relation to this fixed fundamental series. Not one might recur until the other notes have sounded. Not one might appear which did not fulfill its function in the whole structure. There would no longer be a free note. That is what I would call 'strict composition.'
>
> (*Doctor Faustus*, 191)

Though nothing practical comes of Adrian's implied world view, his flirtation with barbarism, with the "abandonment of the artist's social and technical freedom for disciplines restoring the past . . . (perhaps) echo Nietzsche's question— where are the barbarians of the twentieth century?"[20] Howling glissandi as a barbaric, unsentimental return to nature, combined with atonal liberation and iron constructivism point toward a parallel between Adrian's music and German history: they are both "restorative in the revolutionary sense and to that extent fascistic."[21] Interpretive parallels, or perhaps better homologies, are what we tend to realize between the art of music and the art of the novel in *Doctor Faustus*. However, they are complex relationships, suggesting as they do a new maze rather than the *solution* to a puzzle. Commenting on the "montage principle," Mann lists a number of borrowings by means of which he places obstacles into any innocently fictional reading: "Living persons . . . Nietzsche's experience in the Cologne bordello . . . the devil's quotations from Ecce Homo . . . borrowings . . . from Nietzsche's letters . . . the biography of Tchaikovsky . . . Quotations of this kind have something musical about them . . . they are . . . reality transformed into fiction . . . thus creating a strangely protean and attractive mingling of the spheres."[22]

Yet again, even such close guidance is suggestive more of ways of reading than of thematic answers. On the other hand, we may feel inclined to accept as interpretative subsumption Mann's own words on the novel's "central idea: the flight from the difficulties of the cultural crisis in the pact with the devil, the craving of a proud mind, threatened by sterility, for an unblocking of inhibitions at any cost, and the parallel between pernicious euphoria ending in collapse with the nationalistic frenzy of Fascism."[23] This, however, is a projection, a plan which, however helpful in alerting us to possibilities of writing and reading, predates Sunday May 23, 1943, when both the author and his narrator, Professor Serenus Zeitblom, begin to "write." And what Zeitblom, Leverkühn, Stephen Dedalus, Hurtle Courtnee-Duffield, or Marcel produce is an inferrable function of what they themselves 'are,' which in turn is a function of the relationship between what they produce, how they produce and their placing by an inferrable authorial aesthetic-ideological goal: we find ourselves in a kind of method- ological circle, the hermeneutic circle par excellence, which is vicious unless we turn it into a hermeneutic helix.

Even if we acknowledge that the *Künstlerroman* wishes to provide primarily the aesthetic frame within which art creation is possible, we nevertheless hope that the protagonists' aesthetic discourse will be fulfilled by some form of prac- tice. In Stephen Dedalus's case we are granted a few rare glimpses, as for ex- ample, the villanelle, the Shelleyan tone of which echoes an era unaffected by the production of *die nicht mehr schönen Künste*.

> Are you not weary of ardent ways,
> Lure of the fallen seraphim?
> Tell no more of enchanted days.
>
> (*Portrait*, 217)

The poem and the preceding aesthetic discourse can be read as a question-and- answer structure. Yet it is probably too simple to say that "Joyce seems to have proceeded from definition—Stephen's—to demonstration—his own."[24] Both Stephen's credo that "the lyrical form is in fact the simplest verbal vesture of an instant of emotions, a rhythmical cry" (214) and the villanelle are grasped as anachronistic aspects of the presented world and thus in the first instance as predicates of the artist, that is, if we see fictional characters as composite pred- icates as does Gilbert Ryle. At the same time but in a less direct way, our constructions of "definition" as well as its "demonstration" act as modal variants on what we may wish to hold to be the inferrable authorial position.

More than in any other *Künstlerroman*, the overwhelming flow of words of Proust's *A la recherche du temps perdu* appears to drown our very inclination to draw demarcation lines between created art, art theory, the artist and his response to life, and indeed, the inferrable authorial view. Critics tend to agree that this should not be surprising since the fusion of realms of experience is at the center of the novel's presented world and presentational process. Why shouldn't it therefore also be at the heart of the overall interpretive "instructions" which we glean from the novel? And yet, since the distinctions between art, artist, and inferred author are the result of perspectives rather than entities in themselves, we may still pursue them guardedly and provisionally. Perhaps *A la recherche* merely highlights the general principle that the focus of any particular passage may always imply its dialectic relationship with the whole text. For it is not from any quotation, however promising, that the art, artist, or inferred authorial stance emerge most convincingly, but from the whole of the text. Attractive passages are merely different adumbrational aspects of the same total body of the text and its enveloping structures. With this proviso, let me focus on one portion of the text in which intensively lived semiosis and writing are fused into a unified manner of seeing and, I would argue, a latent interpretive method:

> An image presented to us by life brings with it, in a single moment, sensations which are in fact multiple and heterogeneous. The sight, for instance, of the binding of a book once read may weave into the characters of its title the moonlight of a distant summer night. The taste of our breakfast coffee brings with it that vague hope of fine weather which so often long ago, as with the day still intact and full before us, we were drinking it out of a bowl of white porcelain, creamy and fluted and itself looking almost like vitrified milk, suddenly smiled upon us in the pale uncertainty of the dawn. An hour is not merely an hour, it is a vase full of scents and sounds and projects and climates, and what we call reality is a certain connexion between these immediate sensations and the memories which envelop us simultaneously with them—a connexion that is suppressed in a simple cinematographic vision, which just because it professes to confine itself to the truth in fact departs widely from it—a unique connexion which the writer has to rediscover in order to link forever in his phrase the two sets of phenomena which reality joins together.
>
> (*A la recherche*, III, 924)

Marcel is not giving us his answers as to the propositional meaning of experience. Instead he performs a classical phenomenological description by generalizing from his own acts of consciousness and those he infers from his fellow artists. Beginning with (1) a monothetic focusing on (2) a theme (e.g., "*Le goût du café au lait matinal*"), he describes possible additional items of consciousness which are pulled into (3) the horizon of the one experience ("*sensations multiples et différentes*"). Yet the thematic centre is in itself available only as (4) an aspect, a glimpse of reality (e.g., "*la vue, par exemple, de la couverture d'un livre*"). And yet a single aspect is sufficient to realize a highly saturated semiosis; this is possible on the grounds of our habitual performance of (5) appresentation. In addition to what we immediately confront, we add further absent, but available aspects ("*les rayons de lune d'une lointaine nuit d'été*"). Indeed, the monothetic realization of "an hour" explodes into (6) the polythetic aspects of "*un vase rempli de parfums, de sons, de projets et de climats*," resulting in (7) the synthetic experience of reality as a connection of different sign systems ("*Ce que nous appelons la réalité est un certain rapport* . . . "), while (8) the summary noema of *"réalité"* is constituted by (9) the noesis of *"rapport,"* a linking *"que l'écrivain doit retrouver pour en enchaîner à jamais dans sa phrase les deux termes différents."*[25] Quite apart from its mirroring of phenomenological cognition, what we are being offered here in fictional form is nothing less than Proust's intuitive grasp of a directional theory of meaning.

Pablo Picasso is reported to have once said that "painting is a blind man's profession." How appropriate this statement is if we apply it to the fictitious artists of the *Künstlerroman*! And therefore how much less certain can be our constructions of its protagonists' tasks! Against such noetic restraint Leo Bersani's summary interpretation of Marcel's vision strikes us with its full, dead weight of noematic certitude. "He re-creates his past as he writes about it, but he re-creates it definitively; the point of view he develops during his work gives to his life its permanent character. . . . There is no suggestion that he can learn any more than he now knows, and even his uncertainties seem final."[26]

By contrast, Rudolph Splitter's emphasis on Marcel's reminiscences as "a metaphor for metaphors" allows us a good deal more interpretive room, especially since he sees metaphor as a "metaphor for signification in general, for the essential artistic process of 'reading' (deciphering) the phenomenal sign and 'translating it' into a verbal one."[27] On the whole, Splitter's psycho-analytic approach to Marcel's development as an artist acknowledges the destabilization of literality in modally affected discourse.

> . . . the symbolic figure of the artist dying in the process of giving birth to a work of art is not simply a myth to be believed in but a sign that has to be read and interpreted. It is just this opposition between art and life, between imagination and reality, between inner and outer worlds, that Proust's text attempts to overcome: not by turning 'reality' into a purely subjective, ideal realm but by revealing that the relations that govern the self—the structures in which it is "inscribed"— are inescapably symbolic.[28]

In Thomas Mann's *Doctor Faustus* the artist has to be constructed as split into two figures, the musician and the biographer, "arcanum and confession."[29] This complicates our reading enormously, because our understanding of each figure modifies our grasp of the other and so heightens the rapport between Mann's "curious brand of reality" and "total artifice."[30] In order to "write nothing less than the novel of an era," the author says, "disguised as the story of an artist's life, a terribly imperiled and sinful artist," he had to introduce "as much ridicule of the biographer, as much anti-self-important mockery as possible."[31]

How, then, can we describe Serenus Zeitblom with his often clumsy and outmoded literary style, his "old-fashioned humanism?" Can we trust his self-characterization as an "inconsiderable background figure?"[32] Is Professor Zeitblom at least readable in part as retrospective self-critique by the author of his own early style? Why is Serenus Zeitblom so defenseless both to his friend's fiendish aberrations as well as to the downfall of his society? Is it, as George Lukács has suggested, that Zeitblom, "*ein Nachfahre der deutschen Humanisten*," offers neither a positive alternative nor "an Archimedean point from which to view fascist trends from the outside?"[33] The narrator's name certainly is suggestive of a happily unperturbed flower of the times. On the other hand, how are we to reconcile these aspects of Zeitblom with his ability to trace and interpret in depth and to link into a broad context the personal tragedy of Leverkühn and the political catastrophe of Germany? Again, to resolve these contradictions is not the aim of interpretation. The hermeneutic task is not to bring to light once and for all, but to shed light, again and again, on what by definition can be known only in a process as process.

Mann's attempt to create a fictitious artist whose sickness and death can act as a metaphor for the moral collapse of a nation is probably the most ambitious undertaking of any *Künstlerroman*. Because what he "is" fills a novel and far transcends realist aspects of characterization, any statement about his personality must remain fragmentary. Should we concentrate on his belief that "a silly order is better than no order at all,"[34] his Faustian character, or Erich Kahler's view that "the demon resides within him from the start, in his migraine, in his enormous intelligence, his coldness both somber and blasé?"[35] Yet the more we assemble the features which are traceable throughout the text, the more clearly we come to realize that we are not in the process of constructing a realist fictive character, but rather a complex typification capable of carrying the artistic-technical and social-ideological weight which the narrative as a whole is designed to carry. "Dionysiac inebriation, sacred ecstasy and hellish drunkenness"[36] reveal a social pathology crystallized in a fictive persona.[37] Or, as Lukács synthesizes discipline and barbarism, "Adrian Leverkühn, the honest ascetic, absorbs into his work all the dehumanizing motifs of the age preceding and culminating in fascism."[38]

Critics have been trained to follow a spoor relentlessly once they have taken up the scent. And yet, how can we be so sure of our task when we remind ourselves of the paradox thrown in our way by the author? "How necessary the mask and the playfulness . . . in view of the earnestness of my task . . ."[39] And what are the processes which are involved not only in the actualization of that "cosmic figure" Adrian, but in any of our constructions of the protagonists of the *Künstlerroman*?[40] The act of reading first binds us to the actualization of such aspect clusters as the protagonists' art, their reflexivity about themselves and their art, their attitudes toward the world as objects and social reality, the kind of presentational process they employ, as for example, the polyphony of other voices, especially authorial voices, and the technical-thematic aspects of narrative situation. However, the resulting 'compound predicate' is at the same time formal-schematic and propositional-noematic, and so needs to be deformalized or concretized and transformed into a dynamic noetic process. For writers do not 'bring novels to life,' readers do.

In the case of Stephen Dedalus this means the volatile concretization of his sacred and virginal art, his self-torture and "self-doubt," his "mystical aestheticism," his "hydrophobia"[41] and rejection of any involvement in social political life. It also means the construal of the protagonist's illusion of encountering reality as did his imaginary artistic predecessors, for the "millionth time," to "forge," that is, create uniquely and independently. Technically this reading rests on the transformation of the narrational speech act from initial authorial guidance mixed with free indirect presentation to a predominance of dialogue and eventually first-person individuation by way of diary entries. Yet like Stephen's art this concluding discourse never quite acquires thematic weight.

Unlike Joyce's title in which both the indefinite article and the qualifier "young" act as authorial disclaimers, Patrick White's *The Vivisector* invites the construction of an authorial stance. This is reinforced by the "confession" of "My pursuit of that razor-blade truth has made me a slasher" in *Flaws in the Glass*.[42] Here, too, the rubric proves broad and almost empty, permitting a host of interpretive contradictions. What is Hurtle meant to signify? "Idealized artist and moral leper," "destroyer-cum-creator," or "victim as well as vivisector," pairs running like an unstoppable train to the holy synthesis of dirt and beauty in a divine creation.[43] Is he perhaps the Faustian artist ("You may not live, you must create; you may not love, you must know.") that Erich Kahler sees in Adrian Leverkühn?[44] Or is Hurtle above all a picaresque survivor, viewing society from a vantage point below or to the side? Or, perhaps worst of all, is he the "secret betraying *The Vivisector* as the weakest of [White's] major novels," for in that novel it becomes evident that White has "a rather flat notion of character," as Adrian Mitchell notes with New Critical finesse?[45]

In spite of such critical certitudes Hurtle never materializes to that degree, and why should he, or better perhaps *it*? When the critics realize in the end that their quarry—when it is cut up, placed on the hide and given to the dogs— is a highly indeterminate something, they split into three groups: (1) those who declare that White is incapable of producing anything but flat characters (that will teach him to say nasty things about Professor Kramer); (2) those who frantically breathe details into the clay text until the protagonist emerges live from between the covers; and (3) those who welcome the logico-technical limitations of literary discourse as its very strength. In fixing concretizations, the first two positions are not merely epistemologically naive, but reactionary; by contrast, the third approach responds to the linguistic schemata by way of an infinite free-play of readings as a process of imaginative linkage between verbal and non-verbal signs. Autobiography or voluntary memories have much in common with the *Künstlerroman* and sometimes their discursive strategies are indistinguishable. Certainly, they share a high degree of meaning deferment. As Paul de Man observes, "autobiography veils a defacement of which it is itself the cause."[46] Autobiography is often seen by critics as the documentary counterpart of the *Künstlerroman*. Yet while it seems safer to link language and the social semiotic in the autobiographical form and only tentative inferences can be made from its fictional relation, the processes of telling involved in autobiography are anything but reliable. As John Pilling attempts to show, Boris Pasternak's *Safe Conduct* (or *The Grammar of My Heart*) of 1931 is "the almost perfect self-effacement." Because it is "restrained and reticent,"[47] as are many similar documents, we can neither take it for granted nor disregard it. Autobiographies, like all stories, mean more than they say and should be read between the polar expectations of self-effacement and confession, both of which are modal constraints on propositional content.

Much as we would like to argue for many voices in *A la recherche du temps perdu*, we are constantly tempted to confuse Marcel's "je" and Proust's "je."[48] And perhaps a case could be made for the suggestion that the planes of experiencing and narrating selves tend to merge toward the end of the novel and in so doing also approximate to the plane of authorial control.[49] Certainly, the denial of Marcel's family name throughout the novel appears waived when we close the book and we find the narrator's name tied to the author's on the cover. Perhaps Proust too is stepping outside himself through his work in order to see himself in multiple forms, as Marcel says one should:[50] *"Par l'art seulement nous pouvons sortir de nous ... Grâce à l'art, au lieu de voir un seul monde, le nôtre, nous le voyons se multiplier ... "* (III, 895f.).

The procedure proposed here is not a positivist retrieval of authorial intention, but, since the destabilization of the meanings of all discourse is being argued, what we take to be authorial attitudes are reincorporated in the hermeneutic helix as less magisterial propositions so that they become a part of the general task of deciphering signs. This is how Gilles Deleuze understands Proust's problem and that of the reader: as "the problem of signs in general" and specifically the "deceptive signs of love, sensuous material signs, and lastly the essential signs of art (which transform all others)"[51] (including the author, one might add).

In the absence of an autobiography, to balance Joyce's *Portrait* against an alternative authorial stance we would have to look forward to later works rather than return to *Stephen Hero*, since both *Künstlerromane* project Stephen's role as "priest of eternal imagination, transmuting the daily bread of experience into the radiant body of everliving life" (221). By comparison, *Ulysses* and *Finnegans Wake* allow the construction of a more secular as well as more democratic conception of art. In these later works we find, as Richard Ellmann puts it, a "recognition of universal intermingling of sensations and concepts" so that "hierarchies disappear" and all aspects become "common elements."[52] As a paralinguistic text in loose support of this reading could be quoted Joyce's refusal to publish the very kind of poetry which Stephen's aestheticism must regard as the ultimate accomplishment. Such a reading would permit a more constructive opinion of Joyce's techniques, a perspective which might have tempered George Lukács's wholly negative view of the matter.

We may deplore the absence of any clear authorial leverage in Joyce. On the other hand, when we do seem to have found it in certain autobiographical acts, they do not necessarily satisfy the expectations of definitive interpretation either. A case in point are the complementary narratives by Miles Franklin, *My Brilliant Career*, and the much later *My Career Goes Bung*.[53] "Why do I write?" asks the narrator of the earlier "yarn." Apparently, to "get a hearing" for her protest against her "monstrous, purposeless, needless existence." (*MBC*, IX, 228). In *My Career Goes Bung*, published forty-five years later, we are informed that one of the two reasons for writing that earlier story was to establish "a new style of autobiography" in revolt against the "orthodox style" (9). Which of the two then is the more reliably autobiographical account? One would assume the second, only to note its Defoean subtitle, "Purporting to be the Autobiography of Sybilla Penelope Melvyn," and a little later to find it characterized as "This second portrait of Sybilla Penelope" (8). And when the book ends with "Beauty is abroad. Under her spell the voices of the great world call me. To them I give ear and go" (234) we cannot help but activate a whole discourse genre of endings in the manner of the *Künstlerroman*.

In addition to the difficulties involved in making decisions as to whether we are dealing with autobiographical or novelistic-fictive acts, there is further com-plication in the relationship between Thomas Mann's *Doctor Faustus* and *The Genesis of a Novel*—not due to hermetic structure but to the very explicitness, the high degree of documented awareness, of both the narrator in the novel and the author of *The Genesis*. When Mann says that music was "only a paradigm for something more general, of culture, even of man and the intellect itself"[54] we may take this as an interpretive vector pointing toward a reading of the novel as a socio-pathology of German history. This in turn shifts our attention to the schizoid aspects of the society portrayed and the novelistic techniques employed: a society characterized by an opposition between the bourgeois, moderate, classical, sober, industrious, dependable, Apollonian and the drunken release, super-human subjectivity, intoxicating intensification of self, the bold Dionysian genius;[55] as to the technique, the novel presents the fission of Mann and his own artistic possibilities into Leverkühn, an Aschenbach on a larger canvas, and Zeitblom, his worthy, worried, but ineffectual friend.[56] For Mann "had flirted with irrationalism, chafed at the limitations of mere intellect . . . and hoped for a new, simpler order in art and ethics."[57] And yet, Mann, like Zeitblom, with his classical education (he played the "viola-d'amore" with "modest virtuosity") attempts through the novel and inside the novel "to lay bare the moral back-ground of this impotence in the best German middle class intellectuals"[58] in the face of that "monstrous flowering of the German soul, the rise of National Socialism."[59]

Yet even if we accept such summary views as possible directives with a host of possible meaning fulfillments, we now become aware of the dubiousness of the Nietzsche reception underlying the whole structure of Mann's novel and his commentary as well as a broad range of critical opinion. Interpreting Mann's critique of the reading of Nietzsche in the first half of the twentieth century, T. J. Reed suggests that "the conditions for misunderstanding and distortion were ideal."[60] Both Mann and his critic see this reception as a deviation from the right Nietzsche reception. The 'correct' one would have been an ethical guar-antee in itself. Derrida's rereadings of Nietzsche, for example, have replaced these assumptions by the quite different notions of more or less interesting, useful or dangerous forms of reception. In this sense, *Doctor Faustus* is not so much an "epilogue to Germany's cultural development and to her political and social misdevelopment," as George Lukács saw it, but rather a prologue to a rereading of the novel, Mann's commentary, and their critical reception.[61]

The Vivisector, the speaker in *Flaws in the Glass* tells us, "is about a painter, the one I was not destined to become . . . a composite of several I have known, welded together by the one I have in me but never became."[62] In these reflections White is sensitive to the elusive nature of past and present meanings:

> Setting out to portray a convincing artist, I wanted at the same time to paint a portrait of my city: wet, boiling, superficial, brash, beautiful, ugly Sydney, developing during my lifetime from a sunlit village into this present-day parvenu bastard, compound of San Francisco and Chicago. I had a lot of exploring to do. It was not so much research as reliving the windswept, gritty, or steamy moods of the streets, coaxing dead-ends, narrow lanes, and choked thoroughfares to release those voices, images, emotions of the past, which for my deplorably atypical Australian nature evoke guilt rather than pleasure.

> What is seen as success, my own included, has often filled me with disgust. No doubt the 'normal' members of the affluent class will pounce on this confession as explanation of what they think a distorted view-point in all I have written; while to me the refractions from that many-sided crystal, truth, are more diverse than they would have been had I remained blinkered by the values of the Australian rich (151).

White's awareness of montage in the assembly of fictive personae, of the replacement of "research" by "reliving" and reimagining, and of the "distorted viewpoint" as a necessary artistic and cognitive principle should warn us against conveniently tagging White's work onto the tail of English Literature as a minor deviation well in critical hand. Nor can the autobiographical insights Patrick White grants us claim any privileged interpretive status. For perhaps somewhat anachronistically, White writes to know who he is by "putting himself on stage"[63] in the "theatre of his imagination," a theatre more fictional than historically "real," in order to "accommodate the illusion of reality life boils down to."[64]

Few writers have parodied the myth of autobiographical certitude as thoroughly as Vladimir Nabokov, and for this reason it may be best to read all autobiographical commentary against the background of the transformations which his titles undergo: *Speak Memory: A Memoir* (1951), *Conclusive Evidence* (the American edition), *Drugie Berega* (*Other Shores*, 1954, which is meant to correct the "amnesic defects of the original")[65] and *Speak Memory* (in the edition of 1967). There is no "conclusive evidence," nor have we any way of deciding on the corrections of a defective memory; whenever Nabokov's "memory" speaks, it speaks differently, and so nicely confuses further rather than streamlines the hermeneutic task.

In autobiography, "as an alignment between the two subjects involved in the process of reading in which they determine each other by mutual reflexive substitution,"[66] and more compellingly so in the *Künstlerroman*, the modal qualifications of the given propositions are such that the search for authorial certitude is not only futile but contradicts the reading processes encoded in its text. If the polarity between fiction and factuality is undecidable in autobiography,[67] its very stipulation as an interpretive model for the *Künstlerroman* is fundamentally misguided for these reasons: our meaning constructions are impeded and destabilized by a special set of agonistic discursive formations. As a result, the reader has to come to terms with a complication of the processes of mediation: gestures toward a forever deferred art, highly schematic directives for the construal of an artist, snippets of art criticism and theory, and the inference of a socio-political world via the highly subjective acts of the protagonist. This strategy of significatory deferral is further complicated by an intertextual network of literary motifs and topoi, as for example the Faustian contract, the figure of the pariah, sexual transgression and autism, the picaresque, Oedipal search and riddle structure, as well as the pattern of apprenticeship borrowed from the *Bildungsroman*. Lastly, our inferences of autobiographical acts from related sources function not so much as a means of interpretive stabilization, but on the contrary, as a further source of modalization.

In this the *Künstlerroman* highlights the bending of propositional content by modal forces as a necessary aspect of the act of reading. At the same time, because of the genre's paradoxical subjectivity of self-revelation and self-concealment as well as a high degree of intertextual overdetermination, the *Künstlerroman* makes problematic the opposition between and intersection of dialect and ideolect, system and utterance. The continuous substitution of seemingly reliable propositional contents by others—for reasons given above—and the non-verbal semiosis or deformalization of the formal linguistic matrix of the text within loose intertextual constraints result in a highly noetic form of concretization as the most appropriate manner of reading the genre.

By challenging the notion of literal meaning and by drawing our attention instead to the tentative and negotiatory nature of a range of signifying operations the *Künstlerroman* plays an important role in the description of discourse: it portrays meaning as a continuous and always incomplete process of joining linguistic and non-linguistic signs. In this the *Künstlerroman* acts as a paradigm for the indirect procedure by which we construe our world.

IV

LITERATURE AND HUSSERL
A CRITIQUE OF NOEMATIC MEANING

> The incomparably more important and fruit-
> ful analyses belong to the noetical side.
>
> Edmund Husserl, *Ideas*

Before placing Husserl's noematic meaning in our schema of saturated and reduced discourses, the sign systems of "Pandora" and "Occam," I want to address a recent tendency in the reading of Husserl which finds its perhaps most outspoken expression in Michel Pêcheux's *Language, Semantics and Ideology*. A highly fruitful and challenging account of how ideological effects pervade discourses, Pêcheux's analysis is bent on showing how Husserl's analysis is vitiated by an idealist metaphysic and a subjectivist theory of meaning in which individual consciousness is the "zero point" and the "origin" of representations, and so of meaning.[1] We leave aside for the moment Husserl's idealism in the sense of an attempt to anonymize a general *mathesis* from the specifics of directional acts of consciousness.[2] It is Pêcheux's charge of the subjective *origin* of meaning which needs to be challenged.

I suggest that Pêcheux's reading rests on a confused notion of Husserl's epistemological and ontological projects. Almost all of Husserl's work is written from a first person epistemological perspective. From this angle of inquiry, ontological statements or those concerning the being/status of the world are *inferences*. In other words, Husserl proceeds from the descriptions of *his* acts about himself and the world to ontological generalizations, from individual instantiation and their attachments to broader observations. This, incidentally, is precisely how Pêcheux documents his response to Althusser's teaching and his own subsequent extension of Althusserian claims. In this sense, we cannot help but be phenomenologists, embarrassing as it may seem to some. It is with something like a sleight of hand, therefore, that Pêcheux ends his Husserl analysis with a reference to the *Philosophy of Arithmetic*, (1890) as if it played a central role in his oeuvre as a whole. In fact, Husserl quite radically turned away from its claims on the advice of Frege.

Positivism knows the ontic status of the world and its individual inhabitants:

it pretends to stand outside and observe it. Husserl's epistemological descriptions unfold over the span of roughly half a century, from a subjectivist description of arithmetics, to the noetic/noematic description of language and thought, to the question of how egos are realized through processes of "appresentation" (*Cartesian Meditations*) to the exploration of the *Lebenswelt* in *The Crisis* and *Interest and Judgment*. As it turns out, the ontology of the *Lebenswelt* becomes the necessary ontological inference which acts as origin for individual acts of consciousness.

According to Husserl, "I experience the world (including others)... as an intersubjective world, actually there for everyone, accessible in respect of its objects to everyone." [3] Or, in opposition to Pêcheux's reading, "the experienced world exists in itself, over against all experiencing subjects." [4] In *Experience and Judgment* Husserl defines the life-world in these terms:

> ... the world in which we are always already living and which furnishes the ground for all cognitive performance and all scientific determination.
>
> In view of this the objective world is, to be sure, equated with the life-world of humanity, the all-embracing community wherein mutual understanding is possible. [5]

It needs to be emphasized that this ontology, Husserl's life-world, is an inference from a description of individual acts of consciousness, as is Pêcheux's own view of his discursive world. Though Husserl obviously does not write from a materialist perspective, there is nothing in the *Lebenswelt* which would deny the workings of ideological effects.

Therefore meaning itself does not originate in subjective consciousness, but consciousness plays an important role in the instantiation of discourse. If Husserl's meaning were as subjective as Pêcheux suggests, little sense could be made of the distinctions between "ideal," "descriptive," "objective," and "essentially occasional" meanings, nor those between formalization vs. deformalization and generalization vs. specification. This is how Husserl argues:

> *Ideal* concepts... express something which we cannot see... *descriptive concepts*... express the essential nature of things. [6]
>
> We shall call an expression *objective* if it pins down (or can pin down) its meaning merely by its manifest, auditory pattern [its signifier] and can be understood without necessarily directing one's attention to the person uttering it, or to the circumstances of utterance... [7]
>
> We call an expression essentially subjective and occasional, or more briefly *essentially occasional*, if it belongs to a conceptually unified group of possible meanings in whose case it is essential to orient actual meaning to the occasion, the speaker and the situation. [8]

When Husserl says that any expression including personal pronouns, demonstratives, and other "subject-bound determinations" such as ego-centric particulars (here, there, now, later...) "lacks an objective meaning"[9] he is not asserting that they are irretrievably buried in a subjective consciousness. Quite the opposite: "Ideally speaking, each subjective expression is replaceable by an objective expression which will preserve the *identity* of each *momentary meaning intention* ..."[10]

That "we are infinitely removed from this ideal" has to do with the complexity of the occasional apparatus and the *momentariness* of instantiation, a point enlarged upon by Derrida in his paper "Differance." Yet if we could isolate the event of meaning, Husserl says, we would have an objective meaning, a noema: "The subjective acts which confer meaning on expressions are variable, and that not merely as individuals, but, more particularly, in respect of the specific characters in which their meaning consists. But *the meanings* themselves do not alter. ..."[11]

With Husserl's assistance, then, we arrive at a reading which is precisely the opposite of Pêcheux's; it is not Husserl's subjectivist definition of meaning, but his logico-mathematical conception of it which must be questioned. How does Husserl link the ideal meanings of formal-logical discourses with those in everyday speech? For this he developed a procedure which insists on the distinction between generalization versus specification on the one hand and formalization versus deformalization on the other.

> A sharp distinction must be drawn between the relations of generalization and specialization on the one hand, and on the other the reduction of what has material content to a formal generality of a purely logical kind, or conversely the process of filling in with content what is logically formal. In other words: generalization is something wholly different from formalization, which plays so marked a part, for instance, in mathematical analysis. Specialization is also something entirely different from deformalization, the "filling out" of an empty logico-mathematical form, or of a formal truth.[12]

Accordingly, when we perform logic we are dealing with ideal meanings (definitionally ruled concepts) from a high degree of specificity to a high degree of generality. By contrast, the concepts of everyday discourse are not only specific or general, but at the same time more or less filled with "material" content. By increasingly formalizing such concepts, Husserl says, we can arrive at fully formal meanings or eidetic noemata. This is a crucial point for both Pêcheux's and the present analysis. Husserl's procedure of anonymization of "essentially occasional" expressions is argued to produce, at least in principle, neutralized and therefore also ideologically unaffected meanings in all discourses.

Meanings are the result of directional acts, each of which is associated with a noema, a meaning unit, even if this event lasts but a fleeting moment. "To be directed simply is to have a noema."[13] The dominant explanation of what noemata are is summed up well by Dagfinn Føllesdal in "Husserl's Notion of Noema," the central thesis of which is that "the noema is an *intensional* entity, a generalization of meaning (*Sinn Bedeutung*)."[14] This is supported by Husserl himself who sees the noema as being "nothing but a generalization of meaning (*Sinn*) to the field of acts" and "a *Sinn* (in the widest sense)," as well as more recently by J. M. Mohanty, who states that "all mental acts have their correlative *noemata* or *senses*" and "to be intentional is to have a (correlative) sense or noema."[15] The intentional reading of noemata is opposed, for example, by Guido Küng in "The World as Noema and as Referent," where he proposes that the noema is to be associated with sense but in a much broader manner than analytical usage allows.[16] This makes for an attractive phenomenology, yet in my view one which fails to dislodge Føllesdal's reading of noema as idealization. The following argument tests how idealized noemata square with the meaning generated from a highly saturated discourse, a poem. The example chosen is T. S. Eliot's "The Hollow Men" (1925); the first stanza will bring to mind the tenor of the poem.

> We are the hollow men
> We are the stuffed men
> Leaning together
> Headpiece filled with straw. Alas!
>
> Our dried voices, when
> We whisper together
> Are quiet and meaningless
> As wind in dry grass
> Or rats' feet over broken glass
> In our dry cellar
>
> Shape without form, shade without colour,
> Paralysed force, gesture without motion;
>
> Those who have crossed
> With direct eyes, to death's other Kingdom
> Remember us—if at all—not as lost
> Violent souls, but only
> As the Hollow men
> The stuffed men.

Called by one critic a "minimalist" poem with reference to the fine arts, T. S. Eliot's "The Hollow Men" will serve in this chapter as an illustration of what we typically tend to do when we face a relatively opaque chain of literary signification.[17] This is precisely the kind of semiosis absent from the vast majority of theories of meaning. In questioning Husserl's noematic ideality, this chapter by implication also queries the assumptions concerning meaning as definitional sense and the notion of literality in analytic approaches to natural language. This broader critique does not follow the attack on conceptuality found in

Jacques Derrida's writing but emerges from a scrutiny of the basic ingredients which we activate in producing meaning in culturally saturated discourse. From this perspective the purity of analytical signification turns out to be a special possibility of semiosis rather than its foundation.

To keep matters brief a highly selective assemblage of critical comments will have to stand in for a full-scale reading. Framed by two epitaphs at the beginning and a chorus at the end, the poem unfolds its vision of despair in five sections. It is "intensively allusive," referring as it does to the Gunpowder Plot, Julius Caesar, Shakespeare, Valery, Dante, Conrad, and the Lord's Prayer, as well as to a number of Eliot's other texts. Depending on whether we focus on Eliot's precursor poems,[18] or the *Zeitgeist*—Europe between the two World Wars— or on broader intertextual relations, the noemata which we tend to attach to the poem's expressions will vary accordingly. Let us call such meaning modi-fication the noetic phases of reading, in Husserl's sense.

A Dantean noetic modification will stress "paralysed force, gesture without motion" in reference to the wretched souls in *Inferno* (III) who have not had the energy to perpetrate either good or evil, a reading which will in turn affect the initial series of predications about the opening subject "We" ("hollow," "stuffed," "leaning," "quiet," "meaningless").[19] A more historical reading might emphasize the Guy Fawkes motif and so construct the concluding lines in terms of an ironic conversion of the "idea" of revolution into the "reality" of the final whimper of the hanged; a religious noesis may wish to discover an overarching process of "death, burial and resurrection"[20] with the image of the "rounded" prickly pear substituting for the crown of thorns.[21] In spite or perhaps *because* of such noetic multiplicity, Husserl's *Mannigfaltigkeiten*, some critics claim that "nothing quite vital grows" in this text and "the words become increasingly indeterminate, equations left insoluble by the presence of too many variables,"[22] or the poem is a "semiaudible hypnotic mumble," holding "the teasing fascin-ation of an almost-erased inscription," but in the end not much more than "a muted swan song" announcing the "virtual surrender to the silence which has haunted so many modern writers."[23] Other critics have managed to expose to our view with disarming clarity the poem's progression from the hollow men's kingdom of death without faith (I), through the evasion of Charon's eyes from canto three of the *Inferno* (II), the arid world of "frustrated love" (III), "the valley of the shadow of death," where the "star becomes rose" and "the rose becomes the rose window of the church," the multifoliate rose of *Paradiso* (IV) and finally to the "frustrations of reality" and the transformation of "game ritual into liturgical form" (V).[24]

Polysemy in itself of course does not question Husserl's distinction between noetic act and noematic content, it merely multiplies their relations. What is crucial in this respect, however, is that no matter how far we pursue any noetic hierarchy we are never able to rest assured of the identity and ideality of such noemata as "the hollow men" or the "twilight kingdom." The question which must be raised then is whether the literary text and its typical readings highlight the problematic nature of Husserl's noematic ideality and if so, what kind of modification would have to be made to his theory of meaning to enable it to account for what we actually do when we participate in complex signification. Husserl himself has offered us the legitimation for such a move in the *Logical Investigations*, where we read that "*der genannte Gegenstand ja gar nicht als existierender zu gelten braucht.*"[25] However, before we can suggest an answer to our question we need to take a closer look at some of Husserl's relevant tenets.

A special piece of equipment in Husserl's tool kit for the description of the directionality of consciousness is his distinction between noematic and noetic phases of acts of consciousness. Though there are references to noemata and noeses strewn throughout many of his texts, their treatment in the *Ideas* is the most fundamental and comprehensive found anywhere in his work. It is from Husserl's *Ideas* then that this chapter will take its main cues. A promising entry into the field is the following metaphor: "The stream of phenomenological being has a twofold bed: a material and a noetic," of which, as we already know, the noetical side is by far the more important.[26] Yet no matter how much attention should be paid to either, Husserl stresses that there is "no noetic phase without a noematic phase that belongs specifically to it."[27] It is then not conceivable that we should be able to interpret without producing some interpretation, to remember without arriving at a memory, to glance without "furbishing its noun," to image without being granted something imagined or, as Husserl puts it with respect to the concept, "to the signifying in conceptual thought (*Bedeuten*) corresponds the conceptual signification (*Bedeutung*)."[28]

Based on these observations Husserl stipulates "a parallelism between noesis and noema," such that "the formations must be described on both sides, and in their essential correspondence to one another."[29] By "parallelism" Husserl does not mean that these formations are structurally symmetrical; what he wishes to emphasize is that the noematic content always entails its particular noetic constitution. That they are structurally different is made clear when Husserl draws the distinction between the noematic field as "that of the unitary" and noesis as "that of the 'constituting' variety factors (*Mannigfaltigkeiten*)."[30]

Yet rather than presenting us with a linear concept of the noetic moving toward the noematic, Husserl complicates the issue with yet another metaphor when he suggests that "a number of noeses are built up, the one above the other," so that consciousness is conceived of as a hierarchized structure in which multiple pairs of noesis and noemata crisscross and so make up the complex reality of phenomenological being.[31] When in analysis Husserl needs to look at specific noetic-noematic relations this must not be construed to mean that the reality of ongoing acts can be collapsed into one plane of monodirectional processes.

Another crucial point in Husserl's schema is his description of the noetic as the field of *Mannigfaltigkeiten*. How do these noetic multiplicities relate to their parallel and unitary noematic counterparts? According to Husserl, "not only does every addition of new or modification of old noetic characters constitute new noematic characters, but thereby *eo ipso* new ontological objects constitute themselves for consciousness."[32] As our noetic attention shifts, so too is the previous noema transformed into a new one, and so on *ad mortem*. This leads Husserl to explore a number of noetic transformations or "modifications" which affect our realizations more dramatically than others. Memory is one of these, the imagination another, but the most important of them for Husserl is what he terms the "neutrality-modification."

In a special section (III) of *Ideas* that focuses on "Neutrality Modification and Fancy," Husserl notes that we "observe that certain noeses, whether of necessity or following fixed possibilities of their nature, are conditioned by modes of attention, and in particular through positive attention in the quite special sense of the term."[33] The positing kind of noesis appears to be the dominant one, certainly for philosophers, and Husserl is no exception. This should not come as a surprise since it is the positing attitude which allows for statements, assertions, or more broadly, judgments. By neutralizing our attitude of positing, Husserl suggests, we shift from the pragmatic to the realm of as-if. In turn "the process of fancy in general is the neutrality-modification of the 'positing' act of representation, and therefore of remembering in the widest conceivable sense of the term."[34] For Husserl the important difference between the neutrality modification and that of fancy is that the former occurs only once for any set of noemata, while the latter can be repeated indefinitely. The neutrality modification allows us to put the *Lebenswelt* out of play, and as long as we apply it the lifeworld is available to us as an as-if construct without being posited as real. An example of modification by fancy is the Chinese box structure in pictorial representation and in literary texts, which can be entertained in endless permutations and without any logical limits.

At this point a number of related questions need to be asked in order to foreshadow the significance of the literary text for this kind of theory of consciousness. First, is there any logical necessity for Husserl to stipulate meaning constitution primarily as positing or does this inclination "unconceal" some unacknowledged desire? Second, does this move not require him to privilege certain speech acts over others? Third, does not the broad separation of noesis into positing and neutralizing the posited push a significant portion of signifying acts—all those in which fancy plays a role—and doesn't fancy play a large part in much of the communication of the *Lebenswelt*—outside the field of "serious" description of signification?

The next section addresses the question of how the noetic is linked with the ideality of the noema and how this ideality squares with the demands of the *Lebenswelt*. I shall mention only in passing Derrida's critique of Husserl's ideal meaning and focus instead on the question of why Husserl's contentions are indisputable in the realm of formal logic and strictly technical language but cannot be transferred without significant modification to the region of everyday signification. In conclusion, I shall attempt to show that the fundamental question of the modification of noemata by noetic acts can be illustrated more fully by way of literary than by other kinds of sign systems.

In his study, *Edmund Husserl's Theory of Meaning*, J. N. Mohanty argues that

Husserl was able to combine the strengths of both Platonist and antiplatonist views, in that his theory caters to the ideality of meaning in the sense of "identity, objectivity, and universality," as well as to "empirical verification."[35] Since Mohanty offers a highly authentic reading of Husserl's texts, I shall use his study as a stalking horse in the pursuit of the question of noematic ideality. The main reason which Mohanty gives for ideality being a necessary condition of meaning constitution is that without it "thought would lack communicability and logical thinking would be an impossibility." Unfortunately, what Mohanty means when he says that "expressions retain a *degree* of identity of meaning in discourse" is not made clear.[36]

Throughout his writing Husserl poses the question of noematic ideality, even where he does not refer to the issue in these terms, but he does so in three significantly different phases. The first can be characterized as the project of "eidetic language;" the second as the view of language as "concretization;" and the third as the perspective of language from the *Lebenswelt*. Though this is too rough a classification, the first phase is most clearly expressed in the *Logical Investigations*, the second in *Formal and Transcendental Logic*, and the third in the *Crisis*.

When we speak of Husserl's eidetic view we should distinguish between the ideality of word meanings and the "idea of a pure grammar."[37] It is in regard to the latter that Husserl says that "*an dieses ideale Gerüst ist jede [Sprache] gebunden*," and "no language is thinkable which is not determined essentially by this apriori."[38] Husserl's notion of concretization or "*Verleiblichung*" in *Formale und Transzendentale Logik* rests on the assumption that speaking is a soul-endowing or animating meaning intention, a "*beseelendes Meinen*."[39] In spite of its untheorized humanism this view has the advantage of collapsing speaker and listener into one "uttering" position, yet it does not entail, as Mohanty sees it, the "ideality" of noemata.[40] The third or "constitutive" phase of Husserl's theory of meaning is divided by Mohanty into "an attempt to trace language back in the first place to the noetic act which makes it possible" and the investigation of the genesis of meaning from "the more primitive [sic] *Lebenswelt*."[41] This shift to viewing language from the broadest possible base, the *Lebenswelt*, "means a transition from language to speech, to interpersonal communication," and so from *langue* to pragmatics.[42]

At the same time one cannot help but note a fundamental problem in both Husserl and Mohanty which has to do precisely with this transition, namely the relation between noematic ideality which remains unaffected by socio-cultural noeses, on the one hand, and by the shifting complexity of the *Lebenswelt*, on the other. For Mohanty "there is a noetic experience which produces the identity of the word, a meaning-intending act which produces the identity of meaning, and an act which constitutes the two, the physical expression and the meaning, into an inseparable unity." With certain qualifications this summary could stand, yet it should not lead Mohanty to say that "the objectivity of linguistic expression is rooted in the subjective acts of the speaker."[43] As Heidegger and more recently

Derrida have shown, such subjective acts are spoken by language itself and by "the play of linguistic and semiological differance," respectively.[44]

For the study of discursive phenomena Husserl's last phase is by far the most exciting, because it promises to review noetic modifications in terms of reciprocity and meaning negotiation rather than formal ideality. "The environment (*Umwelt*) which constitutes itself in the experience of the Other, in the reciprocal understanding and in agreement is called by us the communicative environment."[45] Like the later Wittgenstein, who realizes that all language games are not only themselves *Lebensformen* but are embedded in larger *Lebensformen*, so Husserl, too, in the end feels compelled to attempt to root his eidetic forms in the larger systems of the *Lebenswelt*. How does this affect the noetic-noematic relation?

As Mohanty sums up the situation, "the noema of the intentional correlate dissolves into the subjective experiences, the mere intentions, of which it represents a limiting end," while "the noetic acts reveal themselves as merely leading up to the intended object whose autonomy however they do not affect."[46] This is a crucial point. While in formal operations both the noetic and the noematic are strictly circumscribed by actual definitions and so will (assuming the rules of the language game are not violated) always produce noematic identity and ideality, the same cannot be said for culturally saturated signification. When "Husserl finds the logical in the nature of all language" he is certainly right, but when he assumes that therefore language is fundamentally eidetic, he has committed the fallacy of composition.[47]

And yet, that Husserl was in the end not altogether happy with his highly propositional theory is signalled by his fascination with so-called "not-objectifying acts" such as the expression of desire and hope, with questions and orders, in short, with speech acts.[48] The inclusion of a noetic or "pronouncing function" in the functions of an expression should have further shaken Husserl's eidetic convictions, but they did not do so sufficiently; nor did his discussion of "occasional expressions," nor yet his distinction between names positing existence and those which do not.[49]

Since Husserl's discussion of ordinary language always draws on formal logic we need to ask how socio-culturally saturated signification ("For Thine is the Kingdom," "Packer cricket is the ruin of the sport") and its formal counterpart ("S is p," C_2H_5OH) are related. What would we have to do, we should ask, if we were to transform instances of the former into expressions of the latter. Following roughly the stages of Husserl's own theory of meaning we are led to address in turn meaning and object (*Gegenstand*), pronouncement, and communicative environment, a triadic relation not entirely unlike that of propositional content and reference, deixis, and frame. If the subject "Packer cricket" (S), its predicate "the ruin of the sport" (p), and the copula "is" were subjected to a process of eidetic reduction from those three perspectives, the result would be a triple dematerialization or formalization—not generalization, as Husserl makes clear in *Ideas*.[50] Consequently, *meaning* would be dereferentialized, *pronouncement* stripped of deictic reference, and the frame neutralized, so that aspects of history, region, class or ideology no longer affect the expression. In short, symbols can now be substituted for the words and so the principle of predication would remain, an empty sediment in our laboratory still. Somewhere along this route we should have reached the point where noematic ideality and identity have disensconced themselves. But at which point? And do not the expressions "For Thine is the Kingdom" and "Packer cricket is the ruin of the sport" make sense precisely because they are embedded wholly in that triple horizonal text of reference, deixis, and social frame?

And yet Husserl, as well as the majority of theorists of meaning, would insist that we cannot explain communication without stipulating the ideality of sense. The traditional support for meaning identity and ideality typically relies on a number of ordinary language expressions which deserve our attention: "the author of Waverley;" "the conqueror of Jena;" "the vanquished of Waterloo;" "Bucephalus is a horse;" "Mayflower is a horse;" and not to be forgotten, "the cat on the mat." Because such expressions direct our glance very firmly in a certain *direction* we tend to assume the noematic ideality of their meanings. Are we not taking for ideality what is in actuality merely the narrow focus or close angle of the *directionality* of certain language schemata? If we were to choose as our examples expressions with a "wide angle" of directionality— examples studiously avoided by the majority of theories of meaning—such as "academic freedom," "my grandfather had a strong sense of honor," or T. S. Eliot's line, "This broken jaw of our lost kingdom," noematic ideality and identity are unavailable even as an illusion. In fact, when we are dealing with such expressions we intuitively replace the expectation of ideality by the production of explanatory texts.

The possibility then suggests itself that the difference between "simple" and not so simple expressions is that in the use of the former we have produced meaning so frequently that we are able to construct it without any difficulty and at high speed, while in the use of the latter we are forced to proceed more cautiously. Perhaps then we tend to confuse our habitual and spontaneous concretizations of the directional schemata of some expressions with the ideality of their meanings and then elevate this error to the level of general principle.

Instead of noematic ideality and identity I would stress the process of noetic modification at the center of culturally saturated signification. Apart from formal and technical usage, where in Heidegger's words, the "merely identical" rules, ordinary language is characterized by Heidegger's notion of the "same."[51] In everyday speech and more so in its ludic extension, literary discourse, noematic ideality is neither necessary nor even possible. The reasons against the possibility of meaning ideality can be summed up thus: (1) natural languages are permeated by *noematic opacity* which stems from the fact that the semantic aspects are not fully and properly defined; (2) this circumstance is aggravated by *noetic opacity* which is introduced in instantiation, without which language does not exist and which requires the conjecture of concealed speech acts in the sense of psychological, social, philosophical and ideological motivations, a conjecture never identical with 'originary' meaning intentions; and (3) there is also *opacity of the frame* or broadly *semiotic opacity* which has to do with the never identical constructions of the wider socio-cultural contexts within which utterers are bound to "read" all texts.

Whether language communication operates against the background of a Habermasian ideal of possible consensus or is more adequately described by Lyotard's agonistics of language games, language praxis is always characterized by a high degree of partial understanding as well as a considerable amount of misunderstanding, features not to be eradicated by making speech partners into better logicians.[52] Certainly, noematic ideality does not appear to be a necessary condition for the occurrence of communication. All that is needed is for utterers to be able to decide whether or not they are operating within the same—not the identical—semantic field. Where a higher degree of specificity is called for meanings are negotiated further, or are replaced by technical signification where noematic ideality and identity can be guaranteed by definitions proper.

What is it then that the literary text and its readings can add to this description? I suggest it 'exaggerates' noetic acts and so foregrounds features which we need to perform if we wish to participate in culturally charged semiosis. The literary text demonstrates that we do not—as Husserl understands signification—proceed from the polythetic to the synthetic and the monothetic, from phenomenon to meaning endowment and identity, along the sequence of "phenomenon—eidos—logos," as in Hülsmann's analysis, or from random flow to the structuring schema and to logos.[53] In fact, at one level the literary text tends to generate the converse process: from "flickering imagistic concentration," as Bergonzi says of the poetic style of "The Hollow Men," to the production of hierarchies or simply sequences of explanatory texts.[54]

In this process the following items each play their special noetic role: the meanings of expressions (especially metaphors), deixis, socio-cultural frame and appresentation and, overriding all such specifics, the politics of reading with its interpretational regimes which tend to favor at different historical moments text autonomy, authorial context, text and the forces of economic production, literary and general intertextuality, and inter-semiotic relations, among many others.

Literariness underlines the historical nature and semantic inconclusiveness in the meanings of expressions and as such draws our attention to the fact that lexical definition is an idealizing freeze frame which denies historicity and semantic drift. Such "definitions" are actually chains of signifiers of unspecified length from which the "ideal abiding aspect" is absent.[55] Because of its emphasis on noetic instability the highly literary text also questions the widely accepted description of meanings in terms of classes. One could with equal justification say of the meanings of expressions what Alfred Schutz said about "things in their intuitive environment": they "vacillate in their mere typicality; their identity with themselves and their being like other things is just an approximation."[56]

This state of affairs is brought into sharp focus by so-called metaphor, a linguistic formation which is not just at the heart of literariness but plays an important role also in everyday discourse. In metaphor we are not simply dealing with a double or triple eidos, nor with any form of eidetic synthesis, but again with directional schemata which are never fully determinable. Metaphors accentuate the slipperiness of meaning by depriving us of the relative, though false, semantic security of its separate signifiers. Thus, the directional schema of "hollow men" has a relatively "wide angle" which we tend to fill with a much larger text in order to endow it with meaning. The length of such a new chain of signification, though, is not delimited *logically*, nor even by contextual constraints, but only *pragmatically* and *politically*.

Deixis, or the overall manner in which expressions are instantiated, is a special case of noesis which I argue once more affects their very propositional content. Mohanty, in support of Husserl, takes the opposite side:

> Looked at from one point of view, the noema or the intentional correlate dissolves into the subjective experiences, the mere intentions, of which it represents a limiting end. From another point of view the noetic acts reveal themselves as merely leading up to the intended object whose autonomy however they do not affect.[57]

However, this does not hold true in that most radical of deictic noeses, irony, through which the very same signifier may receive opposing noemata or may be otherwise qualified into various shades of meaning. One may wish to object by pointing out that identity is not affected, irony merely supplies an oppositional noema: a noematic doubling. Yet this assumes a clear polarity of straight versus ironicized meanings, while in actual discourse there is always a large number of possible meaning nuances between the stipulated extremes of a 'neutral' meaning and its negation. Neither "tenderness" nor "kiss," neither "valley" nor "rose" remain unaffected. Indeed, not a single signifier in "The Hollow Men" escapes deictic modification. Moreover, even in much of everyday speech, apart from its strictly technical usage, deictic noeses shade the meaning of expressions away from the assumed basis of 'neutral speech,' a case which does not exist, nor is it necessary to stipulate.

In culturally saturated expressions, i.e., those in which meaning, reference, and deixis cannot be separated out from the broad semiotic frame of their communicative environment, the *appresentations* which we perform in order to fill the schematic skeleton of the speech system are themselves culture specific and so constitute noetic acts which have a bearing on the directionality of the noemata they produce.

Lastly, the politics of reading with its various interpretive regimes always overdetermines all those acts. Depending on which reading pedagogy we have been the victim of or have revolted against, we may wish to foreground the noeses of textual autonomy, T. S. Eliot's poetic biography—the precursor text approach—or to favor literary and general intertextuality, i.e., explore the text's relations with the Bible, Dante, Shakespeare, Valery, and Conrad, as well as those other texts of myth, history, and philosophy, or to pursue intersemiotic questions, such as those of imagistic and minimalist art. What all these noetic strategies have in common, and what they share with the noeses of much of everyday discourse, is that they generate additional texts and as a consequence new noetic-noematic relations, none of which can be said to be stable, let alone to have identifiable resolutions. Husserl (anticipating Derrida's critique) nearly came to this conclusion himself when he wrote, exasperated, "every subjective expression could be replaced with an objective one if only we could get hold of its momentary meaning—intention in its identity!"[58] Alas, we conclude, we cannot!

V

MEANING AS SENSE AND DERRIDA'S CRITIQUE OF THE CONCEPT

Language—I want to say—is a refinement, *im
Anfang war die Tat*. Ludwig Wittgenstein,
"Cause and Effect: Intuitive Awareness"

In "The Monadology" (1714) Gottfried Wilhelm Leibniz asserted two kinds of truth, a distinction which has had an enormous influence on the theory of meaning to the present day. He sharply separates "truths of reasoning" from "truths of fact." The first kind comprises truths by analytical necessity; the second kind, contingent truths, require a body of reasoning to prop them up. To avoid an infinite regress of explanation Leibniz introduced the procedure of "sufficient reason" which allows us to align contingency with analyticity.[1] Kant was later to call this bridging of reason and the phenomenal the "synthetic judgment." What this means for a directional theory of meaning is threefold.

First, all formalized systems which produce necessary truths (leaving aside critiques of necessary truths) such as mathematics or symbolic logic, i.e., systems which are ruled by stipulated definitions, are severed from other discourses. In the directional theory of meaning proposed here, formalized sign systems are merely a special case. Second, all natural languages, i.e., those verbal signifying systems characterized by contingency, are described as if they are analytical structures, on the grounds of sufficient reason. This violates the nature of language as a set of schemata which are open in the direction of meaning fulfillment Third, discursive formations which are neither analytical nor could be handled by the procedure of sufficient reason, such as jokes and literary language use, are regarded as "spurious," as in Strawson's seminal paper "On Referring."[2] Viewed directionally, such discourses do not produce essentially different meanings but significations at the other end of the spectrum compared to analytical sense.

There is a striking parallel between Leibniz's yoking together of the pair of necessary and contingent truths under the concept of sufficient reason on the one hand and, on the other, explanations of the pair of logical sense and opacity in natural language under the umbrella of propositional clarity. Viewed in this manner, we could say that the logic of sufficient reason has been the dominant tendency in the theory of meaning roughly from Frege to the early Wittgenstein and beyond to speech act theory. What has been repressed in this history of description is the rationale for terminating a chain of signification at a certain point. What in terms of meaning making, we must ask, is 'insufficient,' 'sufficient,' and 'superfluous?'

The alternative to the assumption of sufficient reason is a pragmatics which grants to speakers and readers a range of choices: whether to cut explanation short or extend it at leisure; whether to be satisfied with the mere indication of the direction in which they should think or to insist on an imaginative quest for entailed beliefs, desires, and the politics of utterance. In this we are guided to a large extent by the very discursive formations which we encounter, except that it is always possible to read against the codified rules. Ordinarily we simply accept the convention that technical discourse curtails our referring and deictic acts, while its literary counterpart invites their ingenious elaboration.

This kind of alternative description has been waiting in the wings, as it were, while analytical descriptions since Frege have occupied the center stage. Yet we can observe a gradual weakening of the strict definitions of natural meanings from within analytical procedures themselves. Not that in the end, once we reach the sort of position advocated by Davidson, analyticity turns into a Heideggerian or Derridean description. What appears to be happening, though, is that the rift that existed, say, between Ryle's theorizing and that of the philosophy of Being, has narrowed to the point where a common concern emerges: a holistic description of signification. This chapter will give an overview of selected theorists of meaning in the analytical tradition to be concluded by a brief analysis of the ambivalent position held by Donald Davidson and Derrida's attack on analyticity itself.

Literary and ordinary readers are timid when they step on the slippery hardness of the ice of philosophy. We walk gingerly in this terrain, slip, slide, and fall to the laughter of expert skaters, the logicians. But why not take the risk and perhaps acquire a few minor skills? After all, logicians have not been exactly shy when it comes to saying things about literary meanings. My starting query is: What have the logicians done to *meaning*? The startling answer which I derive from reading logical analyses of ordinary language is that meaning constitution has been trivialized. Consider the following position:

> Because speaker's meaning and sentence-meaning do coincide in the vast majority of cases, our concepts of various performative actions do not tell us and do not need to tell us how they should be applied in those cases where there is a lack of coincidence. As long as the facts of the case are clear, that is, as long as we can specify the speaker's meaning and the sentence meaning and take note of

the points where they do and do not coincide, there is no philosophical reason
to accommodate borderline cases to one concept or another.[3]

The view of the transparency of communication and its toggle-logical basis
require the surgical separation of that which appears murky in language exchange and that which is lucid and unambiguous; the first feature cannot be
covered by definition and is therefore to be excised, while the second yields
to full definitional control and so qualifies for the label of meaning. Though
much more cautiously than Charles Landesman, the author just quoted, Gottlob
Frege in "*Über Sinn und Bedeutung*" draws the crucial distinctions which have
dominated the debate about meaning during much of this century. Frege con-
ceives of the links between "a sign, its sense [*Sinn*], and its reference [*Bedeutung*]" in such a way that "to the sign there corresponds a definite sense and
to that in turn a definite reference."[4]

At the same time, a reference, an object, can serve more than one sign. Frege's
term for reference, *Bedeutung*, with its sense of "meaning" and root in *Deutung*
(as for instance in *Traumdeutung*) and *deuten*, to interpret and point, suggests
that he wished to reserve at least a portion of meaning for this part of the
operation of understanding words and statements. For this reason, I would prefer
the definitions of sense meaning for *Sinn* and referential meaning for *Bedeutung*. One should perhaps note in this context that when Wittgenstein uses the
word *Bedeutung*, the translators usually render it as "meaning" in English.

By making these distinctions Frege is able to separate well-formed expressions
with referential meaning from those without reference. "In grasping a sense,"
he says, "one is not certainly assured of a reference."[5] This allows for all fully
formalized systems, languages which do not refer outside their frames but in-
ward toward their logical grammar and the definitional structure of sense. Where
there is a referential meaning in proper names or propositions, the latter "express" their sense and "designate" their referential meaning.[6] In this way, Frege
accommodates non-formalized discourses within one and the same analysis.
However, as Michel Pêcheux rightly points out, this "subordination of the contingent to the necessary" is a major blindspot in Frege's theory.[7]

In addition to sense meaning and referential meaning, Frege also introduces
the notions of sign and *Vorstellung*, idea, or better, imaginational projection. In
distinguishing among sign, sense meaning, referential meaning, and *Vorstellung*,
Frege in my view offers the basis for an intersubjective theory of meaning.
Consider the following four quotations.

> The sense of a proper name is grasped by everybody who is sufficiently familiar
> with the language or the totality of designations to which it belongs.[8]
>
> The idea [*Vorstellung*] is subjective: one man's idea is not that of another.[9]
>
> This constitutes an essential distinction between the idea [*Vorstellung*] and the
> sign's sense [*Sinn*], which may be common property of many and therefore is
> not part or a mode of the individual mind.[10]

... the idea which we have in that case, is wholly subjective; in between lies the sense which is indeed no longer subjective like the idea, but is yet not the object itself.[11]

The logical-positivist theories which Frege's analysis helped launch paid close attention to *Sinn* which is sharable and not to be confused with either the object or an image/idea. If we re-emphasize those discarded operations, *Vorstellung*, reference and object (though 'object' would need to be turned into a significatory process), a much broader view of meaning ensues. Had Frege pursued this line of thinking and distinguished more carefully the sense meanings of mathematics from those of natural languages, he probably would have been able to develop a tripartite semantics with objective, intersubjective, and subjective components. Michael Dummett, who has done impressive work on Frege's philosophy, goes one step further and describes Frege's definition of *Sinn* as a subjectivist explanation of meaning.

> Despite his reiterated emphasis on the objectivity of sense, Frege in fact described language as governed by the private understanding of it possessed by each speaker: the sense that a given speaker attaches to a word is the manner in which he takes it as contributing to determining the truth-value of any sentence in which it occurs. What, on such a view, makes language a possible instrument of communication is the ascertainability by one speaker of another speaker's private understanding of it; what makes it an efficient instrument of communication is the approximate coincidence of the private understandings of different speakers. Frege thus in effect assumes that an account of what confers on the expressions of a language the meanings that they have can be given by appeal only to the knowledge which each individual speaker has concerning the language.[12]

Put slightly differently, what Dummett calls a "speaker's private understanding" of a language is already based on intersubjective agreements concerning its use, so that any act of meaning endowment in the event of individual instantiation is never a purely private act but the realization of language within an intersubjective matrix of linguistic usage shared by a semiotic community. From this perspective, there is no such thing as a purely private understanding of language, but there is no room for an objectivist conception of the discourse of everyday life either. Dummett rightly draws our attention to "the approximate coincidence of the private understandings of different speakers" in Frege's theory, yet he does so disapprovingly. From the perspectives of a liberal, directional theory of meaning and a broad range of discursive practices, Frege's ambivalence is welcome. *Sinn* is neither subjective nor objective: "in between lies the sense ... which may be common property of many."[13]

Another feature of Frege's theory which is relevant to the reading of literary texts and also to communication in everyday life is his view that one can restrict oneself to sense meaning or, if one wishes, proceed to further meaning constituting operations. "One should be satisfied with the sense, if one wanted to go no further than the thought."[14] This tolerates different degrees of meaning making with respect to one and the same expression and so supports the view that different discourse frames are in need of different 'amounts' of deformalization and different kinds of transformations of the textual surface. In different discourses *Sinn, Bedeutung*, and *Vorstellung* play distinct roles.

Lastly, we sense the potential for an entire theory of indeterminacy in Frege's observation that "an object is anything that is not a function, so that an expression for it *does not contain any empty place*." Reference, thoughts of objects, is determined or saturated while sense remains indeterminate: "It is by this very indeterminacy that sense acquires the generality expected of a law."[15] From this crucial locus in Frege's writing lead two possible paths: one, to a theory of indeterminacy, pursued in very different ways for example by Roman Ingarden, W. V. Quine and Donald Davidson; the other, to an emphasis on sense at the expense of referential saturation.

Alas, as Frege's case shows, the logician tends to suppress the champion of the cause of fuzzy meanings. From the perspective of significatory saturation Frege does have his lapses: in the end he too is bound to return to the flip-flop basis of all formal procedure, true and false statements. Ironically, this very bedrock of positivist philosophizing reveals its metaphysical source when Frege says that "it is the striving for truth that drives us always to advance from sense to reference," and "we are therefore driven into accepting the truth value of a sentence as constituting its reference."[16]

To this one could object, as I shall in chapter 8, that in many of the linguistic transactions of everyday speech we do not consider the question of truth at all. There are any number of reasons for the habitual linking of sense meanings with referential or quasi-referential meanings. Perhaps I feel inclined to transcend sense because I distrust its formal emptiness and wish to fill it with the fuzzy but rich textuality of the phenomenal world familiar to me. Or perhaps it is because sense constitutes only part of understanding, a directional schema which gains full meaning only when it is linked with an encompassing social semiotic, no matter whether or not what is said corresponds reliably to the phenomenal states of affairs designated.

In 1905, seven years after the publication of Frege's "*Sinn und Bedeutung*," Bertrand Russell presented his rival theory of meaning in "On Denoting."[17] It begins with the classical position which couples knowledge of the world to that of language: "All thinking has to start from acquaintance."[18] According to Russell, language has propositions with denoting phrases, of which the most primitive contain "everything," "nothing," and "something," and propositions without denoting phrases. Propositions with denoting phrases have meaning, those without do not. Furthermore, propositions with denoting phrases can denote something with which I am acquainted or something I know only by virtue of denoting phrases. "Acquaintance" refers to knowledge of "things we have presentations of" and "knowledge about" to one of things which we know only by descriptions.[19]

In spite of his dissociation of these knowledges Russell merged Frege's sense meaning and referential meaning in one single "denotation." Translating Frege's terms into "meaning" (*Sinn*) and "denotation" (*Bedeutung*), Russell notes that the distinction was useful to a point, yet was bound to run into difficulties when it had to deal with the assertion of identity. "One of the first difficulties that confront us, when we adopt the view that denoting phrases express meaning and denote a denotation, concerns the cases in which the denotation appears to be absent."[20] By contrast, in Russell's theory, "there is no meaning, and only sometimes a denotation."[21]

When there is a denotation, Russell draws these three distinctions: "(1) A phrase may be denoting, and yet not denote anything . . . (2) A phrase may denote one definite object . . . (3) A phrase may denote ambiguously, e.g., 'a man' . . . "[22] The first kind of phrase covers all fictive statements, the second comprises uniquely referring expressions, and the third all ambiguously referring phrases. I shall argue later that even the second group of unique references loses its apparent stability if we look at it particularly from the perspective of modal opacity. For the time being, denotation appears to be the reliable anchor for my operations of meaning making.

Having abandoned the Fregean pair, Russell posits that if a proposition has a denotation, this could be regarded as its meaning. In this, he treats propositions like names, such that they identify a denoted entity in a descriptive manner. This is an important part of Russell's Theory of Description.

> By a "description" we mean a phrase of the form "the so-and-so" or of some equivalent form. For the present we confine our attention to the *in* the singular. We shall use this word strictly, so as to imply uniqueness . . . Thus a description of the form "the so-and-so" will only have an application in the event of there being one so-and-so and no more.[23]

As John Lyons has noted, the theory of unique description and ostensive definition can be defended even today if Russell's empiricist belief in atomicity is dropped and the descriptive denotations are situated in a network of shared semantic fields.[24] Certainly, the fact that Russell's Theory of Descriptions has come under attack by P. F. Strawson and Gilbert Ryle should not blind the reader of literary texts to the possibility that however deficient the theory may appear from one perspective, it may still be able to relinquish insights into the process of meaning making from another. For example, Ryle's refutation of the theory of names is especially unconvincing in the realm of literary signification, though we should note that his target was specifically Russell's link between names and empirical entities. Nor of course can the qualification of Ryle's theory by way of literature turn Russell into a textualist. Given these provisos, from the point of view of playful language use, both in ordinary discourse as in the use of nicknames or in literature, the rejection of the meaning equation of the name "Fido" with the dog Fido does not apply.[25]

Neither in its formulation of "Proper names are appellations and not descriptions," nor in the form of "Saying is not naming and naming is not saying" does the "Fido"-Fido critique hold in literary discourse. Quite the contrary, in literary reading naming is indeed saying; in literature proper names are conventionally read with the expectation that they are both appellations and descriptions. To a less obvious extent, this is also true of everyday speech, where we often welcome the opportunity of linking the name of a person to his or her social image beyond the mere act of identification.

The names Dewey Dell, Jewel, Darl, or Cash in William Faulkner's *As I Lay Dying* have both naming and saying functions. Also, it is difficult if not impossible to decide where the one function stops and the other begins. For as I read the name I construct at the same time the first tentative expectations as to the projected fictive personae's characterization. Since there is no external referent which is being named and described, fictive naming is part of the overall predication of imaginable subjects to be constructed by the reader. In Thomas Mann's short story "Tobias Mindernickel" the protagonist's name entails *in nuce* the macrostructural thematic development of the entire narrative. His name is a descriptive appellation in that it identifies the central fictive persona and at the same time alludes to the biblical authoritarian figure Toby and the double inferiority expressed by the German *minder* (lesser, inferior) and *Nickel* (a metal and a coin of little value). Mindernickel injures and in the end accidentally kills his little dog in a pathetic attempt at securing his companion's dependence. In this way, the action sequence fulfills the descriptive promise implied in the word Mindernickel which names both the protagonist and the tale. This is the kind of qualification we need to add to the "Fido"-Fido argument.

From the point of view of literary meaning it is also worth reconsidering Russell's position with regard to the vagueness of word meanings. Even if we complement Russell's theory of ostensive definition of words with the more recent conception of language as rule governed system, his insistence on the unalterable haziness of the sense meanings of natural language remains attractive.

> The meaning of a word is not absolutely definite: there is always a greater or less degree of vagueness. The meaning is an area, like a target: it may have a bull's eye, but the outlying parts of the target are still more or less within the meaning, in a gradually diminishing degree as we travel further from the bull's eye. As language grows more precise, there is less and less of the target outside the bull's eye, and the bull's eye grows smaller and smaller; but the bull's eye itself never shrinks to a point, there is always a doubtful region, however, small, surrounding it.[26]

Russell's explanation goes a long way toward supporting what I have called propositional opacity and the view of expressions as directional schemata which act as guide rails for the construction of meaning against the social semiotic background of negotiations about language use. This relative openness is a fundamental requirement for any explanation of the role which imaginational acts play in the process of meaning conferment in referentially and modally saturated discourses. What remains doubtful in communication is questioned or deformalized further by individual users of language, though this process never amounts to any precise closure of meaning. Unfortunately, Russell's liberal account of opacity of word meanings stands in sharp contrast to his rejection of utterance modalities being able to blur propositional sense. I shall discuss later his assault on "egocentric particulars" which mark the intrusion of the speaking subject into propositional content.

P. F. Strawson's paper "On Referring," published in 1950, represents a milestone in the philosophy of meaning and an advance beyond Russell's theory in a number of respects. Of particular interest for the construction of socially rich meanings are the following of Strawson's observations: his distinction between grammatical and logical subjects; the triple distinction between expression and sentence, their use, and their utterance; the separation of referring from ascribing; and the attention he pays the context of utterance.

In his interpretation of Russell's example, "The present King of France is bald," Strawson submits that "The present King of France" can be considered the grammatical but not the logical subject of the assertion.[27] This allows for all statements which, though well formed, do not have an actual referent. One could likewise say then that the great majority of fictional sentences and their equivalents, in everyday speech and especially in political discourse, sometimes have grammatical but no logical subjects. It would seem that in the frames of literary reading I primarily pay attention to grammatical subjects insofar as they function as founders of nominal meanings and initial points of identification which in the course of my reading receive further aspectual predication. Even in "writerly" reading, to use Roland Barthes's term from *S/Z*, where the representational is weakened in favor of linguistic self-referentiality and ruptured modalities, the grammatical subject still holds sway over its logical cousin.[28]

In distinguishing among a sentence, the use of a sentence, and its utterance and, analogously, among an expression, its use, and its utterance, Strawson, like the later Wittgenstein, shifts the emphasis from the relation between world and language to usage: " 'Mentioning,' or 'referring,' is not something an expression does; it is something that someone can use an expression to do. Mentioning, or referring to, something is a characteristic of a use of an expression, just as 'being about' something, and truth-falsity, are characteristics of a use of a sentence."[29]

Transferred to the domain of literary uttering, Strawson's tripartition of sentence, use, and utterance parallels the triad of the iterability of signifier/inscriptions, the engagement with a reading frame, as for example the discourse genre of the sonnet, and the event of imposing a particular prosodic contour on the inscription. In this way, a rationale is discernible in the differences between the stability of the line, "Where are the songs of Spring? Aye, where are they?", its far less stable, historically shifting conventional use as a literary statement, and the fluidity of its actual instantiations.

Instead of speaking, as does Russell, of propositions denoting something, Strawson proposes a referring and an ascribing use to expressions and sentences.

Thus, in the act of referring I identify something and by ascribing I attribute further features to the object so identified; I describe it in greater detail.[30] According to his view of language as a rule governed system, Strawson recognizes "rules for referring, and rules for attributing and describing."[31] As a result, we are in a position to choose whether we wish to employ language for referring or ascribing purposes; however when we do so, we perform these acts within the shared rule structures of a language game.

From the viewpoint of literary meaning making this allows for saying that such nominal identifications at the beginning of narratives, such as "Emma Woodhouse," "Call me Ishmael," "In my younger and more vulnerable years," "I went to live in East Germany" in *Twelve Years: An American Boyhood in East Germany* by Joel Agee, or "Corde, who led the life of an executive" in Saul Bellow's *The Dean's December*, are read in a referring or, more precisely, in a quasi-referring manner. The remainder of these novels then could be seen as guiding my ascriptive use of language, in that my subsequent meaning constructions all have a more or less immediate bearing on my linguistic and semiotic actualization of those agents and narrators.

Finally, as far as the context of utterance is concerned Strawson has this to say: "the context of utterance is of an importance which it is almost impossible to exaggerate; and by 'context' I mean, at least, the time, the place, the situation, the identity of the speaker, the subjects which form the immediate focus of interest, and the personal histories of both speaker and those he is addressing."[32] As brief as it is, this outline sketches a program of deictic contextualization which goes beyond the scope of traditional attempts at defining meaning and in fact beyond the actual achievements of speech act theory to date. Strawson's "at least" appears to acquiesce even to something as precarious as *modal opacity*, introduced earlier.

Unfortunately for the needs of literary meaning, Strawson's account has a few serious flaws. The author brushes aside the uses of language in fictional contexts as "spurious" and so restricts his focus to a language use which is closest to logical and technical discourse. Like John L. Austin, Strawson avoids etiolated and parasitical forms of speech; but unlike the former, who is careful to point out the strategic reasons for his omission, Strawson takes his restricted analytic perspective for granted.[33] Meaning is understood as "a function of the sentence or expression" and "to give the meaning of an expression . . . is to give general directions for its use in making true or false assertions."[34] Regrettably, Strawson here returns to the level of toggle logic and the question of verifiability and in so doing has to leave uncanvassed a vast area of language use in which the switching from truth to falsity and vice versa is not at issue. Nor does he pursue the notion of directionality hinted at in this passage.

Truth and falsity, verification and verifiability have loomed large in the philosophical discussion of meaning. I will leave the much debated question of truth and fictionality to one side, having dealt with this issue elsewhere.[35] I believe that for the discussion of literary reading and related operations in everyday speech the questions associated with truth and falsity are singularly misleading.

This is the case quite apart from the fact that in its straightforward form veri-ficationist theory is now all but discredited in the philosophy of language itself. A brief commentary on two representative positions, one favorable and one critical, will have to suffice here.

In "Meaning and Verification" Moritz Schlick provides a classical view of ver-ification theory.[36] According to Schlick, to give meaning to a sentence is to "transform it into a proposition." However, the sentences concerned must be of a kind which can be applied to reality and so tested as to whether the propositions into which I can transform them are either true or false. On this theory, sentences which violate the rules of language in such a way that no truth-falsity test can be administered are meaningless. What is required to be able to make the appropriate judgment is "a description of the conditions under which the sentence will form a *true* proposition, and those which make it *false.*"[37]

As a consequence of this argument, there is no way of understanding any meaning without ultimate reference to ostensive definitions, and this means, in an obvious sense, reference to "experience" or "possible verification."[38] This implies that the meaning of a proposition is fully dependent on the method of verification, and sentences for which no such relationship can be discovered do not simply fall outside the theory, but are declared to be meaningless. This is obvious nonsense, and one cannot help wondering how such a theory could ever have become as powerful as it did. In the theory of verification "there is no gradual transition between meaning and nonsense. For either you have given the grammatical rules for verification, or you have not; *tertium non datur.*"[39] This is toggle logic in its purest form, and in this form it can handle only a very narrow set of statements, unable to reach beyond empirical and tautological propositions and disqualified from saying anything about the modal intricacies of everyday discourse, let alone the imaginational language games of literary speech. Unlike in *Hamlet* and, for that matter, in social discourse at large, mean-ings here do not "grunt and sweat under a weary life" (III, i, 1.77) but surface untainted as neat conceptual entities.

In "On Meaning and Verification" J. L. Evans offers a succinct critique of the theory. He finds its central error to lie in the attempt to give a simple all-embracing answer to the question, "How do sentences mean?"[40] In this it fails. Evans awards the theory the consolation prize of an *ignoratio elenchi*: though it could not "limit the range of meaningful sentences," it succeeded in eluci-dating the meaning of the terms "tautology" and "empirical."[41] It is not sur-prising then that the Verification Principle was gradually weakened and finally abandoned altogether. Evans analyzes this surrender as having taken place in a number of stages. First, meaning and method of verification were identified; then the concession was made that though the two concepts could not be identified, statements were still regarded as meaningful only if they could be verified. The second surrender occurred when the thesis was weakened to the claim that "a statement, in order to be meaningful, need not be verified or verifiable 'in practice.'" And lastly, the position was modified to say that if a statement is to be regarded as meaningful, "some sensible experience must be relevant to determining its truth or falsity." This, Evans suggests, could be interpreted as having rendered the verificationist thesis "sufficiently harmless," or even as constituting "complete capitulation."[42]

On the other hand, in his rebuttal of verificationism and the Relational Theory Evans assumes a stance which, from the angle taken in this study, has its own shortcomings. According to the theory which he advocates, "the meaning of a word is simply the rules which govern its use, and to ask for its meaning is to ask for the rules." So far so good. But Evans also believes that in considering the question of meaning "no reference need be made to any extra-linguistic facts." We need to make the correction here that as far as meaning is concerned, reference to the extra-linguistic facts of non-verbal sign systems is inevitable. In Evans's purely propositional version, language is still a kind of chess game which denies its knotty entanglement with semiosis at large.[43]

Half a century before Evans, Ferdinand de Saussure introduced the chess analogy to linguistics in his lectures known as his *Course in General Linguistics*.[44] This analogy can be found frequently in the study of language, as for instance in Ryle[45] and in Wittgenstein.[46] In a more recent account of language as communication Stephen R. Schiffer makes use of the move of the game analogy: "For communication to be possible," he says, "it is not necessary that it be known what people will utter; what is essential is that it be known that if someone utters x (in such-and-such circumstances), then he will mean such-and-such."[47] This surely begs the question. It is only when a speaker is embedded in the totality of a semiotic system, which includes language, that he will know what "such-and-such" refers to.

It is important to see that there are many features in chess and in language which are fundamentally distinct, and any hasty comparison is therefore likely to confuse rather than clarify the issue. The root of these differences is that chess is purely propositional and formal and can therefore be played as a closed system, which language can not. This is not to say that a "semiotic of chess" is an illegitimate or fruitless approach.[48] At the same time we need to acknowledge that the formal features of chess are its necessary and sufficient conditions, a scenario too simple to account for social discourse: Chess is a closed system, in which the rules are fully defined and quantifiable. This is not the case in natural language where formal relations constitute only an aspect, however significant, of the total, open and dynamic structure. The moves on the chess board are like tautological propositions; they do not point outside the game itself, but remain within its formal domain. The fact that we can, if we so wish, imagine possible referents to illustrate the constellations of a particular game does not afford us a close analogy with what happens in the performance of everyday speech. For in a wide range of language use I cannot do without such linkages, while in chess they are a hindrance rather than a necessity.

With chess I cannot denote, refer or project within flexible directional guidelines as I habitually do in ordinary speech. Chess does not name nor describe anything other than its own moves. Only in chess can I reasonably claim to be able to make unambiguously correct moves, while only a very small segment of language can be said to be comparable at this level. Further, the power relations which occur in chess and in natural language cannot be equated. The 'pure' power relations of the chess game have only a superficial likeness to those which characterize ordinary language. In the latter, power relations are always contaminated by the modalities of everyday life. To describe them in terms of the formal-propositional relations of chess falsifies matters as much as simplifies them. And lastly, the language of chess yields total control over its reduced realm. By contrast, social discourse is negotiatory and hermeneutic, character-ized by question and answer, and so holds a fundamental potential for eman-cipation.

Perhaps it is safe to say that whenever the chess analogy is made to apply to complex phenomena such as language or nature it is bound to lead us astray. On the other hand, it is at its most persuasive when it is used to explain a specific set of relations. In *The Character of Physical Law*, delivered as lectures at Cornell University in 1964 and broadcast on BBC 2 in 1965, Richard Feynman compared nature to a vast game of chess with the unsatisfactory result of a global and homogeneous explanation quite in disagreement with what physics has to say today. A much more convincing case is made with the help of chess by John Gribbin in his book *In Search of Schrödinger's Cat: Quantum Physics and Reality* (1984) where the author explains the single case of Heisenberg's tables of quan-tum numbers. "Quantum transitions," he says, "are described in a similar no-tation linking paired (initial and final) states." Neither in chess nor in quantum mechanics "do we have any indication of how the transition from one state to another is carried out, a point brought out most strongly by the knight's move and by castling." It is this specificity which gives explanatory power to the analogy. The same applies to its use in the theory of language.[49]

One of the philosophers who has tried to fulfill Strawson's program of de-scribing the background of utterances as part of the process of meaning con-stitution is H. P. Grice. First, a brief comment on his famous distinction between "natural" and "non-natural" meanings, between such signs as spots on our body indicating a disease and language signs or gestures, advanced in "Meaning" in 1957. Useful as this distinction is, it must not be construed to mean that so-called natural meanings are to be located somewhere outside the social semiotics of a community.[50] Quite the reverse is the case. Natural meanings are natural only in the very limited sense of their having to do with physiological phe-nomena; their far more important side, the fact that they can be read in a systemic manner and, as I argued in chapter 1, are not available to us in any other way places them squarely in the dynamics of significations. Only in regard to their being signs within an all-subsuming semiotic, a culture, can they be related to and distinguished from their conventional cousins.

Of greater importance for the clarification of *propositional* and *modal opac-ities* are Grice's concepts of "conventional" and "conversational implicature," what he has to say about the intentions of speakers and writers, as well as his principle of co-operation.[51] Here are attempts, along with those made in speech act theory, to come to grips with a vast number of assumptions which we intuitively make when we engage in conversation and other forms of meaning 'exchange.' Grice's moves seem to open the door at least a little to let into the air-conditioned halls of semantics a whiff of the social world at large. Yet in the end Grice too fails to pursue the notion of "occasion meaning" and instead opts for a semantic solution which permits him to retrieve deviance under the umbrella of linguistic convention: "We require a good reason for accepting that a particular use diverges from the general usage."[52] Unfortunately, the larger goal of extending the definition of meaning from semantics to a "social semiotics," which is promised in part of his work, seems abandoned.

Meanwhile on the Continent, different groups of writers had challenged the centrality of truth and falsity and the *tertium non datur* rule. One such group of theorists descended from Husserl's phenomenology and included Martin Heidegger, Merleau-Ponty, Alfred Schutz, and Roman Ingarden, each of whom inspired other theorists skeptical of an analysis centered on truth principles. Heidegger's critique, for example, is most influentially continued by Jacques Derrida, Schutz has had considerable impact on ethnomethodology, and Ingarden's work on the ontic heteronomy of the literary work of art has provided much of the foundation for reception aesthetics.

Perhaps more exciting than the well-known opposition to truth-conditional theory from phenomenological quarters are the alternative ways of approaching meaning which have been generated from within logical positivism. The main innovators here are the later Wittgenstein and John Langshaw Austin, the founder of speech act theory. I shall deal with the potential for a non-truth oriented and broadly semiotic theory of discourse in Wittgenstein's later writings in chapter 6. Suffice it here to mention that a semiotic reading of Wittgenstein finds support in Garth Hallett's book *Wittgenstein's Definition of Meaning as Use*, where the author argues that use "refers to a far larger context than the purely verbal one . . . to include a whole new dimension . . . a 'form of life,' woven into the whole texture of social intercourse, . . . as much part of our natural history as 'walking, eating, drinking, playing.' "[53] Though Wittgenstein never goes as far as to say so, from this follows, as I am arguing from various angles, that natural language, unlike chess and other formalized systems, does not signify by itself, requiring as it does the bedrock of social semiotics, and not just the world of 'objects.'

Judging by the perspective favored in this study one might expect the author to be enthusiastic about the Austinian revolution. And it certainly is a major step toward breaking the stranglehold of strict sense on meaning. But as an explanation of the relation between linguistic operations and their semiotic embedding, speech act theory got off to a poor start. As much as Austin's work is to be regarded as a breakthrough compared to the context-free definitions of meaning, it is disappointing from the perspective of the very modalities his work promised to address. From the outset, Austin confined his analyses to the serious part of ordinary language, shying away from the less easily formalizable bending of propositional content produced by unreliable speakers. I will not offer here a critique of Austin's avoidance of the so-called parasitic forms of speech, but refer the reader instead to Derrida's light-hearted yet poignant analysis of the restrictive metaphysical presuppositions underlying Austin's theories, as well as those of his main successor, John Searle.[54] Rather than regarding "infelicity" as a risk, Derrida proposes in "Limited Inc abc . . . ," that speech act theory ought to take its own task more seriously by addressing itself to the funny and pleasurable parts of language, to precisely what are presumed to be deviations from the serious center of discourse and so fulfill a promise the theory appeared to have made at its inception.[55]

From the position taken here, where surface meanings are affected by further, complex meaning operations, a serious shortcoming of Austin's theory is that he never allowed illocution to become part of meaning itself.[56] Illocution remained a force outside the act of constructing propositional sense, the latter being an intensional entity sandwiched between speech intention and possible effects on a hearer. By contrast, in the view which I believe the explanation of literary reading as well as a good portion of ordinary language requires, modal forces such as illocutions affect propositional sense and interact with it in the event of overall meaning endowment. Locutions, I would argue, do not exist by themselves, except as merely analytical stipulations for the purposes of separating a number of aspects of meaning which in the actual events of discourse always coincide.[57] Equally serious is the fact that the entities "speaker" and "hearer" remain unquestioned idealizations in Austin's theory, a feature carried over into the writings of John R. Searle.

As to Searle's extension of Austin's theory, I want to make a number of criticisms. First, I would question the sweeping opening of *Speech Acts* where linguistic communication is characterized as perfect meaning exchange. "How is it possible," the author asks, "that when a speaker stands before a hearer and emits an acoustic blast such remarkable things occur as: the speaker means something; *the hearer understands what is meant*."[58] As described here, meaning exchange occurs in only a select class of utterances or, if applied more broadly, only to a part of general discourse, namely its formal relations. The second criticism is in regard to the discrepancy between the twelve criteria which Searle introduces at the beginning of his paper, "A Classification of Illocutionary Acts," and the mere four which he then finds are sufficient to identify his five categories of illocutionary acts. This leads the author to the reductive conclusion that there is "a rather limited number of basic things we do with language."[59] The surprise, I think, should be directed not so much at discourse but at the taxonomy proposed.

This formal reduction of language to "a rather limited number" of operations stands in contrast with Searle's observation in "The Logical Status of Fictional Discourse" in which he comments on Iris Murdoch's *The Red and the Green*: "What we visualize when we read the passage is a man pottering about his garden thinking about horses."[60] Unless Searle were to say that we never use language in this way outside of literature, it appears that we also do other and certainly not very basic and formal things. What Searle fails to consider and what his method is not designed to handle is the possibility that such a semiotic grasp as visualization is more than a pleasurable adjunct to subjective reading; that it is perhaps a fundamental part not only of a naive kind of signification but of all literary reading, as well as a considerable portion of everyday speech. As seen from my angle of emphasizing the instantiation of language, I would say that Searle pays too much attention to the system and its formal conditions and too little to its denting by a vast number of modalities. It is ironic that it is a neglect of the modal aspects of discourse which should so limit Searle's speech act theory. Perhaps the stumbling block to a broader view of meaning in Searle is the conviction that the meaning of expressions and the background from which they emanate are of necessity separate entities rather than features of one and the same process. As Searle writes at the beginning of his essay, "The Background of Meaning," the view he espouses "is that in general the meaning of a sentence only has application (it only, for example, determines a set of truth conditions) against a background of assumptions and practices that are *not* representable as part of the meaning."[61] This, to a point, supports what I am after, except that his surgical removal of "the meaning of a sentence" from other semiotic practices is unacceptable.

My final criticism addresses the argument put forward in his more recent work, *Intentionality: An Essay in the Philosophy of Mind*. Given the central assumption of meaning as an entity within a theory of speech acts, Searle is predictably compelled to look for increasingly broader frames of explanation. This is encouraging. The reader is all the more disappointed when he finds that in dealing with the directionality of meaning intending acts Searle retraces a good deal of the kind of work done by Brentano and the Husserl of the *Ideas* and Schutz in his *Collected Papers*. Especially Husserl's analysis of the noema-noesis distinction or Alfred Schutz's descriptions of our sedimented stock-of-knowledge and the taken-for-grantedness of the life-world are rephrased without proper reference to those original studies. Nor does Searle take any note of Husserl's explanation of "appresentation" in the *Cartesian Meditations* which precisely anticipates this kind of argument: "If one believes one is seeing a whole house, the front of the house actually looks different from the way it looks if one believes one is seeing a false facade of a house, even though the optical stimuli may be identical in the two cases."[62]

Likewise disappointing is Searle's total neglect of semiotic explanations of non-linguistic relations which the book explores as a backdrop for speech acts. I also refer the reader to chapter 1, where I gave a brief account of Searle's notion of "literal meaning" which I think does not square with the interaction between linguistic signs and their "background" as sketched by Searle.

And yet it is not speech act theory as such that sets these boundaries but rather a commitment to propositional sense unaffected by what occurs outside linguistic expressions. A notable exception with respect to this mainstream conviction among speech act theorists is Louise Pratt, who in her more recent work and especially in "Ideology and Speech-Act Theory" (1986) revises an earlier linguistic-propositional bias to accommodate social political dimensions.[63] Such a move is more serious than it may first appear, for it requires an explanation as to how precisely the lexicon, as well as its combinatory use in texts, is affected by unstated yet powerfully present entailments, such as "ideological effects."[64] In the 'final' analysis and beyond Pratt such an investigation involves no less than the questioning of the definitional certitude of meaning as sense.

In the opening section of chapter 2 we encountered Donald Davidson as the philosopher of "radical interpretation" and "interpretive holism." Here we need to look at the way in which he links meaning and truth. I have chosen him as the last representative of the analytic tradition because he seems to me on the verge of undermining the very foundations of the theory of meaning produced by that tradition. Looking at his papers as Davidson himself arranged them in the volume *Inquiries into Truth and Interpretation*, we are struck by a visible shift from titles concerning truth, facts, and Convention T to titles foregrounding moods, performances, belief, inscrutability, metaphor, and finally communication. This seems to me a telling insight into a scholarly career which gradually acknowledges the hermeneutic pressures put on positivist philosophical semantics. As Davidson notes in a late paper, "trying to make meaning accessible has made truth inaccessible."[65] So we are no longer dealing with a theory which fixes meaning by way of truth but one which is prepared to sacrifice the notion of strict truth in order to get a handle on the relationship between meaning and its background. And a non-strict 'truth' is a pretty useless concept; it certainly can no longer do the kind of work we would expect of this metaphysically burdened notion. Inevitably, Davidson's move leads to a semiotic definition of the field of description. This is precisely what Davidson appears to be acknowledging when he says, "we have erased the boundary between knowing a language and knowing our way around in the world."[66]

I have anticipated a result which is close to the kind of theory of meaning advocated here. It is a long and in some ways an astonishing intellectual journey which Davidson makes before he reaches his recent conclusions. Consider Davidson's starting point in Alfred Tarski's truth convention and such semantic concepts as denotation ("'the victor of Jena' denotes Napoleon"), satisfaction ("snow satisfies the condition 'x is white'") and definition ("the equation '$x^3 = 2$' defines (determines uniquely) the cube root of the number two").[67] However, we must not blame Tarski for the application of his truth notions to the semantics of natural languages, for, as he warns, "it is only the semantics of formalized languages which can be constructed by exact methods."[68] As to colloquial language, "the results are entirely negative. With respect to this language not only does the definition of truth seem impossible, but even the consistent use of this concept in conformity with the laws of logic."[69]

Should Davidson have heeded Tarski's advice? If he had, he would certainly have saved himself a good deal of work, and he would by now be one of the champions of an intersemiotic theory of meaning. On the other hand, Davidson's writings turn out not simply to be a circuitous confirmation of Tarski's foresight but also a useful demonstration of the inevitable bending of analyticity by culturally saturated signification. In "Semantics for Natural Languages" Davidson undertakes to establish a set of rules which would supply "for every sentence in the language a statement of the conditions under which it is true." The kind of theory of truth which he develops from Tarski's logic entails "for each sentence s, a statement of the form 's is true if and only if p' where in the simplest case 'p' is replaced by s."[70] This, according to Davidson, establishes the meaning of the sentence, for the expression "is true if and only if" stands for "means that."[71]

From the perspective of meaning as intersemiotic process between linguistic and other forms of social signification the logical use of the copula 'is' must be regarded as illegitimate for two reasons. First, identity can be shown to occur only in definitionally ruled, i.e., fully formalized languages. This is what prevented Tarski from attempting a logical semantics for natural languages. Second, we cannot assume that the different sign systems, natural language and the sign systems making up the remainder of the social semiotic, are commensurable at all. Collaboration between different sign systems almost certainly does not rest on nor does it require synonymy or identity. I shall cite Roman Jakobson in the next chapter to the effect that the assumption of semiotic commensurability in any strict sense is misguided. Yet Davidson needs evidence from both language and its background to apply the Convention T. "The truth of an utterance," he says, perhaps ironically, "depends on just two things: what the words mean, and how the world is arranged."[72]

Davidson, no doubt, is very much aware of the difficulties. When we describe natural languages, "Tarski's Convention T," he concedes, "is no longer available as a formal test."[73] Once we apply the Tarskian strategy to non-formalized languages "it makes more sense to assume a partial understanding of truth, and use the theory to throw light on meaning, interpretation, and translation."[74] Truth now varies depending on the time of utterance, the utterer, and "even, perhaps, the audience."[75] And yet Davidson still defends congruence of meaning between utterers.[76] How can this be done? By making a number of radical assumptions on "sincerity" and "rationality," for in Davidson's world only rational speakers have anything to "say."[77] Assumptions need also to be made, as we saw earlier, about the belief systems of both sender and receiver of expressions, casting a complex background against which the slightly fuzzy T-sentences for utterances can then be construed.[78]

Taken seriously, the background construal required for the securing of meaning amounts to nothing less than the invocation in conceptual terms of the entire social semiotic of which speaker and hearer are a part. And indeed, in his discussion of metaphors we remember that Davidson saw no limit to where they can take us. Here Davidson approaches Umberto Eco's "criterion of interpretability" argued in *Semiotics and the Philosophy of Language*, which "allows us to start from a sign in order to cover, step by step, the entire circle of semiosis."[79] Similarly, for Davidson, the reading of any "single utterance requires evidence for the interpretation of *all* utterances of a speaker of a community."[80] As attractive as this observation looks because of its holistic character, so fundamental is the *aporia* it produces for a philosopher of Davidson's training: in order to be able to apply his truth convention, however modified, he needs to transform all non-assertive utterances into indications.[81] On the one hand, Davidson requires bodies of belief, on the other, beliefs must themselves be available as a language; though he wishes to describe meaning in the process of social transaction, reference is argued to be superfluous in such a description.[82]

To come to grips with meaning as a form of exchange between the system of natural language ("what words mean") and non-verbal systems ("how the world is arranged") Davidson needs to realize that truth-conditional inquiry is in the way of interpretation. He must give up being, as Shakespeare puts it in *The Merry Wives of Windsor*, a "hunter for a truth." (IV, iv, 1.3) For the hermeneutic task is to address all discursive formations, rational and schizophrenic, indicative and non-assertive, sincere and insincere, conventional and deviant as well as their non-verbal background. As far as Davidson's analysis goes, meaning still emerges as an *entity* to be shown to be the case rather than a *process* to be described as a dynamic. I am not saying that truth-conditional inquiry should be abandoned; what I am saying, with Tarski's support, is that it must be restricted to the discourse in which it can accomplish its task without strain: formal logic. As Davidson's case demonstrates, when commitment to truth remains the focus of a theory of meaning, no matter how one tries to widen the methodological straitjacket (and Davidson cannot be accused of not trying), the entire field of non-verbal semiosis is transformed into something it is not: more indicative sentences. Whether Davidson's position can be pushed to the point where it is prepared to go over the top and view meaning in a Heideggerian or Derridean manner must remain a matter for speculation. When we enter the world of Derrida's *écriture* our bearings are radically reoriented, though I believe that his main commitment remains philosophical through and through.

In "The Time of a Thesis: Punctuations" Jacques Derrida tells us that he sees all his writings as part of a coherent enterprise. "All the problems worked out in the Introduction to *The Origin of Geometry* have continued to organize the work I have subsequently attempted . . . "[83] This enterprise is neither literary nor merely rhetorical but committedly philosophical, with its focus on "the philosophical text in its formal structure, in its rhetorical organization, in the specificity and diversity of its textual types, in its models of exposition and production."[84] At the same time Derrida is fully aware that the sort of theorizing he practices is not in the mold of any standard philosophy, except in *Speech and Phenomena*, of which he says, "it is perhaps the essay which I like best . . . in a classical philosophical architecture *Speech and Phenomena* would come first."[85] However, I do not wish to drag Derrida back to a tradition from which he is obviously keen to escape. What he cannot escape from is the responsibility of having made an interjection in the debate.

Derrida's philosophizing is marginal in a double sense: it treats specific philosophers marginally, so that the Plato scholar and Husserl specialist turn away from Derrida disappointed; more importantly, it is marginal also in the sense of showing how issues which have traditionally been regarded as peripheral acquire central significance from a new perspective. Two themes have fascinated Derrida in this way: unacknowledged metaphysical commitments and the 'purity' of the concept. Both have to do with the description of meaning. The first is closely associated with Derrida's critique of presence, the assumption crystallized in Husserl's early writing that meaning presents itself to consciousness in any stable form, a critique summed up in the metaphor, "rising towards the sun of presence, it is the way of Icarus."[86] The second theme, which primarily concerns us here, is Derrida's unrelenting assault on the dominance of analyticity in philosophy, an attack which he launches from within conceptuality by striking at the very foundations of definitional purity. Beyond a critique of individual philosophical notions, Derrida's aim is nothing less than the "overturning and displacing of the conceptual order."[87]

To proceed analytically would have defeated the very purpose Derrida set for himself, and after all, "immediacy is derived. Everything begins with the intermediary."[88] Instead of relying on a linear logic he chooses a heterologous approach of *entrelacement*, after Plato's dialectical art of weaving or the "science of *symploke*."[89] This strategy is not meant to amount to a classically philosophical method; rather, it is a critical procedure which consists of a bevy of critical devices now known as "deconstruction," Derrida's translation of Heidegger's *Destruktion*, or critical dismantling. What deconstruction does has been neatly summed up by Rodolphe Gasché in *The Tain of the Mirror: Derrida and the Philosophy of Reflection*. Deconstruction attempts "to account for the heterogeneity constitutive of philosophical discourse, not by trying to overcome its inner differences but by maintaining them."[90] This, Derrida tries to accomplish with the aid of specific tools, such as "trace," "supplementarity," "iterability," "re-mark," "*sous rature*," "always already," "hymen," "marge," "pharmakon," "mise-en-abyme," "metaphor," and "differance." Each of these "infrastructures" is designed to chip away at the marble of morphologically and geometrically grasped concepts in order to reveal their fundamentally metaphorical nature. Instead of sharpness of distinction, instead of full synonymy and identity, we have "undecidability." Here is how Derrida presents his critical tools to the reader.

An adaptation of Heidegger's *frühe Spur* (matinal trace), Derrida's "trace" can be known only as a reference to another trace, as "the erasure of selfhood," characterized by the threat of "its irremediable disappearance." As the "disappearance of origin" the trace at the same time "becomes the origin of the origin." There is no such thing as an "unerasable trace," for that would make it a "full presence;" it is always between appearance and erasure. In this the trace displays a peculiar economy: "its force of production stands in necessary relation to the energy of its erasure." All specific traces can also be thought of as derivative as to an "originary trace" which attaches to "the *pure* movement which produces difference."[91] Thinking in terms of "traces" nudges us into seeing all signification as transitory processes and conceptual solidity as an illusion.

"Neither presence nor absence," supplementarity is the effect of the supplement which "adds only to replace." Again stressing movement over structure,

Derrida draws our attention to the historical process of conceptual shifts whereby certain aspects of a concept are incessantly being replaced by others. In this sense, the supplement "intervenes or insinuates itself *in-the-place-of*" something else. Supplementarity also means that nothing is ever supplemented for good. The supplement "is not simply added to the positivity of a presence, it produces no relief, its place is assigned in the structure by the mark of an emptiness."[92]

"Iterability" draws our attention to the difference between the eidetic or "that which can always be repeated as the *same*," as in mathematics, and signification in natural languages where all repetition produces difference. Only signifiers and not signifieds are iterable. Since, according to Derrida, there are no signifieds in formalized languages iterability produces ideality: "the ideality and invisibility of the *eidos* are its power to be repeated." In all other forms of signification supplementarity intervenes in the process of repetition.[93]

The "re-mark" or "*le supplément de marque*" is a product of "the text's workings," according to which signifiers are forever marked by others and so can never achieve an un-marked neutrality: "in the act of inscribing itself on itself indefinitely, mark upon mark, it multiplies and complicates its text, a text within a text, a margin in a mark, the one indefinitely repeated within the other: an abyss."[94]

The procedure of "*sous rature*" or putting under erasure, crossing a term out yet leaving it thus qualified, is a practice adopted from Heidegger. It allows Derrida to talk about something about which we can no longer speak in a conventional way. The "always already" structure is often invoked by Derrida to point to the impossibility of deciding on conceptual origins. Rather than being able to isolate a concept in its simplicity and purity, there is always already another chain of signification involved which contaminates our vision.[95]

"Hymen," "marge," and "pharmakon" are devices highlighting conceptual undecidability. They "have a double, contradictory, undecidable value that always derives from their syntax." This affects all signs in such a way that the clear opposites of a conceptual inside and outside become dubious. Instead of pure conceptuality in the analytical sense "one is simply dealing with greater or lesser syntactical units at work, and with economic differences in condensation."[96]

By employing the term "mis-en-abyme" Derrida insists again and again on the endlessness of chains of signification, a fact which confronts our habitual assumption of the frozen sign. This move also undermines the procedure of sufficient reason, for sufficiency is nothing but another kind of signification, a philosophical metaphor, imposed on significatory differentiation in order to arrest its movement.

"Metaphor" is as important to Derrida as it was to Nietzsche, for the main reason that it supplies the syntax of all signification. Language itself guarantees that a term such as "concept" is fundamentally metaphorical. In this sense, metaphor is "a classical philosopheme, a metaphysical concept." Yet it is one of those metaphysical signifiers of which we cannot easily rid ourselves. As Derrida concedes in "White Mythology: Metaphor in the Text of Philosophy," if one wished to conceive and to class all the metaphoric possibilities of philosophy, one metaphor, at least, always remains excluded, outside the system: the metaphor, at the very least, without which the concept of metaphor could not be constructed, or, to syncopate an entire chain of reasoning, the metaphor of metaphor.[97]

I have placed "differance" at the end of this catalogue because next to metaphoricity it seems to me the most complex and powerful of Derrida's notions. Derrida himself aligns "differance" with some of the most ambitious moves made in Philosophy: Hegel's *Aufhebung*, variants of differentiation as argued by Nietzsche, Freud, Saussure, and Levinas and, most eminently, Heidegger's ontic-ontological difference.[98] "If there were a definition of differance," says Derrida in *Positions*, "it would be precisely the limit, the interruption of the Hegelian *relève*." Or, as Steven Shaviro understands the term, differance is the "inversion of the *Aufhebung* in a *mis-en-abyme*."[99]

"Differance" is also the radicalization of Husserl's description of the fleeting 'now' which always carries the shadow of its immediate past, its retentions, with it and yet always already anticipates its protensions, the immediate future into which it gears. These insights, Derrida says, should have led the Husserl of the *Phenomenology of Inner Time Consciousness* to abandon noematic closure of the sign and with it the ideality of meaning. In "Differance" Derrida completes Husserl's task, as it were, by accentuating the dual process inherent in all signification, spatial and temporal differentiation: differing and deferring. As such, "differance" acts as a master trope subsuming all possible differences. Yet would this not turn it into the apex of yet another "violent hierarchy?"[100]

Derrida is at pains to avoid this charge. When he himself asks, "What differs? Who differs? What is differance?" we wait in vain for a definitional answer. Instead, we receive glimpses of descriptions scattered throughout his writings, many of which are negations rather than assertions: "differance" is the "sameness which is not identical," "the order of the same," and yet "nonidentity."[101] It is "neither a word nor a concept," it "is not, does not exist and is not any sort of being-present," to the effect that "it cannot be exposed." Using a Heideggerian phrase, Derrida says it is "irreducible to every ontological or theological—onto-theological—reappropriation." Though "differance" is the "subversion of every realm," it "commands nothing" and "rules over nothing."[102]

Fortunately for those readers who suffer from theoretical vertigo in this *Eiger Nordwand* of philosophizing, Derrida does offer the odd affirmation to hang on to. With its double meaning of spatial and temporal differentiation "differance" tries to capture the primordial workings of textuality. As such, "differance" describes "the origin or production of differences and the differences between differences, the *play* of differences."[103] In *Of Grammatology* it is the "(pure) trace" and the "formation of form," in *Positions* the systematic play of differences of traces of differences, of the spacing by which "elements relate to one another," as well as "a configuration of concepts" which are "systematic and irreducible."[104]

At the same time, "differance" is the "movement by which language, or any code, any system of reference in general, becomes 'historically' constituted as a fabric of differences." Since differance as the "nonfull, nonsimple 'origin'" cannot be derived from anything, it requires a "*de jure* commencement." At the same time it is conceived at such a high level of generality that it "can refer to the whole complex of its meanings at once, for it is immediately and irreducibly multivalent." With reference to Husserl's analysis of inner time, "differance" is described as making "the movement of signification possible only if each element that is said to be 'present,' appearing on the stage of presence, is related to something other than itself but retains the mark of a past element and already lets itself be hollowed out by the mark of its relation to a future element."[105]

In his commentary on Husserl's *Origin of Geometry* Derrida once again stresses the close link between his most general term and signification at large in that "differance already suggests a mode of writing (*écriture*) without presence and absence—without history, cause arche, or telos—which would overturn all dialectic, theology, teleology, and ontology." Derrida believes that this new "mode of writing would exceed everything that the history of metaphysics has conceived in the form of the Aristotelian gramme: the point, the line, the circle, as well as time and space themselves."[106]

By sketching his notion of "differance" from various angles Derrida faces the dilemma of trying to undermine the foundations of philosophical reasoning without having to resort to the kind of foundational procedure he is out to attack. Yet if anything in Derrida's writing amounts to a founding strategy, then it is the way in which "differance" becomes the master metaphor for signification. Not only the representational side of signification and the univocality of conceptual structures are affected by "differance." The speaking subject also belongs to its sphere of influence. As with other meanings, the speaking subject is both constituted and qualified by the differing-deferring dynamics of "differance": the "signifying subject would not be self-present, insofar as he speaks or signifies, except for the play of linguistic and semiological differance."[107] Two issues are being addressed here simultaneously: the determination of utterance by the relevant sign system as well as its discursive formations, and the contention that the result does not yield a presence, a secure set of conceptually clean or stable meanings.

What appears at first paradoxical turns out upon closer scrutiny to be a statement which is both antisubjectivist and anti-idealist or, to put it positively, systemic and pragmatic. Although the speaking subject cannot constitute itself, but rather always emerges as a function of signifying systems, none of its discursive instantiations is able to produce the kind of univocal sense meanings which analytic theories have posited. According to Derrida, then, neither that which is presented by expressions nor its manner of presentation is capable of guaranteeing meaning as pure conceptual sense; all meaning is always already contaminated, "besmeared with sluttish time." (Shakespeare, Sonnet 55, 1.4)

Since Derrida's entire oeuvre is dedicated to the task of disrupting assumptions of semantic stability wherever they occur, his work appears to be more closely related to what I have set out to do than is actually the case. To illustrate this point I shall concentrate briefly on *differance*, though what I have to say applies equally to other infrastructures. Let us gather Derrida's various descriptions of *differance* under the umbrella of 'differential potential' or the 'possibility' of differentiation. Because of Derrida's own usage of the term and those descriptions, *differance* is no longer a mere signifier but has become a specific sign among others. The fact that it is a particularly wobbly one should not be discouraging, for the same degree if not the same sort of instability applies to signs such as 'democracy' or 'freedom.' Nor is the fact that *differance* is a neologism of importance. All non-analytical signifiers are ultimately both underdetermined and indeterminate. Further, like any other sign *differance* refers both to other linguistic formations as well as outside language to non-verbal signs. In this way *differance* is not entirely free but curtailed by the play of general semiosis. Derrida is therefore unnecessarily coy in keeping us in the semi-dark as to what relationship exists between the sign *differance* and other signs.

Nor should the impossibility of meaning as presence be a hindrance to description. Since meanings are not entities but linking processes, significatory deferral is no surprise. Dynamic structures are unstable *ex hypothesi*, and yet they can be described by a chain of signification which is logically limitless but pragmatically curtailable. To insist on the matching of the slipperiness of this dynamic with an even more slippery rhetoric is to confuse (deliberately) the *definiendum* with the *definiens*, or at least that which is to be signified with the signifying act. Because our defining descriptions tend to be conceptual and that which we wish to clarify belongs to semiological practice, this fusion also entails the rejection of the distinction between the logical and the pragmatic.

If in Derrida's work logocentrism is untenable and there is only *pragmatics*, an argument at least partly compatible with a directional theory of meaning, then there is also always the possibility of constraint. Yet we look in vain for a declaration in Derrida as to the pragmatic boundaries of his enterprise. Obversely, we do not know how radical his position is either. We can only take his word for it: we only always deal with an "indefinite drift of signs."[108] But this is where we require a minimal degree of precision. For to take seriously that even *pragmatically* we cannot restrain signifying chains would mean that we could not survive, physiologically, socially or politically. I leave the political critique of Derrida's theorizing to Habermas in chapter 10 and conclude that Derrida's account of signification does not square with social semiosis as a life-supporting system. For social semiotic entails not only the possibility of indefinite significatory bifurcation or an endless pyramid of fractals, but also the possibility for these patterns of dissemination to gel into equally endless, inverted pyramids of syntheses, which act as provisional closures and constraints. The moment when fractal fission turns into new combinatory structures cannot be explained from the vantage point of any one sign system in isolation but only by a holistic view of social semiosis at large.

This chapter has dealt with the struggle of the apophantic 'as' of assertion to control meaning as strict sense by negating its existential-hermeneutical 'as.'[109] From this Heideggerian position one could regard Derrida's writings as the supplement to a deconstructive 'as' which characterizes signification as the infinite chain of 'something else.' Whatever its other merits, the weakness of this sort of explanation stems from its failure to show how overall semiosis accommodates semantic drift. One way of arguing constraints on meaning instability is by way of grammar. How a directional theory in which meanings are ill-defined processes linking linguistic expressions with the background systems of a general social semiotic squares with the concepts of *langue* and *grammatics* is the question posed in the next chapter.

VI

THE LIMITS OF *LANGUE*

> There is a circle here, for if one distinguishes
> rigorously *langue* and *parole* . . . one does not
> know where to begin. . . .
>
> Jacques Derrida, *Positions*

> The task of *liberating* grammar from logic re-
> quires beforehand a positive understanding of
> the basic *a priori* structure of discourse in
> general as an existentiale.
>
> Martin Heidegger, *Being and Time*

The aim of this chapter is to question the role which highly abstract notions of *langue* and similar formal schemata play in relation to the system of *instantiations* or that network of discursive operations which actually takes place in communication. Even if it is not possible to liberate grammar entirely from logic, as Heidegger suggests we should, we can at least attempt to find a level of theorization closer to discursive actualities and less exclusive of other sign systems than is the Saussurean *langue*. The chapter concludes with a discussion of the *semiotic corroboration* thesis which says, put simply, that what we call reality is the product of the interaction of at least two different sign systems.

Before we can talk about *langue* and other abstractions we need to elaborate a little on our description of *meaning* as a *linking process between verbal and non-verbal signification*. By this I want to suggest that we understand the majority of language expressions, specifically indexical ones, to the degree at which we are able to complement if not match them by our schematic grasp of tactile, olfactory, kinetic, proxemic, aural, visual and other forms of reading the world. I concur here with Bateson that far from language constituting a replacement of non-verbal forms of signification, language and non-linguistic sign systems develop side by side toward ever more complex formations. Moreover, in my view they interact with one another to constitute 'reality.' This is qualified by Thomas A. Sebok who believes that "the two kinds of sign systems, though they are often in performance subtly interwoven, serve ends largely different from one another."[1]

If the main purpose of using sign systems is social survival, as I assume it is, then their mastery means a highly competent negotiation of the world toward that goal. It should not follow then that different sign systems could have contradictory roles, even if some of them, as Sebeok shows, have highly specialized tasks. Further, the semiotic contradiction thesis would entail the stipulation of ontically unrelated realities. However, this flies in the face of what I term the intersemiotic test by means of which we can check the meaning of 'The surgeon opens the wound' by an imagined variation of a projected state of affairs in different sign systems. This does not demonstrate that the chosen kinds of signification are entirely commensurate. What it does establish is that the cohesion of our readings of the world is brought about by the possibility of the *relative* corroboration between distinct sign systems. The basis on which this is possible is, I propose, the schematic, and hence accommodating, nature of all signifying acts.

To return now to our starting point: our dominant sign system, language, by virtue of its indexical function, cannot but partake in this dynamic of mutual significatory corroboration. As a consequence, our linguistic construals of reality gather meaning according to the rate of corroboration by non-linguistic signs. This activity should not be understood as a *filling out* of the linguistic schema but rather as a complementation by means of a different kind of schema. For all signification is schematic at different levels of formalization, *langue* being just one such schema at a high level of abstraction.

If our directional theory of meaning as linking process between verbal and non-verbal signification requires the notion of *directional schema*, how does the theory differ, for example, from Kant's "schematism?" The summary answer is that the difference is brought out by a rephrasing of Kant's argument in textual terms. Kant's "schematism" remains useful because it is the most general, even if unnecessarily complex, way in which any sort of perspectival schematization has been argued and so subsumes similar systems at lesser levels of abstraction, including the kind of formalization which produces the Saussurean *langue*, the schema of dematerialized *paroles* or linguistic instantiations.

In order to subsume objects under concepts, says Kant, the "representation" of the former must be "homogeneous" with the latter. But "pure concepts" cannot be discovered in empirical intuitions; they are "heterogeneous" entities. "How, then," Kant asks, "is the *subsumption* of intuitions under pure concepts, the *application* of a category to appearances, possible?" The answer in the *Critique* is that we require "a third thing," something which satisfies the requirement of "homogeneity" with both object and concept. The exact meaning of "homogeneity" is not completely clear, but will turn out to be unimportant in a textual rephrasing of the argument. What is important is that Kant refers to the third element in terms of *mediation*, a "mediating representation" which is both empty and yet sensible, a "transcendental schema." Time and space are the *a priori* conditions of schematization which in turn makes understanding possible. "The procedure of understanding in these schemata" Kant calls "the *schematism* of pure understanding." Although the schema is "always a product of the imagination" it must not be confused with the image. According to Kant

> ... the *image* is a product of the empirical faculty of reproductive imagination; the *schema* of sensible concepts, such as of figures in space, is a product and, as it were, a monogram, of pure *a priori* imagination, through which, and in accordance with which, images themselves first become possible. These images can be connected with the concept only by means of the schema to which they belong. In themselves they are never completely congruent with the concept.

Reality is thus a "continuous and uniform production" by means of schemata. At the most general level there are the schemata of cause, reciprocity, possibility, actuality, necessity, quality, relation, and modality. With the help of these relational structures the schemata "subordinate appearances to universal rules of synthesis, and thus fit them for thoroughgoing connection in one experience." In this way Kant's schematism produces "the unity of all the manifold of intuition in inner sense, and so indirectly the unity of apperception which as a function corresponds to the receptivity of inner sense." Without the mediation of schemata Kant's categories are purely logical, incapable of representing objects. Likewise, without schemata, empirical intuitions would remain meaningless. The schema then is a "phenomenon, or sensible concept, of an object in agreement with a category."[2]

What does it mean to textualize Kant's schematism? It means to flatten out his complex hierarchization to the effect that we can express what he accomplishes from the viewpoint of sign systems without losing valuable distinctions. Let us replace Kant's hierarchy of objects, images, representational schemata, and categories by significations of various kinds at different levels. At the primary level of understanding linguistic schemata compete with the schemata of non-verbal signification such as visual, tactile, olfactory, proxemic, kinetic, aural, and other schemata. At the same time we must allow for the "elasticity of discourse" or its "aptitude to flatten out, in a linear way, semiotic hierarchies."[3] In this way language not only covers the 'same' ground as non-verbal systems but also allows for its meta-function and an infinite number of pyramids of formalization. At the same time, Kant's unsatisfactory treatment of 'image' and its non-visual, non-verbal relations has been subsumed under the schematic. The relationship between linguistic directional schemata and non-verbal sign systems, then, is one of different schemata complementing one another. Accordingly, meaning can be defined as the linking process between the schemata of language and those of non-verbal sign systems.

Since we are not able to talk about non-signified objects, what remains of Kant's theory is a field of schematic significations which permits further significations at various levels of dematerialization or formalization. The question to which we must now return is not so much the possibility or necessity of schematizing, of which *langue* is a special case, but its limits and consequences. A general way of putting the necessity of thinking in terms of grammar is Michael Halliday's notion of "grammatics," our necessary relational textualization of phenomena. What is not so easily acceptable is his claim that since non-verbal sign systems have not received as yet adequate systemic descriptions, the best we can do is to apply linguistic grammatics to them.[4] This leaves unanswered Kant's question of how it is possible to apply linguistic schemata to them. It certainly assumes that the conceptual problems of linguistics are identical with those of non-verbal signification. When we do construct grammars for whatever kind of signification we need to consider at least the following questions:

> Wherein does the power of grammars lie?
> How far should the possibilities of grammars be developed?
> What makes a grammar a closed or an open structure?
> What is the relation between grammar and instantiation?
> Can grammars ever be anything but provisional?
> What are the reasons for the solidity of grammar?
> What is the relation between grammar and modality?
> What are the pedagogic implications of grammar?
> What is responsible for the seductiveness of grammar?
> What kinds of texts are grammars?

At the same time we need to think about the relationship between grammar and instantiation, *langue* and *parole*. We must ask how instantiations compare with their abstractable schemata:

> In what does the relative particularity of instantiations lie?
> In what way can they be said to be 'closer' to the social?
> What distinguishes their historicity from that of grammars?
> How can we explain its massive dependency on modalities?
> Do instantiations transcend grammar and if so in what way?
> Can we say that instantiations favor diffusion rather than concentration of power?

Not all of these concerns are being addressed here; I am quite happy to pose more problems than I can solve, to use a standard phrase. What I do want to take on is the limiting framework which an emphasis on *langue* establishes for the description of the discursive. There appear to be two serious limits set for *langue*. The first is that it is an abstraction, a timeless grid, derived from the teeming mass of discursive operations. Derivative and ahistorical, *langue* is a closed conceptual system which stands in a conflictive relation to the actual 'system' of discourse, the continuously fluctuating sum of language instantiations. With the assistance of *langue* we lend discourse, or language in social use, a stability which actually does not occur. This is not to deny that under certain conditions of legitimation a historical set of instantiations can become stabilized to a considerable degree, as for example, spelling and grammar in written language. In these cases the normative potential of *langue* has been realized by a particular politics of signifying. Yet even under such constraints language remains historically dynamic, and portions of it are always also in a "far-from-equilibrium state," randomly producing an array of possible "bifurcations," as

Prigogine and Stenger describe certain chemical relationships, which are ready to give rise to new discursive formations.[5] This evolving system of instantiations poses the most fundamental limit for *langue* because any description of language in action must address actual phenomena without producing merely a data bank or an empty grammar. As T. S. Eliot formulates the paradox, "The detail of the pattern is movement." ("Burnt Norton," v, 1.23)

There is a second less obvious yet equally radical limit to *langue: semiotic opacity*. By this I mean the intricate but murky relationship between discursive formations as directional schemata for meaning and the manifold of non-verbal sign systems which we activate when we produce meaning. In habitual language use this process of activation is always abbreviated and extremely fast, while it can be elaborated and thus slowed down in critical practice. As an abstraction, *langue* resists processes of semiotic concretization or embedding in two directions. There is resistance backward to the reconstruction of what semiotic relations could have been entailed in an expression and forward to the description of the kinds of materials, the *Lebensformen* and *institutions*, which we are being directed to *realize*.

These two fundamental limits of *langue*, the historical occurrence of instantiated language and semiotic opacity, provide a perspective from which we can characterize various schools of language theory. The first limit would seem to set apart theories of *langue*, deep structure, and generative grammar as well as linguistic structuralism, the "formalist-logistic tendency," as Michel Pêcheux calls it, from theories of enunciation and discourse, or the "linguistics of parole."[6] A similar split can be described by taking the second limit as our perspective. Here we can distinguish positivist language philosophy and formal semantics from a theory of meaning as use, a certain form of pragmatics, phenomenological description, ethno-linguistics, and semiotics. This division does not go with Pêcheux's schema; it cuts across it. Unhappily, Pêcheux argues his case by relying on a narrow definition of meaning as sense which, as I shall try to show later, undermines his theory of ideologically determined discursive formations and so places him in the very "formalist-logicist" tradition whose philosophical idealism he rejects.

In previous chapters I have tried to show that literal meanings, while certainly possible in culturally saturated discourse, are the result of a pragmatic and political curtailment of the process of meaning endowment rather than its logical core and natural consequence. As an alternative to meaning being regarded as strict sense, a generous, meandering and exploratory way of meaning constitution, or 'reading,' has been offered. This bias seems justified if we see language acting as a more or less open, directional schema for meanings in contrast to the assumption that words and expressions are ruled by definitions proper. Given this slant, formal-logical operations are deemed a special case of meaning rather than its rule. At the same time the logical positivist separation of a theory of meaning from the theory of reference cannot be maintained: meaning, as I have argued, turns out to be sequences of operations which progress from a directional starting point toward broadly semiotic realizations and are terminated not logically but only by pragmatic fiat.

As a result of the two-directional openness of expressions, forward toward a propositional content and backward to the motivations informing speech act and speech situation, a double vagueness emerges which plays a part in all meaning construction: *propositional opacity* and *modal opacity*. Chapter 2 explored ways of responding to the former, while chapter 3 addressed a special variety of the latter, the modal force exerted on reading by generic conventions, exemplified by those of the *Künstlerroman*. Chapters 4 and 5 offered critiques of idealized sense to shore up the case for a directional theory of meaning. The global objection to the vectorial description of meaning and its relative vagueness is the contention that such a theory denies the very possibility of communication and its realization in a community of speakers. Yet the question of the dynamic cohesion of culture does not have to be resolved at the linguistic level; rather, it can probably be more forcefully argued at the broader level of semiotic competence which includes language signs but is not fully defined by them. Against this background, the present chapter explores whether or not *langue*, language as system, is able to furnish the ingredients required for our habitual acts of filling the semi-determinate schemata of expressions. Given these premises, we ask again whether meaning is described more fruitfully as a linguistic or a broadly semiotic activity.

Before we can enter this debate, however, we must endorse once more the stipulation of a *textualist view* of reality. By this I do not mean that the world is a linguistic construct, but rather that we cannot conceive of reality in any form other than as a structured meaningful whole or a network of significations, in short: a semiotic. This may not be the only solution to the "ontological fallacy" according to which we cannot argue for the existence of reality without making assumptions about it. But the textualist perspective, certainly in its 'realist' version, does have the advantage of synthesizing a wide range of notions of reality. It allows for a reformulation of the Kantian dualism of appearances regulated by conceptual schemata and *Dinge an sich* beyond our reach and avoids the positivist assumption of commensurability between the real and a language with which to describe it.

In a textualist universe, language describes what is already signified by other means, i.e., non-verbal sign systems. In this sense we never bump into reality as such; we bump into signifying processes. Textualism also brings up to date a compatible phenomenology which sees reality as a system of "typifications" and provides a philosophical platform for poststructuralist thought. It could be argued that Wittgenstein resolved this issue a long time ago when he wrote that "The limits of my language mean the limits of my world."[7] In the *Tractatus* at least, and quite contrary to the Derridean universe, this text world is at the same time the world of logic, for "logic pervades the world: the limits of the world are also its limits."[8] Unlike Hegel's cosmos where logic underpins and transcends everything, Wittgenstein's world is bounded by language which in turn puts strictures on logic. It is a logic allowed for by the kind of language available. Had Wittgenstein written nothing after the *Tractatus*, there could have been considerable agreement on how to read 'language' in this passage. As it is, his later writings, especially the *Philosophical Investigations* introduce a number of complications. Two are of particular interest: a reading which leaves the claims of the *Tractatus* largely intact, but suggests that they apply only within the special realm of analyticity, while *The Philosophical Investigations* addresses the larger question of language pragmatics; and another reading which emphasizes Wittgenstein's idea that all language games are embedded in forms of life (*Lebensformen*), i.e., ways of eating, greeting, in short, ways of *doing*, or social semiotic. In this case, "language" is not tied to logic as tightly as the *Tractatus* appears to say it is and moreover involves operations other than linguistic ones.

A hard-headed linguistic interpretation of Wittgenstein's statements in section 5 of the *Tractatus* finds support in Louis Hjelmslev's *Language: An Introduction*, according to which "The content of language is nothing less than the world surrounding us, and the minimal particular meanings of a word, the particular meanings that are individuals are the *things* of the world . . . "[9]

A mischievous reading of this passage might construe Hjelmslev as a radical textualist whose world lacks all substance and is nothing but the sum of particular significations. However, the remainder of his work leaves no doubt that we are dealing with a writer firmly on realist ground who sees a tight connection between the simples of linguistic naming and those of empirical fact. Nor does the theory allow for the kind of semiotic corroboration that I am advocating here. Such a strict linguistic-atomistic view of the world faces two kinds of problems. One has to do with its "ostensive" regularity whereby language is an empirical ordering system leaving aside ludic or psychological features of the "content plane." Julia Kristeva makes this point when she says that this sort of "linguistics has no way of apprehending anything in language which belongs . . . with play, pleasure or desire." Such issues "infringe its epistemological purity" and are therefore relegated to "stylistics, rhetoric, poetics: aleatory forms of discourse which have no empirical status."[10]

The second kind of problem that Hjelmslev's "particular meanings" face is their independence from other signifying systems. The yet unclarified relation between language and other sign systems plays a central role in the debate between Jakobson and Russell, where Jakobson argues against Russell's 'knowledge by acquaintance.' According to Russell, "no one can understand the word 'cheese' unless he has a non-linguistic acquaintance with cheese," to which Jakobson retorts that "the meaning of the word 'cheese' cannot be inferred from a non-linguistic acquaintance with cheddar," in other words, "without the assistance of the verbal code."[11] Significantly, Russell and Jakobson agree on the necessity of the cultural embedding of language. Their disagreement is over the way such a relationship can be theorized. Russell's 'ostensive' theory stands against Jakobson's more complex semiotic solution which says that verbal signs stand in a transmutational relation to nonverbal systems. Thus all understanding requires "intersemiotic" transformations.[12] It is in this sense that Jakobson quotes Peirce via Dewey: "the meaning of any linguistic sign is its translation into some further, alternative sign, especially a sign 'in which it is more fully developed.' "[13]

Neither Russell nor Jakobson were satisfied with the view that 'understanding' language meant grasping minimal sense. And for good reason, for the suggestion that 'sense' constitutes the necessary and sufficient conditions of meaning reflects nothing more than a preference for Occam's logical tradition of reasoning over catholic pragmatics. While we can agree that minimal sense is necessary since it establishes a directional schema, we should not claim sufficiency *without* at the same time also giving description of the circumstances under which a particular meaning process is judged to be sufficient.

Russell's solution was discarded because it introduced an entity as woolly as 'experience,' something the structured perspectives of linguistics and language philosophy found difficult to handle. It also invoked the possibility of a 'private' acquaintance successfully demolished by Wittgenstein in the 'private language' argument. However, with the assistance of Peirce and Jakobson, it is now possible to retrieve Russell's notion of "acquaintance" by reformulating it in semiotic terms and thus granting it a regularity it formerly lacked. In this sense, having 'eaten cheese' adds to our linguistic grasp a network of other sign systems (visual, tactile, olfactory, gestural) which impinge on the *use* of the term, i.e., on its meaning in Wittgenstein's vocabulary. Put more strongly, the greater our semiotic acquaintance, i.e., the greater the quantity of the sign systems we are able to bring to bear on a verbal sign, the more *meaningful* the term..

In this view the construction of meaning is again a matter of degree and dependent on cultural saturation as opposed to minimal sense. Once more, the question as to when meaning endowment is sufficient cannot be answered *logically* but requires a pragmatic, political frame. Nor is a purely linguistic activation of the language schema a sufficient condition for meaning making in a broad range of circumstances. If we wish to theorize the way we tend to fill linguistic schemata we can draw on a number of quite different theories. I shall refer in chronological order to three phenomenologists, a philosopher of language in the analytical tradition, and a semiotician. In the *Cartesian Meditations* Husserl introduces the notion of "appresentation," or "a kind of making co-present," or "analogical apperception," or "analogizing transfer" to characterize our habitual ways of adding absent but typical features to that which we imagine, see, remember, or project: "An appresentation occurs even in external experience, since the strictly seen front of a physical thing always and necessarily appresents a rear aspect and prescribes for it a more or less determinate content."[14]

Such additional presentations assist us in realizing a coherent world, instead of the relatively few adumbrational aspects of things of which we can be aware at any given moment. Depending on our attitude or tension of consciousness these appresentations produce a still highly schematic or a detailed reality.

Roman Ingarden adapted Husserl's notion of appresentation to his description of ontically heteronomous constructs in *The Literary Work of Art* and *The Cognition of the Literary Work of Art*. He saw literary language to be highly schematic and therefore in need of filling out, a process he termed "concretization." Accordingly, reading a literary work is the actualization of the linguistic surface by further, though not necessarily fully, determining its "lacunae of indeterminacy." It is sometimes forgotten that Ingarden's writings on literature were meant to contribute to phenomenological ontology and that he chose to describe the typical acts without which we cannot achieve literary reading. In this way he wished to distinguish construals of an ontically simple kind, such as the idealities of definitions or the materialities of physical objects, from compound construals which rely on a mixture of different acts. As a result of his studies, the literary work of art turns out to be ontically heteronomous, i.e., it requires for its existence the performance of acts which constitute distinct ontic regions, not only linguistic ones.[15] What I am arguing beyond Ingarden is that only analytical operations can be performed within the boundaries of a formalized grammar, while social discourse requires, in addition, acts outside linguistics.

Alfred Schutz, who extended Husserl's later ideas concerning the structures of the life-world (*Lebenswelt*), argued for a pre-predicative or proto-predicative typification of reality. If we substitute "semiotic structures" for his term "typification" we shall see that his account is compatible with the kind of observation made more recently, for example, by Umberto Eco. Schutz formulates the claim thus:

> Type-construction, as well as type structure, is in principle conceivable without language. . . . The founding relations are such that the structure of language presupposes typification but not vice versa. . . . Language is a system of typifying schemata of experience, which rests on idealizations and anonymizations of immediate subjective experience. . . . These typifications of experience detached from subjectivity are socially objectivated, whereby they become a component of the social a priori previously given to the subject.

Schutz is not saying that non-verbal signs do not link up with language in some way. Nor is he saying that typification, type constitution at a more general level, produces non-linguistic semiosis. On the contrary, he insists that "typification is most closely entwined" also "with language." What he does want to emphasize is the quite unpopular notion of the primacy of typification over linguistic acts.

> By far the largest province of life worldy typifications is linguistically objectivated. Whatever is typically relevant for the individual was for the most part already typically relevant for his predecessors and has consequently deposited its semantic equivalents in the language. . . . Language can be construed as the sedimentation of typical experiential schemata which are typically relevant in a society. . . . The originary formation of language is thus unthinkable without the subjective capability for type-constitution.[16]

Typifications then are basic structures with which we understand the world and of which linguistic formation is only one, even if the most powerful, kind. We can also say that whenever we use linguistic structures our other typifying schemata (proximic, kinetic, tactile, olfactory, gestural, visual, etc.) do not vanish but continue to supply the background configurations of reality from which the stencils of language are cut out, thus activating selected semantic fields.

It is a great pity that Wittgenstein said as little as he did about *Lebensformen*, because had he done so we would probably be in a much better position than we are now to project a kind of "unified field theory" for signifying systems, a general semiotic. This is not to claim that there is commensurability between sign systems at the level of their various abstractable grammars. Scholars as diverse as Hjelmslev and Jakobson deny the possibility of a congruence; Hjelmslev goes so far even as to deny it exists between natural languages.[17] What I am arguing is that if we could find a way of extending Wittgenstein's rudimentary remarks on *Lebensformen* to form a theory, we would then be in a position to show how the language of a speech community is informed by and interacts with the community's other and especially non-verbal sign systems. For there is little doubt that they do interact. The difficult question is: how do they do so and how can one describe what we suspect to be the case? Wittgenstein took a number of steps in the direction of offering a solution.

Even if Wittgenstein is adamant that we must not look for things as if they corresponded to substantives,[18] he insists that there is a link between the verbal and the non-verbal, via forms of life: "the *speaking* of language is part of an activity, or of a form of life [*Lebensform*]."[19] There are a number of other remarks on the matter scattered throughout his later works. A succinct summary description is offered by Theodor R. Schatzki: "The term "form of life" refers to the totality of practices, activities, and ways of being in which a person, or a group of people, is able to participate in virtue of becoming a member of a particular social organization."[20]

Conversely one could say that a social organization exists by virtue of a specific dynamic of "forms of life." And, we must add, it is the specificity of organized or *formed* life which gives rise to (and not merely goes along with) concept formation and language. It is in this spirit that Wittgenstein speaks of an education radically different from ours which "might also be the foundation for quite different concepts": For here *life* would run on differently... this is the only way in which *essentially* different concepts are imaginable."[21]

Again we are reminded of the tight link between a non-linguistic semiotic and sign systems capable of a high degree of formalization, such as natural languages. This is sometimes forgotten when Wittgenstein's characterization of meaning as "use" is quoted.[22] Use is not simply an independent linguistic practice, it is a practice tied to *Lebensformen*. Yet Wittgenstein goes even further. In a little known passage he also speaks of a priority relation between language and other forms of doing, in which language comes *after* "the deed." "Language—I want to say—is a refinement, *im Anfang war die Tat*."[23]

What are we to make of this?[24] We can assume with some certainty that Wittgenstein did not quote Goethe to parody the "In the beginning was the Word" from certain versions of *Genesis*. Nor does he wish to keep the two practices separate. And yet the kind of interaction between the two that Wittgenstein had in mind is not entirely clear. From the bias of this study, I would favor a reading which sees language as a sophisticated sign system on top of other forms of signification. Though language requires those other structures to give it substance, it in turn transcends them in various ways: in the sense that it can address the 'same' phenomena as other sign systems and, in addition, can theorize its own operations. Wittgenstein's "refinement" then appears to point to the ability of language to straddle *all* other signs by way of description, summary, taxonomy, as well as comment on itself by way of its metafunction. "Refinement" also directs us to the multitude of levels of abstraction from a level close to phenomenal indication to near empty conceptuality. This sort of refinement is absent from non-verbal sign systems. Yet this kind of observation should not lead us to separate the two forms, verbal and non-verbal sign systems, as radically from one another as semantics in its positivist, structuralist, and generative versions have done. All three—positivist semantics, structuralist linguistics, and generative deep structure grammar—can be argued to be guilty of an idealism that Wittgenstein seems to urge us to avoid: the excision of isolated linguistic meanings from general semiosis, the abstraction of a *static langue* from the dynamic system of instantiations, and an inferrable and general deep structure which rules a number of specific linguistic surfaces. Not that such abstractions are not permitted or workable. It is their ideological dominance which is at issue.

One of the considerable merits of Michel Foucault's contribution to this debate is its sustained effort to discover a level of analysis of discourse which avoids the abstracting closure of *langue* and so is able to stay within reach of instantiations without collapsing the investigation into a mere description of *paroles*. Instead of establishing a grammar underlying a chosen statement Foucault asks the question of how it is "that one particular statement appeared rather than another." This inevitably leads him to the stipulation of discursive fields which can be analyzed only by attending to the "exact specificity" of the occurrence of statements. In order to understand the statement in this way we must "determine its conditions of existence; fix at least its limits; establish its correlations with other statements that may be connected with it, and show what other forms of statements it excludes."[25]

The main difference between a tradition which works by establishing an inferential order of identities and differences and Foucault's approach is that his kind of description produces what he terms "systems of dispersion." Once we have discovered a certain regularity among statements which amount to such a system Foucault suggests that we are then dealing with a "discursive formation." Not that this non-grammatical arrangement of statements is altogether without rules. Foucault insists that the rules which we can stipulate to be responsible for the appearance of a certain coherence among statements are quite different from those of a *langue*. The "rules of formation" of discursive regularities are the derived "conditions of existence" of related statements. In order to describe these we need to do three things: 1) "map the first surfaces of their emergence," that is, grasp the historical moment when a group of statements first began to constitute a discursive formation, such as "dementia, neurosis or psychosis;" 2) analyze the "authorities of delimitation," that is, the specific historical institutions which give rise to discursive formations; and 3) distinguish between "grids of specification," that is, chart the way in which discursive formations are "divided, contrasted, related, regrouped, classified, derived from one another" to constitute a field of knowledge.[26]

Instead of projecting increasingly sophisticated semantic grammars and looking at discourses as "signifying elements referring to contents and representations," Foucault urges us to regard them as "practices that systematically form the objects of which they speak." If we can characterize a discourse of a number of related statements by the "regularity of a practice," then we have achieved the definition of a discursive formation in its specific historicity. In other words, Foucault is not interested in *langue* but in *language*.[27]

Equally useful to the concerns of this book are Umberto Eco's Peirceian notion of "abduction" and its two subcategories of "overcoding" and "undercoding." Abduction, in Eco's words, "represents the first step of a metalinguistic operation destined to enrich a code."[28] When we overcode a text we "assign additional meanings" or we break the linguistic units down "into more analytical entities."[29] In undercoding linguistic expressions we make interpretive assumptions as to the thematic centrality of certain sections of a text and so proceed from "nonexistent codes to potential codes."[30]

In his more recent *Semiotics and the Philosophy of Language* Eco refines these distinctions, adding "creative abduction" to the list and distinguishes the main category, abduction, from the traditional notions of deduction and induction. While deduction proceeds from an established rule to a given case in order to gain an unknown result and induction is the derivation of a rule from a result and an inferred case, in abduction there is a feedback loop which informs our progress from a tentative rule to a tentative case which produces a result.[31] Creative abduction is a form of abduction in which the interaction between the three stages is highly exploratory rather than analytically restrictive.

Taking us back to Augustin's theory of signs, Eco offers a devastating critique of Saussurian language theory linguistics in which "the linguistic model was crystallized into its 'flattest' form, the one encouraged by dictionaries and unfortunately, by a lot of linguistics."[32] Eco sees this juncture of Saussure's structuralism and logic—one could place Frege next to Saussure here—as the beginning of the dominance of "meaning as synonymy and essential definition."[33] However, this is merely a particular and baneful historical development and in no way a tradition which we need to continue. I fully concur with Eco's view that as a result of this restrictive definition of meaning the world, "the continuum, the pulp itself of the matter which is manipulated by semiosis, escapes semantics."[34]

Eco's critique is also directed at the radical distinction between a theory of meaning, a theory of evidence, and a theory of pictorial depiction as it is formulated, for example, in G. Harman's *Semiotics and the Cinema*. There is no reason, according to Harman, "to think that these theories must contain common principles."[35] This of course paves the way for a legitimation of different disciplines and knowledges which do not interact in any pertinent way. This, Eco rightly argues, is quite misleading on the grounds that each of these theories requires interpretive, inferential processes for their existence, for "the understanding of signs is not a mere matter of recognition (of a stable equivalence); it is a matter of interpretation."[36] Yet it is also aberrant because it flies in the face of the semiotic fact that we do not experience the world in neatly compartmentalized ways but as an interaction of signs, verbal as well as non-verbal. This interaction produces the continuum of our social world.

There are, of course, some good reasons why so many philosophers of meaning opt for starkly linguistic explanations. The most obvious one is that language is the most flexible and therefore also the most powerful system, applicable as it is to any of the more specialized sign structures; language covers the "same" ground, as it were, as visual, tactile, and other typifications. At the same time it can do so at a relatively specific and highly abstract and summary level. Because of this range, it can be self-referential in a way no other sign-system can be. This is known as the meta-level of language. Here we could distinguish two senses of meta-language, a linguistic and a semiotic one, whereby the linguistic meta-level of language signifies its ability to describe itself as language while its semiotic meta-level furnishes descriptions of any other sign system. However, the fact that language appears to cover the 'same' ground as other semiotic systems as well as being able to account for what happens in them by way of its semiotic meta-structure must not lead us to believe that what is being covered is identical. Instead of identities we are dealing with instances of corroboration by different sign systems.

This leads to the concluding claim of this chapter, the "semiotic corroboration thesis" according to which *reality is the corroboration of different signifying systems*. Let me illustrate. Our proxemic, kinetic, tactile, and visual readings are all confounded when we lift what we thought was a rock but what turns out to be a well-designed foam rubber movie prop. We can injure our bodies in this way just as much as we can when we jump from a height of two inches with the belief that the drop is about two feet. Pain tells us that our reading was erroneous (we didn't get the irony of reality) but it does not correct our judgment. Correction is a function of re-reading by way of more than one sign system: the more sign systems, the more real our reality. As long as we are trapped in any one sign system, there is no way of distinguishing between fictions (however fascinating) and actuality. Conversely, the greater the number of different sign systems corroborating a referent the more difficult it is to maintain a fiction. The mathematical predictions of subatomic structures cease to be a fiction when the altogether different semiotic of an experimental apparatus corroborates the hypothesis. From this perspective, not only representational language but also the language of theory is tied to semiosis at large. There exist claims that even the most abstract systems such as formal logic and mathematics are ultimately rooted in our non-linguistic intuitions.[37]

Another way of positing the corroboration thesis is to say that *reference* is the linking procedure between different sign systems, and since meaning is described here as a linking *process* rather than a definitionally ruled analytical entity, reference must be taken into consideration. This, however, requires a *textual* view of reference; instead of regarding reference as a link between words and objects in the world we need to see it as a relation between different sign systems, as argued in chapter 1.

A brief word also on the notion of corroboration. It is used here in a broader sense than the one we find in Karl Popper, in that it focuses on our pretheoretical grasp of the world. But even though Popper's usage of the term is restricted to scientific theory, some of his conceptual demarcations apply equally to the thesis stipulated here. Toward the end of chapter 6 of *The Logic of Scientific Discovery* Popper specifies that instances of corroboration are hypothetical and so "cannot be asserted to be 'true' statements;" they are always merely " 'provisional conjectures.' " More broadly, "corroboration can only be expressed as an appraisal." According to Popper, what has been appraised to be corroborated is also open to falsification: "The appraisal which asserts corroboration (the corroborative appraisal) establishes certain fundamental relations, *viz.* compatibility and incompatibility. We regard incompatibility as falsification of the theory."[38]

The same is true in general semiosis, which could be seen as a steady process of elimination of falsified corroborations in favor of other, not yet falsified, forms of intersemiotic acts. Let me elaborate on the notion of *semiotic corroboration* with the help of selected observations made by Charles Sanders Peirce.[39]

According to Peirce's semiotic, all thinking "must necessarily be in signs" (5.251). Indeed, "all this universe is perfused with signs, if it is not composed exclusively of signs."[40] Without signs we would "have no power of thinking" (5.265). And "whenever we think, we have present to the consciousness some feeling, image, conception, or other representation, which serves as a sign" (5.283). By far the greater part of our significatory activities is dependent on habit, an important concept in Peirce's theory. And because signs tend to be ruled by habit they "are, for the most part, *conventional or arbitrary*" (3.360).[41] These signs are not all linguistic, even though we are in the habit of conceptualizing them as such, but include non-linguistic significations which interact with one another and our habitual abstractions. Even theorizing is thus in the end tied to general semiosis. As J. Jay Zeman notes, "Peirce held that philosophy, and indeed logic itself, must ultimately return to experience for validation" (2.227).[42] Let me quote Peirce at some length on this point.

The meanings of words ordinarily depend on our tendencies to weld together qualities and our aptitudes to see resemblances, or, to use the received phrase, upon associations of similarity; while experience is bound together, and only recognizable, by forces acting upon us, or, to use an even worse chosen technical term, by means of associations by contiguity. . . . It is not the language alone, with its mere associations of similarity, but the language taken in connection with the auditor's own experiential associations of contiguity, which determines for him what house is meant. It is requisite then, in order to show what we are talking or writing about, to put the hearer's or reader's mind into real, active connection with the concatenation of experience or of fiction with which we are dealing, and, further, to draw his attention to, and identify, a certain number of particular points in such concatenation. . . .

The subjects are indications of the things spoken of, the predicates, words that assert, question, or command whatever is intended. Only the shallowness of syntax is manifest in its failing to recognise the *impotence of mere words* [my stress], and especially common nouns, to fulfill the function of a grammatical subject. Words like this, that, lo, hallo, hi there . . . compel the hearer to look about him; and so they, more than ordinary words, contribute towards indicating what the speech is about (3.419).

As Peirce develops the argument, such interaction between non-linguistic signs and language occurs not only in situations of actual ostension, of pointing to 'objects,' but also in the imagination. "Some of these signs (or at least one of them)," writes Peirce,

are supposed to excite in the mind of the receiver familiar images, pictures, or we might almost say, dreams—that is, reminiscences of sights, sounds, feelings, tastes, smells, or other sensations, now quite detached from the original circumstances of their first occurrence, so that they are free to be attached to new occasions. The deliverer is able to call up these images at will (with more or less effort) in his own mind; and he supposes the receiver can do the same. . . . Not only is the outward significant word or mark a sign, but the image which it is expected to excite in the mind of the receiver will likewise be a sign—a sign by resemblance, or, as we say, an icon—of the similar image in the mind of the deliverer, and through that also a sign of the real quality of the thing. This icon is called the predicate of the assertion. . . . there may be a complex of such icons, forming a composite image of which the whole is not familiar (3.343).

Perhaps I should emphasize at this point that when Peirce talks of "mind" he is not presenting a subjectivist semiotic. The individual mind is incidental to his explanation, even if signification normally happens to involve specific minds. To make the logical independence of signification clear, Peirce introduces the notion of "quasi-mind." In his own words, "every sign—or, at any rate, nearly every one—is a determination of something of the general nature of a mind, which we may call the 'quasi-mind' " (Ms 283, 111). As to the question of whether or not Peirce's semiotic is nevertheless mentalistic since it repeatedly uses terms such as "mind" and "mental," he underscores that "what further is needed to clear the sign of its mental association is furnished by generalizations too facile to arrest attention here, since nothing but feeling is exclusively mental" (5.492).

So when Peirce writes that "a form of words which fails to produce a definite picture in the mind is meaningless," he means first of all that no signification has taken place and second, that we can therefore not make any sense of the expression (3.514; cf. also 2.316). When signification is meaningful, we can distinguish three grades of "clearness" of meaning. The first we could call intersemiotic; it "consists in the connexion of the word with familiar experience," such as visual, tactile, or aural signification. The second grade of clearness "consists in the abstract definition, depending upon an analysis of just what it is that makes the word applicable." Finally, there is a grade of clearness that we could term the clearness of argument. It "consists in such a representation of the idea that fruitful reasoning can be made to turn upon it, and that it can be applied to the resolution of difficult practical problems" (3.457).

Nevertheless, whatever degree of clarity one attaches to Peirce's three forms of signification, there is no such thing as an absolutely precise sign. This may come as a surprise, given the fact that Peirce was above all a logician. Yet he can be cited as being in support of the various kinds of opacity discussed earlier; he insists that "no cognition and no Sign is absolutely precise, not even a percept." The indefiniteness that Peirce notes is "of two kinds, indefiniteness as to what is the Object of the Sign, and indefiniteness as to its Interpretant, or indefiniteness in Breadth and in Depth" (4.543).

This double underdetermination or perhaps even indeterminacy of signification is of fundamental importance for Peirce's complex epistemic scheme, for it offers a probabilistic and approximating rather than strict definition of meaning. It is in the form of various kinds of more or less indefinite interpretants that we grasp the world. But how are we to understand Peirce's interpretant? From dozens of descriptions let me choose the following: "A Sign, or *Representamen*, is a First which stands in such a genuine triadic relation to the Second, called its *Object*, as to be capable of determining a Third, called its *Interpretant*, to assume the same triadic relation to its Object in which it stands itself to the same Object" (2.274).

Like any other concept in Peirce's writing the interpretant has to be seen as part of the triadic nature of our grasp of reality, a large epistemic framework characterized by firstness, secondness, and thirdness. Firstness refers to our intuitive grasp of the world, secondness to propositional understanding, and thirdness to the combination of propositions into arguments. This tripartition of cognition is all-pervasive in Peirce's work. It surfaces in the distinction between signs as icons, indices, and symbols, or "likeness . . . correspondence in fact [and] imputed character" (1.558), or resembling, ostensive, and abstract kinds of signification. The triad reappears in the subdivision of symbols into terms, propositions, and arguments such that symbols as terms "determine only

their grounds or imputed qualities," symbols as propositions "also independently determine their objects" and symbols as arguments "also independently
determine their interpretants" (1.559).

Peirce distinguishes the "immediate Interpretant" which allows us to cognize
the world from the "Dynamical Interpretant" which enables us to be "conscious
of our Percepts." Moreover, as Peirce observes, "subsequent Interpretants furnish new Semes of Universes resulting from various adjunctions to the Perceptual
Universe. They are, however, all of them, Interpretants of Percepts" (4.539).
From this cognitive baseline we build our reality by means of other kinds of
interpretants such as "emotional," "energetic," and "logical" (5.475f.).

Writing in a post-Kantian mode with a strong Kantian flavor (for Peirce, Kant
is after all "the King of modern thought") (1.369), Peirce insists that "The *Ding
an sich* . . . can neither be indicated nor found" (5.525). What can be indicated
and found is a reality which is "dynamic" and not "qualitative." It is characterized
by what Peirce terms "forcefulness." But how do we know whether we are
dealing with a fictional real or the actual real? In this context Peirce makes the
crucial observation that "no language (as far as I know) has any particular form
of speech to show that the real world is spoken of" (2.337). This function is to
be fulfilled by other, non-linguistic sign systems: " . . . *tones* and *looks* are sufficient to show when a speaker is in earnest. These *tones* and *looks* act dynamically upon the listener, and cause him to attend to realities. *They are, therefore,
the indices of the real world*" (2.337; my stress).

Tones, in Peirce's theory, "are signs of visceral qualities of feeling." Other
kinds of signs, such as odors, likewise play an important role in cognition; they
"bring back old memories" and are capable of occupying "the entire field of
consciousness, so that one almost lives for the moment in a world of odor."
Peirce singles out "contiguous association" as one distinct way "in which odors
are particularly apt to act as signs." And in near-Proustian fashion he observes
that "they also have a remarkable power of calling to mind mental and spiritual
qualities." This, Peirce says, "must be the effect of resemblance-association . . . "
(1.313).

Yet such significatory associations are by no means marginal to the processes
of cognition, for in his view "every state of consciousness [is] an inference; so
that life is but a sequence of inferences or a train of thought" (7.583). The
significant difference in the cognition of reality is not one between a noumenal
real and phenomena as inferences, but one between different kinds of inferences—"uncontrolled inference from contiguity, or experiential connection,"
which Peirce regards as "the most rudimentary of all reasoning" attributed to
lower animals (7.445), and "inference from resemblance," which "perhaps implies a higher degree of self-consciousness than any of the brute processes"
(7.446).

Whether higher or lower forms of inferential processes are involved, the
constitution of reality is not an individual or idiosyncratic affair. This point is
not argued from a physicalist point of view but rather from the perspective of

a semiotic community. The real, he says, is "independent of the vagaries of me and you," adding that "the very origin of the conception of reality shows that this conception essentially involves the notion of a COMMUNITY, without definite limits, and capable of a definite increase in knowledge" (5.311).

As a result of such an increase, reality is in a permanent state of development. Peirce speaks of "an endless series of representations," since "the meaning of a representation can be nothing but a representation." Meaning in this view is "nothing but the representation itself conceived as stripped of irrelevant clothing. But this clothing never can be completely stripped off; it is only changed for something more diaphanous. So there is an *infinite regression* here" (1.339; my stress).

To return now to the starting point of this excursus into Peirce's semiotic, at the rudimentary level of finding our way around in the world we construe meanings with the help of a variety of sign systems. Together they constitute our reality which is independent of individual idiosynscracies, yet never fully determined, always in a certain state of flux, and fundamentally community based. It is only as a member of a semiotic community that I am capable of reading the corroboration of two or more sign systems as the real, nor can I construe the real in the entirety in which I am aware of it in any other way.

This does not preempt the production of highly abstract kinds of semiosis, such as the formal systems of logic or mathematics. Nor does it question the possibility of the theorization of natural language in terms of *langue*. What the semiotic corroboration thesis does assert is that if natural languages are theorized as systems of the Saussurean kind, which Eco criticizes for their dependence on synonymy and essential definition, it is difficult to argue for the linking processes between the linguistic and the non-linguistic. By idealistically shrinking semiosis to a relation between signifiers and signifieds which make up signs, as does Saussure, and so reducing signification to vehicle and concept (or image), all kinds of doing becomes subordinated to language, itself a subspecies of general semiosis, with lamentable epistemic and political consequences.

This is the kind of problematic with which I shall confront Jean-François Lyotard's otherwise attractive notion of the "differend" in the following chapter.

VII

PHRASES IN DISPUTE
TOWARD A SEMIOTIC DIFFEREND

> The differend is the unstable state and in-
> stance of language wherein something which
> must be able to be put into phrases cannot
> yet be.
>
> Jean-François Lyotard, *The Differend*

In spite of its negotiatory tone and structural modesty, Jean-François Lyotard's *The Differend: Phrases in Dispute* is anything but casual theorizing. For from beneath the presentation of the role of language in social conflict there emerges a broad philosophical argument concerning the "real," as well as a narrower theory of discourse, in which the differend plays its role. Lyotard draws on thinkers ranging from Plato and Aristotle to Kant and Wittgenstein to raise nothing less than the time honored question of how we project reality by means of language. Throughout his study he turns again and again to his central example, Auschwitz, "the most real of realities," and yet one that questions the very possibility of historical knowledge.[1] From this limit Lyotard gradually unfolds a theory of reference as part of a realist textualist view of the world, a construal rooted in the conflictual structure of "phrases." It is to these phrases and to Lyotard's textualist universe that we must turn if we wish to understand the "differend."

I have termed Lyotard's position a 'realist textualism' because he allows for an "extralinguistic permanence" to which deictic reference points but for which we cannot argue without committing the ontological fallacy: "for nothing can be said about reality that does not presuppose it." Brute reality, then, can only be an inference from a textual reality made up of "chronological, topographic, toponymic, and anthropological systems."[2] This significatory reality is all the more reliably established the more it is cross-referenced by "independent testimonies."[3] In this system of textual evidence the empiricist's eyewitness loses his central role in favor of "future corroboration;" reality is never given "once and for all," it has literally become "a matter of the future."[4]

In this textualism the place of analysis is the level of "phrases," a term whose concept subsumes the broad vocabulary of traditional language philosophy and the theory of meaning. Words, expressions, and sentences, as well as their combinations, become part of the economy of the phrase and its networks, its "genres of discourse." Because every phrase "entails a *there is*" it constitutes a "phrase universe"[5] which consists at least of an addresser, an addressee, a sense, and a referent.[6] Phrases have a referential and a deictic side. Reference is established by sense (signification), name (nomination), demonstration (ostension), and an independent meta-phrase which compares these three (validation).[7]

In the course of Lyotard's argument the theory emerges as to how significations, names and ostensions relate to one another. "Cognitive phrases are backed-up by ostensive phrases"[8] and linked with Kripke's "rigid designator" or name[9], although, in agreement with Tarski, "reference cannot be reduced to sense."[10] We should note, though, that Kripke's realist metaphysic cannot be simply yoked to Lyotard's textualist position. According to Lyotard a named referent acquires reality if it is also the potential carrier of an "unknown sense," i.e., a phrase which cannot as yet be formulated. This is why Lyotard characterizes nomination by the "inflation of sense": we cannot prove "that everything has been said about a name;" that is, barring contradiction, there is no limit to the descriptions or "throng of senses" we may wish to attach to a named entity.[11] Ostension also has its unstated shadow: for every assertion, 'there is x,' there is an entailed negation, 'and it is not y.' Lyotard's referent can be strong or weak: strong, if it is backed up by a "network of names" and their "relations;" weak, if it is supported only by a "sense" in heterogeneous "phrase universes."[12] What Lyotard seems to be saying then is that nominative networks produce strong reference and predicative phrases result in weak reference. This cannot be demonstrated without also drawing at the same time on non-linguistic signs, as I shall argue below.

Of equal importance in Lyotard's theory are deictics, an addresser's designation of a "given."[13] As did Bühler (1936) and Bertrand Russell half a century ago, Lyotard distinguishes the "I-here-now," (Russell's ego-centric particulars), as "current" deictics from its generalized form, in which "names transform *now* into a date, *here* into a place." In its most anonymous form, this "quasi-deictics" of names constitutes a "world" made up of names independent of individual instantiations of ostension.[14] And since names and their networks produce stronger referents than sense relations, generalized deictics plays a crucial part in the establishment of Lyotard's reality. Again, such a linguistically constituted reality would be extremely flimsy.

In Lyotard phrases combine to form "phrase regimens," each of which in turn projects "a universe." The phrase universes are always social since they always contain at least one addresser and one addressee, in addition to a name, a sense, and a reference: "the social is always presupposed...within the slightest phrase."[15] At a higher level of organization phrases enter into "genres of discourse" which rule the manner in which phrases can be linked with one another. Phrase regimens which group linguistic expressions into descriptive, ostensive, prescriptive, constative, or performative passages are marshalled by genres to function in the rhetoric of persuasion, argumentation, refutation, pleading, and so forth. In this way the multiplicity of heterogeneous phrase regimens can affect a phrase's modalities, in short, "what is at stake." Not that genres of discourse themselves are in harmony with one another. Quite the contrary. Such genres as logical, religious, or economic discourse are fundamentally hostile toward one another, a condition which is responsible for social agonistics at large. This, Lyotard argues, does away with the kind of "anthropocentrism" which still informs Wittgenstein's language games.[16]

There are always strong and weak instances within one and the same genre. Initially and for a long time, the Christian narrative, for example, was able to out-perform other religions because it was able to rephrase everything from the new and powerful perspective of love, a device which survives in such narratives as "republican brotherhood" or "communist solidarity."[17] However, all traditional genres pale before economics, which reconstitutes traditional discourse in terms of exchange. The economic phrase negates time—the heart of narrative—dismissing as it does "the occurrence, the event, the marvel, the anticipation of a community of feelings."[18]

There is one set of phrases, however, which does not amount to a genre of discourse: politics. In its parasitic realization of the agonistics which exists between different genres, politics is nothing less than the linkage of the "multiplicity of genres" itself.[19] This allows Lyotard once more to argue for a deanthropomorphized state of affairs. The stakes which are tied to heterogeneous genres of discourse rather than people are responsible for social agonistics in the first instance.[20] Thus the differend, "the case where the plaintiff is divested of the means to argue," is the inevitable consequence of language.[21] Hence the necessity of a critical theory of phrases; but there is also the need for a critique of Lyotard's textualism.

Neither Lyotard's differend nor his system of phrases is in dispute here. What is being questioned is his entirely linguistic presentation of reality. It is only after seventy pages that Lyotard feels the need to make an explicit semiotic concession, a yielding which is as grudging as it is short lived. "A wink, a shrugging of the shoulder... can be phrases."[22] Yet in this same sentence the semiotics of gestural, proximic, kinetic, tactile, olfactory, visual, and aural sign systems are collapsed at one stroke onto the plane of language. As I argued earlier, there is no doubt that language is by far the most powerful signification system in that it can both address itself to the "same" items addressed by other forms of signification and subsume their presentations as well as its own by way of its meta-function. This "imbalance" in no way undermines the claim made in the previous chapter, namely that reality is the corroboration of different sign systems. Let us see what this means for Lyotard's theory.

Lyotard's "here it is" and the "shown referent" are phrases substituted for and summing up proximic-kinetic, pictorial, and gestural acts of signification. In order to jump from phrases to an "extralinguistic permanence" (or vice versa) Lyotard not only eliminates the phenomenological pre-predicative cogito, but also any possible non-predicative semiotic.[23] This requires a certain bending of the concepts of one of his main sources, Saul Kripke. Kripke's string of events, which includes both phrases and such non-language items as "birth and meetings," is simply levelled onto the plane of linguistics.[24] Yet ostension is a broadly semiotic structure rather than a merely linguistic one: it can operate completely without words in painting, mime, or gesture (cf. G. *Bedeutung*—meaning, reference: *bedeuten*, to point at/to), even if ordinarily it is generated by a number of sign systems.

In physics, the textualization of reality is always expected to be corroborated by the structures of an additional sign system. To have been able to support certain theories of elementary particles by the semiotics of the hydrogen bubble chamber earned Luis W. Alvarez the Nobel Prize in 1968. This is not to argue once more for a dualist empiricism, but rather for a broader and, more importantly, heterogeneous basis of signs on which to build a textualist view of reality.

Lyotard's linguistic preoccupation also enforces his distinction between "objects of perception" and "objects of history." Accordingly, "the object of perception arises from a field (which is a loose complex of ostensives with deictics); the object of history arises from a world (which is a fairly stable complex of nominatives)."[25] Yet why should visual signification of necessity produce loose ostensive-deictic structures if compared with their linguistic nominations? One would be equally justified in arguing precisely the opposite case, juxtaposing high resolution digital images to hazy sets of nominatives. As the 'super realism' of new generations of digital image machinery begins to produce visual and aural "accuracy" beyond the human capacity of discrimination we will have to question this bias toward the phrase.

Another consequence of going along with Lyotard's emphasis on the "phrase" at the expense of other signifying systems is our inability to distinguish between the fictional real and the actual real. But, one might object, it is at the very point of a textualist view of reality that those distinctions can no longer be drawn. And yet, even within a fully textualist view of reality fictions stick out: they are final, in the sense of presenting completed directional schemata for meaning, while presentations of the actual are forever open to corrections from any signifying order. Only to the latter does Lyotard's succinct remark apply in any strict sense: "reality is . . . a matter for the future."[26] Swift's canon of names, endorsed by ostensive phrases, which invites the reader to project the world of Brobdingnag cannot be vindicated any further. This alone distinguishes *Gulliver's Travels* from Galileo's *Discorsi*, though both can be enlisted in the argument for a textualist view of reality. To press the point a little further, in both cases the reader is required to go beyond the merely linguistic: in Swift's text in order to overcode and imaginatively fill the schema of the text, in Galileo's in order to discover non-linguistic evidence which corroborates or denies his claims.

It is perhaps on the grounds of these and similar objections that Lyotard admits certain non-linguistic signs to the realm of phrases. Or perhaps "phrases" are not linguistic at all, but rather make up a broadly conceived semiotic in which language merely occupies the most powerful position. This is the impression we get from Lyotard's critique of Kant's theory of cognition: " . . . the constitution of the given requires an exchange of roles between addressor and addressee instances, and thus requires two phrases or quasi-phrases: respectively, the one where impression occurs and the one where the putting into (spatio-temporal) form occurs."[27] Whichever the most appropriate reading of Lyotard in this regard, what is missing is a theory of non-linguistic or quasi-phrases. Such a theory would have to argue, among other things, for the congruity between sign systems, an assumption Quine, for example, even rejects for the description of different languages.[28] To allow for Lyotard's position, at least a homology would have to be found between gestural and pictorial, static and dynamic, two- and three-dimensional, aural and tactile, pictographic and alphabetic semiosis, in H. P. Grice's sense of nonnatural meaning, which has not as yet been demonstrated.[29] As Roman Jakobson observes in his paper "On the Relation between Visual and Auditory Signs," there "exists a profound dissimilarity between the spatial and temporal arts" and between "spatial and temporal signs in general." Nevertheless, for Jakobson too the construction of "an overall model of sign production and sign perception and separate models for different types of signs" remains an urgent task.[30]

What is at stake here is nothing less than to show how Lyotard's considerable grammatical apparatus of phrases applies equally to other forms of signification. Validation; strong and weak referents; current and general deictics; silence; phrase regimen and universe; rigid designator; definition; cognitive, exclamative, declarative, and logical phrases, etc. would have to be accommodated in a liberally semiotic version of Lyotard's schema. Yet as hopeless as such an enterprise may look at the moment, it is precisely a semiotic extension which Lyotard's argument needs if he wishes the differend to cover what he claims it does.

The differend is seen from a number of overlapping perspectives: it is the victims' "inability to prove" their case, the fact that the adjudication of a dispute is conducted in the language of one party, "while the wrong suffered by the other is not signified in that idiom," or, the moment in language when something that needs to be formulated "cannot yet be."[31] In Lyotard's nonanthropomorphic scheme the injustice which arises from the linguistic regulation of dispute does not have its origin in some kind of universal evil, nor in human nastiness, nor in any form of laches, nor even in the poor management of language. As we have seen, the cause of such differends is a *structural* "hostility," a systemic agonistics which attaches to language in principle as a result of the ineradicable heterogeneity of phrases and genres of discourse. Barring its linguistic bias, this is a highly persuasive account.

The same can be said of what is arguably the most comprehensive summary statement of Lyotard's theory to date, Geoffrey Bennington's *Lyotard: Writing the Event*.[32] Bennington faithfully reflects Lyotard's massive investment in the linguistic by emphasizing the role of "sentences" ("phrases") in the constitution of reality. "In this conception," writes Bennington, "neither reality nor the subject stands prior to and in principle independent of a sentence." Reality is an act of attribution by a sentence to a referent, which in turn is "positioned by a sentence," just like a subject which "is also positioned by a sentence." In this manner sentences present a universe "which consists of four poles or posts: the three . . . sender, addressee and referent, but now also meaning (*sens*). None of these four poles preexist the sentence which presents them and their relationship or situation. What we call subjects, reality, meaning are, then, effects of the concatenation of sentences."[33] Nothing precedes the sentence, such that we are led to a logical and chronological linguistic foundation of the real. In Bennington's reading, "there is always a first sentence":

> Reality is, then, neither simply given and awaiting more-or-less adequate transcription, nor is it magically produced by a demiurgic act of creation on the part of the speaker, but is an unstable state attributed to referents on the basis of operations of nomination, ostension and description. . . . Reality is established as the result of playing a language-game with specifiable component parts.[34]

Yet Lyotard's linguistically signifiable, showable, and namable reality is nevertheless "located by a world."[35] Here we note a rift in the theory, as well as a blurred area not sufficiently clarified by either the philosopher or his disciple. How do sentences and world relate to one another? If reality is positioned by sentences but located by a world, how then is this world related to sentences? If sentences are prior to everything else, world must also be the result of sentences. That would grant them a certain foundational stability. Yet we are told that "sentences are on the move, in the possible ways of linking onto them with more sentences." The circularity of the account needs to be stressed, though in a different sort of account this would not necessarily be a flaw. As Bennington reiterates, "reality is never given, but always situated by particular narratives *as* referents: just as storyteller and addressee do not precede the story told but are positioned by it."[36]

And yet there is a way out of this circle, for at the same time "a subject gathers the properties of events as phenomena and constitutes their reality by carrying out the temporal synthesis of that series of events." How do both Lyotard and Bennington square this with sentences and discourse in a strictly linguistic sense? They cannot. A much broader semiotic approach is needed. And so the notion of a "non-linguistic sentence" is introduced. "Surely," asks Bennington, "Lyotard cannot be claiming that everything that happens is linguistic? Not if a sentence is not necessarily linguistic." This is a crucial shift in the emphasis of the theory.

To be fair to Bennington, he acknowledges the importance of this move. "If a referent is always (only) what is situated as such in a sentence-universe," he argues, "then saying anything about anything would involve linking onto a (possibly) non-linguistic sentence with a linguistic sentence." This new state of affairs demands careful consideration. For one, what would a non-linguistic sentence look like? And what sort of grammar would have to be envisaged to make it function in a network of non-linguistic sentences? And we must also ask how such non-linguistic sentences relate to Lyotard's "extra-linguistic permanence" mentioned earlier. Could they be part of it or even constitute such a permanence?

But would this not make it difficult to align permanence with the idea that "a subject gathers the properties of events as phenomena" since the latter must change with the subjects? In short, Lyotard's linguistic emphasis as well as Bennington's account of it run into serious difficulties when it comes to fundamental questions concerning cognition. And it is in their critique of Kant that their linguistic emphasis on such notions as sentence, reality, and subject becomes shaky.

According to Bennington, what Lyotard wants to say about cognition is that "perception 'itself' (and not just reports of perception) can and must be analyzed in terms of sentences."[37] For this we require two kinds of sentences. "First a sentence (or quasi-sentence ...) in a 'language' or idiom called 'matter'—of unknown sender, addressed to a receptive addressee. This is a sentence with no referent and an unclear meaning, a 'sentimental' sentence in Lyotard's terms." The second sentence reverses the relation between sender and addressee such that the "addressee of the first becomes the sender of a sentence in a language or idiom called 'form.' This sentence does have a referent, called 'phenomenon' and this referential function of the second sentence hangs on the capacity to apply criteria of space and time to the first sentence: the second sentence is what Kant calls 'intuition'." In Bennington's formulation of Kant, "we shall never know the thing itself, only the phenomenon as organized in the language of our second sentence, of which we are the *sender*."[38]

This is not what Kant says at all. For Kant the phenomenal is what it is as a result of both noumenal constraints (which we cannot know) and our cognitive faculties (not sentences). Thus both Lyotard's sentences and non-linguistic sentences, whatever they may be, are part of the world of appearances in Kant's scheme. To attribute to the noumenal any kind of signification, however vague, is a misrepresentation of *das Ding an sich*. Moreover, to separate two kinds of sentences, linguistic ones and their non-linguistic cousins, or "quasi-sentences," along the lines of the Kantian phenomenal and noumenal deprives us of the possibility of conceiving of reality in other than linguistic terms.

This is a problem as much at the hub of Lyotard's theory as it is in Bennington's critique. What is lacking in both is an argument for other than linguistic types of cognitive structures. What is missing is a description of the structure of non-linguistic sentences. What is also required is a broadly social semiotic which includes the linguistic as its most powerful sign system. But there are also visual, tactile, aural, and other kinds of signification to which we resort not only when words fail us. Having relegated the non-linguistic or quasi-sentence to the realm of "matter" and the non-cognitive, Lyotard and Bennington are left with a monopolistically linguistic vision of the world. Ironically though, Lyotard cannot, without damaging the very argument of the differend, make the linguistic the guarantee of reality by relegating non-linguistic sign systems to a realm with no "referent and an unclear meaning," with an "unknown sender," and merely a "receptive addressee." As I shall argue, we need a broadly semiotic view to make the kind of case Lyotard himself suggests by way of the differend, wherever it occurs. Consider the following examples.

In describing the relationship between certain Greek and Latin terms, Heidegger suggests that "designations are no arbitrary names." Instead, they relay the special way in which reality unfolds for classical Greek society. Heidegger deduces this linkage between linguistic forms and other structures of the life world from the discrepancy he notes in the transference of Greek names to the Latin vocabulary. This process he calls "the appropriation of Greek words by Roman Latin thought." Through it, "*hupokeimenon* becomes *subjectum, hupostasis* becomes *substantia, sumbebekos* becomes *accidens*." This is far from an innocent procedure; Heidegger discovers "beneath the seemingly literal and thus faithful translation" . . . a "*trans*lation of Greek experience into a different way of thinking." We need not bother here with Heidegger's conviction that therein lies the beginning of "the rootlessness of Western thought," nor with his assumption of the homogeneity of culture.[39]

What is important is that his example corroborates Lyotard's assertion that "the contact between two communities is immediately a conflict." However, as he suggests with reference to the Cashinuahua, this is not primarily because "the names and narratives of one . . . are exclusive of the names and narratives of the other."[40] For this is possible only because names and narratives are what they are by virtue of the "forms of life" which surround them and which we need to know if we are to activate the schemata of a language. As Wittgenstein notes, "the speaking of a language is *part of* an activity, or of a form of life (*Lebensform*)," such as "giving orders, and obeying them," or "play-acting," and so forth.[41]

As suggested earlier, we can only speculate why Wittgenstein did not pursue this crucial link. Perhaps, in part, he feared that *Lebensform* might be misread as "things," when at the same time he was at pains to deflate the very idea of a "thing corresponding to a substantive."[42] No matter what his reasons were, his formulation opens the way to a broad pragmatic-semiotic explanation of how language "comes to life" both in the sense of being generated in conjunction with other sign systems and in the sense of being activated by them in the process of "understanding." If we take seriously Wittgenstein's formulation of a "way of looking at things (*Anschauungsweise*),"[43] literally as well as metaphorically, Wilhelm von Humboldt's description of "the variety of languages" as not just "a variety of sounds and signs, but in fact a variety of world views" makes new sense.[44] Visual, tactile, auditory, proxemic, kinetic, olfactory, and other sign systems corroborate with language to form an inextricably, though always evolving, textual grid, which is our world. To have drawn our attention to this fact is the merit of Heidegger's passage.

The following examples are introduced to shore up the claim that non-linguistic significatory processes are stipulated as a necessity for both the generation (encoding) and reading (decoding) of phrases. In describing the Australian landscape in New South Wales, Charles Darwin emphasizes "the extreme uniformity of the vegetation," the "scanty" foliage, its "peculiar pale green tint, without any gloss."[45] This and similar texts were the foundation of a genre of discourse with which to depict the Australian flora, its dominant topos the uniformity of its drab green. The Reverend J. R. Wollaston, on his way to Fremantle, gives a similar if even less flattering account: a "dingy looking forest . . . the trees . . . want freshness; their foliage . . . the most sombre uniform hue." All he can see is "an impervious mass . . . of one uniform colour, a dark dirty green, over which on a hot day, the hazy, African-looking atmosphere hangs like pestilence."[46]

No doubt A. D. Hope had a different tone in mind when, about a hundred years later, he put these lines in his well-known poem: "A Nation of trees, drab green and desolate grey in the field uniform of modern wars."[47] Foreign forms of life and their significations produce linguistic schemata which declare the Other ugly. To the Aboriginal reader and increasingly also to the new Australians, these descriptions reveal an impoverished way of seeing in conflict with a semiotics that feels "at home." This is not to say that there can ever be a "right" way of signifying. At best we are dealing with a textual reality characterized by a minimal differend.

When in 1688 William Dampier portrayed Aboriginal Australians as "the miserablest People in the World" who, apart from their "Human Shape . . . differ but little from Brutes," he was among the founders of a disastrous "discursivity."[48] By not discovering "one graceful feature" in their appearance or behavior Dampier helped to instantiate the history of a differend which still impairs social progress on this Continent. In a structural sense Dampier's cocksure assessment lives on: in the way official designation of Aboriginal culture finds it difficult to let Aborigines speak for themselves or get a dialogue going. One such dialogue illustrates well the claim that the legal differend is in the first instance a semiotic conflict rather than a dispute of phrases. A number of Aboriginal elders were invited to a television panel discussion to meet members of a Commission which had addressed the issue of land rights and sacred areas. It took a long time for the opponents to find their uncommon, common ground. An elder, frustrated by a panel member's insistent question as to whether he had any documents to prove his claims, walked up to his opponent and slowly asked with a pleading gesture: "Do you know rock?" The member of the Commission hastily assured him that "of course" he knew what a rock was. This did not convince the Aborigine and after slowly repeating "rock" several times he shook his head and walked off the stage.

The audience was stunned because, I think, they sensed the hopelessness of indicating in English the complexity of a semiotic without which it is impossible to legitimate Aboriginal claims. The point is that the level of *comparatio* cannot be language itself, but only the non-predicative level of a semiotic which embraces all forms of life. True enough, the cognitive phrases of "knowing rocks" and their celebratory, revelatory, or mystical counterparts are irreconcilable, as Lyotard would say. Yet to do something about it you need to know the semiotic reasons for the linguistic conflict. The differences between the two forms of life, assuming a degree of homogeneity in each only for simplicity's sake, are fundamental and probably beyond description. Simplifying again to make the point, economic utilization of the land is opposed to its worship, private property to common good, litigation to tribal censure, linguistic narrative to story telling accompanied by sand drawings, mime, and dance, commerce to community. And yet what "worship" means remains propositionally and modally opaque, overrun by the economic genre and its dynamics: exchange. "In an exchange," says Lyotard, "the debt must be canceled, and quickly. In a narrative it must be recognized, treasured and deferred." And he seems right in suggesting that "communities woven through narrative must be destroyed by capital."[49] In that case we may witness not so much "a last phrase" as a dying gesture.

However, there is a way in which this particular differend is being challenged now, in the writings of an increasing number of Black Australian writers. Works by Lionel Fogarty, Jack Davies or Colin Johnson (Mudrooroo Narogin), to name only a few, are no longer written to fit into the canon of colonial English literature and so to accentuate the differend; they do not apologize for the way they transform English, nor do they flinch at the prospect of offending the sensitivities of a readership traditionally shielded from the directness of the political text. Colin Johnson has this to say on the reception of Lionel Fogarty's verse:

> The general English critic's response to Lionel Fogarty's poetry has been a deafening silence from publishers, fellow-poets and critics. This is only to be expected. The guerrilla is ignored until his actions become too daring and a threat, then the army is sent in to put him down.[50]

Johnson also points out that Aboriginal people share the fate of marginalization with many others "that became immersed in the European flood which flowed out from the fifteenth century onwards. The Aboriginal response to this threatened drowning has been and is similar to that of many other peoples."[51] He insists that Aboriginal culture is not dead, but only conveniently declared a Stone Age phenomenon by those who wish to continue to exclude its rightful contribution. For Colin Johnson, writing in English is a continuation of a powerful Aboriginal tradition of story telling, even if the level of both the content and the expression have been transformed by the clash of the cultures.[52]

Unlike his three novels and some of his poetry, which were snatched up by the presses, Colin Johnson's 48-page "Bicentennial Gift Poem" entitled "Sunlight Spreadeagles Perth in Blackness" has to this day not yet been published in its entirety. It is safe to assume that the reason is not that Johnson is an unknown writer or that he could not be trusted to produce a poem of quality. Written in 1985, the poem is an ironic, bitter, profound, lyrical, aggressive, and above all substantial poetic-critical statement by an Aboriginal poet in the face of a highly commercial, often insensitive, and garish campaign celebrating the great accomplishments of two hundred years of White settlement in Australia. What do publishers expect an Aboriginal writer to say on such an occasion from the position of a minority which has narrowly survived genocide? Whatever the answer, the refusal to publish Johnson's poem must remain both a puzzle and a scandal.

The poem opens with three lines, the motifs of which are repeated in various combinations throughout the text

> In any passage of the sun and moon
> Fragments flutter,
> The ancestors and children of this time

Johnson uses a cosmic image to indicate temporality instead of technical time and identifies the Aboriginal people of past and present as the floating remains of a fragmented culture: "the ancestors of my broken thoughts." As the title suggests, the focus is on the city of Perth, Western Australia, but the speaker roams freely to other places and to a general level of abstraction at which the broader motifs of Australia and the two cultures are treated. Throughout the poem the speaker changes from the initial announcer to various personalities, as the poetic form changes from short lyrical stanzas to narrative passages and Nyoongar lines.[53]

Australia is seen as "a wrecked black body swarming with white termites" and "a filthy unessential world / Filled with the ruins of mountains innocent / Except for the trace of iron in their souls." Here, the European commercial attitude to the land stands in contrast with an older spiritual outlook. Perth is described as a "colonial outpost teetering on the world's edge" swamped by homesick American sailors, a place in which "the Nyoongars wander disowned and owning," its environment destroyed by European greed:

> The water lilies die one by one
> To the poisoned bellyup fishes,
> I have never done this to you

And much later in the poem:

> Instead of the impotent lives of your unjust
> Fishing out the waters of my spirit breathing
> In the breath of every breathing creature
> Never to be plundered unless amends were made

Throughout the text two figures recur as polarities of past and present, the Nyoongar hero Yagan, murdered last century, and the fictive figure of King Willy, an old homeless Aborigine who denies social reality by way of drunken dreams. In a prose passage Johnson links the death of Yagan with the deaths of Aboriginal people in white institutions.

Yagan's land, Yagan's land! Here is his tree, scratch it and it bleeds his ancient blood, scratch it and it bleeds the blood of a Nyoongar spitting out his teeth in a police station, coughing up his lungs in a charity hospital, vomiting his blood from a shattered skull in Fremantle prison just a short gasp and a death away.

As King Willy sleeps on park benches or squats in street corners he reminds the reader of Noorak, an old Aborigine from *Long Live Sandawara* who tells a city youth about the heroic deeds of their slaughtered leaders, except that King Willy is a further development of Noorak in that he never rises from his dreams, a wholly passive symbol of a demoralized community.

Recollections mingle with attempts at forgetting and a denial of the present: "We lose this time . . . We forget this agony." What cannot be forgotten are the bitter memories of injustice, insult, enslavement, humiliation, and the imposition of a new and hateful identity. "Beaten and buggered" for "defying the whiteness" by a law which was "never the ass, but a great big white man with authority to beat and maim and hurt." Yet the insults still cut more deeply:

> We'll remember 'Boong,'
> And 'Nigger' and 'Coon'
> And all the rest of the scum
> You lashed us with

As a consequence of two hundred years of white rule, old identities have been replaced by new ones. On the one hand, the poem catalogs typical occupations and positions in terms of which Aborigines were seen: "Stockman / Fruitpicker / Casual worker / Castoff / Bludger / Fringedweller / Landowner and land holder: The ones who never had to arrive;" and on the other, the speaker identifies himself thus: "I am the corpse rotting in the tree," not merely with reference to Aboriginal burial custom.

Or, more harshly, "We are the offal stinking to high heaven / We are your penned up cattle," and, reminding the white reader of the practice of transporting the remains of dead Aborigines to Europe for scientific study, the speaker identifies himself with "the measurements of my bones / Cast into museums and words collected into Primitive." A concise prose section rounds off this European vision of Aboriginality: " . . . the classification of grunts deemed the language of blacks close to the missing link and apedom clothed in close kinship ranks massed together as a biological thinking species of beyond the stone age."

Both missionary education and English as the conquering language system are motifs in Johnson's work. Having rejected the straitjacket of the mission and its sacred lies the poet demands

> Bury the oldtime mission Aboriginality,
> Give it to the white man with a cross
> . . .
> Let the stench of two hundred years
> Drive him to the far horizon and beyond . . .

The differend is realized by the author in the paradox of having to use English to say what he must say and yet wishing he did not have to do so. This produces a powerful conflict in the poetic speech act, resulting in the spitting out of aggressive obscenities and a despair at being fettered yet again: "These English words / All I can say is / Fuck, cunt, kill . . . These words, my words . . . the stone knife cuts gentler than your gentlest words. Your words are blows aimed against the setting sun." And yet the rejection of English is illusory; it is not only the medium of the differend but the very basis of the poet's protest. He appeals to the ancestors to "Make me a man never ending . . . Make me harden into an axe" in order to be ready to call for a new rebellious spirit among his people.

> Rise, Black Children, wipe out the centuries,
> Tear at their truth and find the lies,
> All they hide and hide in the shadows of their smiles.

In the end, the Black Australian text confronts the differend of the texts of white celebration, demanding "Justice two hundred years denied." To conclude from this that it is after all a linguistic differend which is being challenged by an agonistic linguistic discourse would be quite wrong. What is needed to understand why writers like Colin Johnson are now capable of transforming themselves from plaintiffs into prosecutors is something broader than a strictly linguistic explanation. To achieve the position which he has taken up in this text Colin Johnson does two things beyond verbal signification. First, he places himself, in a reconstructive manner, into Aboriginal culture as a social semiotic in tune with the Australian environment: "I have never done this to you" and "Never to be plundered unless amends were made." Second, unlike the Aboriginal elders in the televised 'debate,' for whom obscenities are out of bounds, Johnson launches his literary-political attack by acquiring that very sign system of aggression which subsumes the verbal yet is not identical with it. It seems that in order to defeat the differend the plaintiff must not only acquire the idiom of the court but also its non-verbal social semiotic.

VIII

A STRIPTEASE OF MEANING ON THE LADDER OF DISCOURSE

> Words, expressions, propositions ... obtain their meaning from the discursive formation in which they are produced.
>
> Michel Pêcheux,
> *Language, Semantics and Ideology*

What could "a burlesque act in which a female [*sic*] performer removes her clothing piece by piece in view of the audience" or any less sexist description of "unconcealment" possibly contribute to the discussion of discourse? What does "striptease" entail in a procedure which begins with the richly dressed and decorative acts of meaning endowment in literary reading and works its way down the rungs of a ladder at the bottom of which is revealed the stark "sense" of formal logic and its digital offspring? Is what is finally disclothed perhaps disappointing because it is fully sharable? The tease, a tantalization without the intention of fulfilling an aroused desire, perhaps rests on the realization that in order to be entirely and publicly available, in order to be meaning without fringe and penumbra, meaning must be empty. Perhaps it is only when meaning is individually unfulfilled that it can become 'pure' sense.

This chapter attempts to sketch a number of discursive practices which all partake of a construable minimal sense without being adequately defined by it. One can also argue the cohesion of all discourses via discursive microstructural tropes, as for instance metaphors and macrostructural features, such as narrative strategies, which are present in the vast majority of discourses and, in a minimal sense, even in the final reduction of the discursive, the digital. At the same time we need to be aware of tendencies in different discursive operations toward weighing certain features in a distinct manner, as for example reference, meaning, degree of propositional and modal opacity, truth, deixis, and cultural frames. Our ladder of discourse acts as a heuristic device illustrating observations of this kind.

There are many ways of designing ladders of discourse. I could begin with formal logic and add rung after rung by increasingly loading and so bloating the starting definition of meaning as sense. I could do this by the introduction of cultural reference and deixis, by ambiguities and unresolvable problems of polysemy and synonymy. Even where such a ladder is not explicitly offered but merely implied, this is the rarely acknowledged metaphor underpinning much of formal semantics. However, to proceed from the relative safety of propositional sense to the opacities of everyday speech and literary discourse is to assume tacitly that natural language deep down is a homogeneous system gone wrong in the course of history; or, that if it is a largely heterogeneous organism, it is nevertheless preferable to impose on it a disambiguating matrix rather than be swamped by its murky intricacies. In either instance the heterogeneity of language is regarded as a deviation from what ought to be the case. This is not to deny that the formal method has yielded impressive and elegant results and will continue to do so as semantics learns to accommodate ever more complex modal structures.[1] Its main disadvantage lies in the fact that in order to achieve this modal semantics has had to develop an analytical apparatus quite beyond the grasp of ordinary readers. Meaning is a semiotic and not a linguistic phenomenon. Verbal expressions only 'mean' in conjunction with other sign systems. By contrast, definitional or analytical sense, or minimal meaning, can operate as a purely grammatical relation, as for instance in formal logic, mathematics, and the digital. As argued in previous chapters, the equation of meaning with sense in saturated discourses is an illegitimate or at least unwarranted move which leads to a kind of description favoring propositional bias. With an emphasis on analyticity and propositional content also goes a grammatical expectation about truth, falsity, and verification. The ladder of discourses proposed here has an altogether different set of presuppositions: it looks at a selection of discursive forms in relation to reference, explicit modalities or marked discourse, inferrable modalities, truth/falsity, reading conventions, and cultural frames, etc. Such a perspective is likely to produce a set of distinctions and similarities between language systems in use which is quite different from those in traditional language philosophy.

The ladder of discourses which I wish to propose, then, does not start empty, waiting to be filled by the analyst rung by rung; it is fully occupied by a multitude of natural and artificial languages. I shall begin by describing the acts which I typically perform on the top rungs of the ladder instead of striving upwards from formal definition to the rich fuzziness of living speech. For in the performance of saturated social discourse I am always already at the top of our ladder, intuitively and yet not uneconomically engaged in the interpretation of complex ambiguities. On the other hand, I must apply special acts of reduction to these habitual readings if I wish to descend the ladder toward technical and formal speech: from (1) literary discourse to (2) mythic language, (3) historiography, (4) juridical language, (5) everyday speech, (6) technical language, (7) scientific statements, (8) the discourse of formal logic, and (9) the digital. The particular selection of discursive operations chosen is of course arbitrary and so could be varied infinitely. On the other hand, the principle of the ladder as a dynamic order should be maintained.

(1) Literary Discourse

When I read literary texts in a literary manner I execute multi-stratified and compound transformations of the linguistic surface. Also, as I noted in the examples chosen in the previous chapters, some texts make me construct primarily a presented world and so perform quasi-referential acts, while others encourage me to imagine primarily the presentational process and so perform quasi-deictic acts. More simply, what is implied here is the difference between the text as a *speaking picture* (emphasizing the presented world) and the text as *picturing speech* (foregrounding the presentational process). In principle these two poles are always present in all signifying systems, except that the reading of literary texts, more than other forms of reading, foregrounds their dialectic relationship. This is emphatically the case when the text surface represses its speech acts in favor of its propositional content or vice versa. In other words, reading in a literary manner throws light on the relationship between propositional and modal opacity. The literary text tends to encourage such a reading. Consider the following as an example.

> My mistress' eyes are nothing like the sun—
> Coral is far more red than her lips' red—
> If snow be white, why then her breasts are dun—
> If hairs be wires, black wires grow on her head:
> I have seen roses damasked, red and white,
> But no such roses see I in her cheeks,
> And in some perfumes is there more delight
> Than in the breath that from my mistress reeks.
> I love to hear her speak, yet well I know
> That music hath a far more pleasing sound.
> I grant I never saw a goddess go;
> My mistress when she walks treads on the ground.
> And yet by heav'n I think my love as rare
> As any she belied with false compare.

Literature occurs whenever a certain kind of writing is instantiated by a certain kind of reading. This writing/reading comprises a large number of discursive operations which are summarized for simplicity's sake under the heading of literary discourse. I place it at the top of our schematic ladder by reason of a number of distinctions which can be drawn between literary writing/reading and other language performances. In summary, everything that can be done in other discourses also occurs in literary discourse. Moreover, much that is curtailed, denied, and prohibited in specialized languages can be celebrated in literature. To say that literary reading conventions impose the same strictures as do juridical scientific or logical rule is quite misleading, since it is precisely a characteristic of the literary that these very conventions compete with one another and are constantly challenged, altered, and supplemented.

Shakespeare's Sonnet 130 is a relatively simple text, chosen to avert the charge
of having illustrated an average by means of a highly complex example. Yet any
literary reading will produce even here a degree of complexity absent from
non-literary performances. By this I mean that no matter what specific linguistic
item we consider, our literary reading will handle differently these very 'same'
features once we enter another discourse. This applies to extension, reference,
propositional content, intension, existential qualifier, shifters, denotation, connotation, concretization, speech acts, explicit and inferrable modality, as well as
to presupposition or 'preconstruction,' and many other perspectives.

Without warning the first line engages the reader with a parody of the Renaissance catalogue of beauty, and for another eleven lines, the first three stanzas
of the sonnet, the poetic speaker lists the main points of the beloved not in
words of praise, but by negation. His love's eyes are "nothing like the sun;" her
lips cannot match the red of coral; the color of her breasts is not the white of
snow; her hair compares poorly with golden threads; her cheeks are quite
inferior to "damasked roses;" her voice falls short of the sound of music; while
her gait, far from being divine, is simply human. Stanza four, or lines 13 and
14, appear at first as a simple reversal of the negative catalogue by the poetic
"I" who now confesses his love in spite of what he wrongly condemned as
shortcomings.

This is where our reading runs into difficulties. The 'yet' certainly turns matters
around, but we have by now come to appreciate a speaker's ironic-sarcastic,
distancing modalities and bridle at his swearing "by heav'n" that he will now
speak sincerely. If he thinks his "love as rare / As any she belied with false
compare," he is allowing for variant readings. First, his love is so rare that it
doesn't exist, since the Petrarchian fad produces ludicrous fictions. Second, it
is the speaker who has produced the "false compare" and not the beloved, and
third, her/his very existence, assuming she/he did exist, would not belie but
prove correct this comparison. "Falsity" makes most sense here if it is read in
two directions: as the speaker's pretended falsity and the actual and ridiculed
falsity of the catalogue of beauty.

Whichever ambiguities we wish to emphasize, in the end we do want to ask
what the poem does in this sort of reading. Clearly, it ridicules a poetic fad,
while at the same time displaying the poet's easy mastery of the sonnet form,
the traditional thematic, and the details of the love catalogue. In this the poem
suggests that Shakespeare is interested much more in intertextual questions
than in specific portrayals. Thus, the collective referent for this, as for many
other texts, is literature itself rather than either the immediate propositional
content (and hence the presented world) or the poem's immediate modalities
(presentational process).[2] If this is so, what the poem also does is to draw our
attention to a number of subordinate specific referents: Petrarch, English Renaissance imitators, perhaps one or more particularly silly sonnets which riled
the author, actual pictures of beauties drawn according to the tradition, even
perhaps the fact that this very tradition represses other forms of relationships,
for the treatment of which there is ample evidence in the Sonnets.

Indeed, reading in a literary fashion alters the function of reference itself: it splits into a number of directions to which signifiers 'refer:' the euphonic qualities of the words (e.g., rhyme), the self-reference of the speaker not just by way of shifters (my, I) but by *every word* this parodic speaker utters; references to any possible mistress or friend; reference to convention; self-reference to the poet who for one transcends the fashion he parodies. Reduplicating the poetic speech act as we are led to do by the syntax, we also duplicate the referents of each noun in the negated catalogue. The "sun" refers both to our habitual notion as well as to the "sun" of love poetry, to Romeo's "Juliet is the sun," but now merely a weak metaphor of praise, and likewise with "coral," "snow," and so forth. This double referential system, one straight and one in quotation marks, should logically come to an end in line 12 where the speaker brings the tradition down from its idealistic nonsense back to earth (ground), yet the parodic distrust, once activated, carries over as we have seen to the concluding rhyming couplet. It is a peculiar observation that once we have noticed the evident parodic impulse of some texts all our literary readings become affected in this way. When Umberto Eco defined a sign as anything we can lie with, he gave a logical and so minimal umbrella description to all signifying systems. Literary discourse differs from most other discourses in that it makes the most of this potential.

Another way of distinguishing discourses is by a tripartite schema proposed by Michael Halliday and refined for literature by John Frow. In his *Language as Social Semiotic* Halliday understands the semantic aspects of language in their double function of constituting "a projection, or realization of the social system" and "the lexicogrammatical system" by which the social system is projected and by which it is realized as a projection. According to Halliday, the semantic potential of language is available to the individual speaker in different kinds of "register" or the "configuration of semantic resources that the member of a culture typically associates with a situation type."[3] Which situation type a speaker is dealing with can be understood by virtue of three concepts: the "field" of social action, the "tenor" of social relations, and the "mode" of symbolic organization. With field, tenor, and mode go three semantic components: an ideational, an interpersonal, and a textual component. The ideational component "represents the speaker's meaning potential as an observer" and contains such items as "objects, actions, events . . . of the world and of our consciousness" and also "language itself" as well as "metaphenomena' . . . already encoded as facts and as reports." The interpersonal component "represents the speaker's meaning potential as an intruder" and the textual component "represents the speaker's text-forming potential."[4] This tripartition of the semantic field allows for the discussion of significant relationships within social discourse. Halliday's triple emphasis is on the "field" of what is presented (the quasi-referential side of texts), on the "tenor" of its speech processes (the deictic references of discourse), and on the self-referentiality of texts (their printed, oral, dramatic, or televisual mode).

A combination of the Bakhtinian concept of "genre" with Halliday's "register" leads to a system of discourses of the kind proposed by John Frow in "Discourse Genres."[5] Here language use is differentiated as to whether field, tenor, or mode are dominant. Accordingly, a dominance of *field* can be observed in the languages of science and professional jargon, administrative discourse, journalese, sports commentary, news casting, historiography, philosophical dialogue, or the language of technical analysis; *tenor* is seen to be foregrounded in face-to-face conversation, invective and boasting, gossip, prayer, epistolary style, the language of showmanship, or amatory discourse, while the dominance of *mode* generates oratory, sermon, cant, natural narrative, sacred or scriptural discourse, parody and impersonation, jokes, graffiti, riddle and word games, as well as literary genres and subgenres.[6] In this schema discourse is protected against the threat of subjective denting of the system; discourse becomes the "production of a unified cluster of semantic, structural and contextual meanings in accordance with generic norms."[7] Genre constitutes the frame of the "sayable" and so "allows the unsaid to be said without being said, i.e., without the speaker taking responsibility for the enunciation of the message. And by defining that which can be taken for granted it establishes the stable field of meanings, the ideological second nature, which constitutes the real."[8]

In spite of some advantages for the linguistic study of the literary text the approach shares some of the drawbacks of all methods overemphasizing the system. In any semantic theory the "stable field of meaning" is discovered at considerable cost. The cost here is the suppression of the permeability of language typification and the irreality of the "limits of the sayable."[9] Any theory of meaning should be able to reconcile the thematic core of meaning with its fringe which may turn thematic the very next moment in history; it must be able to establish a structural and yet dynamic relationship between system and instantiation of utterance. In Frow's schema it is assumed that the system always determines the utterance. And although I cannot explain utterance without the stipulation of a system, I could not talk about the system, much less query it, without the performance of a never quite systemic utterance. The irretrievability of any originary utterer from the inscription cannot be disputed. In each utterance event the speaker, by imposing a particular prosodic contour which carries a vast amount of inferrable information about himself or herself, nonetheless takes "responsibility for the enunciation of the message."[10] In so doing the speaker makes thematic a discourse genre in a particular manner and by denting it dissolves its currency into a fluidity from which new genres emerge. The heuristic value of "discourse genres" is considerable; however, the faith in the "stability of the real" should be queried.[11]

The main reason that I do not adopt the Hallidayan triad is because it constitutes a category mistake in that "tenor" and "field" belong to one level of operation, syntactic/semantic/semiotic, while "mode" requires an altogether different and prior response on the part of the reader/listener: the establishment of the very basis on which our constructions of tenor and field can occur. A stratified model in the tradition of Ingarden's findings concerning the ontic heteronomy of the literary work draws this distinction to our attention. In such a schema the ideational (field), interpersonal (tenor) and textual (mode) components are by no means absent but appear at certain levels of the kind of transformation which we tend to perform in discursive operations. In literary discourse they can be described in the following manner.

By speaking the literary text interpretively, i.e., by supplying it with an actual or silent intonation and stress pattern, I first transform the linguistic surface reductively into the more general deep structures of propositional content and its modal conditions and so grasp minimal quasi-referential and quasi-deictic conceptualizations. The imposition of a prosodic contour also means that I execute further expansive, conceptual-imaginational projections beyond reductive deep structures. In addition, there are activated such self-referential linguistic constructions of "mode" as a review of the textual surface in the light of intertextual parallels, genre frame, parodic variations, and intralingual differentiation, with a view toward establishing semantic patterns. Further, I perform concretizing transformations of both the "field" of the presented world and the "tenor" of the narrative and poetic speech processes and finally, again reductively, transformations of interpretive ideation. And as I pay attention to the interaction of these transformations along the forward axis of reading, say of a string of words of 85 cm in an average sonnet and about 4.3 miles of text in *Ulysses*, I am ready at the same time to realize a complex interaction (Ingarden calls it a "polyphony"), though not necessarily a harmony, of inter-related aspects from the phonic to the ideational level.[12]

In this explanation of my reading performance I wish to stress that I pay equal attention to the propositional and modal sides of my constructions, even though in practice particular texts will guide me to favor one at the expense of the other. In principle, both appear to be grasped and imaginatively explored according to the double matrix of typifications anonymized from my experience of literary practice and the praxis of the life-world: the structure of spatial and temporal relations (world and locus of speaking), acts and events (happenings and speech acts), agents (characters and narrators), values, and ideological stance. In such reading I am also aware of the at least double modality of the actual author's inferred position vis-à-vis the text and the presentational modalities inside the text. Further, when I read narrative texts I am prepared especially for the actualization of the triple deixis of author speech, narrator speech, and the speech of the presented personae or agents. And, lastly, I have learned to cope with multiple, subordinated modal operations, as in Chinese box arrangements of narrators handing over their temporary authorities to yet further narrators. The following two tables present in schematic form the *Transformations* which I typically perform on the linguistic surface of literary texts if I read them in a literary manner and the *Double Matrix of Literary Reading* which permits me both to construct a coherent verbal and imaginative fictive world and to relate this construction to the social life-world, without which I could not conceive of alternative possible worlds or counterfactual states of affairs.[13]

As a result of the multiple transformations (Table 2) which I perform within

TABLE 2 **Transformations in Literary Reading**

Text surface ("My mistress' eyes are nothing like ... ")

Transformation 1	1.1 abstracted propositional content	1.2 inferrable modal conditions of propositional content
	(reduced signifieds)	
Transformation 2	2. textual surface is self-referentially reviewed in the light of linguistic and intertextual contexts with a view toward establishing semantic patterns	
Transformation 3	3.1 deformalization or concretization of quasi-referential verbal schemata	3.2 deformalization of quasi-deictic information
	(signifieds in the light of non-verbal semiosis)	
Transformation 4	4.1 set of abstracted values of presented world: aesthetic, religious, political, and ideological	4.2 set of abstracted values of presentational process as in 4.1
	(reduced high-level signifieds)	
Transformation 5	5. synthetic abstraction of overall work-ideology on the basis of tension between or congruence of 4.1 and 4.2	
	(high-level subsumptive signifieds)	

the double coordinates of referentiality and deixis (Table 3) I have learned to distrust the seeming stability of literal meanings. Instead, I tend to modify them by designing feedback linkages between the self-referential, imaginational, and ideational transformations on the one hand and the text surface on the other. Despite the high degree of fluidity of these aspects, I tend to aim in the end at a summary reconciliation of all these acts into a synthesis, however tentative and lopsided, of an overall work ideology. This is neither the grasp of a contained sense meaning nor the apex of a pyramid of deep structures, but rather the synthesizing act of the projection of a schematically imagined world and an authorial stance which of necessity includes myself as gaze and ideological force. Whether such construals are totalizing and so amount to a form of hermeneutic closure or are deliberately 'off-center' to produce a counter-reading is not in conflict with these transformations.

One of the reasons for the high complexity of these acts is the fact that literary discourse can subsume all other forms of language, from the parodic handling

TABLE 3 **The Double Matrix of Literary Reading**

	Aspects of the presented world (quasi-referentiality)	Aspects of the presentational process (quasi-deixis)
formal relations	logical relations and numerical quantities in presented world	formal aspects of speech acts
spatial aspects	spatial structures of presented world	spatial locus of speaker
temporal aspects	temporal structure of presented world	temporal locus of speaker
agents	presented personae characters agents	speaker, narrator poetic I biographical situations and zero-points of orientation
acts events	act and event structure	narrating, confessing, concealing, divulging, fore-shadowing, confiding, lying; multiple narrating
social matrix	social relations	speaker's social position in relation to presented world
super-structure	dominant, aesthetic, religious, moral, political codes	speaker's dominant values
ideological abstractions	dominant ideological structure of presented world	speaker's ideological stance as inferred
overall meaning making	reader's construction of quasi-reference	reader's construction of quasi-deixis

of other literary texts to the formal operations of chess and formal logic. This is not implied in the simplifying metaphor of the ladder, yet it supports my proposal to situate literary reading at its highest rung. At the same time, the inclusive character of the literary text is achieved at the expense of being devoid of facticity in any immediate sense. In literary reading my modal and referential realizations are redirected to collaborate in the establishment of a quasi-world in which the truth-by-correspondence rules of factual language do not apply. These realizations rest on considerable modal variations of propositional contents, the latter being affected by visual, kinetic, proximic, tactile, and other forms of semiotic grasp. I believe, as does the linguist John Lyons (though he does so for different reasons), that such readings cannot be brushed aside as emotive or purely subjective deviations from sense meanings; they too are structured and intersubjectively shared to a high degree.

The Aquinian *adequatio rei et intellectus* which I may discover in Gerard Manly Hopkins's sonnet "As Kingfishers Catch Fire, Dragonflies Draw Flame" requires more than the propositional grasp of "each hung bell's Bow swing finds tongue to fling out broad its name." In fact, our ability to abstract such a content relies on the imaginative variation of my non-verbal understanding of the world where kingfishers do not catch fire as well as on the ideational subsumption of its *quiditas* under "what in God's eye" everything is.[14]

Christopher Norris is therefore not quite right when he says that "fictions are marked as a distinctive and peculiar class of utterance precisely insofar as they work to inhibit the usual inferential advance from 'sense' to 'reference.'" One could argue on the contrary that fictions, more than technical language use, guide us to project playfully and experimentally imaginary referents; realist fiction even invite us to do the same with actual referents such as the city of Dublin.[15] In principle, this complex interaction of meaning construction provides a model by which we can understand similar procedures of meaning conferment in the discourse of the everyday world and their reductions to various degrees of formalization in a series of other discourses.

(2) Mythical Discourse

Different types of discourse and their conventional readings constitute different possible worlds and utterance acts. Likewise, different kinds of critical commentary do different things with texts. They may not all sparkle, yet they must all be acts. When Harold Bloom declares that "criticism is spark and act, or else we need not read it at all," he is shrinking the spectrum of critical voices to his own tenor. Both the more artistic and the more logical form of criticism may wish, for instance, to address such narrative origins as "Genesis." When Bloom does so, it is to make a point about the absence of the "crucial referential aspect" of chaos and the disallowed question "What was there prior to Creation?"[16] Here we note the content orientation inherited by deconstructive American criticism from its New Critical forebears. Other critical discourses tend to pose different queries, as for example the obverse of the referential question: where was the narrator standing when he witnessed the Lord saying " 'Let there be Light' "? As Lévi-Strauss observes, "the order of myth excludes dialogue: the group's myths are not debated, but transformed when they are assumed to be repeated." However, the question of the absorption of the speech act by the presented world in myth is not of primary interest to the structural study pursued by Lévi-Strauss. His is a macro-structural interest in which the surface text is incidental. This is why he can say that "poetry is a kind of speech which cannot be translated except at the cost of serious distortion; whereas the mythical value of myth is preserved even through the worst translation." Myth functions "on an especially high level where meaning succeeds practically at 'taking off' from the linguistic ground."[17]

Both the ellipsis of chaos and the suppression of the narrational speech act point in the same direction: towards the authoritative-authoritarian positing of a world. Post-Cervantesian, post-Sternean, post-metafiction readers, naturalized into decoding the dominance of the presentational process over the simulacrum of a presented world, find themselves barred from identification with the reader stipulated in the text. Their readings are of necessity characterized by a tension between their logos arguing about the concealed speaker of the text and the narrative mythos, the divine facticity of the propositionally given. On the one hand, there is the frustrated attempt to construct variants of possible utterance situations giving rise to the narrative, and on the other, the performance of the codified ritual of imagining the presented world of the Creative Act. Congregational readers do not face this dilemma; for them the question of the narratorial speech act is embedded and resolved in the frame set by "the word of God."

In the first case, the textual undermining of constructions of the utterance stance of "Genesis" drives me to speculate on the political motivation of the denial of modality: only when debate is denied can cosmo-logos act as control. In the second case, the reader welcomes the suppression of the modemes and with it the transformation of the text into mythic, divine proposition: the word-world is all that is the case. In this reading, "skepticism is not irrefutable, but obviously nonsensical, when it tries to raise doubts where no question can be asked," for as in Wittgenstein's *Tractatus*, "doubt can exist only where a question exists."[18] In the mythic-authoritarian text the construction of modality is disallowed. While in formal logic the absence of modality in its deictic-referential and ideological sense at least guarantees the full sharability of its propositions, the suppression of modality in the mythic-authoritarian text constitutes a denial of negotiatory speech and so of historical progress.

(3) The Discourse of History

When I read historiographic narrative, how far are my acts of meaning making constrained by historical fact, or by what some historians call evidence? Recent debates have addressed the extremes of "documentary objectivism" and "relativistic subjectivism" in historiography from a new middle ground. As Dominick LaCapra argues in *History and Criticism*, the two positions do not present useful alternatives.

> They are mutually supportive parts of the same larger complex. The objectivist historian places the past in the 'logocentric' position of what Jacques Derrida calls the 'transcendental signified.' . . . The relativist simply turns objectivist 'lo-

gocentrism' upsidedown. The historian places himself or herself in the position
of 'transcendental signifier' that 'produces' or 'makes' the meaning of the past.
And in the semiotic variant of relativism, the past does indeed seem submerged
in all-pervasive semiosis.

Instead LaCapra prefers the Gadamerian notion of a "dialogic interchange
with the past." He uses such concepts as "transference" and "alterity" to point
to the problematic relation between an opaque past and an unclear present. In
so doing he draws our attention to "the relation among texts, discursive practices,
and sociopolitical institutions. And yet he does not want to abandon "the virtue
of traditional historiography at its best" with its "ability to join meticulous research with a form of critical rationality in the investigation of the past." These,
LaCapra believes, can be retained by being sensitive to "certain contestatory
'voices' " beyond "mere hermeneutic echoes that resonate on the level of pure
meaning [but] have implications for the conduct of social and political life."[19]
Is there then any non-textual framework beyond LaCapra's "contestatory
voices" such as 'history itself' which rules the sense meanings of the text as
well as the imaginational projections which I may be able to entertain? A possible
answer is the reformulation of Althusser's position as offered by Frederic Jameson in *The Political Unconscious*. History here is seen as "an absent cause"
which is "inaccessible to us except in textual form," so that "our approach to
it and to the Real itself necessarily passes through its prior textualization, its
narrativization in the political unconscious." In this view, history is "ground and
untranscendable horizon."[20] Yet since this is not a ground on which I could
experience any horizonal guidance for my acts of meaning conferment, what
do "ground and untranscendable horizon" amount to when I confront the historical text? Consider the following passage by William L. Shirer.

The answer was given two days later, on March 23, in the Kroll Opera House in
Berlin, where the Reichstag convened. Before the House was the so-called En-
abling Act—the "Law for Removing the Distress of People and Reich (*Gesetz zur
Behebung der Not von Volk und Reich*)," as it was officially called. . . .

'The government (Hitler promised) will make use of these powers only insofar
as they are essential for carrying out vitally necessary measures. Neither the
existence of the Reichstag nor that of the Reichsrat is menaced. The position and
rights of the President remain unaltered . . . The separate existence of the federal
states will not be done away with. The rights of the churches will not be diminished and their relationship to the State will not be modified. The number of
cases in which an internal necessity exists for having recourse to such a law is
in itself a limited one.'

The fiery Nazi leader sounded quite moderate and almost modest; it was too
early in the life of the Third Reich for even the opposition members to know
full well the value of Hitler's promises. Yet one of them, Otto Wells, leader of
the Social Democrats, a dozen of whose deputies had been detained by the police,

rose—amid the roar of the storm troopers outside yelling, 'Full powers, or else!'—
to defy the would-be dictator. Speaking quietly and with great dignity, Wells
declared that the government might strip the Socialists of their power but it could
never strip them of their honour.

'We German Social Democrats pledge ourselves solemnly in this historic hour
to the principles of humanity and justice, of freedom and socialism. No enabling
act can give you the power to destroy ideas which are eternal and indestructible.'
Furious, Hitler jumped to his feet, and now the assembly received a real taste of
the man. 'You come late, but yet you come! (he shouted) . . . You are no longer
needed . . . The star of Germany will rise and yours will sink. Your death knell
has sounded. . . . I do not want your votes. Germany will be free, but not through
you!' (Stormy applause)
. . .
The vote was soon taken: 441 for, and 84 (all Social Democrats) against.
. . .
Thus was parliamentary democracy finally interred in Germany.[21]

In Jameson's account, historiography is urged "not to elaborate some achieved
and lifelike simulacrum of its supposed object, but rather to "produce" the
latter's "concept," a concept informed by Necessity or "why what happened (at
first received as "empirical" fact) had to happen the way it did." When Jameson
rightly attacks the simple representationality of traditional historiography and
replaces it by an "exorable form of events" and "narrative category" of Necessity,[22] he is analyzing discourse in terms of the propositional, the "simulacrum"
of a projected world, and its post-mythical narrative nexus, causality. Phrased
in the language of Halliday's linguistics, Jameson is approaching discourse by
means of "field" and "mode," leaving unaddressed the question of "tenor," or
the question of the intrusion of the speaker into the spoken.[23] From the perspective by which I have distinguished these aspects, Jameson's focus is on
propositional content and narrative organization while the fundamental issue
of the modalities of utterance, in particular the biographical-ideological motivation of the speaker of the text, remains masked.

In reading Shirer's text I cannot but construct, similar to my performance of
literary reading, the double vision of a possible world and the world which
contains the speaker of the utterance. As a result, it is not only the simulacrum
of the heroic Social Democrat Otto Wells, the wily Hitler, and the howling
brownshirts outside the Kroll Opera House, but also the modal side of these
representations which I project.

Who or what, we need to ask, speaks Shirer's text? The answer that offers
itself is a speaker who addresses me from a position of Western democratic
judgment not yet tainted by Vietnam and Watergate, a position from which evil
reveals itself unambiguously. An ideological stance can thus be inferred as a
view of the world in which Fascism is tied to a particular historical German
naivete and political immaturity. This should not be questioned. However, the
unreflexive certainty of Shirer's judgment is, in its superficiality, not altogether

unlike the belief of a large number of German intellectuals who thought that Nazism could be used as the engine with which to pull the German economy into top gear and then dismissed when it was no longer required.

There is nothing in the sense meanings of the given texts which either contains or prohibits such readings. But since I know that statements require speakers I habitually construe them to the best of my knowledge and ingenuity. To say that such modal readings are unnecessary or even illegitimate additions to the discourse is to claim at least two things: 1) the neutrality of mediation in historical writing and 2) that whatever the enveloping utterance situation may be, it has no effect on the propositional sense which we can formalize from the text. Beyond historiography as the representation of a world and the "adequacy of any story telling framework in which History might be represented,"[24] the construction of meaning in historical writing includes the projection of the world of which the speaker of the utterances is an integral biographical part. Such projection requires deictic discursive formations as well as a non-verbal situational background beyond propositional sense and so transcends the boundaries of historical meaning as evidence.

In spite of Hayden White and Dominick LaCapra, historiography still appears committed to Rancke's ideal of presenting reality *"wie es eigentlich gewesen."*[25] Yet its referents float somewhere between the technical and the literary to the extent that it employs numerical relationships and empirical objectivity on the one hand and, on the other, the intertextuality of rival histories as well as imaginative projection not unrelated to those of literary reading. As to modality, historical discourse assumes a factual speech act while at the same time minimizing the reader's exploration of the unsaid and its motivations. As in literature, and unlike technical, scientific, or formal logical writing, the propositional contents of historiography are heavily overdetermined by ideological forces and its cultural frame. Its hermeneutic, too, places historical discourse somewhere between the literary and the technical in that it is neither ludic like the former nor strictly instructional like the latter; neither is it revelatory, as is the mythic, nor strictly coded, as is the discourse of the law.

(4) Juridical Discourse

In *Measure for Measure* Shakespeare explores the situation in which the reading of legal language and its application is foisted on someone who senses that he may very well fail his duty: "Let there be some more test made of my metal Before so noble and so great a figure Be stamped upon it," pleads the deputy. Yet the Duke insists, and one is entitled to ask with Angelo, "The tempter or the tempted, who sins most?" So in spite of his self-doubt Angelo is vested with the Duke's "terror" and "love" in order to be able to "enforce or qualify the laws."

Unfortunately, Angelo is a rigid reader, incapable at first of filling with life the schemata of legal speech. He is too precise, "a man of stricture and firm abstinence," and at the same time "but man, proud man, Drest in a little brief authority" who, when tempted, quickly "bids the law curt'sy to his will" and gives his "sensual race the rein": "Let's write good angel on the devil's horn." Unmindful of the Duke's admonition, "Mortality and mercy in Vienna Live in thy tongue and heart," Angelo administers the letter of the law and falls.

It is the precision of propositional sense, from which the life of psychological needs and social appetites have been excised, which effects the corruption of the very laws the Duke intends to have restored. What is instructive in the present context is that Angelo's strict reading of the juridical propositions results in far greater disruptions of the social world than did the negligent reading of the law during the Duke's reign. Given the 'weakness of human nature' as portrayed in the play, Angelo's interpretation is bound to produce fundamental contradictions in the meting out of justice: the puritan moral fiction of stricture is reversed into its counter image of monstrous corruption. Only a process of meaning making which from the outset fills the juridical linguistic schemata with a broad view of social reality allows for, even if it cannot guarantee, a reasonable rule.[26]

The distinction between the letter and the spirit of the law marks a tension present in most forms of discourse. In juridical language it determines the very structure of meaning constitution. The sterility of sense meaning is confronted by the fertility of social and political phenomena. Does a 'proper' reading of juridical language then mean simply the more generous casting of the linguistic net or the broader application of the web of sense meanings? I do not think that this satisfactorily explains what goes on either in the legislature or in the law courts. To take an example, "the right of the people to keep and bear Arms, shall not be infringed" suggests that the kinds of situations of personal defense which the legislature of the United States of the late eighteenth century had 'in mind' are at odds with the imaginable situations of bearing arms in an advanced technological society. Yet we can only note this discrepancy if we fill the directional schemata of juridical discourse with imaginary referents. Without such acts legal language would remain a mere linguistic exercise.

The propositional content of the Constitution of the United States is reasonably clear to the extent that its various ambiguous readings could be listed. A team of linguists and philosophers of language could adequately provide that service. However, the Supreme Court in which the judicial power of the United States is vested has a far less enviable task. It must act as an arbiter as to whether the discourses of inferior courts contradict or comply with the spirit of Federal Law. This highlights an essential feature of all hierarchical schematization and of language typification in particular: the fundamental gap between the *definiendum* of social semiosis and the *definiens* of a system of formalizing abstraction.

Contrary to the operations of formal logic, where the starting basis (put simply) is a set of fully sharable axiomatic agreements from which all further operations follow, legal discourse starts with the superimposition of a linguistic mesh over the labyrinth of the social life-world.[27] As a result, there must always be a question mark over the application of the verbal schema to a particular set of social phenomena. To match the social semiotic and a specific language we require the play of reference which produces a multiply variable quasi-world. Though such acts are bound to occur within much stricter guide rails than meaning endowment in literary reading, I cannot see how without the concretization of the legal language by an imaginational variation of my world, that is, language and all non-verbal sign systems, one could negotiate Angelo's role.

Compared with historiography, juridical discourse occupies the opposite pole on a possible spectrum: it does not describe past social action (though it entails it) as much as it attempts to preview a future maze of social phenomena. In this, legal language tends to be formal and prescriptive, where historical writing aims at relative particularity and description. This is not just the case in a formal logical sense. As Michel Pêcheux remarks in a comment on Frege's notion of the generality of a law:

> ... the term 'law' can be understood in its different sense, including the *legal sense* in which someone 'falls within the provision of the law' which has a penalty ready for him: this means, I believe, that the legal is not purely and simply a 'domain of application' for logic, as is held by the theoreticians of legal formalism ... but that there is a constitutive *relationship of simulation* between legal operators and the mechanisms of conceptual deduction, and especially between legal penalty and logical consequence.
>
> (*Language, Semantics and Ideology*, 71f.)

Pêcheux draws our attention here to a degree of indeterminacy and "non-saturation" which we tend to overlook when we think of juridical discourse. The very terms "*judgment, proof, indices, evidence*," says Pêcheux, are affected by this "promiscuity."[28] But beyond logical extension and like meaning making in historiography, both the forward design of law making and the application of existing laws require acts of fantasying. The success of a legal code rests partly on how ingeniously it allows for the projection of possible social situations, actual occurrences, and their counterfactual alternatives. At the same time, the employment of material semiosis in the *Lokaltermin*, the on-the-spot investigation of criminal jurisdiction, demonstrates the necessity of the concretization of juridical linguistic schemata beyond the propositional sense of the law.

A similar point is made by Brendan Cassidy in "Whose Law, Which Discourse?" when he rebuts the common assumption of an "unproblematic language structure" which regards the codified rules of law "as a matter of recognition and enforcement." This, he writes,

> belies the intrinsically imprecise nature of language and the capacity of social agents to 'construe' it in different ways. Contrary to the popular view ... it is not possible to 'know' the law in a definitive way, because the 'law' can only be known after its enunciation in specific instances as a set of effects on the participants. If predictive certainty was possible, then one of the main justificatory claims for the existence of a specially trained legal apparatus (lawyers, judges

and other adjudicative personnel) would become rather hollow. The occupational claim as it stands amounts to an argument for the employment of special skills in determining connections between general rules and particular events.[29]

However, "debates in modern jurisprudence have stopped far short of the questions opened up by contemporary critical theory." Far from acknowledging the imprecise nature of its linguistic expressions, the juridical text, writes Christopher Norris in *The Contest of Faculties*, is characterized by the "need to preserve the authority of law as a discourse immune to any form of antinomian critique." And yet it is a fairly obvious observation to make that "it is not hard to find parallels between case law and the business of interpreting literary texts."[30]

In literature as in jurisprudence we require, for example, both actual and imaginary reference in order to link the word with our grasp of the world. This is achieved by semiotic processes beyond the linguistic and certainly beyond the constraints of the traditional authority of the Law. From the perspective of a directional theory of meaning one could say that in the application of law linguistic schemata are filled with non-verbal significations according to the historically shifting rules of a regulatory practice of surveillance.

(5) The Discourse of Everyday Life

When I look at the 'discourse of the everyday world' which facilitates social interaction, I may be deluded into thinking that I am constructing meaning in a factual, technical, or perhaps even formal sense. To be sure, such language use does occur, yet it is not characteristic of daily discourse in general. Although pragmatic speech does not encourage me, as does its literary counterpart, to read as richly and experimentally as possible, my habitual use of the language of the life-world has taught me to be prepared nevertheless for the realization of full cultural referentiality and modality. Though I am normally satisfied with shortcuts to propositional meaning, I always also hold a fuller set of interpretive recipes in readiness should things go wrong in communication and a more delicate negotiation of meaning be required, or when I sense that in a specific exchange the politics of language override its referential task.

The degree with which I endow natural discourse with meaning appears structurally determined by my judgment as to its position in my "system of relevances."[31] In this sense, a whimperative such as, "Would you please pass me the salt, darling?" can be actualized in its minimal sense as an imperative or understood with its full interpersonal and social implications of a marriage on the rocks. This requires our acquaintance with what Strawson regards as part of the context of utterance, the personal histories of the participants in the utterance situation.[32] Another aspect which relates much of everyday speech to literary reading rather than to technical speech is the relative indeterminacy of lexemes and the resulting propositional opacity discussed earlier. To disregard this observation leads to the assumption that the so-called definitions of ordinary language behave very much like the sense definitions of formal discourse. I have argued against this view in detail in chapter 5. Suffice it to say at this point that a good many studies of language take the identity of these two kinds of definitions as established or as close enough an approximation to the facts. But beyond this fundamental opacity, I would also wish to say that without a comprehensive grasp of cultural referentiality and modality, the manner in which a culture speaks its language against its own historical, semiotic background, meaning making in the life-world would be severely handicapped. In support of this claim consider the following simple examples.

(1) to drink beer
     to drink water
     to drink wine
     to drink liquor

(2) the baby drinks
     the giraffe drinks

(3) I do not drink.

(4) *Essen und Trinken hält Leib
     und Seele zusammen.*

(5) *Bevono nostri patri, proponziponziponz
     Bevono nostri matre, proponziponziponz*

"Imbibe" or "swallow a liquid" are very loose guidelines for an understanding of the verb "drink" in context, and it is only in context or specific discursive formations that I can speak of the meaning of a word. The sense of "drink" is substantially modified by its grammatical object (1) as well as by its different grammatical subjects (2). And it is arguable that a semiotic realization of the typical manner in which a giraffe drinks is a more economic way of meaning making than a verbal network which I draw upon at the moment of utterance. For if I know what a drinking giraffe looks like, I understand the expression "in a flash."

In the more complex examples (4) and (5), propositional sense could not be realized without the simultaneous construal of a social semiotic. "I do not drink" in the sense of "I do not drink alcoholic beverages" is tied to the right-eousness of a puritanical tradition, while *"Essen und Trinken hält Leib und Seele zusammen"* supplies a metaphysical rationalization of good living. The receivers of this message will transcend its propositional sense to the extent to which they are acquainted with the Catholic Church's role in the production of wine and beer, or perhaps the Bavarian beer purity law of 1516. Likewise, the semantic-semiotic content of the verb *"bevere"* in example (5) is modalized by virtue of my familiarity with the place value of drink in Italian culture. On this view, we arrive at the observation that we are always dealing with differing degrees of meaning fulfillment against a non-verbal background and a set of intersubjective-ideological constraints. Moreover, we must also draw the conclusion from this that there is no such thing as identical meaning exchange between speakers of different social classes, cultures, or even generations in this sort of discourse.

Perhaps the transfer of meaning is less problematic in the pragmatic discourse of daily business which one may suspect is regulated largely by truth-by-correspondence rules. Consider the following transcript.

Discourse between a customer (A), a sales lady (B), and a sales manager (C)

A: These four sleeping bags, please.
B: Certainly. How do you ... ?
A: Cash, by check.
B: (Types the relevant numbers into the register)
    One hundred seven dollars and forty cents, please.
A: (Fills in the check) Here we are ...
B: Any identification?
A: Certainly, my Yale ID card ...
B: Thank you. Any other identification?
A: Will my passport do?
B: Hmm, thank you (studies the passport). Any other document with a picture? A driver's license?
A: Yes, wait a minute, here, how about this, my international driver's license.
B: Well, I don't know. Don't you have a Connecticut licence?
A: No, I'm sorry. I'm staying only for a short while. I am from Australia, on study leave.
B: I'll have to ring our head office in New York.
    Perhaps they ...
    (Calls the Main Office in New York)
    No, I'm sorry, they won't accept this.
A: What do you want, a blood test?
B: I am sorry, but that's what they're saying.
    Perhaps I should get our sales manager.
    (Returns with the sales manager)
C: Can I help you?
A: I sincerely hope so!
C: Well, you must understand. There are a lot of bad checks.
A: There must be, judging by ...
C: What positive ID have you got?
A: Well, now you have my passport, driver's license, Yale ID card. Here is also a bank statement from the bank down the road, a library card, my local address, an Australian bank card, letters addressed to me ...
C: Still, we can't be too sure.
A: I'd be happy to leave my fingerprints ...
C: No, no. You don't understand. How do I know that this is you (points at one of the documents) and that this check is OK?

A: I don't think you could ever be absolutely sure, could you? Any old reliable
   customer could give you a bad check and leave the state.
C: (Nods) I don't know.
A: I suppose it comes down to which is stronger, your caution or your desire
   to sell.
C: OK, then.
A: Thank you.
B: We do have to be careful, you know.

How is meaning construed in this exchange? What goes wrong and how is
agreement reached in the end? The entire, lengthy discourse would not have
taken place had A been able to produce a standard Connecticut driver's license.
In its absence, the relationship between the sense of A's statements (sense a),
the sense of the text of his documents (sense b), the sense of the wording of
A's check (sense c) and the material referent A itself are not linked by B and
then C in the normal manner; to them the relationship between sense and
referent is problematic. Only when C feels it is worth taking the risk that senses
1 and 3 have one and the same referent, namely A, does he authorize the sale.
Let us assume then for the moment that it was the 'truth' and its verification
which were at stake here.

To use one of Gottlob Frege's examples, C is in a position not unlike that of
a person who has seen both evening and morning star but requires an authority
to guarantee that their common referent is the planet Venus. For, as Frege points
out in his paper "On Sense and Reference" (*Über Sinn und Bedeutung*, 1892),
the reference of "evening star" would be the same as that of "morning star,"
but not the sense."[33] Without the authority of a scientific community or, in A's
case, the road traffic authority of the state of Connecticut, even in its mediated
form of A producing a driver's license, the connection between sense and referent cannot be made, at least not without a leap of faith. Frege goes on to
argue his case somewhat metaphysically by asserting that "it is the striving for
truth that drives us always to advance from sense to reference" and concludes
that "we are therefore driven into accepting the *truth value* of a sentence as
constituting its *reference*." Yet the question of truth would not have arisen had
A been able to participate smoothly in the socially accepted discourse game.
The sales manager's responsibility would then have shifted to a higher form of
authority, such as the police, should it turn out that A had not been the correct
referent after all.

According to the verification principle as proposed by the logical positivism
of the Vienna Circle, "no statement is meaningful unless it can be verified by
observation."[34] If this was so, then the present example and with it a considerable number of utterances of workaday speech would be meaningless. Even
for the more exact utterances of natural science the verification principle did
not remain a convincing test for long. Since Karl Popper pointed out that corroboration and falsification rather than verification are applicable to the judgment of scientific statements, the verification thesis has begun to lose its appeal.

In one of its weakened forms, the thesis appears as the verifiability principle in Ayer's *Language, Truth and Logic*. According to Ayer, "a sentence is factually significant to a given person if, and only if, he knows how to verify the proposition which it purports to express."[35] Applied to our example, this would mean that to C the various bits of language presented by A, i.e., senses 1 to 3, are not factually signified since they do not allow him to know how to verify the propositions they entail. First, it may never be really possible to accomplish such verification and second, in the end C does accept A's statement as factually significant, although not on the grounds suggested by Ayer's theory.

If the verification principle is qualified further, we arrive at what has become known as the truth-conditional theory. According to this, truth conditions are "a precisely specifiable account of the conditions which determine the truth-value of the propositions conveyed by the sentences when they are used to make statements."[36] But in the example in question, it is not that C does not understand the account of conditions provided by A's documentation. Rather, C rightly suspects that such an account could be taken to considerable lengths without yielding the kind of assurance C is looking for. As does the majority of actors in the social life-world C wants a meaning shortcut: a reasonable assurance that the transaction can be regarded as regular or, on the other hand, sufficient doubt to be able to cancel the sale. As so many situations in the discourse of everyday life, the example before us typically lacks the all-or-nothing conditions required by verification theory. C must construct meaning by other means, and so C, from the full scale of semiotic cues furnished by A and his family nearby, intuits a much more fuzzy set of meanings than is given by the statements at hand; C assures himself in the end that he can accept responsibility for the sale in good faith after all by concretizing the linguistic schemata with a range of socio-psychological, non-verbal typifications which he draws from the utterance situation as a whole. Yet we merely assumed that truth played such an important role in this transaction. What has been demonstrated instead is that such mainstays of traditional language philosophy as definition, satisfaction, predication and truth and falsity are not at the center of much of everyday discourse. What is at stake in this sort of exchange is nothing but *legitimation*. All the saleswoman and her manager wished to be assured of was that a specific form of legitimation guaranteed by the Connecticut driver's license and *prescribed* by their Main Office was fulfilled. Thus, the issue of truth is shifted from ordinary social discourse to the apparatus of juridical control. Similar displacements, assuming that 'truth' was ever at the center, occur when the politics of language competes with practical goals as in persuasion, insinuation, manipulation, and a multiplicity of other not primarily referential forms of discourse.

(6) Technical Discourse

Hold container upright, 6 to 8 inches from skin or clothing, and spray with a slow sweeping motion. Saturation is unnecessary. For maximum

protection: spread evenly with hand to moisten all exposed skin. Reapply
as needed.

Such discursive operations form a large portion of our daily routine. Instead
of regarding the technical as an autonomous realm, I suggest that it too requires
discursivity since here too exists a negotiatory relationship between the signifier
and user, even though this relationship is drastically curtailed in comparison
with our performance of the literary. Our habitual response to technical language dictates the construction of straightforward propositions. The references
of "holding," "containers," "skin," etc. are minimally realized as are whatever
"preconstructions" are needed for basic grasp. This suggests that a modicum of
quasi-referential projection occurs when we imagine how to follow technical
instructions.

A useful set of distinctions is drawn by Jürgen Habermas in his early paper
"Science and Technology as Ideology" where he juxtaposes negotiatory social
behavior or "symbolic interaction" to the technical realm or "purposive-rational
action." The two are distinguished by the way they relate to (a) action-orienting
rules, (b) level of definition, (c) kind of definition, (d) manner of acquisition,
(e) function of action type, (f) sanctions against violation of rules, and (g) what
Habermas uneasily calls " 'rationalization' " or a kind of embedded goal. Accordingly, "symbolic interaction" is characterized by social norms, intersubjectively shared ordinary language, reciprocal expectations about behavior, role
internalization, conformity to norms, social penalties, and its 'deep structure
reason' aiming at the "extension of communication free of domination" and
hence its potential for "emancipation."

By contrast, systems of purposive-rational action are recognizable by technical
rules, context-free language, conditional predictions and imperatives, skills,
problem solving, technical breakdown, and the extension of power of technical
control. In instrumental or technical language, as in strategic discourse, the
"growth of productive forces" and hence the necessity of increasing control are
central. It is this kind of rationality which is in irreconcilable opposition to the
emancipatory potential of the discourse of the public sphere.[37]

In Habermas's later work this opposition is not abandoned but incorporated
in a more sophisticated schema of validity claims. Suffice it to say here that as
far as technical discourse is concerned, propositional content, modality, satisfaction, and reference all reflect the reductions Habermas notes in his table. What
his critique leaves untouched are certain semiotic extensions which, however
purposefully directed, are nevertheless habitual in our performance of the technical. Specifically, Habermas's "context-free language" cannot mean that technical discourse functions like formal logic: it is the perspectival utilization of
formalized sign systems and as such requires the semiosis of technology as its
backdrop. Whether this directional argument can be shown to establish semiotic
extensions as necessary conditions I will not attempt to resolve here, for as I
wish to remind the reader, my interest is not in the logical establishment of

necessary and sufficient conditions but of what we typically *do* when we use any specific discourse: *this is what it is.*

Another, yet very different, perspective is provided by Heidegger who speaks of the "merely technical." This phrasing should not be understood as Heidegger's failure to grasp the power which attaches to technology. Quite the contrary. Heidegger in fact shows how technology, *das Gestell*, or the scaffolding or apparatus, is a late flowering of Greek philosophizing.[38] In realizing technology Western culture has had to pay the heavy price of largely abandoning its philosophical hermeneutic and so of emptying its culture of thought. To reduce culture to the technical is to renounce our potential for interpretation and forward vision which needs to be steeped in the past. Our technological preferences have deprived the species of its hermeneutic task. And yet, for Heidegger technology too "is a way of revealing;" what is revealed is "Enframing." But once our discourse is technical through and through, language can fulfill only a small portion of human speech as the discourse par excellence of "understanding," as an "as-structure." By this he means that we are nothing if not beings who interpret by cognizing the world as something else. This something can be thoughtful and thus rich, or lacking in thought and so at best technical. In the first instance we understand "in terms of the *totality* of involvements," in the second form the totality "recedes" into understanding. At the heart of technical discourse we find the syntax of "assertion" which Heidegger regards as a "derivative mode of understanding." Discourse, then, occurs between the two poles of an "existential-hermeneutical 'as'" and the "apophantic 'as' of assertion." What Heidegger has to say of mathematics also applies to technical speech: "Mathematics is not more rigorous than historiology, but only narrower, because the existential foundations relevant for it lie within a narrower range."[39]

If all understanding is to face the world in terms of 'as' rather than in itself, then all representational systems and in particular language, its most elaborate form, make us grasp whatever we attend to *as* something else. Dictionaries give a typographical picture of this opposition which, pursued to its logical conclusion, leads us inexorably to Derrida's endless chain of signifiers. In technical discourse this chain is linked not by the purpose of representing the world as hermeneutically meaningful but only by its common goal of univocal characterization and hence commodificatory reproduction. Here the *as*-dynamic of understanding is reduced to minimal predication: identification.[40]

Perhaps we should press Heidegger's and Habermas's readings a little further and ask: what kind of semiosis are we dealing with that answers to identity and reproductivity, or in Derrida's terms, iterability? Technology could be regarded as a form of semiosis in which *techne* is ruled entirely by *logos*. To put it in this way may strike the reader as a sleight of hand. What I want to say is that to the degree that materiality is transformed by formal logical principles, such as mathematics or chemical signification, it can be regarded as technological. While thus a hammered copper bowl is minimally technological, a synthetic vase is so entirely: a product achieved by transforming natural materiality via the 'funnel' of formal logical semiosis into an unnatural materiality, a technological product.

In this the formal semiosis to which nature is subjected is crucial, for it allows the possibility of iterability and so, at least theoretically, endless reproduction. One could say then that in technology formally empty semiosis, i.e., chemical or mathematical signification, has handed on its feature of iterability to the material world. Across the divide of formal semiotic transformation two materialities confront one another: nature and its *Doppelgänger*, technology.

We need to ask, however, whether this shrinkage to "identity" implies a total stripping of cultural and ideological features. Althusser and Pêcheux, who quotes him on the issue, argues that we must not "ignore the action of the ideological effects in all discourses—including even scientific discourses."[41] The problem with this position is its generality; we do not know how ideology shows itself in different discourses. I would like to show that the difference between discourses can neither be resolved by saying that they are ideologically marked nor by asserting the opposite. We need to show *how* different discourses display their relationship to ideology. I suggest that in technical discourse ideological effects appear in two ways: massively at the level of its socio-historical frame: what *kind* of technology we are dealing with; much more subtly at the propositional level. For here we need to ask what kind of propositions are typically generated and how are they affected ideologically. While in literary or historical discursive formations it is easy to show how the whole propositional apparatus and its extension are ideologically saturated, in technical discourse ideology is reduced to 'domination.' In this assessment I again take the advice of Habermas who criticizes Herbert Marcuse's differentiation between exploitative dominating and non-exploitative, non-dominating technology. If it works, Habermas persuades us, technology dominates its parts and through them also society. Only non-technical, political-critical structures are capable of regulating technical discourse. It is strange that even on this one point there should be a glimmer of agreement between Heidegger and Habermas.[42] Specific ideological effects cannot be shown to affect the internal features of technical discourse; it transcends societies and cultures without having its propositional content altered.

(7) Scientific Discourse

Scientific discourse is here anonymized from technical and ordinary language, in the company of which it normally appears. With this proviso, scientific language, such as that used in physics or chemistry, does not describe the world directly as an "unambiguous one-for-one mapping of reality," but in terms of a particular, agreed upon perspective.[43] The precision of all scientific viewing is achieved at the expense of a full, though from a scientific viewpoint imprecise, grasp of the world. In reading scientific statements conventionally, I construct propositional sense against the double background of a formal system of definitions proper and the expectational horizon of corroboration or falsification. With reference and modality severely curtailed, the transformations of the textual surface which I typically perform are shrunk to a portion of the first transformation of literary reading, its propositional side and a trace of modality. For both the propositional and modal remnants are to be covered by minimal identification and quantification.

These constraints characterize what is known as *scientific method*: description of problem and object of inquiry, hypothesis and inductive generalization, description of experiment, statistical analysis of variance, statements about corroboration of hypothesis, falsification and reformulation of hypothesis, prediction of comparable cases, description of scientific consensus or disagreement, and nomological formulations or laws.

Not that this method has remained unquestioned. Karl Popper has emphasized that the provisional nature of hypothesis does not end with corroboration and that even "the laws we find are always hypotheses." And while we should not stop to discover "strict laws—prohibitions—that can founder upon reality," we should be wary of "issuing prohibitions that draw limits to the possibilities of research."[44]

A similarly fervent defender of the freedom of scientific research but radically more skeptical than Popper as to the relationship between reason and science is Paul Feyerabend. Both in *Against Method* and the more recent *Science in a Free Society* Feyerabend questions the conviction that reason should be the center of scientific advance. "Reason," he writes, "at least in the form in which it is defended by logicians, philosophers of science and some scientists does not fit science and could not have contributed to its growth." Far from being a final crystallization of logical insights, what we call scientific method is anything but universal. Where there are standards, says Feyerabend, they are a result of the "research process itself" rather than the accomplishment of an abstract rationality. "The idea of a universal and stable *method* that is an unchanging measure of adequacy and even the idea of a universal and stable *rationality* is as unrealistic as the idea of a universal and stable measuring instrument. . . ."[45]

Apart from this sort of critique which reminds us of the non-logical ingredients in science, scientific discourse tends to obey the rules of referential and modal reduction. Where scientists feel that their work contravenes some ethical or other commitment they can remodalize the scientific discourse by linking it back to its frame: funding source, public and political interests, economic value, or metaphysical assumptions. In this way, full referentiality and cultural modality are reintroduced and political judgments can be made which cannot be handled by the reduced discursive formations of scientific speech.

In his persuasive account of *The Postmodern Condition: A Report on Knowledge*, Jean-François Lyotard suggests that science, in order to legitimate its claims on national funds, resorts to a discourse outside its own domain: "The state spends large amounts of money to enable science to pass itself off as an epic" and, a little later, "Scientific knowledge cannot know and make known that it is the true knowledge without resorting to the other kind of knowledge, which from its point of view is no knowledge at all," i.e., the large-scale narrative which constitutes the discourse of the socio-political life-world.[46]

Lyotard's claim that narrative is alien to science rests on an oppositional set of assumptions which cannot be taken for granted. I would favor quite a different view and suggest that science is a late discursive formation which has repressed its "epic" aspects in favor of analyticity, such as full reference to the phenomenal world and the deictic features of speech instantiation. The resulting analyticity of its discourse (mathematics, chemical formulae) is only one side of science, the other being the necessity of the reapplication of its discourse to the phenomenal world. This, however, can never be fully achieved without recourse to its own buried narrative, so that science must allow the return of a repressed discursive formation whenever it engages in the larger socio-political sphere.

(8) Formal Logic

On the bottom rungs of our ladder meaning is shrunk to minimal sense. Here we find the discourse of logic and mathematics, as well as that of the digital, a formalized language which I shall address separately. In reading its paroles conventionally I must impose a further set of reductions on my acts of meaning making. Let us say for the moment that in logico-mathematical language I intend actual definitions, complete in themselves and independent of materiality on the one hand and concretization on the other. This state of affairs changes radically when formal discourse is embedded in a literary text, as for instance the moves of a chess game in Beckett's *Murphy*. Since logico-mathematical concepts can naively be said to be fully defined, they can by the same naive assumption be shared in their entirety by a community of speakers. It is this identity of acts of sense making which can 'properly' be called objective. Here my acts of meaning conferment could be said to collapse into the proposition itself. Since no transformations take place, the utterers of formal logic cannot modally affect its propositional contents. I cannot, for example, as I can in referentially saturated speech, reverse the sense of a logical proposition by an ironic speech act, such as an ironic intonation. From this perspective otherwise separable meanings coincide: author meaning, speaker meaning, sentence meaning, and utterance meaning are all subsumed under one and the same proposition. This is possible, because in purely formal discourse there is no referring act which points outside the system, nor is there any deictic act which points back to a speaker: logico-mathematical discourse can be described as a language in which referring and modal acts are classes without members. The inscriptions of formal logic, unlike those of everyday speech and literary language, would seem then not to act as directional schemata to be filled by an intersubjectively linked group of speakers: formal inscriptions are agreed upon to constitute a "pure" realm of meaning. This, at least, is how logicians and mathematicians viewed the matter until Gödel's critique of *Principia Mathematica* and other formal systems in 1931. Husserl, for example has this to say about logico-mathematical discourse:

> All theoretical science consists, in its objective content, of one homogeneous stuff: it is an ideal fabric of meanings. We can go even further and say that the whole, indefinitely complex web of meanings that we call the theoretical unity of science, falls under the category that covers all its elements: it is itself a unity of meaning.[47]

Husserl's notion of the science of logic is still the basis on which contemporary logicians build impressive schemata too complex and difficult for me even to mention here. At a simple level, they have defined such formal relations as 'but,' 'although,' 'since,' ' or,' and 'if . . . then,' in a manner that their 'meaning' can be "explained entirely in terms of combinations of truth and falsity ('truth values') of the assertions that it connects or applies to." The relationships between different truth values can be expressed in terms of truth functions, the most economical representation of which is the construction of 'truth tables.' One could describe the semiotic of truth tables as partly 'linguistic' (as far as we need to read the language of symbolic logic) and partly non-verbal (as far as it uses the convention of spatial order).

As the authors of *The Fundamentals of Logic* describe it, "the truth table simply lists the possible combinations of truth and falsity for propositions, and for each possible combination records whether the truth function would be true or false." There are two possibilities for each proposition *P*. Three propositions, say *P*, *Q*, and *R*, produce two to the power of three combinations and so on.

P	*Q*	*PQ*
T	*T*	*T*
T	*F*	*F*
F	*T*	*F*
F	*F*	*F*

The two left columns give the possible truth values for *P* and *Q* separately. The right column lists the solutions for *PQ*. Descending from the first line, *PQ* is shown to be true if *P* and *Q* are both true. But *PQ* is false if *either Q* is false while *P* is true *or P* is false while *Q* is true *or*, as in line four, both *P* and *Q* are false. We can imagine infinitely more complex examples by increasing the number of propositions to be related. However, no matter to what degree of complexity formal logical relations can be constructed, we should not be taken in by the kind of belief expressed by Kupperman and MacGrade: "The reader should see all this as precisely defining the meaning of *PQ*."[48]

For the absence of referentiality and deictic designation of its utterance situation does not mean that formal logic could claim full definitional certitude or an absolute *neutrality*. In order to perform its operations at all, I have to enter into certain agreements of procedure; my reading rests on the acceptance of a particular kind of frame.

> ... Whilst we have faithfully observed the rules of the calculus, so that *at that level* we have eliminated all the assumptions there is an extra hidden assumption, smuggled into the proof at the metalevel: namely the assumption that the calculus itself with its variables, its operators and its rules, is a valid instrument of cognitive inquiry. And it is the same with an axiomatic system; we have to assume the axioms are self-evident—we cannot prove them *within* the system. Rationality, in order to function at all, has to assume the rationality of its own procedures.[49]

Except for a brief word of caution now and then I have treated formal logical relations as exempt from the kind of critique I am advancing by way of a directional theory of meaning. The reason for this is that the various opacities I have described, propositional and modal opacity in natural language and semiotic opacity as a vagueness attaching to the relationship between verbal and non-verbal sign systems, are different in kind if compared with the principle of *undecidability* which can be used to reject the naive belief in the univocality of logical systems.

This does not mean that the critique of formal systems proposed by Gödel, Skolem, and others does not also apply to natural languages. Indeed, it does to the degree to which natural languages contain logical relations, which means that undecidability is an element of vagueness in addition to the principles of opacity outlined. Though one could make a case for seeing what I have called propositional opacity as an extension of Gödel's theorem. Gödel's famous paper *"Über formal unentscheidbare Sätze der Principia Mathematica und verwandter Systeme I"* (1931) demonstrated beyond any doubt that in any logical system, including those of elementary arithmetic, we come across propositions which can be neither proved nor disproved within that system. With reference to Russell and Whitehead and the set theory of Zermelo-Fränkel-von Neumann, Gödel writes:

> These two systems are so extensive that all methods of proof used in mathematics today have been formalized in them, i.e., reduced to a few axioms and rules of inference. It may therefore be surmised that these axioms and rules of inference are also sufficient to decide *all* mathematical questions which can in any way at all be expressed formally in the systems concerned. It is shown below that this is not the case, and that in both the systems mentioned there are in fact relatively simple problems in the theory of ordinary numbers which cannot be decided from the axioms. This situation is not due in some way to the special nature of the systems set up, but holds for a very extensive class of formal systems.[50]

Derrida refers to Gödel's undecidability principle to bolster his own attack on the univocality of the concept. And indeed, the infinite regress of further and further metapropositions on top of metapropositions governing logical systems does lend support to Derrida's critique in a fundamental way.[51] What needs to be asked again, however, is how communication is possible in any sign system. The answer given before still holds. For practical purposes the Leibnizian chain of sufficient reason to back up our significations is pragmatically employed to the degree to which a semiotic community deems it necessary. What the present discussion adds to this is that if full identity and synonymy are ultimately not even securable in formal systems, how much less should they be taken for granted in natural language. This requires a rethinking certainly of such notions as *literal* meaning in social discourse, a stipulation wholly untenable on many grounds, not the least of which is the demolition of absolute certitude in formal systems.

(9) The Digital

This sort of critique need not shake our faith in the practical applicability of logic but only in its assumed absolute certitude. Logic has yielded its most powerful practical results yet in digital discourse. To call digital information processing a discourse at first looks like a *tour de force*. There are two reasons for this. One, the digital cannot encode the phenomenal world as such but requires precodification by other sign systems; that is, it is a secondary language. Two, the digital cannot be read as are other codes; it remains hidden as the rationale which determines the electronic opening and shutting of logic gates. There is only a small step from the truth tables of logic to the electronic gates of computing. The truth-falsity relations of, for example, 'and,' 'or,' negation, 'not-and,' and 'nor,' reappear as And-gates, Or-gates, Non-gates, Nand-gates, and Nor-gates. The Nand-function can be illustrated in this way.

$I1$	$I2$	O
0	0	1
0	1	1
1	0	1
1	1	0

This simply says that current will not flow ($=0$) through exit O only if all entry variables ($I1$ and $I2$) are on charge ($=1$). All other positions result in current at O. Even in its most complex arrangements this toggle-logic does not appear to be discursive in the sense of ordinary language.

However, there are also some good reasons why we should include the digital as the final rung on our ladder. First, digital signs can be made visible and when they are, they display syntagmatic and paradigmatic features which align them with other language systems; second, the digital is capable of addressing anything and everything available in other sign systems and so occupies an important position in general semiosis; and third, in terms of the various reductions observed in our survey from literary to formal logical operations, the digital suggests yet another systematic curtailment of discourse.

If we design a little program which makes our PC 'self-reflexive' and ask it to print out the first line of a novel in English, hexadecimal and binary code we receive something like this:[52]

I   n   my   y o u n g e r   a n d   m o r e
49 6E 20 6D 79 20 79 6F 75 6E 67 65 72 20 61 6E 64 20 6D 6F 72 65 20

v u l n e r a b l e   y e a r s . . .
76 75 6C 6E 65 72 61 62 6C 65 20 79 65 61 72 73 2E 2E 2E   (hexadecimal)

y	e	a	r	s	
84218421	84218421	84218421	84218421	84218421	(8-bit bytes)
01111001	01100101	01100001	01110010	01110011	(digital)
79	65	61	72	73	(hexadecimal)

We note that both the hexadecimal and binary code use up more space than natural languages. Yet the visual representation should not give the impression of binary inefficiency. What the digital adds in length is far outweighed by the voracity of its "multiplex time" which sucks the coded world through its funnel, as it were, at speeds beyond human comprehension. Let us look at its 'discursive' operations from a number of angles.

Viewed syntagmatically, a number of thresholds have to be crossed before phenomena can be digitized and dedigitized: they are sorted into semiotic units by an appropriate system of Peripherals (camera, microphone, seismograph, printer) and proceed to input ports; if analog they pass through an ADC (analogue-digital converter), if not, as in the case of word processing, they are transformed into numerical units; from the input ports signals are sent to the CPU (central processing unit) which interacts with a Program Memory (ROM); the digitized signals are stored in a Data Memory (RAM) from where they are retrieved and processed once more by the CPU before they are sent via the DAC through output ports to another set of Peripherals (printer, monitor, oscillograph). During this process incoming signals in the form of electronic impulses pass through a number of states. For example, they are analyzed by way of the regular pattern of a Central Clock or tact generator; ramp generators and a binary counter identify them digitally; at the same time ports, CPU, ROM, and RAM employ gates or routine logic chips (AND, NAND, OR, NOR), flip-flop gates (NAND flip-flop, NOR flip-flop, etc.), or 'gate arrays' (combination chips up to 'megachips' or 1 million chip combinations), whereby all gates (chips) are technical applications of logical truth tables.

From a paradigmatic or polyphonic perspective the digital can be described in terms of band width, i.e., in numbers of frequencies available at any given time and also as a simultaneous flow of digits in parallel processing. In both cases, the syntagmatic and paradigmatic view, speed is a function of directness of wiring (now printed microcircuitry), but more importantly a function of the frequency of the tact generator (megahertz). The speeds now achievable are measured in gigaFLOPs (billions of float-point operations per second), the aim being to reach teraFLOPS (trillions of operations/sec) in the foreseeable future by a combination of linear supercomputers and parallel processors. What is crucial in all this is that at the level of phenomena we are dealing with parallel, slow, simultaneous systems, whereas at the level of the digital the complex flow of the phenomenal world has been transformed into what is referred to as time multiplex, which is strictly linear and extremely fast, a kind of narrow channel into which the phenomenal world is directed as into a funnel. It is the speed of the time multiplex phase which makes linearity appear as simultaneity. All digitized simultaneous phenomena, such as music, only seem to happen simultaneously, but since each frequency is addressed separately 'bit by bit,' this false simultaneity is in reality nothing more nor less than a linear high speed bit stream.

Apart from its technical function, the computer presents itself also as a semiotic body with organs metaphorically named from the outside to the inside, from peripherals to a series of specialized parts, gateways, memories, and orifices. In this way, the computer engineer manages to maintain a link with the human body already denied by the digital. As to the discursive operations of the digital in relation to those of its fully deictic and referential counterparts, a few observations can now be made. (I shall leave aside a comparison of the digital with its cognitive relations).

(1) As a discourse, the digital cannot process phenomena directly but depends on prior semiotization by a nondigital technology; (2) the digital transforms qualitative identities (e.g., the complexities of deixis and referentiality of a speech situation) into a series of quantitative identities or a series of numerical names; (3) thus, the digital flattens complex simultaneities into seriality, so that the length of the syntagm or the number of frequencies make up for complexity; (4) speed (FLOPS) makes up for the disadvantage of linear spread or length of the bit stream; (5) there is no theoretical limit to the dehierarchization of the phenomenal, that is, whenever its semiotization appears as a hierarchy; (6) the digital is readable as such but only through retranslation; (7) the digital does not itself offer any hierarchization of knowledge, but makes its digits available through its concomitant technology (RAM, ROM, DAC, Ports) to those with an interest in hierarchization and access-power.[53]

As to Pêcheux's insistence on the all-pervasive ideological effects inside all discourses, here too we need to be specific. The bits and bytes of binary language are unaffected by cultural and ideological forces except that what they codify is already always ideologized. On the other hand, there is an important feedback relationship not at the level of propositional contents but at the level of syntax. By this I mean that the style of the digital operation itself is affecting social practice and thus contributes significantly to a shift in late twentieth-century textuality. As I have argued elsewhere, in this sense the digital furnishes a deep structure to match the new surfaces of our culture. In summary this deep structure consists of: seriality; replaceability; speed; indistinction; indifference; forgetting; dissolution of subject; availability; shelvability; masking of mediation; repeatability; iterability; either/or syntax; chain reaction of the textual; data flow; fusion of the actual and the fictive; fragmentation; dehistorization; random access; dissolution of reference; rapid creation and satisfaction of desire; packaging and speed of delivery; or exchangeability of images. From a technical and commercial perspective these are enormous advantages if compared with the cumbersome procedures of other information systems. Ideologically viewed, these very same features undermine critical practice and lend structural support to depoliticization and commodification.

Some readers may reject our ladder of discourses because it aligns traditionally separate sign systems. I have tried to show that their differences cannot conceal their common ancestry in saturated social signification. Moreover, as Wittgenstein notes, they are also linked by the relentlessness of pedagogy. "We learn with the same inexorability that this is a chair as that $2 \times 2 = 4$."[54] Yet the stipulation of homogeneous meaning for all forms of language, as we find it in the majority of studies in semantics, must remain a logician's dream. What emerges by contrast from an overview of a number of distinct discourses is that the acts of meaning conferment which I employ in each case vary sharply. This is not to say that by formally reducing these acts I cannot arrive at a lowest common denominator; I can indeed empty all meaning making to the level of minimal sense. And yet, by generating a unitary construct of meaning which can be rediscovered in all discourses we have not gained as much as we may have expected. For we are still confronted by two options and an irreducible difference.

We either define meaning as minimal sense and are left with the task of describing which other acts must be performed in order to be able to account for meaning remnants in the richer discourses, or we take as our point of departure a comprehensive description of meaning conferment as it occurs in literary reading and then define all other operations as reductions on a ladder of increasing formalization. The second procedure, the one chosen in this chapter, proves wrong the assumption that only literary readings and social discourse are "culturally freighted phenomena."[55] What has been shown instead is that all discourses are culture laden, except that some display their freight while others are designed to conceal it. A directional theory of meaning can provide an appropriate description of such saturated as well as reduced significations.

IX

HYPOCRISIS OR READING AS FEIGNING

For last year's words belong to last year's language, And next year's words await another voice.

T. S. Eliot, "Little Gidding"

—Hypocrite lecteur,—mon semblable, Mon frere!

Baudelaire, "Au Lecteur," *Les fleurs du mal*

Reading, the construction of meanings from texts, is always a duplicitous affair in a far more general sense than the critical focus on *ennui* in Baudelaire's poem suggests. Reading is the pretense of being the writer's "*semblable*" and brother; but there is no identity, only a family resemblance. In this, "Au Lecteur" points beyond its immediate historical situation: the public uproar and the prosecution of the *Fleurs du mal* in the name of bourgeois morality; the refusal of reception on the part of the majority of contemporary readers; and its first concretization as a trailblazing work of decadence by the approving literary avant-garde. For what the speaker in "Au Lecteur" insinuates for the purposes of *Les fleurs du mal* is observable as a general relationship in all acts of reading.[1]

In order to constitute meaning from written expressions the reader must in some way fill the subject position vacated by its writer, who is also its original speaker, as well as other previous speakers. Filling vacant subject positions means that any specific historical reader must perform a series of acts of self-displacement and an imaginative transformation into an alter utterer. At the same time he or she needs to insert the imagined utterance event into his or her own ongoing discursive operations. The actual or imagined intonation and prosodic contour which is thus imposed on a linguistic expression alters its seemingly secure propositional content by setting it against a series of complex modal operations.

If we strictly believe that discourse speaks the speaker, or that word and sentence meanings are stable, or that language games are sets of rules which

165

absorb their users, if in short we wish to deny both modal and propositional opacity, then the imaginational socio-individual, substitutionary act of hypocrisis is unacceptable. Yet if we describe carefully what we habitually do when we construct meanings from written texts, we note that we always feign a subject position which is neither fully our own nor entirely and systemically fixed. What then does "feigning a subject position" mean?

Hypocrisis is understood here as a construction beyond discourse markers of a set of imaginary variations of such items as a speaker's possible spatial and temporal locus of speech, his or her utterance as event, a speaker's acts of speaking, a speaker's "personality," social status, philosophical, moral, religious, or aesthetic convictions, and his or her ideological motivation of speaking. And no matter how comprehensive and tight the guide rails are which are provided in the event of meaning constitution by the material inscription and its propositional content, by frames and various kinds of contexts, any statement must in a special sense become his or her utterance for the event of signification to take place.

Part of the complexity of the act of hypocrisis is embedded in the Greek *nomen actionis* *"hypokrisis"* as listed in Liddell/Scott: "reply... Orator's delivery... tone or manner of animal's cry" or "playing a part." Likewise, the verb *"hypokrinomai"* puts weight on acts of interpretive simulation: "to expound ... to interpret... to use histrionic arts... to exaggerate... to play a part... to feign... to pretend" or "to deceive."[2] Though this list remains undifferentiated as to the special acts I wish to describe as *"hypocrisis,"* its range recommends the use of the term.

Hypocrisis or feigning refers specifically to the fact that I read/speak a logico-mathematical expression *as if I were a logician*, a commercial statement *as if I were a businessman*, a piece of juridical discourse *as if I were a lawyer*; biological, military, agricultural, or political speech *as if I were a biologist, a general, a farmer, or a politician*, respectively. And to the extent to which I am able to feign these subject positions I can be said to approximate 'ordinary' meaning events. As argued earlier, however, this process of approximation covers a broad band from the possibility of reconstruction of sense in the purely formal discourses to a wide range of devious constructions such as fortuitous displacements and deliberate distortions of meaning. With reference to Descartes, Foucault sees what I call hypocrisis as a set of modifications "forming an exercise" as against the constitution of the "system" of propositions:

> The *Méditations* require this double reading: a set of propositions forming a *system*, which each reader must follow through if he wishes to feel their truth, and set of modifications forming an *exercise*, which each reader must effect, by which each reader must be affected, if in turn he wants to be the subject enunciating this truth on his own behalf.[3]

While any reading, if it is to constitute meaning at all, requires acts of hypocrisis, critical reading further relies on the reader's awareness of the relationship between a statement and its frame. This implies that all critical reading is always potentially at least also parodic reading; critical reading entails the possible denial of a given frame and the superimposition of an alien horizon of reading which is not coded as the context of an utterance. By contrast, readings which fail to grasp statements as relative to their framing conventions and discourse genres produce, just as they are produced by, a reader-as-victim. This is not to say that meanings so constituted are *inappropriate* readings, they may on the contrary be precisely the kind of meanings the writer had hoped to bring about.

The reader may object at this point that hypocrisis, then, merely marks the revival of a hackneyed humanist argument. But there is a subtle and yet important difference between a theory which insists on the human subject in discourse and one which requires *instantiation* as a necessity. It is quite thinkable on the theory presented throughout that a highly complex and fully socialized machine could perform acts of hypocrisis and much else that goes with it. It just so happens that humans have so far been the better readers! I have also preferred the term 'instantiations' over 'parole' to avoid a limiting linguistic bias. Instead, I have favored a broadly semiotic view of discourse, a system devoid of *langue* (even though it permits any such construction) but instead constituted by the sum of its *actual* instantiations.

Fundamental objections have been raised to both the humanist parole and the emphasis on the particularity of instantiation. They come mainly from two directions: from the perspective of scientific discourse (analytic or conceptual language) and from ideological practice (dialectic materialism). To illustrate these I have once more chosen the philosophers Russell and Schlick to present the argument from the viewpoint of analyticity and Pêcheux to offer a dialectic materialist position.

Russell's relatively liberal view of meaning (cf. chapter 8) stands in contrast to his attempt at achieving absolute precision on the deictic side of language by exterminating the pest of "egocentric particulars."[4]

> The words with which I shall be concerned in this chapter are those of which the denotation is relative to the speaker. Such are this, that, I, you, here, how, then, past, present, future. Tense in verbs must also be included.

Here Russell rounds up all those items in natural languages which Husserl called "essentially occasional" expressions; i.e., those which make signification a function of an entailed speaker. Unfortunately Russell avoids considering any "preconstructed" speech act, that is, a speech situation which is not marked but nevertheless a necessary construction by the reader in order to constitute meaning, even if only in the form of sense.

> All egocentric words can be defined in terms of "this." Thus: "I" means "The biography to which this belongs;" "here" means "The place of this"; "now" means "The time of this"; and so on. We may therefore confine our inquiry to "this."

To be able to handle the confusing variety of egocentric particulars Russell now reduces them to a single class, that of "this." This is possible only on the assumption that all egocentric particulars have a single function, namely conceptual identification. For all but the most reduced language games this is an *illegitimate* reduction. As the next quotation shows it is the language of physics which is assumed to be the yardstick for this kind of analysis.

> ... no egocentric particulars occur in the language of physics. Physics views a space-time impartially, as God might be supposed to view it.

> There can be no question that the non-mental world can be fully described without the use of egocentric words.

Russell is in no doubt as to what a description is: a conceptual listing of items and identifying relations viewed from the position of Newtonian stability.

> If our theory of "this" is correct, it is a word which is not needed for a complete description of the world. We wish to prove that the same conclusion holds as regards "I" and other egocentric words.

> The connection between "I-now" and "this" is obviously very close. "I-now" denotes a set of occurrences, namely all those that are happening to me at the moment. "This" denotes some one of these occurrences. "I", as opposed to "I-now", can be defined by causal relations to "this," just as well as to "I-now"; for I can only denote by "this" something that I am experiencing.

> For reasons which will appear more fully in later chapters, I think that the phrase "I am" can always be replaced by the phrase "this is," or vice versa.

The phrase "can always be replaced" suggests the notion of inefficient redundancy. Natural languages are viewed as having accrued unnecessary duplications of concepts which a cleansed version of, for example, English, should do without. From the point of view of everyday discourse where identification is only one of several linguistic functions this view is entirely unacceptable. To substitute "this is" for the phrase "I am" in a statement such as "I am so grateful to you for having told her of my disappointment" so that it reads "This is the person who is ... " is to alter completely the modal forces in operation and so also the propositional contact we may wish to construe.

> Thus in every statement containing "this" we may substitute "what I-now notice," and in every statement containing "I-now" we may substitute "what is co-present with this."

> This, so far as I can see, solves the problem of egocentric particulars, and shows that they are not needed in any part of the description of the world, whether physical or psychological.

Russell's strict reduction of a large variety of discourses along with their specific formations and respective uses to one form of conceptual description has had consequences far beyond the immediate baneful effect on the theory of meaning.[5] In the final analysis, I suggest, it is no mere accident that when Russell in his later life needed to analyze complex socio-political relationships he was not able to draw on the reductive analyses presented here. The discourse on the war crimes committed in Vietnam required full discursive referentiality and deixis to be as effective as its advocates wanted it to be.

A similar, purely propositional view of language was proposed by Moritz Schlick who believed that "one of the greatest advantages and attractions of the true positivism" was its "antisolipsistic attitude, which characterizes it from the beginning."

> The words "I" and "my," if we use them according to the solipsist's prescription, are absolutely empty, mere adornments of speech. There would be no difference of meaning between the three expressions,"I feel my pain"; "I feel pain"; and "there is pain." Lichtenberg, the wonderful eighteenth-century physicist and philosopher, declared that Descartes had no right to start his philosophy with the proposition "I think," instead of saying "it thinks." Just as there would be no sense in speaking of a white horse unless it were logically possible that a horse might not be white, so no sentence containing the words "I" or "my" would be meaningful unless we could replace them by "he" or "his" without speaking nonsense. But such a substitution is impossible in a sentence that would seem to express the egocentric predicament or the solipsistic philosophy.[6]

Granted his misgivings as to the solipsistic argument, what Schlick forgets in his analysis is that the replacement of first person by third person pronouns does not really eliminate the former but merely changes them from marked to inferrable modalities. According to hypocrisis we always ask who is speaking the "he" and the "his." To produce a fully conceptual language further reductions need to be performed, especially the elimination of all reference. This degree of neutralization, however, always produces a sign system which apart from minimal syntactic similarities bears no resemblance to the discourse of the social lifeworld.

A theory which does address itself to fully saturated discourse and yet at the same time needs to reduce the significance of instantiation is the one offered by Michel Pêcheux in *Language, Semantics and Ideology*, quoted earlier. Pêcheux, drawing on Althusser, Foucault, Paul Henry, *et al*, sees discourse as one of many social practices in which ideological formations determine the way in which subjects perform. "Individuals are 'interpellated' as speaking subjects (as subjects of *their* discourse) by these discursive formations which represent 'in language' the ideological formations that correspond to them" such that "the interpellation of the individual as subject of his discourse is achieved by identification (of the subject) with the discursive formation that dominates him."[7]

This makes the speaking subject a duplicator of existing formations. In order to cater to discursive deviance Pêcheux therefore distinguishes between two "modalities" within the "relationship of reduplication": a "subject of enunciation" and a "universal subject." The first constitutes the "good subject" who consents to his own subjection to a "universal subject" and so "spontaneously reflects this subject;" according to the second, modality marks the discourse of rebellion, "distantiation, doubt, interrogation, challenge, revolt . . . " This is the discourse of what one might call a " 'bad subject.' " To avoid a pre-Hegelian theory of oppositions, Pêcheux adds the third modality in which the speaking subject neither conforms with nor merely revolts against, neither *identifies* nor *counteridentifies* with the "subject," but achieves a "disidentification effect" as a result of "a subjective process of appropriation of scientific concepts and identification with the political organization 'of a new type.' "[8]

Even in this advanced third way of realizing itself in discourse, the speaking subject does not constitute a practice, for Pêcheux emphasizes that "strictly speaking there is no practice of a subject, there are only the subjects of different practices."[9] This is useful insofar as it explains how ideological effects are produced in all aspects of discursive performance, from the typographical to high level abstraction and how the individual in any of Pêcheux's three modalities has to fulfill given discursive formations. What the theory has not addressed is the fairly dramatic changes which most languages—perhaps with the exception of French, thanks to the Academie Française—undergo, and the role which "founders of discursivity," as Foucault calls them, play in these transformations.[10] In Pêcheux's terms such ruptures can be produced by discursive practices but never by subjects who are hypocritical and deviant. My reading of Pêcheux, though, makes me suspect that he is not telling the whole story: there are a number of quite fundamental discursive changes which the author has taken over from Althusser (interpellation, ideological effect, etc.) and has proposed himself in the observations, "various theses," and "propositions" of his study, alterations which have already become part of the discursive practice of colleagues and students. Perhaps there is something like the edge of a discursive practice at which most writers dream their specific instantiations could make a difference.[11]

Yet how can we conceive of discourse so that the reader is able to play the part which I am arguing is indispensable for meaning to happen? Instead of regarding discourse as "a phenomenon of expression—the verbal translation of a previously established synthesis" we should seek, as does Michel Foucault, "a field of regularity for various positions of subjectivity." Seen in this manner, says Foucault, "discourse is not the majestically unfolding manifestation of a thinking, knowing, speaking subject, but, on the contrary, a totality, in which the dispersion of the subject and his discontinuity with himself may be determined. It is a space of exteriority in which a network of distinct sites is deployed." And later in *The Archaeology of Knowledge* we read that "to describe a formulation *qua* statement does not consist in analysing the relations between the author and what he says (or wanted to say, or said without wanting to); but in determining what position can and must be the subject of it." According to Foucault then the statement is

> One of those objects that men produce, manipulate, use, transform, exchange, combine, decompose and recompose, and possibly destroy. Instead of being something said once and for all—and lost in the past like the result of a battle, a geological catastrophe, or the death of a King—the statement, as it emerges in its materiality, appears with a status, enters various networks and various fields of use, is subjected to transferences or modifications, is integrated into operations and strategies in which its identity is maintained or effaced. Thus the statement circulates, is used, disappears, allows or prevents the realization of desire, serves or resists various interests, participates in challenge and struggle, and becomes a theme of appropriation or rivalry.[12]

This makes sense as long as we know that what is reiterable is not the uttered statement itself, but merely the materiality of its enunciation. For every utterance event is nothing other than the individual filling of a subject position describable to a large extent in terms of an intersection of the forces of a vast net of social praxis. Foucault's explanation here is vulnerable to the attack of being committed to a psychological behaviorism on the one hand and, on the other, of 'merely' having broken up *langue* into a series of micro-*langues* called "discursive formations." Nevertheless, Foucault's argument points to the core of an all-pervasive problematic: how to make visible by way of systemic explanation an event which, as it is occurring, is already sliding away along its historical trajectory. How do we express diachrony in synchronic terms? While materiality grants the statement iterability, each time an inscription "enters various networks and various fields of use" it turns into the material base for yet another set of acts which make up what we call "meaning." Dazzled by the promise of lucidity inherent in wholly systemic explanations, we may wish to brush aside the uniqueness of the event of meaning making as at best insignificant. Yet this would negate a fundamental fact about language, namely that *without the actual performance of linguistic expressions there would be no language at all.* Indeed, a system such as a *langue* is merely a stipulatable structure which never happens in actuality. What does demonstrably occur is a myriad of language instantiations which by themselves constitute a dynamic system, a practice, which already changes its contours as we attempt to describe it.

As far as the special case of meaning construction from written materials is concerned, these texts themselves never actually occur either, but act as the matrix of constraints within which linguistic expressions are actualized. Again, what does occur are the many acts of hypocrisis by which individual speakers constitute meanings within a texture of intersubjective practice. The conflict between the irretrievability of the event of meaning and its systemic explanations must be seen also from the double perspective of the propositional and modal sides of all sign systems. As argued before, the propositional components of any uttered statement—and it becomes a statement only when it is uttered—can be described in terms of their intersubjective features, i.e., as far as they can act as directional schemata for meaning making. At the same time there is what I have called *propositional opacity,* a certain lack of clarity, a surplus not covered by the description of a word sense, an extra which comes into existence as words, expressions, and sentences are used.

With regard to the other side of all propositional content, its modal complement—without which no statement can exist *qua* statement—there too appears a rift in the strategies of explanation. As Foucault demonstrates, we can explore the enunciative level against the screen of conflicting social forces in the discursive intersection of which the speaking subject is "dispersed" and "discontinued" as an individual. On the other hand, there is the equally demonstrable fact that the particular intersection which takes place in the event of an utterance is usually overdetermined modally, i.e., by its speech situation and the speaker's special use of it, so that the uniqueness of discursive instantiations cannot be doubted. To hear Jacques Derrida deconstruct a text by Martin Heidegger ("heath harrower," "pagan," etc.) is to 'know' who is speaking and the speaker is positioned within and against a mesh of concepts, signatures, of margins or spurs. And yet it is Derrida's particular *manner* of speaking which is memorable. And if one were to shrink into one observation Derrida's achievement in *Speech and Phenomena*, one could say that in establishing Husserl's unacknowledged continuation of metaphysical presence Derrida has substituted for Husserl's propositional givenness his own modal equivalent, or to stay with Husserl, Derrida has shifted the weight from noematic certitude to the flow of noetic qualification. In spite of his aim, Derrida too constitutes a presence, not so much by what he says as in the manner of his saying it.

In this sense the shifter "I" is of enormous significance for the theory of discourse. While it is quite easy to show how we can proceed from saturated formations to a conceptual system by shifting the first person pronoun to its frame (e.g., "I agree to play the formal logic game"), it is much more difficult to find cogent explanations as to the role which the "I" plays in referentially and modally charged speech. In spite of Derrida's critique of Husserl's distinction between "indication" and "expression" in *Speech and Phenomena*, the description of the first person pronoun as "universally operative indicator" and its functions is still valuable.

In Husserl's *Logical Investigations* the egocentric predicament is seen in the context of "essentially occasional meaning." Husserl has this to say on the egocentric particular "I": "The word I *names a different person from case to case*, and does so by way of an *ever altering meaning*. What its meaning is at the moment can be gleaned only from the living utterance and from the intuitive circumstances which surround it."[13]

In the case of actual semiotic embedding of verbal codes the feigning of a subject position relies on the construction of speakers and their background by way of what Husserl was later to call acts of "appresentation": we complete or imagine additional presentations to the social given.[14] Something quite different occurs when we confront the "I" of a written text. If we read the first-person shifter

> ... without knowing who wrote it, it is perhaps not meaningless, but is at least *estranged* from its normal sense. Certainly it strikes us differently from a wanton arabesque: we know it to be a word, and a word with which whoever its speaker designates himself. But the *conceptual meaning* thus evoked is *not* what the word 'I' *means*, otherwise we could simply substitute for it the phrase 'whatever speaker is designating himself.' Such a substitution would lead to expressions, not only unusual, but also divergent in sense, if, e.g., instead of saying 'I am pleased' I said 'Whatever speaker is now designating himself is please.' It is the *universal semantic function* of the word 'I' to *designate* whoever is speaking, but the notion through which we *express* this function is *not the notion immediately constitutive of its meaning.*

Husserl's "estranged" 'I' is actually the rule rather than the exception in the vast majority of printed materials, newspapers, instructional texts, texts with anonymized speakers (e.g., authorities), and novels. What is important for 'hypocrisis' is Husserl's distinction between the general or *conceptual meaning*, I would say the sense, of "I" as the speaker's designation of himself, its "universal semantic function," and the specific meaning with which we fill though not 'fulfill' this schema. According to Husserl this kind of meaning endowment requires in addition to a general expression an *indication.*

> Each man has his own I-presentation (and with it his individual notion of I) and this is why the word's meaning differs from person to person. But since each person, in speaking of himself, says 'I,' the word has the character of a *universally operative indication* of this fact. Through such indication the hearer achieves understanding of the meaning, he takes the person who confronts him intuitively, not merely as the speaker, but also as the immediate object of this speaker's speech. The word 'I' *has not itself directly the power to arouse the specific I-presentation*; this *becomes fixed* in the *actual piece* of *talk.* It does not work like the word 'lion' which can arouse the idea of a lion in and by itself. In its case, rather, an *indicative function mediates*, crying as it were, to the hearer 'Your vis-à-vis intends himself.'

In the terminology adopted in this study, Husserl's double directionality, the shifter's "universal semantic function," and "indicative function," can be expressed in this way: the conceptual, designatory, or universal function establishes the directional schema (what *kind* of pronoun) of 'I' over 'he,' 'she,' or 'they,' while the indicative, mediating function allows for the realization of deictic reference (what *kind* of speaker) to whatever degree the respective discourse formation and reading situation direct the instantiation. There is no reading without both these functions, or without hypocrisis, just as there is no discourse without instantiations. It is for this reason that I have consistently blurred the distinction between language and discourse: the former only exists in the guise of the latter. Language as such is the false stipulation of grammar books, which are themselves instantiations and therefore discourse.

What Husserl does not address and what has not been addressed for a very long time by other philosophers of language is the complication that hypocrisis is not as free a semiotic performance as the term *shifter* may suggest. In Foucault's writings we can again find useful hints at the limitations put on hypocrisis, for what applies to the limits of speaking also holds, at least to a considerable extent, for our imaginational variations of discursive processes. Not everyone is able to speak any sort of discourse. We must "describe the institutional sites" from which certain statements are typically made. "What is the status of the individuals who," Foucault asks, "have the right, sanctioned by law or tradition, juridically defined or spontaneously accepted, to proffer such a discourse?" According to certain programs, Foucault argues, we are typically questioning, listening, seeing, or observing subjects. Although our imaginative variations are certainly capable of transgressing the strictly institutional boundaries of which Foucault speaks, these very transgressions are presumably limited in a similar manner. This is an important qualification of the notion of hypocrisis.[15]

Whatever the institutional boundaries of hypocrisis, it is a key element of all language. If there is no discourse outside instantiation, a particular performance by a member of a speech community, (be it human or advanced machine), there is also no discourse without an 'I.' No matter whether this 'I' becomes part of the material base of an expression or remains concealed in the expression's inferrable modalities, the egocentric particular is a *sine qua non* of discourse. In fact, there is a further complication. Egocentricity is part not only of the expression itself, but also of its *frame*. At the level of expression the 'I' stands for "in relation to me such and such is the case;" at the level of the frame the 'I' indicates acceptance, rejection, or qualification of the frame itself within which every statement is situated.

It is of course not surprising that Russell cites physics in support of his purgation of language, for in purely formal languages such as mathematics it certainly appears that deictic references have been successfully eliminated. Yet this view is no longer generally accepted, as I suggested earlier. Even so-called a-perspectival languages, i.e., languages whose propositional contents are not directly affected by such events as intonation or ideological effects, are still informed by the perspectives of their frames and are not valid generally but only with respect to the possible worlds which they project. In this case, hypocrisis is certainly reduced, yet not entirely absent.

In the act of 'full' hypocrisis—the imposition of a prosodic contour, the imaginative assumption of the proxemic, kinetic, temporal, and spatial features of a speech stance, the tentative intuitive, stipulation of a speaker's psychological make-up, his or her social status, the inference of an ideological motivation— the speaker's "interest" always points in two directions: toward knowing the Other and toward securing the Self. In order to understand an 'alien' speech from an inscription I succumb to a certain extent to its directives; at the same time, in order to do so, I must impose my own manner of speaking. In this way I produce what to me appears to be a *plausible* utterance. This relationship has been recognized partially in various ways: as doubly directed "interest" by the late Husserl,[16] as manipulation or striving for consensus by Habermas,[17] less systematically by Harold Bloom as desire for domination and metalepsis,[18] and in Lyotard as the agonistics of social intercourse.[19]

No matter whether we describe discourse in consensual or agonistic terms, hypocrisis is an activity as fundamental as acts of referring and ascribing (Strawson). Because it relies to a large extent on inference, hypocrisis is closely related to our reading instantiations of fiction. Indeed, whether I read a biological or geographic text I need to perform fictive acts to be able to put myself in a biologist's or geographer's position. This intrusion of non-scientific discursivity into science, (which science has been at pains to eliminate) in the form of all social deixis, is a curious case of the 'return of the repressed,' a process in which hypocrisis or reading as feigning plays an important part. Nevertheless, it is of course in literature more than in any other discourse that hypocrisis can explore its ludic hermeneutic potential. A brief reading of Saul Bellow's *The Dean's December* will perhaps illustrate this point.[20]

At the end of the novel the central persona, "the carrier of the largest number of words," Albert Corde, high up in the coldness of Mount Palomar and close to the stars has the last word in the book. Asked whether he really minded the cold so much, he says: "The cold? Yes. But I almost think I mind coming down more."

Some 340 pages of text, the author's status as novelist, his earlier work, the discourse genre of the novel, narrative theories, the rhetoric of U.S. society, the rhetoric of the Eastern bloc, the discourse of ideological conflict, the debate about liberal humanism, the catastrophe mindedness of the age, and still further backdrops prevent me from reading Corde's and, by one remove, also the author's last words at the literal level. In constructing "their" meaning I intuitively or critically pack into this speech act a subsumption of what I sense to be the novel's major structural-thematic aspects. I do so by way of hypocritical substitution. I pretend, for the time being, that I am speaking from the position of Corde/Bellow.

The spatial locus of speech: Corde has accompanied Minna to the top of the telescope in the dome of the Mount Palomar observatory. There he faces "white marks, bright vibrations, clouds of sky roe, tokens of the real thing," from a locus of extremity cleansed of the "blood and mire" of human interaction. This we read against that other cleansing house, the crematorium in Bucharest, though such a construction is disallowed by authorial guidance—"This Mount Palomar coldness was not to be compared to the cold of the death house. Here the living heavens looked as though they could take you in"—the modal force of the statement overrides and reverses its propositional content. The reader who has not as yet fused the two domes (and how could this be avoided?) is likely to do so now. From where he speaks Corde is both removed from and tied to "the slum of innermost being, of which the inner city was perhaps a material representation." And above all, Corde's speech locus is grasped as a point of elevated retreat from communication, from the social sphere where his own garrulous humanity has brought him personal pain and public disgrace.

The temporal locus of speech: Just as the spatial locus of utterance and the place of the presented world coincide in Corde's last words, so too is the temporal locus of speaking identical with the temporal plane of the signified world. Unlike in the discourse of "once upon a time" and all epic preterite structures, and unlike the speech of prophecy where narrating and narrated present are marked as distinct, in Corde's last utterance speaking and experiencing selves collapse into a narrative "now." Yet hypocrisis does more than intuit locutions in a temporal frame. The "now" of "I almost think I mind . . ." is also construed as an after: after Corde participated in the social world of Bucharest, the colonel's rule, the "oppressive socialist wonderland," after he has reviewed and sharpened his critique of the Chicago jungle, after he has buried his mother-in-law, after he has been betrayed by a rivalrous friend, after he has despaired at the failure of the humanist stance, and after he has had to resign his Deanship. At the same time hypocrisis is the realization of a "now" which precedes his coming back down to a world in which Corde will have to accommodate himself, perhaps to a career in journalism: "I'll take it up again, as quietly as I can." If so, he will have to come to grips with the relationship between science, humanistic speculation, and critical social analysis. At the moment of his speaking he is not well equipped to handle such matters, nor are the stars likely to shed light on the conflict.

The speech act: The act of communication through ordinary speech takes a prominent place in Corde's world. "There's the whole thing—having people to talk to. To be able to say what you mean, mean what you say." Because throughout the novel Corde is made to insist on trust, sincerity and impartial accuracy, the reader is led to construct his utterances accordingly. We tend to assume that what he says complies with the conditions of sincerity and felicity. On the other hand, Corde is made to realize that his own speech, like Prufrock's and all language forever, also misses the point: "If we could say what we meant, mean what we said!" a piece of free indirect discourse which hovers in the double sphere of Corde's stream of thought and the authorial voice. How do we rescue the illocution from an inscription? Whatever we do in respeaking it, we are bound to miss something as well as supply an extra, a *semblable* of the original. Corde is painfully aware of this uncontrollable surplus: "The trouble is all in the nuances: Oh, the nuances!" It is the nuances which people misread; it is the indeterminacies which are treacherously concretized. Alien instantiations of his speech bring about his social disgrace, his realization of the dubiousness of his own utterances produce his moral crisis. And who is to say how the reader must fill the directional schema of "I almost think I mind coming down more"? At the surface it felicitously imparts the helplessness, disillusion, and fear of its speaker. All speech conceals as much as it reveals, and Corde's final speech act masks the bankruptcy of his personal humanistic, intellectual-moral stance as a general failure of critical endeavor in the face of the decadence of chaotic corruption and the decadence of oppressive control.

The speaker as persona: Bellow's Corde is "an experienced man and far from young" ("how could you deny the slippage?") who suffers from "fits of vividness" and "fool-fear;" Corde is "organized for observation and comprehension": "What a man he was for noticing . . . As if he'd been sent down to mind the outer world, on a mission of observation and notation." Like his novelist progenitor, Corde deplores the weakness of humanist culture and the fact that the trust, warmth and responsibility of personal relationship cannot act as a general model for social interaction. Corde is read as a man yearning for love and truth and understands himself in contradistinction to his Chicago fellow citizens, "men of power, devoid of culture, lovers of money, fearlessly insolent." But despite his humanist morality he is capable of no mean prejudice: he is hostile to theorizing beyond the personal level. "As long as it was sufficiently theoretical it went over easily enough," Corde judges; he prefers the Dantesque dance of "whirling souls . . . Spinning, streaming with passions, compulsive protests, inspirations." Corde is loved by his scientist wife, respected by her mother, and distrusted, disliked, and disdained by his Provost, to whom the Dean is merely a "disaster" at first, yet a "traitor" in the end. Whatever the interpretive specifics which we wish to bring to the assembly of Corde as a fictional speaker, without their schematic projection on some social matrix the construction of meaning from his last words would not be possible.

The speaker's philosophical stance and ideological motivation: Manifestly in its propositional content or latently in its inferrable modality, all speech is also tied to a speaker's philosophical outlook, his scale of values and, ultimately, his ideological motivation. Whenever I construct meaning from a text I intuit by spontaneous approximation or by careful analysis a speaker's center of ideological gravity. As a result, Corde's last words are realized as burdened with a considerable ideational load. Corde has recognized different pain-levels in the East and West. In Bucharest "the toilet paper was rough" (*damit auch der letzte Arsch rot wird*), the queues long: the pain of depravation. In the West a pleasure society invites, then disallows the voice of moral critique: the pain of betrayal. In this scheme of restrictions Western Europe is an in-between: "They had the trenches in the first war, and the bombing of cities in the second, and the camps. They'd like to retire from history for a while. They're on holiday." This "prevents rigorous positions from being taken. In that respect they share the American condition."

What kind of position does Corde take? "Consider: Eastern Europe as a place to read about endangered humanity," a place where Corde discovers "personal humanity, a fringe receding before the worldwide consolidation," a process he feels was "shaping the future." To Corde this threat is the result of the failure of philosophy, "the grovelling stuff the universities mainly do," of science which "had drawn all the capacity for deeper realization out of the rest of mankind and monopolized it," and of liberal humanism which "lacks scientific knowledge." Corde recognizes the value of comparative socio-political analysis, for he realizes that he understands Chicago better from the vantage point of a communist capital, but this knowledge never amounts to a method or a beginning for an approach to reach a more "rigorous position." Corde remains trapped in his "modern consciousness, that equivocal queer condition." The philosophical-ideological standpoint from which Corde speaks his final sentence is indeed his ultimate equivocation. Can he, should he, will he lend his artistic style to the exposure of lead poisoning? Whence should he take his convictions when he objects to critical theory and when in his eyes "poetry, painting, humanism" have turned to "fiddle-faddle—idiocy?" In the end, the starry heavens grant Corde his unacknowledged desire for social blindness so as to black out the painful vision of a decadence for which there is no personal remedy.

Hypocrisis always acts also at a secondary level, so that we always construct a voice as well as that of its implied designer, the author. Here we speculate about the Bellow of *The Dean's December*, and the question arises as to what kind of author he is at this moment when he projects the helplessness and ultimate irrelevance of American liberal humanism? An author who hasn't realized that Europe is about to find its 'second wind' and that his own society is about to be relegated to a branch line of history. And this possibly because European thought has once more transcended individualist solutions while the U.S. celebrates them in the most bizarre and fundamentalist forms. Has Bellow lost his touch to make Corde a sensitive fool just a level above social idiocy or is it precisely his achievement to have painted the philosophical emptiness of his countrymen in this way? However, hypocrisis does not provide any interpretive closure, it merely asks more and at best critical, speculative questions.

Such readings must not give the impression that they could in any sense be called *private* or suchlike. As instantiation hypocrisis is intersubjective in that the imaginative projection of a speaker, just as the projection of a presented state of affairs, is possible only within the typifying frame of a social semiotic. Thus, my projection is necessarily made up of typical ways of speaking, typical postures of speech, typical semiotic traits which accompany and modify acts of speaking, typical social roles which inform a speech event, typical philosophical, moral, religious, aesthetic, and political convictions, as well as a typical ideological blindness. In short, a range of "recipes for social action," as Alfred Schutz called them, and not just discursive formations are at my disposal as I respeak an inscription. How close or how far the resulting meaning construction happens to be from any original delivery is not at issue here. The point is that without hypocrisis meaning cannot be established, and when hypocrisis in its 'full' sense occurs, it always typically gears into the dynamic semiotic of a community, it is always a social act.[21]

As a strategy hypocrisis has been introduced to caution against a number of popular and falsifying reduction of discourse

> to a language of propositional clarity by removing social semiotic referentiality

> to a language of modal neutrality by the elimination of "egocentric particulars"

> to an idealized *langue* by trivializing the significance of actual instantiation.

Instead, the sum of instantiations available at any given moment in a given social semiotic is the very system we are looking for. Even the book of chess rules is an instantiation, not a *langue*.

Hypocrisis, which is essential for the instantiation of written materials, allows for a number of discursive responses. It comprises both Pêcheux's "identification," in which readers actualize themselves as ideologically docile subjects, and "counteridentification", by means of which "bad subjects" revolt against all authority and yet remain ideologically blind. Hypocrisis also caters to Pêcheux's "non-subjective position" of "disidentification" in which subjects transcend compliance and blind rebellion from the perspective of proletarian, dialectic materialist critique.[22] What Pêcheux does not tell us is how readers achieve these various positions. In particular, it is the imaginative, fictive, and always potentially critical acts which we perform in feigning possible 'subjects' that constitute the workings of hypocrisis.

As pointed out earlier, hypocrisis, even when it resorts to fictions, is not the prerogative of literary readings where nothing is considered dysfunctional and a whole novel can be adduced to bolster the meaning of a single utterance. The imposition of an actually performed or merely imagined intonation which carries a broad spectrum of aspects of feigning and social projection is required for all speech. Without hypocrisis there is no meaning, another example of non-linguistic semiosis backing up language. Where literary discourse invites its readers to explore fully the hypocritical potential of its surface structure, and logico-mathematical propositions remain unaffected by hypocrisis—though they too must be uttered in order to constitute sense—hypocrisis is central to the discourses of the social life-world. It is above all crucial to the recognition of the modalities of political speech, in its overt form as well as in the politics of reading, the topics of chapter 10.

X

THE FICTIONS OF POLITICAL DISCOURSE AND THE POLITICS OF READING

> The problem isn't so much to define a political 'position'... but to imagine and bring into existence new schemas of politicisation.[1]
>
> Michel Foucault

The difficulties of understanding the historically remote and the culturally distant text can be seen, as does Gadamer, in terms of the reconstruction of a question to which the text inscription was the answer. Viewed from the perspective of inferrable modality, what is problematic is the invention of a manner of speaking, a prosodic contour, a speech stance, a speaking personality embedded in a biographical situation and background of discursive formations as well as a set of ideological effects from which arise both that virtual question and the inscribed answer. The political text should likewise be regarded as remote, in that its inscription is the answer to a question which reveals its concealed fiction. This chapter aims to link the fictions embedded in political discourse with the politics of reading by drawing attention to the often neglected speech stance underlying the former and by foregrounding the ideological convictions entailed in the latter.[2] Once again utterance modalities can be shown to override overt propositional contents.

To what extent such modalities or the overall 'manner of speaking' can affect, bend, or replace what is being said has been subtly described by J. P. Stern in his study of the discourse of the Third Reich, an "essay in historical reconstruction," *Hitler: The Führer and the People*. He found that hardly any of Hitler's speeches contained any information which had not before been made available and orchestrated through other channels. Yet what was always powerfully present was a consistent register of tone: "the staccato invective" rising to "abuse and vituperation," the strategic pauses thrown into relief by the speaker's vertiginous insistence on his "personal authenticity." Even his early speeches, Stern notes, were informed by a "frightening, unrestrained violence of tone." There is "layer upon layer of invective, aiming at the creation of "conspirational solidarity." Hitler's appeal to absolute sacrifice, his "constant cajolings" and "invocation of an either/or decisiveness" met with the audience's "bitter delight in apocalyptic visions." In a language reduced to an informational minimum "the strongest affirmation is repetition." In the end we find discourse shrunk to political liturgy. When Hitler shouts "Deutschland!" and the audience delivers the echo "Sieg Heil!" the hermeneutic of question and answer collapses into ritual.

What was it, Stern asks, that could sustain the belief in such speeches? What was the "good faith" that could explain Hitler's political success? Part of the answer which Stern discovers is that the propositional content of that belief could not be retrieved; the other side to his answer is that "the reason why it proved next to impossible to find out what people had believed in was not so much their disingenuousness and willful forgetting as rather their real difficulty in recalling the message now that the voice was gone."[3]

What is regarded as dangerous in political speech is heterogeneous at any time and undergoes rapid historical change. In a post-fascist, high-tech, multinational world of computer capital Hitler's harangues sound ridiculous. What appeals now is a sober insistence on technical advances, the realities of the market, statistical evidence, and the relation between micro- and macro-management. Such texts, too, create their fictions and at the same time conceal their hidden speech acts. However, the discourse of war and destruction is by no means restricted to an evil past. Here is a more recent example of the megalomaniac variety from the influential journal *Foreign Policy*:

Nuclear war is possible. But unlike Armageddon, the apocalyptic war prophesied to end history, nuclear war can have a wide range of possible outcomes.... A plausible American victory strategy... would have to envisage the demise of the Soviet state. The United States should plan to defeat the Soviet Union and to do so at a cost that would not prohibit U.S. recovery. Washington should identify war aims that in the last resort would contemplate the destruction of Soviet political authority and the emergence of a postwar world order compatible with Western values.

The most frightening threat to the Soviet Union would be the destruction or serious impairment of its political system. Thus the United States should be able to destroy key leadership cadres, their means of communication, and some of the instruments of domestic control. The USSR, with its gross overcentralization of authority, epitomized by its vast bureaucracy in Moscow, should be highly vulnerable to such an attack. The Soviet Union might cease to function if its security agency, the KGB, were severely crippled. If the Moscow bureaucracy could be eliminated, damaged, or isolated, the USSR might disintegrate into anarchy hence the extensive civil defense preparations intended to insure the survival of the Soviet leadership. Judicious U.S. targeting and weapon procurement politics might be able to deny the USSR the assurance of political survival.[4]

As has been brought home by recent political shifts in the Eastern bloc, providing the scenarios of a number of possible worlds "Victory is Possible" projects one of the more calamitous fictions of recent times. According to its predictions, sound strategy "wedded to homeland defenses should reduce U.S. casualties to approximately 20 million." This is the prophecy of the manifest text. But there is also a hidden fiction which we can infer from the text by way of hypocrisis: the speakers' conception of Soviet society. Without at least a schematic and tentative construction of that conception the prophecy itself does not make sense. "The destruction of Soviet political authority and the emergence of a postwar world compatible with Western values" entirely negates Russian national fervor and assumes as natural that the U.S. version of Western values is the one the Russians would opt for. The prophecy hinges on the assumption that a U.S. nuclear attack and victory would be greeted as an act of liberation. Neither in a Stalinist nor a post-Gorbachev Soviet Union is this a likely response. The modal fiction beneath such writing is a Russian population rallying to the cry "rather dead than red" and one wholly unable to differentiate between a range of capitalist and socialist alternatives. Without a massive degree of ignorance not only of Soviet society but also of other non-U.S. nations, a fantasy as brutal as presented by these writers from the Hudson Institute could not be entertained. And who (and for what purpose, and for whose gain) would wish to foster such ignorance?

In the interaction of propositional content, modality, and frame—the large-scale semiotic constraints of utterance—political reading is closely related to its literary relation. Both need to construct a double fiction, propositional representations and utterance modalities, and both do so by acknowledging the necessity of interpretive latitude as a result of propositional and modal opacity. As in literature, reading here assumes that nothing is dysfunctional, that the text surface is always to be distrusted and forever qualified by competing acts of hypocrisis and by the imaginative variation of the relation between statement and frame. We could say that in reading the political text we are dealing with a weakened form of 'phenomenological reduction' which, however, will not in the end yield a secure *eidos* but rather a reader's historically anchored and ideologically motivated interpretative choice.

As a result of the combination of a long history of rhetoric and the more recent history of modern literary theory, language philosophy, linguistics, and various literary critical practices, literary reading has been able to take advantage of an impressive even if heterogeneous body of methodologies. It is for this reason that 'literary reading' is now beginning to intrude successfully into anthropology, history, philosophy, and also the political text. An argument for such reading and a related defense of the importance of instantiation can be advanced, not on the grounds of an immediate transferability of a text's propositional contents to other areas, but for formal and political reasons: the kind of literary reading generated by a directional theory of meaning produces a process of signification more attuned to the complexities of sign systems than other forms of interpretation. As such it enters the arena of the politics of reading.

At the center of the attack of the present study is a politics of language and reading which has been more powerful and influential than any other, the formal-logical and analytical notion of meaning as strict sense. That this is not just a theory or philosophy or a collection of these becomes evident when we look at the consequences its tenets have had on the conception of discourses beyond the realm of analyticity and the kind of performance it tends to prescribe for them. Against this bias I have set a broad spectrum of discourses and their respective performances, most of which transcend the prescriptions of the formal theories of meaning discussed. This spectrum, too, constitutes a politics of writing/reading. Between its two poles, one emphasizing socially saturated discourse, the other its reduced variants, have been situated a number of relevant issues: the relative openness of meaning as process, propositional, modal, and semiotic opacity, the question of *langue*, the dependence of discourse on non-verbal semiosis, the relationship between rich and reduced discourses, noetic and noematic meaning, the 'leakage' of conceptuality, and the importance of hypocrisis and instantiation. To dramatize somewhat the possible results of such an enquiry, let me set in opposition tendencies characteristic of these two kinds of politics of reading.

Formal approach (Occam)	Approach from the perspective of literary and other saturated forms of reading (Pandora)
true or false propositions	neither true nor false, but quasi-statements, quasi-questions, etc.
tertium non datur	inclusion of a wide range of possibilities in the middle
necessary and sufficient conditions	rich habitual and other ways of meaning conferment; pragmatic not logical termination of signifying chain
propositional sense	significance of surface text as well as transformations of surface beyond propositions
minimal sense	maximal meaning exploration
meaning as use	meaning as use including the ludic
use understood as performance of language games	use understood as linking process between linguistic schemata and non-verbal sign systems
objective sense	modification of objective schema by socio-cultural reference and deixis
meaning as definition	meaning as directional process linking different sign systems
words and expressions as definable	words, expressions, sentences, and texts as directional schemata for meaning making
names as appellations	names as appellations and descriptions

Formal approach (Occam)	Approach from the perspective of literary and other saturated forms of reading (Pandora)
rejection of *Vorstellung* as part of meaning	importance of acts of fantasying as aspects of meaning constitution within intersubjective constraints
verification and truth conditions	imaginative exploration of language in relation to non-verbal sign systems; corroboration instead of verification
language as game	language as game tied to non-linguistic "forms of life"
equation of meaning and propositional sense	distinction between propositional sense and full meaning exploration
opposition of subjectivity to objectivity	subsumption of subjectivity under a general social semiotic; critique of both subjectivity and objectivity
sense or nonsense	meaningful nonsense and spectrum of meanings between sense and nonsense
completeness of utterance	ongoing chain of intersemiotic relations
homogeneity	heterogeneity
closed system	open system
static state	dynamic relations
meaning exchange	meaning negotiation
perfect understanding	partial understanding and misunderstanding
hierarchy of branching categories	fluidity of typifying schemata
preference of serious discourse	inclusion of etiolations and so-called parasitic language
arbitrariness of sign	contingency of signs in relation to different sign systems
designative and descriptive side of language	dependence of descriptive side of language on deixis and intersemiotic modalities
formalized modals	inferrable, instable modalities
disregard of unconscious aspects of meaning	significance of socio-psychological motivation
disregard of ideological motivation	central role of ideological stance of utterance as interpretive inference

(as well as many other possible contrasts which the reader may feel have been omitted here).

Although the right-hand column illustrates primarily the demands made on meaning from the perspective of the most complex form of reading, there is an implication that the claims made also apply in principle to a large portion of language use in the situations of everyday life. Certainly, the assumption that ordinary speech should follow the rules indicated in the left rubric any more closely than its opposite is not borne out by actual discursive performance.

There are many other politics of reading, some of which have been closely associated with the literary itself and others that have emerged from a variety of knowledges. In what follows I offer brief summaries and critiques of some recent theories from the perspective of what kind of politics of reading they advance. My selection of quotations, though no doubt idiosyncratic, is based on two principles: 1) what statement these theories make in the frame of current debates in the Humanities and 2) how their writers present their politics. This double emphasis then continues the demonstration of the relation between vision and utterance act.

It is no longer persuasive to submit a defense of literature for the classical reasons of *delectare et prodesse* or its being *dulcis et utilis*; or, as Sir Philip Sidney saw in *The Defence of Poesie (An Apologie for Poetry)*, because it presents a golden world which will rub off; or because of its Kantian purposefulness without purpose; or because it stimulates our faculties of the imagination; or because it fosters in us a subtlety of perception and personal moral stance. Nor is the case put forward by Georg Lukács still cogent, that the climax of modern literature, the realist novel, stands as a bulwark against the onslaught of the formal excesses of modernism by holding up the principal laws of the socio-political dynamics of an age in its central category of realist "typicality." Though the Lukácsian "type" is intricate as well as employable in interpretation, the elemental weakness of this apologia for literature in its realist version is that it is precisely in works such as those of Proust's narrative, the German expressionist decade, or Joyce's *Ulysses*, which commit all the Lukácsian crimes, that the typicality of early twentieth-century thought appears captured in its multiplicity and totality.

Nor could one now sensibly write a *Defence of Poesie* based on a narrowly constricted canon, as used to be the case in the now largely defunct 'English Department.' And yet, to declare both literature and literary theory non-subjects, as does Terry Eagleton in *Literary Theory: An Introduction*, is not without its problems: they are fields of inquiry, arbitrarily delineated, as are all such subjects. There never has been a *natural* subject. The real opponent now is not so much the English Department as a theoretical pluralism which tends to appropriate Eagleton's work in competition with speech act theory, semiotics, phenomenology, psychoanalysis, feminist theories, or deconstruction. Nor, to remain with Eagleton's "obituary" of literary theory, does his critical survey of faulty literary practices necessarily deliver what we hope for. While Eagleton succeeds in pointing out the naive and not so innocent concealments of political assumptions and interests throughout the history of literary aesthetics, what the approach gains in moral-political sharpness it loses quite often in terms of the argument about meaning constitution. Political critique and precision of interpretation need to be combined. Without the former, critical analysis is weakened to at best technical competence; without the latter, it defeats its own purpose.

Eagleton's political recommendations for broad cultural studies and the redeployment of rhetoric are sound and have in fact been pursued by many teaching institutions. By contrast, his analysis of proponents of language philosophy and literary theory is at times disappointing. From the bias of this study, writers such as Husserl, Heidegger, and Ingarden receive the same treatment as the victims of Russell's *A History of Western Philosophy*.

Husserl is scaled down to his early noematic mathematization, which leaves to a more sympathetic scholium the Husserl of noetic modification, the critic of the natural attitude, the theorist of intersubjectivity, and the philosopher of the *Lebenswelt*. What is missing specifically in the Husserl section, for example, is the theory of "noetic modifications," the argument concerning "occasional meanings," the pivotal distinction between acts of consciousness as epistemo-logical starting points and their ontic foundation in the *Lebenswelt*, and Husserl's notion of critical dismantling which foreshadows both Heidegger's *Destruktion* and Derrida's deconstruction.

As to Heidegger, to be able to account even briefly for his contribution to literary theory one must take more seriously his statements about language, interpretation, and understanding. What needs to be stressed is his notion of understanding as an "as-structure" which straddles all signification from the most elaborate literary reading to the starkest of technical assertions. In the latter "the as-structure of interpretation has undergone a modification. In its function of appropriating what is understood, the 'as' no longer reaches out into the totality of involvements" and so reduces to a "derivative mode of inter-pretation." What we miss in Eagleton's summary is Heidegger's theory of lan-guage as a discursive spectrum stretching from its most thoughtful and therefore human or "poetic" form to the signification of "mere identity."

The section on Roman Ingarden is far too short if compared, for example, with that on Wolfgang Iser, whose major premises rely heavily on Ingarden's seminal writings. Eagleton's politics of reading here conceals the Polish phi-losopher's important contribution to phenomenological literary theory, which is his insight into the "ontic heteronomy" of the reader's acts in constituting the concretized work. Unlike the production of ideal entities such as defining triangles or acts constituting material objects such as noticing chairs, reading in a literary manner is to combine the heteronomous realizations of *materiality* (sound, print), *ideality* (syntactic rules, high-level abstractions), and *purely in-tentional objects* (mental images) in the forward dimension of the printed lines. The revolutionary and complex feedback model of stratification which Ingarden develops in the course of his two major works is designed as an illustration of the power of a phenomenologically argued epistemology. Its influence on re-ception aesthetics and reader response theory has been absolutely crucial. It is a pity that the difficulty of Ingarden's argument has tended to occlude this fact. Gadamer and Jauss likewise are given short shrift.

Unfortunately, this kind of gloss is part of all critical summary and the present comments on *Literary Theory* are no exception. However, I think that at least some of Eagleton's difficulties stem from the fact that he himself has not de-veloped nor has at his disposal a sophisticated Marxist theory of meaning re-sponsive to the intricacies of a body of works in language philosophy, speech act theory, phenomenology, or linguistics which asks consistently and from very different angles how signification operates. For a Marxist theory which is highly sensitive to nuances of discourse we need to look at the writing, for instance, of John Frow, addressed briefly below. Eagleton certainly has supplied a neat lever with which to upset the tradition, but what we lift turns out to be a little light.[5]

The catholic need to advance a legitimate umbrella for all cultural study is present also in Frederic Jameson's *The Political Unconscious*. Exempt, like Althusser's scientific Marxism, from the delusions of the ideological standpoint, Jameson's "anti-transcendent hermeneutic model" can lay claim to a leniency of "oppressive tolerance." It enjoys "ultimate philosophical and methodological priority" over other hermeneutics which are "more specialized codes whose insights are strategically limited." To reassert, as does Jameson, "the specificity of the political content of everyday life and the individual fantasy-experience and to reclaim it from the reduction to the merely subjective and to the status of psychological projection" is a pressing task. Yet to declare a Marxist view of history the "untranscendable horizon," "cancelling and preserving" the "sectoral validity" of other theories is a decree of Hegelian proportions.[6] In spite of this criticism, Jameson's politics of reading remains an exciting contribution to speculative criticism.

Nor can a defence of literary reading rely wholeheartedly on the text's affinity with the language of the Unconscious. For as Gilles Deleuze and Felix Guattari point out, nothing is gained by a reading in which one text is rewritten according to the matrix of another text, a master key which unlocks the ultimate, concealed meaning of the original. Nor on the other hand could a present day literary apologia exclude the exploration of the various levels of text in *Traumdeutung* or refuse to find a place for the Lacanian subject. The theoretical position presented in this study is as omnivorous as our interpretive strategies; both take their logical justification from the emancipatory potential of discourse and their political stance from a social-democratic vision.

A fervently committed politics of reading in the Althusserian mode is Pêcheux's *Language, Semantics and Ideology*, quoted earlier. Pêcheux launches a large number of attacks directed at such targets as: metaphysical realism and logical empiricism; the subordination of what is contingent to the necessary; subjectivism and its Münchhausen effect; the logico-formal tendency in linguistics and its rhetorico-poetic opposition; speech act theory; or Foucault's archaeology. Let us take each of these in turn.

Metaphysical realism and logical empiricism are shown to be "the two faces of idealism" in that the former is committed to the "myth of universal science" while the latter practices the generalization of "fiction." This has specific consequences for politics, such that politics is to be transformed into "an objective science" which would rid itself of erroneous political practice and, on the other hand, is debased to a cynical game. The apparent opposition between the two tendencies is resolved by Pêcheux by seeing them as part of the same bourgeois political practice: metaphysical realism corresponds to the "bourgeois phantasy of the reabsorption of political struggle" in the technical, "legal-political ap-

paratus," whereas logical empiricism reappears in the form of political partici-
pation as in a cynical "game."[7] These tendencies are merely the practical results
of philosophical positions: both "empiricist theories of knowledge" and their
metaphysical realist counterparts favor ideational universalization over a historical evolution of science because it permits a "realist form" of "a priori
network of notions" and at the same time "an administrative procedure" which
can be imposed on the contingent facticity of workaday reality.[8] Applied to
education and the transmission of knowledge this implies that metaphysical
realism "passes off purely ideological effects as an object of knowledge" and
logical empiricism fictionalizes objects of knowledge into an "arbitrary convention."[9]

Pêcheux's double-barrelled critique of a two-faced idealism reemerges in his
discussion of the subjugation of what is contingent to "necessary truths," a
philosophical tendency he traces from the Port-Royal logicians to Carnap. In
Leibniz "truths of fact" are subordinated to "truths of reasoning" by the device
of "sufficient reason," analyzed by Pêcheux as a "supercalculus . . . inaccessible
to man" which resolves the infinite regress of detailed explication in "the secret
necessity of contingent facts."[10]

In Kant's *Critique of Pure Reason* the distinction reappears as the pair analytic
and synthetic judgment, whereby now the contingent is linked with experience
and so subjectivity.[11] Frege continues the tradition by equating formal and contingent sense, "the only flaw in Frege's lucidity."[12] I disagree with both this
subjectivist analysis of Kant and, as I have shown in chapter 8, with Pêcheux's
purely formalist reading of Frege. Husserl is shown to have sharpened Kant's
transformation of the necessary/contingent pair into its objective/subjective variety, revived by Carnap in his distinction between "theoretical language" and
"observation language." This brings the Port-Royal logician's argument up to
date in the form of a combination of a theoretical concept and an observation
concept, the latter resulting from the replacement of subjective notions about
the contingent to "a universal subject situated everywhere and nowhere and
thinking in concepts."[13]

As is to be expected, subjectivist theories of signification in which the speaking
subject is stipulated as the origin of meaning and of itself fare badly in Pêcheux
politics of reading. Apart from his weak analysis of Husserl, the author persuades
us that all subjectivist philosophy requires the metaphysical fantasy of a Münchhausen effect whereby the subject lifts "himself into the air by pulling on his
own hair."[14] Likewise, Pêcheux sees the funny side of semantics when he compares Jerrold Katz classificatory definitions—e.g., "a bachelor is characterized . . . as: (Object), (Physical), (Human), (Adult), (Male), (Unmarried)"—to the
fantologies of *Les Vérités de la Palice*, the original title of Pêcheux's book which
was to grant "Monsieur de la Palice the place he deserves as the semanticist's
patron saint."[15]

A special attack, early in the book, is reserved for the "logico-formal" and the
"rhetorico-poetic" tendencies in language education, not just in France but in
bourgeois education in general. Once again Pêcheux sees a link between two

apparently contradictory discursive formations by moving to a less abstract level of analysis. Accordingly, logico-formal practices draw on the logic of "concrete realism" which focuses on "simple, indestructible elements" as "the essence of objects." By contrast, the rhetorico-poetic practice is an expression of an "idealist rationalism" by which the mind "represents reality to itself" and so too reconciles concepts and facts. In other words, the two tendencies are also a version of the two faces of idealism—metaphysical realism, and logical empiricism.[16] Likewise, the dominance of formalist-logistic linguistics, e.g., linguistic structuralism, over historical studies in ethnolinguistics or sociolinguistics, and the linguistics of enunciation is presented as a powerful expression of the subordination of the contingent to the analytic, two seemingly contradictory expressions of philosophical idealism.

With regard to speech, Pêcheux argues that we need to review the role of the speaking subject which can never act in any originary capacity: "on the contrary, it must be understood as an effect, in the subject form, of its determination by interdiscourse . . . " It is only the "ideologic-discursive real" which can grant the subject the kind of determination which speech act theory requires.[17] Later in his study the author sharpens his attack by brushing aside the claims of the theory to be able to explain "legal-political and ideological relationships" by the notion of "word game" in which individuals resolve matters in personal combat.[18] Although this criticism is explicitly directed at Anglo-Saxon analytic philosophy, it also applies to Jean-François Lyotard's more recent use of language-game agonistics in *The Postmodern Condition: A Report on Knowledge*.

Finally, to end this selection, Pêcheux rejects the politics of reading offered in *The Archaeology of Knowledge* on the grounds that Michel Foucault unnecessarily retreats from an analysis informed by ideologically determined class struggle to the "sociology of institutions and roles."[19] This criticism is not made, however, without having first acknowledged the book's considerable contribution to the study of discourse and the analysis of the Port-Royal Grammarians.[20]

Given this broad range of opponents singled out in this book for at times devastating critiques, it will not come as a surprise if I now suggest that Pêcheux's politics of reading has a few 'blind spots' of its own: the disappointing equation of sense and meaning; a willfully idealist reading of intersubjectivity; his thesis of the full determination of utterance; the refusal to address the difference between epistemological starting point and ontological inferences; and his hardheaded stipulation of the real.

By identifying sense and meaning Pêcheux continues the tradition of logical positivism and so a form of conceptualization of the contingencies of the social, which he rightly criticizes in Frege as a temporary lapse from an otherwise materialist vantage point and neatly attacks in the general form of an illegitimate subordination of the factual to the analytical. At the same time the definition of meaning as sense robs Pêcheux of the opportunity to demonstrate how ideological effects play different roles in idealized sign systems as against social pragmatic or political discourses. In the former, propositions do not change under different ideological conditions, it is the role of the sign system as a whole which is affected; in the latter, owing to the complexities of reference and deixis such as propositional and modal opacities and habitual inferences, every propositional content can be shown to bear the marks of ideological effects. However, this kind of analysis is severely undermined by the collapse of meaning into sense.

By calling intersubjective consensus "notorious"[21] Pêcheux rejects an idealist reading according to which intersubjectivity is the platform from which being is understood as a shared "thought." It seems it is politics rather than analysis which prevents Pêcheux from appropriating the term for a materialist reading. To say that it is a " 'complex whole in dominance' of discursive formations" which permits specific discursive formations and so instantiations is not only to relegate origin to another level (and from there to Ideology), but is in fact to weaken a not merely verbal but broadly semiotic intersubjectivity which produces all signification. Again, the very arguments of "ideological effect," "subject form" and Pêcheux's three modalities of "identification," "counteridentification," and "disidentification" could be accommodated by a non-idealist notion of intersubjectivity which already contains ideology and so informs all social negotiation. In fact, I suspect that Ideology is the last unacknowledged idealist remnant in Pêcheux's (as in Althusser's) schema which needs to relegate intersubjectivity to the status of idealist nonsense. For if "Ideology" was truly materialist, a practice, rather than an abstraction it would not have to be a universal "outside" (Thesis 2) but should be content to play its dominant role inside the social, intersubjectivity: the relations between subjects engaged in practice.

Pêcheux develops an elaborate argument to persuade his readers that "everyone's discourse reproduces that of another" and that "everyone is a mirror to everyone else."[22] To get off this treadmill he employs Foucault's discursive formations, and adds a " 'complex whole in dominance' of discursive formations imbricated with that of ideological formations," which finally "has no outside for itself."[23] It is difficult for Marxism, even in its Althusserian form, to get away from Hegel's *Geist*.

Changing material conditions and consequently altered practices then produce a new Ideology which passes down those alterations in terms of new ideological effects, which affect discursive formations which allow new utterances to happen: linguistic change! Would it not be a more materialist explanation to say that material changes require new practices which among other things produce new discursive formations?[24]

I have already questioned Pêcheux's reading of Husserl and his refusal to acknowledge the fundamental distinction between the epistemological starting point, rather than origin, of the descriptions of acts (instead of the world) and the ontological inferences which are a consequence. Ontologically, as Pêcheux describes Husserl's findings, the *Lebenswelt* is the origin of 'intersubjective' acts and 'objective' meanings, only Husserl's "solitary mental life" remains within the realm of subjectivity (cf. chapter 4). It is only to this last area that Pêcheux's critique applies.[25]

In Pêcheux's analysis it remains unclear whether the "real" is the real of semiotics, life-forms, in other words, the cultural texts within and by which we live, or a *noumenal* real to be stipulated of necessity, or yet an empiricist's real into which all of us are supposed to bump all the time. Pêcheux's "Theses 1: the real exists necessarily independently of thought and outside it, but thought depends on the real . . . " says something about the dependence of thought on the real, while the "real" remains undefined. If a semiotic-textualist reading is inappropriate, we are returned either to a Kantian *noumenal*, or a pre-Husserlian 'natural attitude,' or at best to the Wittgenstein of the *Tractatus* which still assumes a manageable relation between elements of the world and those of a language of description. What Pêcheux needs, I suggest, is a broadly semiotic, textualist view which subsumes degrees of ideological blindness which strikes us all. What such a view reveals is the heterogeneity of material conditions and practices, such as Pêcheux's and my own.

A politics of reading which is acutely attuned to recent contributions to the Humanities and the Social Sciences is John Frow's *Marxism and Literary History*. Frow argues for a nonreductive study of literary discourse which must be able to address "the specificity of literary structures and systems," while it "cannot and should not be separated from ordinary political struggle." In forging such a critical practice the author acknowledges the "arduous process of reworking alien categories." While committed to a Marxist literary theory Frow is nevertheless "deeply suspicious of the central categories of Marxism itself." This makes for a penetrating study of a wide range of traditional Marxist aesthetics from Lukács to Goldmann and Morawski, pointing to the flawed common ground of the base-superstructure metaphor which struggles with the priority of content over literary form. This metaphor is traced in its different guises, as "reflection, correspondence, interaction, homology, analogy, affinity, expression, testimony, [and] modeling," notions which make it difficult for Marxist theory to come to terms with literary form and discursive strategies. Frow draws our attention to the actual political ineffectiveness and final ethical utopianism of a critic such as Georg Lukács, linking these with his failure to come to grips with the notion of mediation. Instead of being able to accommodate discursive play Lukács is shown to revert to the advocacy "of an absolute generic form" in his preference of the realist novel.[26]

Frow sees as one of the major tasks for "Marxist cultural theory" to take seriously the challenge of post-structural writings because they require a redefinition of "the status of the dialectic" and invite the construal of "a semiotic politics on the ruins of metaphysics." This the author accomplishes himself to the degree to which he is able to rewrite the concept of ideology "in semiotic terms," that is in a significatory theory of "social relations of production, social power, and systems of discourse." What the reader is offered here is an attack on the Marxist version of the truth-falsity orientation which fails to account for ideology in terms other than "false consciousness," a description which requires an unattainable epistemological privilege "complicitous with power."[27]

Frow moves the debate about ideology away from the dichotomy of discourse and reality toward the relation between "discourse and *power*, the intrication of power in discourse." His strategy rests on the textualist insight that "the signifieds of discourse (including the 'referential' discourse of science and history) are generated not from an extradiscursive real to which we may appeal as a final authority but within specific processes and practices of signification." Apart from its different political starting point this links well with a directional theory of signification which regards meanings as linking processes between different sign systems, in particular those between linguistic schemata and non-verbal signs. Meanings, then, are not so much an "abstract potential" as processes "closely tied to the context of utterance." Likewise, the Lacanian distinction between the Real and the Symbolic are not viewed ontologically but as "a social and historical result," for from Frow's perspective material processes are always already also symbolic structures. This has consequences for the theory of ideology in that ideology can no longer be seen as a deduction from the categories of economics or class but rather as discursive effects. "Ideology is thought of as a *state* of discourse." In the same vein Frow suggests that the theorization of the subject needs to avoid its identification with the "origin of utterance" and instead argue the subject, as does Pêcheux, as a discursive effect. What remains crucial for a theory of ideology then is "the possibility of disruption of discursive authority, and the integration of this disruption into general political struggle."[28]

Frow's conception of discourse accommodates well the contradictory nature of discursive organization. "Genres of discourse" are shown to "produce at once an effect of semantic stability [and] an effect of semantic contradiction." This occurs in the social as well as within the individual: "the clash of voices is a clash of power." This, Frow urges, is what discourse analysis must address. Nor should such a description be either ontological or formal in a linguist sense but functional, so that it is able to account for the "variable capacity" of discourse "to produce particular forms of knowledge, and subjects appropriate to those forms."

Marxism and Literary History makes a special point of the historicity of textual effects. The literary text, for example, is seen not as an entity but as a transformational process "of textual production and reception." As such it

> integrates the text into a series of three moments: production, automatization, and defamiliarization (new production), so that the historical dimension of the text involves not only its past (the norms against which it reacts) but its future (the transformation of norm-breaking features of a text into a new norm).[29]

What Frow is after is the description of "particular texts in terms of their specific historical status and their historically changing ideological value." Such a focus hinges on our ability to "identify the movement of power in the variant forms of literary textuality." Yet this identification must always be aware of the historicity of discourse. According to Frow, literary evolution, for instance, "occurs in two contradictory ways: discontinuously, through the production of deviant forms of textuality, and continuously, through the reproduction of the literary norm." Historicity likewise affects literary discourse as a system which is itself systemically linked to non-literary discursive forms.[30]

Special treatment is given to the notion of intertextuality as historical frame. As Frow views it, "the historical dynamic of the literary system is intertextually motivated, and the intertextual relations establish the specific historicity of texts." In this, literary intertextuality is nothing but a special case of "interdiscursivity." Frow occupies a problematic niche in the hall of textualism. After all, it does not seem easy to deny the empiricist real and still advocate an effective politics. Instead of reality and fictions he speaks of linguistically generated "reality effects and fiction effects." And in Lyotardian fashion Frow suggests that the "clash of languages is a clash of realities—that is, of moral universes." Reality then is textual and texts are processes of "relations of discursive contradiction." The text is not given in this theory but established by practices. In this way Frow avoids both the positivist stipulation of an autonomous object of inquiry and the multiple dualism of an outside social and an inside text. This has implications for critical evaluative practice. Instead of seeing evaluations applied to texts from the outside he focuses on "the structured field of evaluations and the critical concepts used to produce them as objects of analysis, and thereby integrating them into the textual process."[31]

Although the author does not hide the fact that *Marxism and Literary History* as a whole is a statement of a politics of reading, the book ends with an emphasis on the "Limits: The Politics of Reading." All politics of reading concerns the positions "from which readings are undertaken and theories generated." Here Frow takes readings by Derrida and Foucault of a passage from Descartes on madness and shows how "the modality of the passage is constructed" by both. He stresses Derrida's attention to the "play of voices in the text of Descartes," contrasting this with Foucault's focus on the "generic conventions" which constitute "the discursive practice of meditation." The juxtaposition of two poststructuralist positions demonstrates the relative superiority of Foucault's more systemic approach; instead of a play of two opposing voices Foucault can point to the discursive regimes which govern a series of different subject positions as well as certain literary elements and choices of specific discursive formations as well as determinations of diction. Frow argues that Foucault is effectively attacking not just a specific reading, but rather the very practice of "interpretation." Frow prefers Foucault in this specific instance on the grounds that he "is able to thematize more fully the conditions of textual enunciation."[32]

Important for any politics of reading is the dynamics of its frame, since "the authority of the frame corresponds to that of the generic conventions it establishes. It works as a metacommunication specifying how to use the text, what one can expect to happen at different stages, and what to do if these expectations are not confirmed." However, we must also realize "that the text never completely *fills* the frame." As to the analysis of the frame itself, the theorist must be aware that "to describe, from within a literary system, the interpretive limits set by the system is at once to describe a set of constraints and to interrupt the limits, the enclosing frame, by framing them within a larger closure." In pursuing such politics of reading we are neither free nor entirely restrained, for "the possibility of unsettling limits is always both given and limited by an actual condition of power." Rephrasing Derrida, Frow insists that "there is no outside of power." At the same time he cannot fully accommodate Derrida's deconstructionist enterprise for to do so would jeopardize a politically committed reading. In Derrida's case, the "deferral of judgment and authority, this refusal to occupy the place of law, has ambivalent political consequences." One such consequence is 'American' deconstructive practice which is largely a "self-serving critique of the political" ill equipped to ruffle the social or even its own "disciplinary boundaries."[33]

All readings, Frow shows, are governed by "interpretive regimes," which, he would have to accept, are themselves subject to semantic drift. What distinguishes these regimes is not only their manifest content but also their readiness to foreground or conceal their political strategies and goals. Frow's politics of reading aims above all at liberating the boundaries of literary studies to include "such genres and media as jokes, 'natural' narratives, biography and autobiography, pornography and popular romances, journalism, and the genres of film and television." The narrow aim here is to evolve "the construction of a general poetics." Frow also addresses the further target of "an extension of the strategies and interests of literary analysis to nonaesthetic discursive domains: to legal discourse, scientific discourse, historiography, philosophy; to moral and religious discourses; and to everyday language." The politics of reading for Frow is nothing less than the "radicalization of discursive power."[34]

A likewise committed politics of reading can be gleaned from the writings of Jürgen Habermas. Since the publication of "Science and Technology as Ideology" and as recently as in "A Reply to My Critics" and *The Philosophical Discourse of Modernity*, Habermas has insisted on the emancipatory impulse of ordinary language oriented toward understanding as against the language of manipulation and technical language designed to accomplish control. This is an attractive position, but it is not so easy to give a satisfactory explanation why this should be so. What is it that makes this kind of language rebellious in the face of constraint? How can we make this assumption when there is ample evidence for language being used as one of the most powerful and all-pervasive tools of domination?

If Habermas is right, then the emancipatory potential of language must have a structural foothold as well as social enactment to be realized. It is not simply that ordinary language asks questions where technical speech is oriented toward unequivocal response. Technical discourse too has its minimal hermeneutic, it too consists of query and reply. Instead, the argument for the emancipatory potential of natural language should rely on the fundamental features of its propositional and modal opacity which tie language to the social from which it receives, as I have argued, its discursive character. The double opacity of language must be continuously resolved by filling its directional schemata with the significations of the social. And as Habermas argued some twenty years ago, the legitimation for the shaping of the social can come neither from the technical nor from technocratic rule but only from the democratic basis of the "public sphere." If we accept this kind of politics it follows that all practices of reading should be likewise grounded in the public sphere.

It is from the public sphere that Habermas's pragmatic theory of signification takes its cues. As such it overcomes the "fixation on the fact-mirroring function of language" of truth conditional semantics, the "cognitive-instrumental mastery" of objectified nature and society, and the "narcissistically overinflated autonomy" of subjectivity. At the same time, such a pragmatics allows for all three, by way of differentiated validity claims under the umbrella of social reason: cognitive *truth, rightness* vis-à-vis social norms, and *truthfulness* in terms of the sincerity claims of individual speakers.[35]

Habermas's politics of reading is articulated most sharply in his critique of a number of thinkers of late modernity in *The Philosophical Discourse of Modernity*, and perhaps not surprisingly, it is Jacques Derrida's position more than any other which is taken to task. The chapter "Beyond a Temporalizing Philosophy of Origins: Jacques Derrida's Critique of Phonocentrism" accuses Derrida of failing to escape the very foundationist tendencies which he himself denounces. Instead of taking the linguistic turn with other modern philosophers Derrida is shown to remain within the paradigm of the philosophy of consciousness which cannot address meaning as a rule-governed pragmatics: Husserl's ideality of meaning is simply replaced by Derrida's "ideality of the sensible form of the signifier."[36] Habermas suggests that Derrida is guilty of "an inversion of Husserlian foundationalism inasmuch as the originative transcendental power of creative subjectivity passes over into the anonymous, history-making productivity of writing" (178). *Graphe*, however, is not argued in terms of a pragmatics of communicative competence, but remains an idealization. Far from overcoming the "foundationalist tenacity of the philosophy of the subject," Derrida offers the even deeper "basis of an originative power set temporally aflow" (178f.). Derrida is charged with the continuation of the tradition of "*Ursprungsphilosophie*" by way of an "*Urschrift*." Unfortunately, says Habermas, Derrida let slip what initially looked like a scientific claim about signification as a grammatology and fell back on a quasi-religious authority which "conceals its true face and thereby incites the frenzy of deciphering interpreters" (183). What is accomplished then is that "the labour of deconstruction lets the refuse heap of interpretations, which it wants to clear away in order to get at the buried foundations, mount ever higher" (183). By supplying us with his new "tools of a negative foundationalism" Derrida has returned "to the historical locale where mysticism once turned into enlightenment." In Habermas's schema of social reason this is nothing less than an intellectual disaster.[37] Certainly, Derrida's project not only runs into technical difficulties as a way of theorizing, as I pointed out at the end of chapter 5, but also undermines itself as a politics of reading.

An extension of Habermas's argument can be found in Rita Felski's *Beyond*

Feminist Aesthetics: Feminist Literature and Social Change, which analyzes a range of feminist literature before concluding with a plea for a "feminist public sphere." The book stresses the "construction of symbolic fictions" as an "important moment in the self-definition of an oppositional feminist community."[38] Felski also insists throughout that writing and reading cannot be properly described in isolation. Technically, subjectivity and narrative have played a leading role in feminist literary practice. At the same time, the "process of identity formation" for feminist authors is seen to have been dependent on a "concept of community." Subject and gendered collective have set the boundaries which permit feminist writing to define itself against society at large. Felski shows convincingly that aesthetic and literary debates about realism, modernism, and postmodernism on their own provide inadequate parameters for the question of feminism and culture. Without an acknowledgment of art as an institution embedded in an ideological framework, reading and writing remain esoteric. For "radical impulses are not inherent in the formal properties of texts; they can be realized only through interactions between texts and readers."[39] Nor should feminist practice have to associate itself exclusively with popular genres and deny the formal complexities of high art; it needs to evolve a theory which cuts across these inherited distinctions. This can be achieved by transcending the rules of textual analysis through the broader political and cultural concerns which characterize a "feminist public sphere."[40]

The feminist public sphere or "counter public sphere" is understood by Felski as a "repoliticization of culture" which would link "literature and art to the specific experiences and interests of an explicitly gendered community."[41] In opposition to Habermas's political universalism, Felski defines the feminist public sphere in terms of a "critique of cultural values from the standpoint of women as a marginalized group within society." The writing and reading practices which constitute this sphere are both gender-specific, in that they address women's interests neglected or undermined in male-dominated culture, and publicly discursive, by using their own but gradually also traditional communication channels to disseminate feminist ideas. The advantage of seeing these practices from the perspective of a feminist public sphere is that it avoids marginalization as an academic pursuit and instead can be argued as a broad social and cultural movement.[42]

Both Habermas and Felski need the support of a theory of discursive signification to show how the public sphere and its feminist counterpart communicate within their own boundaries and with other institutions. Habermas attempted such a theory in "What Is Universal Pragmatics?" where he offered a critique of Austin's speech act theory by substituting the notion of "communicative competence" for the much more restrictive "linguistic competence." The theory goes a fair way toward showing how linguistic processes are facilitated and informed by the social, but is hampered by its continuation of the semantic tradition of regarding meaning as an entity. Neither linguistic nor communicative competence can be accounted for outside a dynamic conception of meaning as a semiotic linking process.[43] Felski is well aware of the absence of a satisfactory feminist theory of discourse. This emerges from some of her early chapters where she offers trenchant critiques of the theory of phallocentricity and the debilitating perspective of a feminist "prison house of language."[44] Yet there are seeds of alternative theories of language in feminist writing which should be taken seriously. A modal description of language seems to be promised in Julia Kristeva's work, a theory of indeterminacy is announced in the writing of Irigaray, and the foregrounding of metaphor in some feminist writing suggests the possibility of an apropositional semantics.[45]

Even if these announcements amount to no more than half promises, they express a double anxiety: that the dominant tradition of language description, and by implication its politics of reading, has a stifling effect on the emancipatory potential of discourse and that new ways of communicating need to go hand in hand with liberating forms of critical practice. But without the support of a generous theory of meaning such practices are ill-founded. Instead of the laboratory meaning of semantics construed at low temperatures, under extremely high pressures, and in the absence of a biosphere, what is required is a directional theory of meaning as process linking diverse sign systems and so the social at large. This implies arguing against meaning as an entity and in favor of its modally always overdetermined directional process. It is by no means accidental that all domination of and through language begins with the declaration of the univocality of its directional schema and the concealment of its modals. A sound politics of reading and a related pedagogy need to make sure that such closure is denied whenever it occurs.

In conclusion, we are now in a better position to review our early question as to the rate of semantic drift in a directional theory of meaning. How is communication possible if our critique of literality, propositional purity, locution, strict sense, and full identity holds? How can social and political visions be shared if they are always and fundamentally shifted by inferrable modalities? How indeed can we argue the coherence of a semiotic community if we have rejected as untenable the accurate transfer of meanings between utterers? Moreover, how can a realist textualist view explain how society gets on in the world if all it can know about is a mesh of sign systems of which the dominant one, linguistic discourse, now looks far less stable than the critical tradition has led us to believe? In short, what are the *constraints* of semantic drift in this sort of theory?

To begin with, some negative answers. The constraints are not logical in any strict sense, such that 'open' could be said to be fully secured by its opposition to 'closed.' Nor are the constraints guaranteed by literality. No such semantic foundation is available at any given time in the history of a language. We are simply unable to furnish criteria of meaning identity for all discursive operations. The fact that meaning identity is characteristic of some discourses, i.e., fully formalized languages, must not, as Tarski has warned us, be generalized to apply to natural systems. Nor does this sort of identity ever lead to literality. For once, literality makes no sense in formal logic since there is no opposite such as figurality, while literality in social discourse is a pragmatic fiction without a founding identity. Strict identity is indeed a constraint, but one which belongs to a small range of reduced discourses and so is derivative rather than the central property of all linguistic signification.

Now some provisional solutions. The constraints we are looking for are neither intrinsically inside language nor outside, attached to the world of objects; that is, as far as we can be sure. Rather, semantic drift is controlled by social semiotic at large, i.e., by historically shifting and always highly differentiated significatory practices in a variety of sign systems. The constraints which we need to be able to explain the cohesion of speech communities are themselves *textual*. This means that any one sign system receives its restraining orders from other semiotic practices, such as proximic, kinetic, aural, tactile, olfactory, and visual signification. Constraints of semantic drift occur along the boundaries of intersemiotic ratification and disaffirmation. Where corroboration of meaning shades into its opposite, this is where we find the controls for semantic choice. In addition to intersemiotic constraints there are also intrasemiotic curbs, semantic checks which are specific to particular discursive operations. As to linguistic signification, these appear to be a function of discursive frames or rungs on a ladder of discourse and of the politics of reading. Let us briefly illustrate these suggestions.

(1) As to intersemiotic constraints, the meaning of 'open' in different expressions was shown not to be secured by literality but more loosely by reference to other sign systems. Thus, instead of merely saying that a word receives its meaning from the discursive formation in which it occurs, we should add that each such regularity receives its function from its non-verbal semiotic backdrop.

(2) Intrasemiotic constraints in language are described well by Foucault's and Pêcheux's theories. Here we have to show that one and the same expression is ruled by different semantic limits in different formations. On the various rungs of a ladder of discourse 'satisfies,' for instance, takes on several meanings, some ruled by definition, as in formal semantics, and others loosely guided by intersemiotic negotiation.

(3) Within each linguistic regularity, as for instance the discourse on postmodern architecture, we find different discursive politics which likewise shift the curbs on semantic drift. The 'freedom' to quote at liberty from past styles is regarded as a liberation from one position, but turns on its semantic hinges to refer to commodificatory blindness from another. Semantic drift here can be understood as the result of a political form of ironic reversal. The constraints of reading politics can also be exaggerated when for example an analytical frame (2) is superimposed on socially saturated discourse. The boundary conditions exerted by the politics of reading are by no means minor, but have a powerful feedback effect on all other semantic boundaries and as such a profound influence on shifts in the social semiotic at large.

CONCLUSION

PANDORA, OCCAM, AND
THE POST-HUMANIST SUBJECT

> Or, is postmodernity the pastime of an old
> man who scrounges in the garbage-heap of
> finality looking for left-overs, who brandishes
> unconsciousness, lapses, limits, confines, gou-
> lags, parataxes, non-senses, or paradoxes, and
> who turns this into the glory of his novelty,
> into his promise of change?
>
> Jean-François Lyotard, *The Differend: Phrases*
> *in Dispute*

Or, a much less humanistic future awaits us. For complexity may not be a human privilege. Put another way, the complexities of the human and those of techno-logos may in the long run become indistinguishable when the survival of the species *homo sapiens sapiens* has to rely to an ever increasing extent on the synthetic maintenance of its bodies and machines incrementally exchange their mechanical simplicity for an organic countenance. For what the literature on minds and Turing machines tends to forget is that both *mind* and *machine* may turn out to be the crucial metaphors in the debate. Postmodernity from this futuristic perspective could be the transitional mode, our present "garbage-heap of finality," before we turn into digital beings.

We have looked at signification from two perspectives, the generosity of mean-ing exploration in pandoric reading and the censorship of Occam's formal-logical idealization. I presented a critique of idealization of meaning as definition by contrasting it with a directional theory (ch. 1); propositional closure was questioned by a fuzzy and semiotically extensional reading (ch. 2); deictic clo-sure was rejected by an argument for modal inference exemplified by way of generic semantic destabilization (ch. 3); the idealization of pure noematic mean-ing as against noetically murky signification was shown to fail when confronted by socially saturated signs (ch. 4); an overview of the history of meaning as sense revealed the gradual weakening of its initial definitional convictions to the point of dissolution in deconstructive critique, while deconstruction was itself questioned for its inability to account for pragmatic constraints on social semiosis (ch. 5); the idealization of language as abstracted system (*langue*) was confronted with its limits: the system of instantiations and the quasi-materiality of non-verbal signs (ch. 6); idealization in the form of a "universe of phrases" was supplemented by a semiotic perspective (ch. 7); the idealization of one sign system (formal logic) was relativized by its role in a ladder of discourses, each requiring specific descriptions of meaning and forms of reading (ch. 8); idealization in the form of a speaker abstractable from inside the text was replaced by the notion of hypocrisis which ties the "speaking subject" to semiosis at large; this, however, has not lead to a rehabilitation of the subject as originator of meaning, but rather to an insistence on the necessity of instantiation of semiosis by a complex system for which an individual reader is usually the vehicle (ch. 9); finally, the idealization of reading itself was found wanting on the grounds that it denies its links with the deictic and propositional distortions of political discourse, and idealization in the form of the construction of a *langue* of ideology was questioned by suggesting that ideology is more fruitfully construed as the combination of particular groups of instantiations for purposes of control (ch. 10). Seen in this way, linguistic ideality gives way to intersemiotic materiality.

Pandora, giver of all gifts, we remember is the goddess of fecundity, rich materials and energy, of earth and seed, of sprouting, flowering and growing, of grain and birth, a summary signification in hope of more materiality, more goods. Occam has been made to stand in for ideality, the principle of economy, essence, and conceptual truth. Between these heuristic idealizations exist our actual discourses: some, highly saturated with the materials of social semiosis, dreams, memories, facts; others, whose processes of signification have been functionally reduced down to the digital stripped of materiality except for that of its signifiers. Conceptual sign systems guarantee the continuation of social existence, saturated semiosis makes it meaningful. Neither can survive without the other. Yet it would be quite wrong to insist on splitting the ladder of discourses along the line of an idealist-materialist opposition. They are all merely different forms of materiality: rich and reduced and most of them in between. In the strictly formal sign systems materiality is suspended, waiting to be recalled as is the case in techno-logos.

How does this square with the large-scale and minute-scale descriptions of the world available at the moment? The quark has been hunted down,[1] far-from-equilibrium states in chemistry have been shown to yield ever new forms of order out of chaos,[2] the speed of change of reproduction and the generation of symmetries at the molecular level of cells is exciting biological science,[3] while multi-strand realities may once more be subsumed under a unified theory in theoretical physics. Some scientists go as far as to conclude from this a foundation for knowing the universe as it is.[4]

From a realist textualist perspective this looks naive. Indeed this new faith in ultimate foundations is at odds with the skeptical trajectory of thought in critical speculative philosophy. If we take a very broad view we can bring up to date the major explanatory hypotheses of the world during the twentieth century in this way: "atomism" with its quest for the ever receding ultimate indivisible or simple (Russell and the early Wittgenstein); the aspect theory of phenomenology (Husserl); "possibilism" to cover world semantics and theories of "counter factual states" (Kripke);[5] and "textualism" to allow for the late Wittgenstein, Heidegger, Foucault and Derrida.

In literature, deconstruction marks the end of an era characterized by the dominance of a variety of forms of criticism in which meaning emerged as an entity legitimated by the authority of distinct schools of scholarship: meaning at the behest of philology; meaning as the result of the unpacking of molecular sentences into atomistic ones; meaning arising from a New Critical autotelic perceptiveness; meaning as the object of speech act classification; meaning as a surface retransformed into a deep structure; meaning as the result of the superimposition of structural grids; or meaning as material practice and ideological effect.

The radical breach in this history, prefigured by Nietzsche and prepared for by the very phenomenology which had to serve as the main target of Derrida's attack, occurs when the clarity of the view shared by those schools is blurred by the shifting of the ground of the argument. Suddenly there is no longer any presence of the signified, no noematic meaning, but only processes of signification or noetic instantiations of discourse, processes which provide meaning with no more than differing degrees of instability.

But why should the institution of Literature be so worried, as it has been for a while, about this particular move in the language game of criticism? After all, deconstruction is developing its own scholarly apparatus and so, far from leading toward chaos, merely adds another authority to those already in play. Because this new player cheats, they say. And in a way this cannot be denied. For deconstruction wants to have it both ways: it insists on an infinite chain of signifiers without stable signifieds and at the same time wishes to signify quite firmly and without theoretical qualms the radical breach in the theory of meaning it believes it heralds. But then, deconstruction loves a paradox, and in any case there is no going back before Derrida's *Speech and Phenomena*, even if the critique is itself vulnerable to pragmatic attacks. However, there is the more serious worry that once the foundations of traditional hermeneutics are in doubt the centerpiece of the humanist structure itself is endangered: the subject. What *langue* is for structuralism, the subject is for traditional humanism: theoretical rationale and thematic focus. In the following I want to look at some of the implications of the construction of subjectivity for my position.

Even a parsimonious view of signification cannot avoid the problem of enunciation and the processes of meaning constitution and so of the subject, for "expressions manifest things, and hence essentially refer us to subjects for whom these things can be manifest."[6] It has been argued in this context that only through the subject's capacity called imagination can we have, "in advance of presentation, a workable criterion for applying or refusing to apply an expression to what should be presented."[7] This criterion could be said to be a differential relation in a semiotic of instantiations which inform the subjective; otherwise we would lack an explanation as to how intersubjective, i.e., social discourse, can function at all. But then again, the limits of such a *grammar* would have to be queried, for the yet-not-formulated and the no-longer-concretizable require a pre-predicative and a post-predicative, a pre-systemic and a post-systemic *field* to be arguable at all. Yet no matter whether those manifestations are seen as minimal sense identifications or richly suggestive projections, the worry about the subject remains.

What is a subject? Leaving subject matter aside, there is the difference between a grammatical and a logical subject (Strawson),[8] the speaking subject (Kristeva),[9] the social subject as individual consciousness within intersubjective constraints (Schutz),[10] the linguistic subject undermining objectivity by way of ego-centric particulars (Russell),[11] the psycho-analytic subject as the author, origin, or father of an expression (Lacan),[12] the subject as implied reader (Iser),[13] the "Subject of Law" (Frow),[14] the disseminated speaking subject that participates in the general play of semiosis (Derrida), the individual player who intervenes in the language games that confront him (Lyotard),[15] the subject as a series of vacant positions to be filled (Foucault),[16] the "subject of semiotics" (Kaja Silverman), or the subject as the ideologically overdetermined "subject-form of discourse" (Pêcheux).[17]

The list could be extended considerably. Relevant to our argument here are especially Kristeva's speaking subject, Schutz's intersubjectively circumscribed subject, Lyotard's intervening subject, Foucault's vacant subject positions, and Pêcheux's subject-form. I am not suggesting that these perspectives are compatible, but rather that they provide insights into the problem of the instantiation of language. For as I have insisted throughout: without instantiation, no language; without hypocrisis, no meaning. No matter how systemic and collective language may appear, it forever requires individual speakers or 'machines' to produce it anew. To turn the traditional phrasing around, only discourse is language in the full sense of the term.

This should not be construed to mean that instantiation could ever be entirely arbitrary. The necessity of enunciation does not deny the fact that when an utterance occurs it always does so within several sets of guidelines. In reading, one such set is intertextuality, which "makes possible precisely a formal analysis of texts: not in the sense that meaning would be taken to be inherent in formal properties, but in the quite opposite sense that it is only within a system of intertextual relations that the function of formal elements can be assessed."[18] One might add that even "informal reading," however rich, cannot completely escape those relations. In one sense "rich reading" can be said to be rich precisely to the extent to which it activates further and further fields of intertextuality.

Given the necessity of instantiation and the fact of multiple constraints, what does happen when a speaking subject fills the vacant subject positions of inscriptions? A synoptic answer would see this event as a function of the polarity between full parsimony or analyticity on the one hand and pandoric or expansive reading on the other. In other words, the answer depends on two opposing, as well as a range of other, conceptions of the process of meaning constitution: one which reduces this process to an atemporal and minimal definition of meaning as strict sense, essence, connotation, eidos, locution, or intension; its opposite, which requires full social semiosis as necessary background; and meaning constitution between these polarities: *tertium datur*.

In the logico-mathematical realm there is no room for any other kind of sense. As we have seen, however, its application to culturally saturated language leads to unhappy results. The paucity reflected in the well-known grammar of examples is the outcome of such misdirected parsimony: "The present king of France is bald . . . the morning star . . . the evening star . . . the cat on the mat . . . Scott, the author of Waverly . . . Napoleon defeated Wellington at Waterloo . . . the dog 'Fido.' "

However, there is another approach, the one favored throughout this study, which opts for as broad as possible a description of signification. Accordingly, there is no identifiable sense outside of and separable from "wishing to say" and "being affected by what is said." Or, more technically, there is no locution isolated from illocution and perlocution, no connotation without *vouloir-dire* and denotation, no noema without the noeses of speaking and receiving, no intension without intention, no linguistic meaning without non-verbal extension: no semantic of language outside its intersemiotic frame.

Wilhelm von Humboldt pointed to such a more generous view when he wrote about the Kavi language on Java, "*Sie ist selbst kein Werk, ergon, sondern eine Tätigkeit, energeia,*" not a work but rather a continuous process.[19] Hegel's temporalization of logic, Nietzsche's critical psychologization of truth criteria,[20] Husserl's notion of type as "vacillating approximation,"[21] Peirce's, and later Derrida's temporization of the sign,[22] Austin's broadening of a purely propositional description of language,[23] Derrida's qualification of speech intention and his metaphorization of conceptuality,[24] Wittgenstein's semiotic conception of language use as meaning,[25] Foucault's multiple saturation of language inscription,[26] or a semiotically amended notion of Lyotard's differend[27] can all be adduced in favor of pandoric reading and a liberal conception of signification.

Minimal sense definition, numerical identity ("this there") and outer horizon (the "endless horizon of coexisting objects . . . being either different from or typically similar to the object I am actually adverted to") serve perfectly well when we are dealing with formal languages.[28] In such operations, filling the vacant subject position means that the subject, the moment when an individual utters/reads an inscription, has the option of becoming a player in the game by denying the significance of his or her semiotic placement by eliminating the "deictic anchorage of utterances" (neutralization of deixis in a broad sense), refraining from referring and ascribing acts (neutralization of reference),[29] and abstaining from challenging the game as such (neutralization of the frame). Perhaps it is useful to point out here that there is an important difference between the kind of challenge which Gödel mounted, which is a challenge from within the realm of analyticity, and the broader metacritical challenge which asks historical and socio-critical questions (Habermas, Lyotard).[30] Traditionally, a player of the formal game who disobeys those three fundamental rules of neutralization is sent off the field of analyticity, to play the lesser game of social critique.[31]

The second pole, a comprehensive conception of meaning making, which proposes an unlimited chain of possible qualitative identifications (what *kind* of "this-there"?) and the notion of inner horizon ("the open frame for further determinability") does not concede any logical boundary for acts of meaning making.[32] That such boundaries are drawn all the time in actual speech rests on pragmatic considerations alone. In principle, there is no absolute basis for the definition of the degrees of determinateness. And the briefest of identifications ("Shut the door") can turn into a full exploration of meanings when its practical aspects are construed to conceal a less innocent intent. Apart from numerical quantities and formal relations, all items of natural language are "open and always rectifiable" concepts, directional schemata, as I have argued, rather than definitionally ruled instructions.

Admittedly, meaning exchange on this theory is a shaky affair, yet the assumption that communication takes place at all does not require the analytical solution of perfect meaning transfer, but rather the more modest thesis of the "reciprocity of perspectives" and meaning approximation.[33] As such communication goes beyond meaning as sense and includes what Kristeva has referred to as "pre-meaning," "pre-sign," "trans-meaning," and "trans-sign."[34] Such surplus significations, where "more is meant than is intended in each expression,"[35] allows for the "counterfactual states" of "possible worlds" in a rich sense produced by literary uses of language and experimental transformations of semiotic systems. They constitute cases of a ludic kind of *petitio principi*, macrostructural versions of the illegitimate move of "begging the question;" but at the same time, and paradoxically, they can act as a critique of the actual or, in Kripke's words, of "the way the dice come up."[36]

However, it is not surplus signification, but on the contrary the process of anonymization of typified experience into binary analyticity which characterizes electronic civilization as we now know it and as it will develop in the foreseeable future. To what realm then, we may ask, will full semiotic grasp be relegated? One possible answer is that saturated socio-cultural narrative repressed in analyticity returns through the political frames of science in its arguments for funds and legitimation, while general discourse threatened by the validity claims of formal language games takes its revenge in meta-narratives which adjudge analyticity and so attempts to place it under their critical purview. To general discourse, analyticity is never fully convincing, even if it no longer asserts the isomorphism, argued for instance by the Wittgenstein of the *Tractatus*, between its propositions and the world. All we can say now in this respect is that all language games, from the logico-mathematical ones to the ludic discourses of literature, facilitate different kinds of meaning imposition on the not-yet-structured and on what needs to be renamed.

Within certain institutional strictures the reader then has a wide range of options between terminating the chain of qualitative identifications and extending it. And apart from the simplest practical examples of language use, everyday discourse is in principle always "unsaturated" (Frege) and requires for its actualization not acts of neutralization, but on the contrary the kind of cultural saturation of which the members of a speech community are capable. This saturation includes the challenge of the limits of *langue* in both its forms, the not-yet-formulated and the no-longer-concretizable. Such extensions stand in a critical relation to what is given in that they constitute projections of possible worlds, each of which being a "modal transformation of the actual." [37]

What threatens signification is censorship. Censorship can be described as any form of restriction on the ways in which the vacant subject positions of discourse could be filled. There are many stages of the censorship between an ideal of 'full' signification and the radical denial of idiom, as for example Lyotard's differend, as well as many levels at which such curtailment becomes effective: at the levels of *intonation* (exclusion of non-standard accents of class, region, foreigners; imposition of prosodic contours in political and other ritual chants), *diction* (Bowdlerism and other abstersive measures), *syntax* (the delegitimation of non-standard English, pidgin), *semantics* (strictures on meaning descriptions, official meanings; strictures on the modal extensions of inscriptions, e.g., the denial of the speech act in "Genesis"), and *ideation* (constraints on interpretive exploration: institutionalized readings).

Important margins of communication are threatened by parsimonious reading programs, though such injunctions do not all come from domains out of sympathy with the literary.[38] Indeed, the insistence on the very possibility of literal readings is an interpretive embargo frequently imposed from within the institution of literature. From the viewpoint of a literal reading, what is a "vacant subject position" is drastically less than is inscribed in Foucault's term. Departmental jealousy is another kind of censorship which rests on the dubious inside/ outside distinction. It is usually voiced as an attack on the critic who has deviated from the center of the reading norm.

As Harold Bloom censors the theorist, "many critics flee to philosophy or to linguistics, but the result is that they learn to interpret poems as philosophy or as linguistics."[39] Similarly, Geoffrey Hartman's view that "in criticism, we deal not with language as such, nor with the philosophy of language, but with how books or habits of reading *penetrate* our lives"[40] harbors the assumption that these books affect us as Literature and nothing else. This negates what Foucault has termed the "polyvalence of discourses."[41] Like Harold Bloom's, Hartman's position also supports a view of the institution of literature as an activity which, as Kuhn has said of science, "is its own exclusive audience and judge."[42] Yet signification in the literary text more than in other discourses is characterized by its "fundamental entanglement with all discourses" and so is forever overdetermined by theoretical principles and reading practices which we can deny, if only at a cost, or search out and put to critical use.[43] For there is clearly the danger that "the current provocative celebration of strong misreadings over weak ones" will reduce itself to merely another flogging of the dead horse of "the positivistic conception of philological accuracy" from the perspective of a not-so-New Criticism .[44]

In the face of the agonistics of social discourse, the reader of inscriptions does not merely fill vacant subject positions at all levels of language from intonation to ideational operations but is always also in a position to transform those acts into creative and metacritical extensions. If the achievement of analyticity lies in its neutralization of reference, deixis, and frame into synonymy and synchrony, that very analyticity turns into censorship when it is applied to natural language. For neutralization means the removal of the semiotic and the diachronic, without which cultural saturation and meta-critical extension cannot occur. Diachrony here does not mean the looking back at securely retrievable meanings, but on the contrary the thinking of the present in terms of projections into the past and the future. As Heidegger formulates it, *"Erst wenn wir uns denkend dem schon Gedachten zuwenden, werden wir verwendet für das noch zu Denkende"* (Only when we turn thoughtfully toward what has already been thought, will we be turned to use for what must still be thought).[45]

It is perhaps ironic that the pandoric rather than parsimonious conception of discourse, with its emphasis on the ludic, literary, and metaphoric should score particularly well in terms of "performativity," the ultimate criterion of power in the age of information technology.[46] For example, the metaphor "octopus," signifying "bureaucracy," may be an "imperfectly intuitable concrete universal,"[47] but in terms of "the relationship between input and output" its "fecundity of expression"[48] is remarkably cost-effective; it generates a lot from a little, a vast discourse from limited resources.

In pandoric as in parsimonious uses of language meaning-as-unstable-process occurs through individual instantiation. In the former, hypocrisis, the necessary act of feigning a subject position, is allowed its full range, whereas in the latter it is reduced to a near-neutral speech act. Though either instances are ordinarily performed by an individual, that particular person is not the subject we are looking for. The subject cannot be an individual who is *subjective* much in the same way again and again. Rather, the subject is an *event* which requires an individual but is not identical with it. The subject occurs, for example, in the act of reading when a reader, the one "who is alone with his text"[49] can read this text only "as the always-already-read."[50] Thus, what we commonly and loosely refer to as the subject is the paradox of a systemically overdetermined event of meaning endowment which in the process of filling the always unsaturated possibilities of signification makes possible the transcendence of its limits.[51] The subject "never *is*;" it can be described only as "the process of signification."[52]

Much as we tend to construe this process in humanist terms it really only indicates the high degree of complexity characteristic of semiosis.[53] The traditional humanistic equation of the writing/reading/speaking subject and the individual self rests on a confusion between the necessity of instantiation and the contingency according to which human readers at this moment in history display by far the greatest reading competence.[54] Yet our reasons are dwindling fast according to which no 'machine' can ever reproduce the complexities involved in filling the directional schemata of language. Already Wittgenstein's understanding "at a flash" has literally become an electronic possibility by virtue of giga flop and tera flop "multiplex time" of digital transformation.

Toward the end of the last century Charles Sanders Peirce introduced the notion of the "quasi-mind" to distinguish the principles involved in signification from the incidental apparatus of the human mind and to protect his semiotic theory against the charge of subjectivist mentalist error.[55] And in spite of the post-Turing debates we have not been able to move radically ahead; where we are now is no more than a primitive beginning.[56] Quite possibly the present dissolution of the humanist subject is only a preparation for the disfiguration of the individual by way of feedback: technology, initially an extension of humankind, will in turn relativize humanity as a complex entropic system. Perhaps there are worse prospects than having monitoring systems guard the ecology of the biosphere against the foolishness of human complexities. If anything humanist is at all worth rescuing in this process it is not the subject but notions of justice, a project not for individuals but for society.

Advanced social perspectives, such as universal altruistic behavior, may turn out to be not a Kantian speculative accomplishment of our duty for the higher values of a non-utilitarian formal ethics but rather the inevitable consequence of our brain stem having grown beyond itself in a feedback relation with the evolution of more and more complex social structures. This is the kind of explanation which goes well with a posthumanist conception of the subject.[57] The hardware of our brain evolves with the ever more sophisticated software of our understanding of the universe as a text which we project with increasing ingenuity. In this process the irretrievable event of the individual humanistic self is no more than an unreliable witness; what counts is whether the species will be able to fulfill its potential for perhaps the ultimate social vision: global justice on a sustainable planet.

NOTES

Preface

1. Nelson Goodman, *Ways of Worldmaking* (Indianapolis: Hackett Publishing, 1978).
2. Thomas G. Pavel, *Fictional Worlds* (Cambridge, Mass.: Harvard University Press, 1986).
3. N. V. Voloshinov, *Marxism and the Philosophy of Language* (New York: Seminar Press, 1973).

Introduction

1. Christopher Norris, *The Contest of Faculties: Philosophy and Theory after Deconstruction* (London: Methuen, 1985) and Reed Way Dasenbrock, *Redrawing the Lines: Analytic Philosophy, Deconstruction, and Literary Theory* (Minneapolis: University of Minnesota Press, 1989); on this question see my "The Two Paradigms: Is a Dialogue Possible?" in *On Literary Theory and Philosophy: A Cross-Disciplinary Encounter*, ed. Richard Freadman and Lloyd Reinhardt (London: Macmillan, 1991), pp. 213–34.
2. I am grateful for this term to John de Reuck who suggests that *semantic foundationalism* describes the untheorized deep level of assumptions concerning literal meanings.
3. Donald Davidson, "What Metaphors Mean," in *On Metaphor*, ed. Sheldon Sacks (Chicago: University of Chicago Press, 1981), pp. 29–45.
4. J. Hillis Miller, *Fiction and Repetition: Seven English Novels* (Cambridge, Mass.: Harvard University Press, 1982), p. 3.
5. Julia Kristeva, "The System and the Speaking Subject," in *The Tell-Tale Sign: A Survey of Semiotics*, ed. Thomas A. Sebeok (Lisse: Peter de Ridder, 1975), pp. 47–66, 50.
6. Jacques Derrida, *Speech and Phenomena and Other Essays on Husserl's Theory of Signs*, trans. David B. Allison (Evanston: Northwestern University Press, 1973); Horst Ruthrof, "Identity and Differance," *Poetics* 17 (1988): 99–112; Jürgen Habermas, *The Philosophical Discourse of Modernity* (London: Polity Press, 1987), pp. 161–84, 184.
7. Geoffrey Hartman, *Criticism in the Wilderness: The Study of Literature Today* (New Haven: Yale University Press, 1980), pp. 162, 203.
8. Jürgen Habermas, "A Reply to My Critics," in *Habermas: Critical Debates*, ed. John B. Thompson and David Held (Cambridge, Mass.: MIT Press, 1982), pp. 219–83; and as early as in "Science and Technology as Ideology," in *Toward a Rational Society: Student Protest, Science and Politics*, trans. J. J. Shapiro (London: Heinemann, 1971), pp. 81–122; esp. pp. 92–94.
9. Harold Bloom, "The Breaking of Form," in *Deconstruction and Criticism* (New York: Continuum, 1979), p. 9.
10. Thomas Nagel, *The View from Nowhere* (Oxford: Clarendon Press, 1986), p. 91.
11. Michael Devitt, "Dummett's Anti-Realism," *Journal of Philosophy* 80 (1983): 73–99; 76.
12. Michael Dummett, "Realism," in *Truth and Other Enigmas* (Cambridge, Mass.: Harvard University Press, 1978), pp. 145–65; and "Truth," pp. 1–28; 24. I am indebted to David Novitz for part of this section, even if my position differs quite radically from the one he advocates in *Knowledge, Fiction and Imagination* (Philadelphia: Temple University Press, 1987).

13. Hilary Putnam, *Reason, Truth and History* (Cambridge: Cambridge University Press, 1983), p. 49.

14. I am grateful to Jeff Malpas for having drawn my attention to the intricacies of the realism debate; see his *The Mirror of Meaning: Donald Davidson and Radical Interpretation*, esp. chapter 7 (Cambridge: Cambridge University Press, 1992).

15. Michel Pêcheux, *Language, Semantics, and Ideology*, trans. H. Nagpal (London: Macmillan, 1986), pp. 183ff.

16. Gottlob Frege, "Thoughts," in *Logical Investigations*, ed. Peter Geach (Oxford: Basil Blackwell, 1977), pp. 3f.

17. Ibid., p. 4; Donald Davidson, "A Coherence Theory of Truth and Knowledge," in *Truth and Interpretation: Perspectives on the Philosophy of Donald Davidson*, ed. Ernest Lepore (Oxford: Basil Blackwell, 1989), pp. 307–319; 308.

18. Mark Platts, *Ways of Meaning* (London: Routledge and Kegan Paul, 1979), p. 33.

19. Putnam, p. 52.

20. Novitz, chapters 1 to 4.

21. For example in Stephen W. Hawking, *A Brief History of Time: From the Big Bang to Black Holes* (London: Bantam, 1989), pp. 124, 125.

22. Friedrich Nietzsche, "On Truth and Falsity in Their Ultramoral Sense," in *The Complete Works of Friedrich Nietzsche*, vol. 2, ed. Oskar Levy, trans. M. A. Mügge (London: Allen and Unwin, 1911), pp. 171–192; 186, 184.

23. Friedrich Nietzsche, "The Wanderer and His Shadow" (1873), in *The Complete Works of Friedrich Nietzsche*, vol. 7, ed. Oscar Levy (New York: Russell and Russell, 1964), pp. 191f.

24. Friedrich Nietzsche, "Of the Prejudices of Philosophers," (1886) in *Beyond Good and Evil: The Complete Works*, Aphorism 20.

25. Friedrich Nietzsche, *The Dawn of Day*, 2, Aphorism 115, *The Complete Works*, vol. 9, pp. 119f.

26. Martin Heidegger, *The Question Concerning Technology* (New York: Harper and Row, 1977), p. 21.

27. Novitz, p. 56.

28. Jean-François Lyotard, *The Differend: Phrases in Dispute* (Manchester: Manchester University Press, 1988), p. 32.

29. Cf. also Richard Rorty, "Nineteenth Century Idealism and Twentieth Century Textualism," in *Consequences of Pragmatism* (Brighton: Harvester Press, 1982), pp. 139–59.

30. Steven Lukes, "Relativism in Its Place," in *Rationality and Relativism*, ed. Martin Hollis and Steven Lukes (Oxford: Basil Blackwell, 1982), pp. 161–305; 302; 304.

31. W. Newton-Smith, "Relativism and the Possibility of Interpretation," in *Rationality and Relativism*, pp. 106–122; 119.

32. Goodman, pp. 3; 94; 128; Richard Rorty agrees with Goodman's "versions" of the world in "The World Well Lost," *Journal of Philosophy* 69 (1972): 649–65.

33. Peter Marler, "Visual Systems," in *Animal Communication: Techniques of Study and Results of Research*, ed. Thomas A. Sebeok (Bloomington: Indiana University Press, 1968), pp. 103–126; 103.

34. Cf. the work of Hayes and Bateson, E. T. Hall, L. K. Frank, A. A. Moles and others; see also the more recent studies, for example, by Adam Kendon, ed., *Nonverbal Communication, Interaction, and Gesture: Selections from Semiotica* (The Hague: Mouton, 1981), and Fernando Poyatos, *New Perspectives in Nonverbal Communication* (Oxford: Pergamon Press, 1982).

35. Goodman, p. 139, n. 26.

36. Richard Rorty, *Philosophy and the Mirror of Nature* (Oxford: Basil Blackwell, 1980), p. 318.

37. Ian Hacking, *Why Does Language Matter to Philosophy?* (Cambridge: Cambridge University Press, 1975), p. 183.

1. The Directionality of Meaning

1. Steven W. Hawking, *A Brief History of Time: From the Big Bang to Black Holes* (London: Bantam, 1989).

2. Martin Heidegger, "The Principle of Identity," in *Identity and Difference*, trans. Joan Stambaugh (New York: Harper and Row, 1974), pp. 23–41, and "Language" in *Poetry, Language, Thought*, trans. Albert Hofstadter (New York: Harper and Row, 1975), pp. 189–210; Charles Sanders Peirce, *Collected Papers*, vols. 3 and 4, ed. Charles Hartshorne and Paul Weiss (Cambridge, Mass.: The Belknap Press of Harvard University Press, 1974), 3.621

3. Jacques Derrida, "Differance," in *Speech and Phenomena* (Evanston: Northwestern University Press, 1973) pp. 129–60.; *Dissemination*, trans. B. Johnson (Chicago: University of Chicago Press, 1981); *Margins of Philosophy*, trans. Alan Bass (Chicago: University of Chicago Press, 1982); and "White Mythology," *New Literary History* 6 (1974): 5–74. Cf. also Heidegger's notion of *Verstehen* as an "as-structure" in *Being and Time* (Oxford: Basil Blackwell, 1962), pp. 188ff.

4. This directional model of meaning also acts as a critical commentary on Habermas's schema offered in *Communication and the Evolution of Society* (London: Heinemann, 1979), with its triad of cognitive, social and subjective speech. His "subjective" expression is replaced by a form of social discourse while the "cognitive" is relegated to a less privileged position. What should be retained are Habermas's arguments concerning "consensus" ideal (*pace* Lyotard), "manipulation," and "communication free of domination" as well as his notion of "validity" claims.

5. M. A. K. Halliday, *An Introduction to Functional Grammar* (London: Edward Arnold, 1985), pp. 319–45; 327, 320; the point of the all-pervasiveness of metaphor in everyday discourse is also made from a different angle by George Lakoff and Mark Johnson in "Conceptual Metaphor in Everyday Language," *The Journal of Philosophy* 77 (1980): 453–86.

6. Aristotle, *Poetics*, trans. G. F. Else (Ann Arbor: Michigan University Press, 1973), p. 57. L. Jonathan Cohen refines the Aristotelian notions of condensation and substitution by way of componential semantics and a process of feature-cancellation; in so doing Cohen remains strictly within a linguistic semantic analysis; "The Semantics of Metaphor," in *Metaphor and Thought*, ed. Andrew Ortony (Cambridge: Cambridge University Press, 1979), pp. 64–77.

7. John R. Searle, "Metaphor," in *Metaphor and Thought*, pp. 92–123; 105.

8. Paul Ricoeur, *The Rule of Metaphor*, trans. Robert Cerny (London: Routledge and Kegan Paul, 1978), p. 6.

9. Donald Davidson, "What Metaphors Mean," in *Metaphor: Problems and Perspectives*, ed. David S. Miall (Sussex: Harvester Press, 1982), pp. 1–13. Cf. also Max Black's objections to Davidson's approach which appear to miss Davidson's point that if "meaning" and "saying" are to be treated in a strictly semantic fashion, then metaphor does indeed not "mean," unless there were a secondary and quite different sort of semantics; "How Metaphors Work: A Reply to Donald Davidson," in *On Metaphor*, ed. Sheldon Sacks (Chicago: University of Chicago Press, 1981), pp. 181–92.

10. Stephen Davies, "Truth-Values and Metaphors," *The Journal of Aesthetics and Literary Criticism* 42 (1984): 291–302; Davidson, "What Metaphors Mean," pp. 31; 36.

11. Davidson, p. 44.

12. Black, "How Metaphors Work: A Reply to Donald Davidson," in *On Metaphor*, pp. 190–92; "More About Metaphor," in *Metaphor and Thought*, ed. Andrew Ortony (Cambridge: Cambridge University Press, 1979), pp. 21–41; "Metaphor," in *Philosophical Perspective on Metaphor*, ed. Mark Johnson (Minneapolis: University of Minnesota Press, 1981), pp. 63–82.

13. Umberto Eco, "The Semantics of Metaphor," in *The Role of the Reader: Explorations in the Semiotics of Texts* (Bloomington: Indiana University Press, 1979), pp. 67–89; 69,

86f. For other broad approaches to metaphor see also Paul de Man, "The Epistemology of Metaphor," in *On Metaphor*, pp. 11–28; or Jacques Derrida, "The *Retrait* of Metaphor," *Enclitic* 2,2 (1978): 5–33, who understands meaning "also in the sense of direction;" 24.

14. Umberto Eco, *Semiotics and the Philosophy of Language* (London: Macmillan, 1984), p. 88; 88f., 127.

15. Gareth Evans, *The Varieties of Reference*, ed. John McDowell (Oxford: Clarendon Press, 1982).

16. Ibid., pp. 311f.

17. J. N. Mohanty, *Edmund Husserl's Theory of Meaning* (The Hague: Martinus Nijhoff, 1964), p. 141; 140.

18. C. M. Meyers, "The Determinate and Determinable Modes of Appearing," *Mind* 68 (1958): 32–49; 45.

19. For a short version of this argument see my "Literature and the Ladder of Discourse," *Analecta Husserliana* 19 (1985): 413–31. The term *semantic foundationalism* was suggested by John de Reuck to focus my attack on literality and related semantic assumptions.

20. Jacques Derrida, *Speech and Phenomena* (Evanston: Northwestern University Press, 1973), *passim*; and "Differance," in Ibid., pp. 129–60.

21. Jacques Derrida, *Of Grammatology*, trans. Gayatri Chakravorty Spivak (Baltimore: The Johns Hopkins University Press, 1978), Part I; 226f., 280ff., 285.

22. "The Apology of Socrates," in *Plato: The Last Days of Socrates* (Harmondsworth: Penguin, 1984), pp. 43–76.

23. Not only in the sense of language as a "social semiotic" as presented by M. A. K. Halliday in *Language as Social Semiotic: The Social Interpretation of Language and Meaning*, (London: Edward Arnold, 1978), but in a more radical sense of always involving other than verbal sign systems. For this sort of application of the term cf. Bob Hodge and Gunther Kress, *Social Semiotic* (London: Polity Press, 1988).

24. Michel Foucault, *The Archaeology of Knowledge* (London: Tavistock, 1972), pp. 95, 108, 115, 153.

25. Ibid., p. 107; Ludwig Wittgenstein, *Philosophical Investigations*, trans. G. E. M. Anscombe (New York: Macmillan, 1953), I.23.

26. Cf. John Frow, "Discourse Genres," *Journal of Literary Semantics* (1980): 73–81; and "The Literary Frame," *Journal of Aesthetic Education* 16 (1982): 25–30.

27. The concepts of "propositional opacity" and "modal opacity" have been developed out of the indeterminacies attached to the more specific narrative notions of presented world and presentational process used in my *The Reader's Construction of Narrative* (London: Routledge and Kegan Paul, 1981), *passim*.

28. John Lyons, *Language, Meaning and Context* (London: Fontana, 1981), pp. 26, 125, 139, 183, 205.

29. In qualification of Derrida's argument in "Limited Inc abc . . . ," *Glyph* 2 (1977): 162–254. Cf. also my brief critique of the limitations of Searle's indirect speech act theory in "The Problem of Inferred Modality in Narrative," *Journal of Literary Semantics* 13 (1984): 97–108; esp. 99–102.

30. Gottlob Frege, "On Sense and Reference," in *Translations from the Philosophical Works of Gottlob Frege*, ed. Peter Geach and Max Black (Oxford: Basil Blackwell, 1966), pp. 56f; Bertrand Russell, "On Denoting," in *Essays in Analysis*, ed. Douglas Lackey (New York: George Braziller, 1973), p. 102; and again P. F. Strawson, "On Referring," *Mind* 59 (1950): 320–44; 321 and 331.

31. Frege, p. 58; and Russell in a reply to Strawson entitled "Mr Strawson on Referring," *Mind* 66 (1957): 385–89; 385.

32. Barry Humphries, Forward to K. Dunstan, *Ratbags* (Sydney: Golden Press, 1979).

33. Wittgenstein, I, 138, pp. 53/53e.

34. Edmund Husserl, *Cartesian Meditations*, fifth meditation (The Hague: Martinus

Nijhoff, 1973); and Roman Ingarden, *The Literary Work of Art* and *The Cognition of the Literary Work of Art* (both Evanston: Northwestern University Press, 1973), *passim.*

35. John R. Searle, *Intentionality: An Essay in the Philosophy of Mind* (Cambridge: Cambridge University Press, 1983), pp. 145f.

36. Dieter Wunderlich, "Methodological Remarks on Speech Act Theory," in *Speech Act Theory and Pragmatics,* ed. John R. Searle, Ferenc Kiefer, and Manfred Bierwisch (Dordrecht: Reidel, 1980), pp. 291–312; 298.

37. "My account is hard to follow: because it says something new it still has egg-shells from the old view sticking to it;" from Ludwig Wittgenstein, *Vermischte Bemerkungen,* ed. Georg Hendrik von Wright and Heikki Nyman (Oxford: Basil Blackwell, 1977), p. 44e.

38. "Fuzzy" is used here in a different sense from the probabilistic, quantitative definition employed by Lofti Asker Zadeh in "Quantitative Fuzzy Semantics," *Information Sciences* 3, 2 (1971), 159–76.

39. Ludwig Wittgenstein, *On Certainty,* ed. G. E. M. Anscombe and H. G. von Wright, trans. Denis Paul and G. E. M. Anscombe (Oxford: Basil Blackwell, 1969), p. 6e.

2. The Rape of Autumn or the Rich and Fuzzy Life of Meanings

1. Jean-François Lyotard, *The Differend: Phrases in Dispute* (Manchester: Manchester University Press, 1988), pp. 130, 137.

2. Bob Hodge and Gunter Kress, *Social Semiotic* (London: Polity Press, 1988).

3. David Birch, *Language, Literature and Critical Practice: Ways of Analysing Text* (London: Routledge, 1989), pp. 150–65; and Marie Maclean, *Narrative as Performance: The Baudelairean Experiment* (London: Routledge, 1988).

4. Terry Eagleton, *The Rape of Clarissa* (Oxford: Basil Blackwell, 1982).

5. Jacques Derrida, "Cogito and the History of Madness," in *Writing and Difference,* trans. Alan Bass (London: Routledge and Kegan Paul, 1978), pp. 31–63. Cf. John Frow's analysis of both Derrida's and Foucault's reading in *Marxism and Literary History* (Oxford: Basil Blackwell, 1986), chapter 8.

6. Hans Robert Jauss, *Question and Answer: Forms of Dialogic Understanding,* trans. Michael Hays (Minneapolis: University of Minnesota Press, 1989), pp. 231f.

7. Donald Davidson, "Thought and Talk," in *Inquiries into Truth and Interpretation* (Oxford: Clarendon Press, 1984), pp. 17–36, 169; and "The Method of Truth in Metaphysics," in *Inquiries,* pp. 199–214, 204.

8. Donald Davidson, "Belief and the Basis of Meaning," in *Inquiries,* pp. 141–54; 153; 144; 146; and "A Coherence Theory of Truth," in *Truth and Interpretation: Perspectives on the Philosophy of Donald Davidson,* ed. Ernest Lepore (Oxford: Basil Blackwell, 1986), pp. 307–319; 315 n. 7.

9. Donald Davidson, "Toward a Unified Theory of Meaning and Action," *Grazer Philosophische Schriften* 2 (1980): 1–12; 7; "Introduction," in *Inquiries,* pp. xiii–xx; xvii.

10. I am grateful to Jeff Malpas for having drawn my attention to a 'hermeneutical' reading of Davidson, even if my argument turns out to be less sympathetic to Davidson's overall position than his. Cf. J. E. Malpas, "Shanks, King-Farlow and the Refutation of Davidson," *Idealistic Studies* 18 (1988): 20–31; see also his "*Agreement and Interpretation,*" (Ph.D. dissertation, Australian National University, 1986), pp. 372.

11. Wlad Godzich, "The Semiotics of Semiotics," *Australian Journal of Cultural Studies* 2 (1984): 3–22; 17ff.. Perhaps "substance-effect" would be better termed "substance-principle" since it is not an effect itself but enables specific historical semiotic events to take place.

12. Cf. the argument against literature and literary theory and for cultural studies in Terry Eagleton, *Literary Theory: An Introduction* (Oxford: Basil Blackwell, 1983), pp. 194–217.

13. In Stephen Booth, *Shakespeare's Sonnets* (New Haven: Yale University Press, 1977), p. 59.

14. Harold Bloom, "The Ode To Autumn," in *Twentieth Century Interpretations of Keats's Odes: A Collection of Critical Essays*, ed. Jack Stillinger (Englewood Cliffs, N.J.: Prentice-Hall, Inc., 1968), pp. 94–97; 94.

15. *Metamorphoses*, Book II, 1.29, in Ovid, *Metamorphoses*, vol. 1, trans. Frank Justus Miller, rev. ed. G. P. Goold (Cambridge, Mass.: Harvard University Press, 1977), pp. 62f.. The topos appears again in *Fasti*, iv, 1.897, "*venerat Autumnus calcatis sordidus uvis*," *Georgics*, 11.4–6.

16. *Virgil's Georgics*, trans. Smith Palmer Bovie (Chicago: University of Chicago Press, 1956), p. 91.

17. *Carmina* 4.7.1.11 and *Epodes*, II, 11.18–20; in Horace, *The Odes and Epodes*, with an English translation by C. E. Bennett (Cambridge, Mass.: Harvard University Press, 1968), pp. 310f. and 364f.

18. "Mutabilitie," Canto VII, 30, in Edmund Spenser, *The Faerie Queene*, ed. Thomas P. Roche (Harmondsworth: Penguin, 1978), p. 1047.

19. "The Fable of Vertumnus and Pomona," 11.10 and 58 in *The Poems of Alexander Pope*, vol. I, Pastoral Poetry, ed. E. Audra and Audrey Williams (London: Methuen, 1961), pp. 337 and 379; cf. Ovid, *Metamorphoses*, Book XIV, 11.629 and 660.

20. *The Complete Poetry and Prose of William Blake*, ed. David Erdman (Berkeley: The University of California Press, 1982), p. 409.

21. William Wordsworth, "Excursion," 5, 11.400–402.

22. Rainer Maria Rilke, "*Herbsttag*" 2, 11.1–4; Georg Trakl, "*Verklärter Herbst*," 1, 11.1–2.

23. Charles Baudelaire, "*Chant D'Automne*," 1, 11.1–2.

24. William Butler Yeats, "The Wild Swans at Coole," 5, 11.3–6.

25. Jacques Derrida, "Differance," in *Speech and Phenomena* (Evanston: Northwestern University Press, 1973), p. 145.

26. For example Ferdinand de Saussure in *Course in General Linguistics* (London: Fontana, 1974), pp. 22f., 88, 110; Ludwig Wittgenstein in *Philosophical Investigations*, trans. G. E. M. Anscombe (New York: Macmillan, 1953), I, 31, p. 15/15e; and Gilbert Ryle in "The Theory of Meaning," in *British Philosophy in the Mid-Century*, ed. C. A. Mace (London: George Allen and Unwin, 1957), pp. 239–64; esp. 248–64.

27. Pure "locutions" in Austin's sense do not exist as part of discourse; the concept is a strictly analytical stipulation which describes something that does not occur, though it is thinkable. In living speech propositional contents are always fully tied to all elements of Austin's triad.

28. E. D. Hirsch, *The Aims of Interpretation* (Chicago: University of Chicago Press, 1976), pp. 1–13; 79ff.; 85f.; 146.

29. John Lyons, *Language, Meaning and Context* (London: Fontana, 1981), p. 242.

30. Letter to Reynolds from Winchester, September 22, 1819. Keats apparently remains quite unaware of the relationship between his observation of the chastity of the scene, his use of language and the formal aspects of his poem and concludes by explaining, "This struck me so much in my Sunday's walk that I composed upon it."

31. Letters 599 and 539 quoted by Jean Z. Seznec, "Literary Inspiration in van Gogh," in *Van Gogh in Perspective*, ed. Bogomila Welsh-Ovcharov (Englewood Cliffs, N.J.: Prentice-Hall, 1974), pp. 1–133; 133, 132.

32. "Le Soleil," 1, 11.3f.

33. 5–6 September, 1889; quoted from A. M. and Renilde Hammacher, *Van Gogh: A Documentary Biography* (London: Thames and Hudson, 1982), p. 198.

34. N.105, 5 in *The Poems of Gerard Manley Hopkins*, ed. W. H. Gardner and N. H. McKenzie (London: Oxford University Press, 1967), p. 148.

35. Letter to Reynolds from Winchester, September 22, 1819. Keats's "innocence" is outdone only by such critics as Aileen Ward, *John Keats: The Making of a Poet* (New

York: Viking Press, 1963) or Charles I. Patterson, *The Daemonic in the Poetry of John Keats* (Urbana: University of Illinois Press, 1970).

36. Cf. "Ode on a Grecian Urn," 5, 11. 8–10.

37. Friedrich Nietzsche, *The Will to Power: An Attempted Transvaluation of All Values*, trans. Anthony M. Ludovici, vol. II, books III and IV (London: George Allen and Unwin, 1924), pp. 45–49.

38. Friedrich Nietzsche, "On Truth and Falsity in Their Ultramoral Sense," in *The Complete Works of Friedrich Nietzsche*, vol. 2, ed. Oscar Levy, trans. M. A. Mügge (London: Allen and Unwin, 1911), pp. 171–92; 180.

39. Martin Heidegger, "The Origin of the Work of Art," in *Poetry, Language, Thought*, trans. Albert Hofstadter (New York: Harper and Row, 1975), pp. 15–87; 33f.

40. Ibid., p. 81.

41. Ibid., p. 35.

42. Ibid., p. 36.

43. Hans-Georg Gadamer, *Truth and Method*, trans. William Glen-Doepel, ed. John Cumming and Garrett Barden (New York: Seabury Press, 1975), pp. 273ff.; 337ff.. His "fusion of horizons" (*Horizontverschmelzung*) is tenable only as a highly flexible metaphor. To attach any strict methodological procedure or the hope of specific disclosures to the phrase would be misleading.

44. Cf. my paper, "Towards an Intersemiotic Definition of Meaning" (in press).

3. The Modalities of the "Künstlerroman"

1. Patrick White, *Flaws in the Glass: A Self-Portrait* (London: Jonathan Cape, 1981), p. 74.

2. I am grateful to Umberto Eco for drawing my attention to the close relationship between the phenomenological method and the conception of vectoriality in semiotics.

3. Cf. Edmund Husserl in *Ideas* and *Cartesian Meditations* and Roman Ingarden in *The Literary Work of Art*.

4. Elizabeth W. Bruss, *Autobiographical Acts: The Changing Situation of a Literary Genre* (Baltimore: Johns Hopkins University Press, 1976), p. 1; Bruss attacks the normative tradition in the criticism of autobiographical writing since Roy Pascal's *Design and Truth in Autobiography*, p. 7.

5. Patricia A. Morley, *The Mystery of Unity* (Toronto: Bryant Press, 1972), Chapter 11, "Ggoddd, the divine vivisector," pp. 209–32.

6. For a definition of the *Künstlerroman* as a genre see Roberta M. Bayer, "*Voyage into Creativity: A Comparative Study of the Development of the Artist in the Work of Hermann Hesse, D. H. Lawrence, James Joyce and Theodore Dreiser*," (Ph.D. dissertation, New York University, 1974). Cf. also Herbert Marcuse's *Der Deutsche Künstlerroman* (Freiburg, 1922).

7. Quoted in Paul Gauguin, *Artists on Art*, ed. R. Goldwater and M. Treves (New York: Pantheon, n.d.).

8. Leo Bersani, *Marcel Proust: The Fictions of Life and Art* (London: Oxford University Press, 1975), p. 201.

9. J. Ann Duncan, "Imaginary Artists in *A la recherche du temps perdu*," *The Modern Language Review* 64 (1969): 555–64; 556.

10. Randolph Splitter, *Proust's "Recherche": A Psychoanalytic Interpretation* (Boston: Routledge and Kegan Paul, 1981), p. 81.

11. Bersani, p. 201.

12. Thomas Mann, *The Genesis of a Novel*, trans. Richard and Clara Winston (London: Secker and Warburg, 1961), p. 163f.

13. *The Genesis of a Novel*, p. 175.

14. Gunilla Bengsten, *Thomas Mann's Doctor Faustus: The Sources and the Structure*

of the Novel, trans. Krishna Winston (Chicago: The University of Chicago Press, 1969), p. 87.

15. Ibid., p. 165.

16. Georg Lukács, *Essays on Thomas Mann*, trans. Stanley Mitchell (London: Merlin Press, 1964), p. 70.

17. Ibid.

18. Ibid.

19. T. J. Reed, *Thomas Mann, The Uses of Tradition* (Oxford: Clarendon Press, 1966), p. 361.

20. Ibid., p. 374.

21. Thomas Mann, in a manuscript note, quoted in Reed, p. 374., p. 35.

22. *The Genesis of a Novel*, p. 30.

23. Ibid., p. 28.

24. Grant H. Redford, "The Role of Structure in Joyce's *Portrait*," *Modern Fiction Studies* 4 (1958): 21–30; 29.

25. Marcel Proust, *A la recherche du temps perdu*, vol. III, *Le temps retrouve* (Paris: Gallimard, 1954), p. 889; English translation by C. K. Scott Moncrieff and Terence Kilmartin (London: Chatto and Windus, 1981), III, p. 924.

26. Bersani, p. 194.

27. Splitter, p. 90. Cf. also *"en rapprochant une qualité commune a deux sensations, il dégagéra leur éssence commune en les réunissant l'une et l'autre pour les sustraire aux contingences du temps, dans une metaphore."* (*A la recherche*, III, 889).

28. Splitter, p. 117.

29. *The Genesis of a Novel*, p. 29.

30. Ibid.

31. Ibid., p. 34.

32. Reed, p. 390.

33. Lukács, p. 91.

34. Ibid., p. 92.

35. Erich Kahler, *The Orbit of Thomas Mann* (Princeton: Princeton University Press, 1969), p. 37.

36. Reed, p. 396.

37. Kahler, p. 39.

38. Lukács, p. 94.

39. *The Genesis of a Novel*, p. 34.

40. Kahler, p. 37.

41. Darcey O'Brien, *The Conscience of James Joyce* (Princeton: Princeton University Press, 1968), pp. 5, 22, 31.

42. *Flaws in the Glass*, p. 155.

43. Morley, pp. 212, 213, 214.

44. Kahler, p. 73.

45. Adrian Mitchell, "Eventually, White's Language: Word's and More Than Words," in *Patrick White: A Critical Symposium*, ed. R. Shepherd and K. Singh (Adelaide: CRNLE, 1978), pp. 5–16, 7.

46. Paul de Man, "Autobiography as Defacement," *Modern Language Notes* 94,5 (1979): 919–30.

47. John Pilling, *Autobiography and Imagination: Studies in Self-Scrutiny* (London: Routledge and Kegan Paul, 1981), p. 50.

48. Marcel Muller, *Les voix narratives dans la "Recherche du temps perdu"* (Geneva: Droz, 1965).

49. Cf. Franz Stanzel, *Narrative Situations in the Novel* (Bloomington: Indiana University Press, 1971).

50. George Stambolian, *Marcel Proust and the Creative Encounter* (Chicago: The University of Chicago Press, 1972), p. 229.

51. Gilles Deleuze, *Proust and Signs*, trans. Richard Howard (London: The Penguin Press, 1973), p. 14.

52. Richard Ellmann, *The Consciousness of Joyce* (London: Faber and Faber, 1977), p. 95.

53. Miles Franklin, *My Brilliant Career* (Sydney: Angus and Robertson, 1974) and *My Career Goes Bung* (Melbourne: Georgian House, 1946).

54. *The Genesis of a Novel*, p. 37.

55. Reed, p. 364.

56. Ibid., p. 389.

57. Ibid., p. 387.

58. Lukács, p. 85.

59. Patrick Carnegy, *Faust as Musician: A Study of Thomas Mann's Novel Doctor Faustus* (London: Chatto and Windus, 1973), p. 3.

60. Reed, p. 380.

61. Lukács, p. 60.

62. *Flaws in the Glass*, pp. 150f.

63. Veronica Brady, "Patrick White, *Flaws in the Glass: A Self-Portrait*," *Westerly* 27,1 (1982): 102–109; 103.

64. *Flaws in the Glass*, p. 154.

65. Pilling, p. 103.

66. Paul de Man, p. 921.

67. Ibid.

4. Literature and Husserl: A Critique of Noematic Meaning

1. Michel Pêcheux, *Language, Semantics and Ideology* (London: Macmillan, 1986), pp. 31–35.

2. Edmund Husserl, *Ideas* I, trans. W. R. Boyce Gibson (London: Collier-Macmillan, 1969), p. 185.

3. Edmund Husserl, *Cartesian Mediations: An Introduction to Phenomenology*, trans. Dorion Cairns (The Hague: Martinus Nijhoff, 1973), p. 91.

4. Ibid.

5. Edmund Husserl, *Experience and Judgment: Investigations in a Genealogy of Logic*, ed. Ludwig Landgrebe, trans. James S. Churchill and Karl Ameriks (London: Routledge and Kegan Paul, 1973), p. 163.

6. Husserl, *Ideas* I, pp. 190f.

7. Edmund Husserl, *Logical Investigations*, vol. 1, trans. J. N. Findlay, (London: Routledge and Kegan Paul, 1970), p. 314.

8. Ibid., p. 315.

9. Ibid.

10. Ibid., p. 321.

11. Ibid., p. 322.

12. Husserl, *Ideas* I, pp. 64f.

13. Dagfinn Føllesdal, "Husserl's Notion of Noema," *Journal of Philosophy* 66 (1969): 680–87; 681.

14. Ibid.

15. *Ideas* III, *Husserliana* 1950, p. 89 and *Ideas* I, p. 233, quoted in Dagfinn Føllesdal, p. 681; J. N. Mohanty, "Intentionality and Noema," *Journal of Philosophy* 78, 11 (1981): 706–717; 709f.. Cf. also Dorion Cairns, "The Ideality of Verbal Expressions," *Philosophy and Phenomenological Research* 1 (1941): 435–56.

16. Guido Küng, "The World as Noema and as Referent," *Journal of the British Society for Phenomenology* (1972), pp. 15–26.

17. Bernard Bergonzi, *T. S. Eliot* (London: Macmillan, 1972), p. 105.

18. A. D. Moody, *Thomas Stearns Eliot: Poet* (London: Cambridge University Press,

1979), and Ronald Bush, *T. S. Eliot: A Study in Character and Style* (Oxford: Oxford University Press, 1983).

19. Bergonzi, p. 104.

20. Genesius Jones, *Approach to the Purpose*, (1964), p. 313, quoted in Robert H. Canary, *T. S. Eliot: The Poet and His Critics* (Chicago: American Library Association, 1982), p. 198.

21. F. W. Strothman and L. V. Ryan, "Hope to T. S. Eliot's 'Empty Men' " *PMLA* 73 (1958): 426–32.

22. Elizabeth Schneider, *T. S. Eliot: The Pattern in the Carpet* (Berkeley: University of California Press, 1975), pp. 101f.

23. Bergonzi, p. 105.

24. George Williamson, *A Reader's Guide to T. S. Eliot* (London: Thames and Hudson, 1955), pp. 156–61.

25. Edmund Husserl, *Logische Untersuchungen*, 2,1 (Halle: Max Niemeyer, 1922), p. 59. Cf. J. N. Mohanty, *Edmund Husserl's Theory of Meaning* (The Hague: Martinus Nijhoff, 1964), p. 23; also *Logische Untersuchungen* 2, 1, pp. 462f.

26. Husserl, *Ideas*, p. 251.

27. Ibid., p. 271.

28. Ibid., p. 278.

29. Ibid., p. 288.

30. Ibid.

31. Ibid., p. 271.

32. Ibid., p. 301.

33. Ibid., p. 269.

34. Ibid., p. 309.

35. Mohanty, *Edmund Husserl's Theory of Meaning*, p. 54.

36. Ibid., my stress.

37. Ibid., p. 60.

38. Husserl, *Logische Untersuchungen*, p. 338. Cf. also Y. Bar-Hillel, "Husserl's Conception of a Purely Logical Grammar," in *Readings on Edmund Husserl's 'Logical Investigations'*, ed. J. N. Mohanty (The Hague: Martinus Nijhoff, 1977), pp. 128–136; and James M. Edie, *Speaking and Meaning: The Phenomenology of Language* (Bloomington: Indiana University Press, 1976), pp. 50–57.

39. Mohanty, *Edmund Husserl's Theory of Meaning*, p. 60.

40. Ibid., p. 59.

41. Ibid., p. 63.

42. Ibid., p. 65.

43. Ibid., p. 64.

44. Martin Heidegger, *On the Way to Language* (New York: Harper and Row, 1971), p. 120; Jacques Derrida, *Speech and Phenomena* (Evanston: Northwestern University Press, 1973), p. 146. Cf. also Ludwig Wittgenstein's 'private language' argument in *Philosophical Investigations*, trans. G. E. M. Anscombe (New York: Macmillan, 1953).

45. Mohanty, *Edmund Husserl's Theory of Meaning*, p. 65.

46. Ibid., p. 75.

47. Ibid., p. 73.

48. Husserl, *Logische Untersuchungen*, 2, 2 p. 207.

49. Husserl, *Logische Untersuchungen*, V.2, 1 pp. 32f., 79–90; V.2, 2, pp. 18–23; and V.1, 1, pp. 59, 462f.. Cf. Mohanty, *Edmund Husserl's Theory of Meaning*, pp. 16, 77f., 23.

50. Husserl, *Ideas*.

51. Martin Heidegger, *Identity and Difference* (New York: Harper and Row, 1969).

52. Jürgen Habermas, *Communication and the Evolution of Society* (London: Heinemann, 1969), and Jean-François Lyotard, *The Postmodern Condition: A Report on Knowledge* (Minneapolis: University of Minnesota Press, 1984).

53. Heinz Hülsmann, *Zur Kritik der Sprache bei Husserl* (Munich: Anton Pustet, 1964), p. 249.

54. Bergonzi, p. 105.

55. Mohanty, *Edmund Husserl's Theory of Meaning*, p. 74.

56. Alfred Schutz, "Type and Eidos in Husserl's Late Philosophy," *Philosophy and Phenomenological Research* 20 (1959): 147–65; 157.

57. Mohanty, *Edmund Husserl's Theory of Meaning*, p. 75.

58. Husserl, *Logische Untersuchungen*, V.2, 1, p. 90.

5. Meaning as Sense and Derrida's Critique of the Concept

1. *Leibniz: Philosophical Writings*, trans. Mary Morris and G. H. R. Parkinson (London: Dent, 1934), pp. 179–94; 184. For a critique of the *principium rationis sufficientis* cf. Martin Heidegger, "The Problem of Reason," in *The Essence of Reason*, trans. Terrence Malick (Evanston: Northwestern University Press, 1969), pp. 11–33.

2. "On Referring," *Mind* 59 (1950): 320–44; 336.

3. Charles Landesman, *Discourse and the Presuppositions* (New Haven: Yale University Press, 1972), pp. 60f.

4. Gottlob Frege, "On Sense and Reference," in *Translations from the Philosophical Writings of Gottlob Frege*, ed. Peter Geach and Max Black (Oxford: Basil Blackwell, 1966), pp. 56–78; 58.

5. Ibid.

6. Ibid., p. 61.

7. Michel Pêcheux, *Language, Semantics, and Ideology*, trans. H. Nagpal (London: Macmillan, 1986), p. 43.

8. Frege, p. 59.

9. Ibid., cf. also Frege's "*Si duo idem faciunt, non est idem.*"

10. Ibid.

11. Ibid., p. 60.

12. Michael Dummett, *The Interpretation of Frege's Philosophy* (Cambridge, Mass.: Harvard University Press, 1981), p. 109.

13. Frege, "On Sense and Reference," p. 59f.. Cf. Christian Thiel, *Sense and Reference in Frege's Logic* (Dordrecht: D. Reidel, 1968), pp. 160f., where he demonstrates that Frege's account of sense is by no means unambiguous.

14. Frege, "On Sense and Reference," p. 62.

15. Frege, "Function and Concept," in *Translations from the Philosophical Writings of Gottlob Frege*, pp. 21–41; 32; "On Sense and Reference," Ibid., pp. 56–78; 72.

16. Frege, "On Sense and Reference," p. 63.

17. Bertrand Russell, "On Denoting," in *Essays in Analysis*, ed. Douglas Lackey (New York: George Braziller, 1973), pp. 103–119.

18. Ibid., p. 104.

19. Ibid., p. 103f.

20. Ibid., p. 108.

21. Ibid., p. 108, note 3.

22. Ibid., p. 103.

23. Bertrand Russell and Alfred North Whitehead, *Principia Mathematica*, vol. 1 (Cambridge: The University Press, 1963), p. 30.

24. John Lyons, *Language, Meaning and Context* (London: Fontana, 1981), pp. 61ff.

25. Gilbert Ryle, "The Theory of Meaning," in *British Philosophy in the Mid-Century*, ed. C. A. Mace (London: George Allen and Unwin, 1957), pp. 239–64; esp. 248–56.

26. Bertrand Russell, *The Analysis of Mind* (New York: Macmillan, 1921), pp. 197f.

27. P. F. Strawson, "On Referring," *Mind* 59 (1950): 320–44; 321f.

28. Roland Barthes, *S/Z*, trans. Richard Miller (New York: Hill and Wang, 1974), pp. 4ff.

29. Strawson, 326.

30. Ibid., 335.

31. Ibid.

32. Ibid., 336.

33. Ibid.

34. Ibid., 327.

35. Cf. the chapter "Ladders of Fictionality," in *The Reader's Construction of Narrative* (London: Routledge and Kegan Paul, 1981), pp. 78–96.

36. Moritz Schlick, "Meaning and Verification," *Philosophical Review* 45 (1936): 339–68.

37. Ibid., 341.

38. Ibid., 347.

39. Ibid., 352.

40. J. L. Evans, "On Meaning and Verification," *Mind* 62 (1953): 1–19; 13.

41. Ibid., 18.

42. Ibid., 2.

43. Ibid.

44. Ferdinand de Saussure, *Course in General Linguistics*, trans. Wade Baskin (London: Fontana, 1974), pp. 22f., 88, 100.

45. Ryle, p. 256.

46. Ludwig Wittgenstein, *Philosophical Investigations*, trans. G. E. M. Anscombe (New York: Macmillan, 1953), Part I, 531, p. 15/15e.

47. Stephen R. Schiffer, *Meaning* (Oxford: Clarendon Press, 1972), p. 155.

48. Cf. I. I. Revzin, "Language as a Sign System and the Game of Chess," in *Soviet Semiotics*, ed. and trans. Daniel P. Lucid (Baltimore: The Johns Hopkins University Press, 1977), pp. 87–92.

49. Richard Feynman, *The Character of Physical Law* (Cambridge, Mass.: MIT Press, 1967), chapter 2; John Gribbin, *In Search of Schrödinger's Cat: Quantum Physics and Reality* (New York: Bantam Books, 1984), pp. 104–107; 106.

50. H. P. Grice, "Meaning," *The Philosophical Review* 66 (1957): 377–88.

51. H. P. Grice, "Logic and Conversation," in *Syntax and Semantics 3: Speech Acts*, ed. P. Cole and J. L. Morgan (New York: Academy Press, 1975), pp. 41–58; "Utterer's Meaning and Intentions," *The Philosophical Review* 78 (1969): 147–77.

52. Grice, "Meaning," 387.

53. Garth Hallett, *Wittgenstein's Definition of Meaning as Use* (New York: Fordham University Press, 1967) p. 70. Ibid., p. 127.

54. Jacques Derrida, "Limited Inc abc . . . " in Glyph, *Johns Hopkins Textual Studies* (Baltimore: The Johns Hopkins University Press, 1977), pp. 162–254, esp. pp. 210ff.

55. Ibid., p. 241–48.

56. "Meaning" in Austin is still the "sense" of "locution" which in a pragmatic speech situation becomes tied to illocutionary forces and perlocutionary effects but remains isolatable in a speech act semantics. In this, Austin stands close to the early Husserl and his noetic modifications of noemata.

57. This analytical carving out of a "locution" results in a fundamental analytical error, namely the assumption, derived from purely formal operations, that sense-meanings (locutions) are strictly definable entities prior to their being affected by use, i.e., by linkage with other sign systems.

58. John R. Searle, *Speech Acts: An Essay in the Philosophy of Language* (London: Cambridge University Press, 1977), p. 3.

59. John R. Searle, "A Classification of Illocutionary Acts," *Language in Society* 5 (1976): 1–23; 23.

60. John R. Searle, "The Logical Status of Fictional Discourse," *New Literary History* 6 (1975): 319–32; 328.

61. John R. Searle, "The Background of Meaning" in *Speech Act Theory and Pragmatics*,

ed. John R. Searle, Ferenc Kiefer, and Manfred Bierwisch (Dordrecht: Reidel, 1980), pp. 221–32; 221.

62. John R. Searle, *Intentionality: An Essay in the Philosophy of Mind* (Cambridge: Cambridge University Press, 1983), p. 55.

63. Louise Pratt, "Ideology and Speech-Act Theory," *Poetics Today* 7, 1 (1986): 59–71.

64. Michel Pêcheux, *Language, Semantics, and Ideology* (London: Macmillan, 1986), e.g., p. 185.

65. Donald Davidson, "A Coherence Theory of Truth and Knowledge," in *Truth and Interpretation: Perspectives on the Philosophy of Donald Davidson*, ed. Ernest Lepore (Oxford: Basil Blackwell, 1989), pp. 307–319.

66. Donald Davidson, "A Nice Derangement of Epitaphs," in *Truth and Interpretation*, pp. 433–46; 445f.

67. Alfred Tarski, "The Establishment of Scientific Semantics," in *Logic, Semantics, Metamathematics*, trans. J. H. Woodger (Oxford: Clarendon Press, 1956), pp. 401–408; 401.

68. Ibid., p. 403.

69. Alfred Tarski, "The Concept of Truth in Formalized Languages," in *Logic, Semantics, Metamathematics*, pp. 152–278; 153.

70. Donald Davidson, "Semantics for Natural Languages," in *Inquiries into Truth and Interpretation* (Oxford: Clarendon Press, 1984), pp. 55–64; 60.

71. Ibid.

72. Davidson, "A Coherence Theory of Truth and Knowledge," p. 309.

73. Donald Davidson, "The Method of Truth in Metaphysics," in *Inquiries into Truth and Interpretation*, pp. 199–214; 204.

74. Ibid.

75. Davidson, "Semantics for Natural Languages," p. 58.

76. Donald Davidson, "Radical Interpretation," *Dialectica* 27 (1973): 313–327; 323. Cf. also his assertion that "your utterance means what mine does if belief in its truth is systematically caused by the same events and objects," in "A Coherence Theory of Truth and Knowledge," p. 318.

77. Ibid., 324.

78. Donald Davidson, "On the Very Idea of a Conceptual Scheme, "in *Inquiries into Truth and Interpretation*, pp. 183–98; "Belief and the Basis of Meaning," in *Inquiries*, pp. 141–54.

79. Umberto Eco, *Semiotics and the Philosophy of Language* (Bloomington: Indiana University Press, 1984), p. 43.

80. Davidson, "Belief and the Basis of Meaning," in *Inquiries*, p. 148.

81. Donald Davidson, "Moods and Performances," in *Inquiries*, pp. 109–121.

82. Donald Davidson, "Reality Without Reference," in *Inquiries*, pp. 215–25.

83. Jacques Derrida, "The Time of a Thesis: Punctuations," in *Philosophy in France Today*, ed. A. Montefiori (Cambridge: Cambridge University Press, 1982), pp. 34–50; 4.

84. Jacques Derrida, *Margins of Philosophy*, trans. Alan Bass (Chicago: University of Chicago Press, 1982), p. 293.

85. Jacques Derrida, *Positions*, trans. Alan Bass (Chicago: University of Chicago Press, 1981), pp. 4f.

86. Jacques Derrida, *Speech and Phenomena*, trans. David Allison (Evanston: Northwestern University Press, 1973), p. 141.

87. Derrida, *Margins of Philosophy*, p. 329.

88. Jacques Derrida, *Of Grammatology*, trans. by Gayatri Chakravorty Spivak (Baltimore: The Johns Hopkins University Press, 1978), p. 157.

89. Jacques Derrida, *Dissemination*, trans. B. Johnson (Chicago: University of Chicago Press, 1981), p. 122.

90. Rodolphe Gasché, *The Tain of the Mirror: Derrida and the Philosophy of Reflection* (Cambridge, Mass.: Harvard University Press, 1986), p. 135. Cf. also Horst Ruthrof, "The

Infrastructures of Deconstruction: Rodolphe Gasché, *The Tain of the Mirror*," *Southern Review* 21 (1988): 203–210.

91. Jacques Derrida: *Writing and Difference*, trans. Alan Bass (London: Routledge and Kegan Paul, 1978), p. 230; *Of Grammatology*, p. 112; *Dissemination*, p. 331; *Of Grammatology*, p. 62.

92. Derrida, *Of Grammatology*, p. 154; 145.

93. Derrida, *Dissemination*, p. 123.

94. Ibid., p. 265.

95. Cf. *Of Grammatology* for Derrida's discussion of the roles which sexuality and writing play in Rousseau's work.

96. Derrida, *Dissemination*, p. 221.

97. Derrida, *Margins of Philosophy*, pp. 219f.

98. Jacques Derrida, "Differance," second half. Cf. also Gilles Deleuze, *Nietzsche et la philosophie* (Paris: Presses Universitaires de France, 1973), pp. 48–55, where he elaborates on Nietzsche's insight that differential relations are already the products of differences.

99. Derrida, *Positions*, pp. 40f.; Steven Shaviro, " 'Striving With Systems:' Blake and the Politics of Difference," *Boundary 2* 10 (1982): 229–50; 235.

100. Derrida, *Positions*, p. 41.

101. Jacques Derrida, "Differance," in *Speech and Phenomena*, pp. 129–160; 129.

102. Ibid., pp. 134, 153.

103. Ibid., p. 130.

104. Derrida: *Of Grammatology*, pp. 62f.; *Positions*, p. 27, 17.

105. Jacques Derrida, "Differance," pp. 141; 135, 140; 137; 142.

106. Jacques Derrida, *Edmund Husserl's "Origin of Geometry": An Introduction*, trans. James S. Churchill (Stony Brook, N.Y.: Nicolar Hays, 1978), p. 6.

107. Derrida, "Differance," p. 145.

108. Jacques Derrida, *Speech and Phenomena*, p. 103.

109. Martin Heidegger, *Being and Time*, trans. John Macquarrie and Edward Robinson (London: SCM Press, 1962), p. 201.

6. The Limits of *Langue*

1. Thomas A. Sebeok, "Zoosemiotic Components of Human Communication," in *Semiotics: An Introductory Reader*, ed. Robert E. Innis (London: Hutchinson, 1986), pp. 294–324; 300; 301.

2. Immanuel Kant, *Critique of Pure Reason*, trans. Norman Kemp Smith (London: Macmillan, 1973), pp. 180–86.

3. A. J. Greimas and J. Courtés, *Semiotics and Language: An Analytical Dictionary*, trans. Larry Crist, Daniel Patte, *et al.* (Bloomington: Indiana University Press, 1982), p. 97.

4. From a conversation with Mike Halliday at the conference "Discipline—Dialogue—Difference" held at Murdoch University, Perth, Western Australia, 3–8 December, 1989. Cf. also his "Language and the Order of Nature" in *The Linguistics of Writing: Arguments between Language and Literature*, ed. Nigel Fabb, Derek Attridge *et al.* (Manchester: Manchester University Press, 1987), pp. 135–54; and "On the Ineffability of Grammatical Categories" in *Linguistics in a Systemic Perspective*, ed. James D. Benson, Michael J. Cummings, and William S. Greaves (Amsterdam: John Benjamin, 1988), pp. 27–51.

5. Ilya Prigogine and Isabelle Stengers, *Order out of Chaos* (London: Fontana, 1988), pp. 13f.; 140–59.

6. Michel Pêcheux, *Language, Semantics and Ideology* (London: Macmillan, 1986), p. 6.

7. Ludwig Wittgenstein, *Tractatus Logico-Philosophicus*, trans. D. F. Pears and B. F. McGuinness (London: Routledge and Kegan Paul, 1963), 5.6 and 5.61.

8. Cf. Ludwig Wittgenstein, *Philosophical Investigations*, trans. G. E. M. Anscombe (New York: Macmillan, 1953), I, 23.

9. Louis Hjelmslev, *Language: An Introduction*, trans. Frances J. Whitfield (Madison: The University of Wisconsin Press, 1970), pp. 120.

10. Julia Kristeva, "The System and the Speaking Subject," in *The Tell-Tale Sign: A Survey of Semiotics*, ed. T. A. Sebeok (Lisse, Netherlands: Peter de Ridder, 1975), pp. 47–55; 48.

11. Bertrand Russell, "Logical Positivism," *Revue internationale de philosophie* 4 (1950): 18; Roman Jakobson, "On Linguistic Aspects of Translation," in *Language in Literature*, ed. Krystyna Pomorska and Stephen Rudy (Cambridge, Mass.: Belknap Press, 1987), pp. 428–35; 429.

12. Jakobson, p. 429.

13. John Dewey, "Peirce's Theory of Linguistic Signs, Thought, and Meaning," *Journal of Philosophy* 43 (1946): 91.

14. Edmund Husserl, *Cartesian Meditations: An Introduction to Phenomenology*, trans. Dorion Cairns (The Hague: Martinus Nijhoff, 1973), fifth meditation, pp. 108f; 111. Cf. also Edmund Husserl, *Logical Investigations,* and *Formal and Transcendental Logic*, trans. Dorion Cairns (The Hague: Martinus Nijhoff, 1969), pp. 313–29 and "Zur Logik der Zeichen (Semiotik)" [1890] in *Husserliana*, vol. 12, ed. Lothar Eley (The Hague: Martinus Nijhoff, 1970), pp. 340–73.

15. Roman Ingarden, *The Literary Work of Art* (Evanston: Northwestern University Press, 1973), and *The Cognition of the Literary Work of Art* (Evanston: Northwestern University Press, 1973), *passim*.

16. Alfred Schutz and Thomas Luckmann, *The Structures of the Life-World* (Evanston: Northwestern University Press, 1973), pp. 233–35. Cf. also Alfred Schutz, "Type and Eidos in Husserl's Late Philosophy," *Philosophy and Phenomenological Research* 20 (1959): 147–65.

17. Hjelmslev, p. 121.

18. Ludwig Wittgenstein, *The Blue and Brown Books* (Oxford: Basil Blackwell, 1975), p. 5.

19. Wittgenstein, *Philosophical Investigations*, I, 23.

20. Theodor R. Schatzki, "The Prescription is Description: Wittgenstein's View of the Human Sciences," in *The Need for Interpretation*, ed. S. Mitchell and Michael Rosen (London: The Athlone Press, 1983), pp. 118–40; 126.

21. Ludwig Wittgenstein, *Zettel*, ed. G. E. M. Anscombe and G. H. von Wright (Oxford: Basil Blackwell, 1967), pp. 387; 388; also pp. 147–75, 210, 219.

22. Wittgenstein, *The Blue and Brown Books*, pp. 4; 69. Cf. also Garth Hallett, *Wittgenstein's Definition of Meaning as Use.* (New York: Fordham University Press, 1967).

23. Ludwig Wittgenstein, "Cause and Effect: Intuitive Awareness," *Philosophia* 6, 3–4 (1976), ed. and trans. Peter Finch.

24. Peter Finch, "Im Anfang war die Tat," in *Perspectives on the Philosophy of Wittgenstein*, ed. Irving Block (Oxford: Basil Blackwell, 1981), pp. 159–78.

25. Michel Foucault, *The Archaeology of Knowledge* (London: Tavistock, 1980), pp. 27f.

26. Ibid., pp. 38f.; 41f.

27. Ibid., pp. 49; 74; 109.

28. Umberto Eco, *A Theory of Semiotics* (Bloomington: Indiana University Press, 1979), p. 132.

29. Ibid., p. 134.

30. Ibid., pp. 135f.

31. Umberto Eco, *Semiotics and the Philosophy of Language* (London: Macmillan, 1984), pp. 39–43.

32. Ibid., p. 34.
33. Ibid.
34. Ibid., p. 45.
35. In *Film Theory and Criticism*, ed. G. Mast and M. Cohen (New York: Oxford University Press, 1979), p. 23; quoted in *Semiotics and the Philosophy of Language*, p. 43.
36. Eco, *Semiotics and the Philosophy of Language*, p. 43.
37. Cf. intuitionist mathematics.
38. Karl R. Popper, *The Logic of Scientific Discovery* (London: Hutchinson, 1975), pp. 265f.
39. Charles Sanders Peirce, *Collected Papers*, volumes I–VI, ed. Charles Hartshorne and Paul Weiss (Cambridge, Mass.: The Belknap Press of Harvard University Press, 1974) and *Collected Papers of Charles Sanders Peirce*, v. VII, Science and Philosophy, ed. Arthur W. Burks (Cambridge, Mass.: Harvard University Press, 1958) (references in the text).
40. Quoted as motto in *A Perfusion of Signs*, ed. Thomas A. Sebeok (Bloomington: Indiana University Press, 1977), p. v.
41. My stress; this observation was made as early as 1885!
42. J. Jay Zeman, "Peirce's Theory of Signs," in *A Perfusion of Signs*, pp. 22–39; 22.

7. Phrases in Dispute: Toward a Semiotic Differend

1. Jean-François Lyotard, *The Differend: Phrases in Dispute* (Manchester: Manchester University Press, 1988), p. 58.
2. Ibid., pp. 32, 33.
3. Ibid., pp. 38, 39; Saul Kripke, *Naming and Necessity* (Cambridge, Mass: Harvard University Press, 1980), pp. 91–93.
4. Lyotard, pp. 43, 53.
5. Ibid., pp. 128f., 84, 14, 139.
6. Ibid., p. 13.
7. Ibid., p. 43.
8. Ibid., p. 41.
9. Kripke, p. 48.
10. Lyotard, p. 41.
11. Ibid., pp. 47, 48.
12. Ibid., p. 50.
13. Ibid., p. 33.
14. Ibid., pp. 33, 39, 40.
15. Ibid., p. 169.
16. Ibid., p. 130.
17. Ibid., pp. 160f.
18. Ibid., p. 178.
19. Ibid., p. 138; cf. p. 141.
20. Ibid., p. 137.
21. Ibid., p. 9.
22. Ibid., p. 70.
23. Ibid., p. 33.
24. Kripke, pp. 91ff.
25. Lyotard, p. 50.
26. Ibid., p. 53.
27. Ibid., p. 62.
28. As part of his argument on "radical translation."
29. H. P. Grice, "Meaning," *The Philosophical Review* 66 (1957): 377–88.
30. Roman Jakobson, "On the Relation between Visual and Auditory Signs," in *Lan-*

guage in Literature, ed. Krystyna Pomorska and Stephen Rudy (Cambridge, Mass.: Belknap Press, 1987), pp. 466–73, 472; and Ibid., p. 466.

31. Lyotard, pp. 10, 9, 13.

32. Geoffrey Bennington, *Lyotard: Writing the Event* (Manchester: Manchester University Press, 1988).

33. Bennington, p. 125.

34. Ibid., p. 121.

35. Lyotard, p. 50.

36. Bennington, pp. 130, 112.

37. Ibid., p. 131.

38. Ibid., pp. 132f.

39. Martin Heidegger, "The Origin of the Work of Art," in *Poetry, Language, Thought*, trans. Albert Hofstadter (New York: Harper and Row, 1975), pp. 15–87; 23.

40. Lyotard, p. 157.

41. Ludwig Wittgenstein, *Philosophical Investigations*, trans. G. E. M. Anscombe (New York: Macmillan, 1953), I, 23.

42. Ludwig Wittgenstein, *The Blue and Brown Books* (Oxford: Basil Blackwell, 1960), p. 5.

43. Ludwig Wittgenstein, *Philosophical Investigations*, i, Section 144. Cf. also his *Zettel*, ed. G. E. M. Anscombe and G. H. von Wright (Oxford: Basil Blackwell, 1967), pp. 157–75, 201, 219.

44. Wilhelm Humboldt, *Werke*, vol.3, ed. A. Flitner and K. Giel (Stuttgart: Cotta, 1963), p. 19.

45. Charles Darwin, *Journal of Researches* (1839), p. 517, in Brian Eliott, *The Landscape of Australian Poetry*, (Melbourne: Cheshire, 1967), p. 19.

46. J. R. Wollaston, *The Picton Journal 1841–44*, quoted in Helen Watson-Williams, "Land into Literature: The Western Australian Bush Seen by Some Early Writers and D. H. Lawrence," *Westerly* 25 (1980): 59–72.

47. A. D. Hope, "Australia" (1939), in *Collected Poems* (Sydney: Angus and Robertson, 1977), p. 13.

48. William Dampier, *A New Voyage Round the World* (1688), in Eliott, *The Landscape of Australian Poetry*, pp. 8f.

49. Lyotard, p. 178.

50. Colin Johnson, "Guerilla Poetry: Lionel Fogarty's Response to Language Genocide," in *Long Water: Aboriginal Art and Literature* (Bathurst: Robert Brown, 1986), p. 73.

51. Colin Johnson, "White Forms, Aboriginal Content," in *Aboriginal Writing Today*, ed. Bob Hodge (Canberra: Australian Institute of Aboriginal Studies, 1985), p. 21.

52. Cf. Colin Johnson, *Wild Cat Falling* (Sydney: Angus and Robertson, 1965), *Long Live Sandawara* (Melbourne: Quartet Books, 1979), and *Doctor Wooreddy's Prescription for Enduring the Ending of the World* (Melbourne: Hyland House, 1983).

53. The Nyoongars are "the Aboriginal nation of South-western Australia" in Colin Johnson, "Sunlight Spreadeagles Perth in Blackness: A Bicentennial Gift Poem," published partly in Hugh Webb, "Poetry as Guerilla Warfare: Colin Johnson's Semiotic Bicentennial Gift," *New Literatures Review* 17 (1989): 43–49 and another part separately, 50–68.

8. A Striptease of Meaning on the Ladder of Discourse

1. Cf. the work of Saul Kripke, e.g., "Naming and Necessity," in *Semantics of Natural Language*, ed. G. Harman and D. Davidson (Dordrecht: Reidel, 1972), pp. 253–355; and his book *Naming and Necessity* (Cambridge, Mass.: Harvard University Press, 1980).

2. See the excellent chapter, "Toward a Poststructuralist Practice: A Reading of Shakespeare's Sonnets," in Howard Felperin, *Beyond Deconstruction: The Uses and Abuses of Literary Theory* (Oxford: Clarendon Press, 1985), pp. 147–99.

3. M. A. K. Halliday, *Language as Social Semiotic* (London: Edward Arnold, 1978), p. 79; 111.

4. Ibid., p. 112.

5. John Frow, "Discourse Genres," *Journal of Literary Semantics* (1980): 73–81.

6. Ibid.: 74f.

7. Ibid.: 78.

8. Ibid.: 79.

9. Ibid.

10. Ibid.: 76.

11. The same criticism applies to Lacan's "Real; " there is no cogent reason why his "Imaginary" and "Symbolic" require a triadic foundation more "real" than they are to themselves, unless he were to argue for *noumenal* entities. The "Imaginary" and the "Symbolic" should be regarded as two textual versions of our world; in that sense they constitute the real.

12. Cf. my suggestions in "Text and the Construction of Meaning: A Phenomenological Approach," *Southern Review* 16 (1983): 110–20.

13. Such counterfactual states of affairs do not have to be homogeneous but can be informed by their opposite, a principle of agonistics, as long as they stand in some recognizable relationship to a set of signifiers. Cf. S. A. Kripke, *Naming and Necessity* (Cambridge, Mass: Harvard University Press, 1980), p. 15.

14. *The Poems of Gerard Manly Hopkins*, ed. W. H. Gardner and N. H. McKenzie (London: Oxford University Press, 1967), p. 90.

15. Christopher Norris, *The Contest of Faculties: Philosophy and Theory After Deconstruction* (London: Methuen, 1985), p. 59.

16. Harold Bloom, *The Breaking of the Vessel* (Chicago: Chicago University Press, 1982), pp. 4, 16f.

17. Claude Lévi-Strauss, *L'Homme Nu* (Paris: Plon, 1972), p. 585; and "The Structural Study of Myth," in *Structural Anthropology* (Harmondsworth: Penguin, 1977), pp. 206–231; 210. Cf. also his *Myth and Meaning* (New York: Schocken Books, 1979).

18. Ludwig Wittgenstein, *Tractatus Logico-Philosophicus*, trans. D. F. Pears and B. F. McGuiness (London: Routledge and Kegan Paul, 1963), I, 2.012 and 6.51.

19. Dominick LaCapra, *History and Criticism* (Ithaca: Cornell University Press, 1985), pp. 137f.; 139ff.; see also Hayden V. White, *Metahistory* (Baltimore: The Johns Hopkins University Press, 1973), and *Tropics of Discourse* (Baltimore: The Johns Hopkins University Press, 1978); therein "The Burden of History" (1966).

20. Frederic Jameson, *The Political Unconscious* (Ithaca, N.Y.: Cornell University Press, 1982), pp. 35; 102.

21. William L. Shirer, *The Rise and Fall of the Third Reich: The History of Nazi Germany* (New York: Simon and Schuster, 1960), p. 198f.

22. Jameson, pp. 12; 101f.

23. Cf. Halliday, *Language as Social Semiotic*, e.g., pp. 62–64.

24. Jameson, p. 49.

25. For a standard view of the objective reconstruction of historical truth see, for example, G. R. Elton, *The Practice of History* (1967).

26. William Shakespeare, *Measure for Measure*, ed. R. E. C. Houghton (Oxford: Clarendon Press, 1970), Acts I and II.

27. Cf. Alfred Schutz, *Phenomenology of the Social Life World*, trans. George Welsh and Frederick Lehnert (Evanston: Northwestern University Press, 1967), pp. 245–49.

28. Michel Pêcheux, *Language, Semantics and Ideology*, (London: Macmillan, 1986), pp. 71f.

29. Brendan Cassidy, "Whose Law, Which Discourse?" in *Social Theory and Legal Politics*, ed. Gary Wickham (Sydney: Local Consumption, 1987), pp. 24–39.

30. Christopher Norris, "Suspended Sentences: Textual Theory and the Law," in *The Contest of Faculties: Philosophy and Theory After Deconstruction* (London: Methuen,

1985), pp. 167–92; 168f. Cf. also L. A. Hart, *Essays in Jurisprudence and Philosophy* (Oxford: Clarendon Press, 1983); Stanley Fish, "Working on the Chain Gang: Interpretation in the Law and in Literary Criticism," in *The Politics of Interpretation*, ed. W. J. T. Mitchell (Chicago: University of Chicago Press, 1983), pp. 271–86; and Ronald Dworkin, "Law as Interpretation," *Critical Inquiry*, 9 (1982/3): 179–200, reprinted in *The Politics of Interpretation*, pp. 249–70.

31. Alfred Schutz, *Reflections on the Problem of Relevance* (New Haven: Yale University Press, 1970).

32. P. F. Strawson, "On Referring," *Mind* 59 (1950): 320–44; 336.

33. Gottlob Frege, "On Sense and Reference," in *Translations from the Philosophical Works of Gottlob Frege*, ed. Peter Geach and Max Black (Oxford: Basil Blackwell, 1966) pp. 56–78; 57; 63.

34. John Lyons, *Language and Linguistics: An Introduction* (Cambridge: Cambridge University Press, 1981), p. 41.

35. A. J. Ayer, *Language, Truth and Logic*, (London: Gollancz, 1946), p. 35.

36. Lyons, p. 171.

37. Jürgen Habermas, "Science and Technology as Ideology" in *Towards a Rational Society* (London: Heinemann, 1971), pp. 81–122; 92ff.

38. Martin Heidegger, *The Question Concerning Technology and Other Essays*, trans. William Lovitt (New York: Garland, 1977).

39. Martin Heidegger, "The Question Concerning Technology," in *The Question Concerning Technology and Other Essays*, trans. William Lovitt (New York: Garland, 1977), pp. 12; 25; Martin Heidegger, *Being and Time*, trans. John Macquarrie and Edward Robinson (Oxford: Basil Blackwell, 1962), pp. 188–214; 189; 191; 195; 201; 195; for his critique of 'assertion' see esp. pp. 196–203.

40. Martin Heidegger, "The Principle of Identity," in *Identity and Difference*, trans. Joan Stambaugh (New York: Harper and Row, 1974), pp. 23–41.

41. Pêcheux, p. 105.

42. Cf. Habermas's attack on the relationship between Heidegger's way of theorizing and his temporary attachment to Fascism in *The Philosophical Discourse of Modernity*, trans. Frederick Lawrence (London: Polity Press, 1987), pp. 131–60.

43. J. M. Coetzee, "Newton and the Ideal of a Transparent Scientific Language," *Journal of Literary Semantics* 11 (1982): 3–13; 12.

44. Karl R. Popper, *The Logic of Scientific Discovery* (1934) (London: Hutchinson, 1975), pp. 247, 250.

45. Paul Feyerabend, *Science in a Free Society* (London: New Left Books, 1978), pp. 16, 98f.

46. Jean-François Lyotard, *The Postmodern Condition: A Report on Knowledge* (Manchester: Manchester University Press, 1984), pp. 28f.

47. Edmund Husserl, *Logical Investigations*, I, (London: Routledge and Kegan Paul, 1970), p. 325.

48. Joel Kupperman and Arthur S. McGrade, *Fundamentals of Logic* (New York: Doubleday, 1966), pp. 124ff.; Alex C. Michalos, *Principles of Logic* (Englewood Cliffs, N.J.: Prentice-Hall, 1969), pp. 3–34. Cf. also G. E. Hughes and M. J. Cresswell, *An Introduction to Modal Logic* (London: Methuen, 1968), pp. 6f.

49. Trevor Eaton, "Literary Semantics: Modality and Style," *Journal of Literary Semantics* VII (1978): 5–28; 9.

50. Kurt Gödel, *On Formally Undecidable Propositions of Principia Mathematica and Related Systems I*, ed. B. Meltzer, intr. R. B. Braithwaite (London: Oliver and Boyd, 1962), pp. 37f. Cf. also his "*Über eine bisher noch nicht benützte Erweiterung des finiten Standpunktes*," *Dialectica* 12 (1958): 280–87; and "What Is Cantor's Continuum Problem?" in *Philosophy of Mathematics*, ed. P. Benacerraf and Hilary Putnam (Cambridge: Cambridge University Press, 1982), pp. 470–85. Also see Jeff Paris and Leo Harrington, "A Mathematical

Incompleteness in Peano Arithmetic," in *Handbook of Mathematical Logic*, ed. Jon Barwise (Amsterdam: North-Holland, 1977), pp. 1134–42.

51. Jacques Derrida, *Dissemination*, trans. B. Johnson (Chicago: University of Chicago Press, 1981), p. 219.

52. I would like to thank Klaus Fahrner for introducing me to some intricacies of computer engineering and for granting my word processor a degree of self-reflexivity.

53. Horst Ruthrof, "Narrative and the Digital: On the Syntax of the Postmodern," *Narrative Issues,* special issue of *AUMLA* (1990), pp. 213–34.

54. Ludwig Wittgenstein, *On Certainty*, ed. G. E. M. Anscombe and H. G. von Wright, trans. Denis Paul and G. E. M. Anscombe (Oxford: Basil Blackwell, 1969), 59e.

55. Joseph Margolis, "Robust Relativism," *The Journal of Aesthetics and Art Criticism* 35 (1976): 37–46; 44.

9. Hypocrisis or Reading as Feigning

1. For a close reading see, for example, Martin Turnell, *Baudelaire: A Study of His Poetry* (New York: New Directions, 1953), pp. 97ff.

2. *Greek-English Lexicon: A New Edition*, comp. Liddell and Scott (Oxford: Clarendon Press, 1968) pp. 1885f.

3. Michel Foucault, "My Body, This Paper, This Fire," *Oxford Literary Review* 4 (1979): 9–28; 19.

4. Bertrand Russell, *An Inquiry into Meaning and Truth* (London: George Allen and Unwin, 1961), pp. 108–115. Cf. also his discussion of egocentric particulars in *Human Knowledge: Its Scope and Limits* (New York: Simon and Schuster, 1948), pp. 85–93, and the paper "Mr. Strawson on Referring," *Mind* 66 (1957): 385–89.

5. Cf. the alternative of a ladder of discourses in chapter 8 above.

6. Moritz Schlick, "Meaning and Verification," *Philosophical Review* 45 (1936): 339–68; 364–67.

7. Michel Pêcheux, *Language, Semantics and Ideology*, trans. H. Nagpal (London: Macmillan, 1986), p. 156.

8. Ibid., p. 156f.; 159.

9. Ibid., p. 159.

10. Michel Foucault, "What is an Author?", in *Textual Strategies: Perspectives in Post-Structuralist Criticism*, ed. J. V. Harari (London: Methuen, 1979), pp. 141–60.

11. Pêcheux, pp. 92; 105; 171ff.

12. Michel Foucault, *The Archaeology of Knowledge* (London: Tavistock, 1978), p. 105; cf. also pp. 106f.

13. Edmund Husserl, *Logical Investigations*, I, trans. J. N. Finley (London: Routledge and Kegan Paul, 1970), pp. 315f.

14. Edmund Husserl, *Cartesian Meditations*, Fifth Meditation, trans. Dorion Cairns (The Hague: Martinus Nijhoff, 1973), pp. 108f.

15. Foucault, *The Archaeology of Knowledge*, pp. 51; 50; 52.

16. Edmund Husserl, *Erfahrung und Urteil: Untersuchungen zur Genealogie der Logik* (Hamburg: Cassen, 1969), esp. p. 519.

17. Jürgen Habermas, consistently throughout his early work and still in "A Reply to My Critics," in *Habermas: Critical Debates*, ed. John B. Thompson and David Held (Cambridge, Mass.: MIT Press, 1982), pp. 219–38.

18. Harold Bloom, *Poetry and Repression* (New Haven: Yale University Press, 1976) and *The Breaking of the Vessel* (Chicago: Chicago University Press, 1982).

19. Jean-François Lyotard, *The Postmodern Condition: A Report on Knowledge* (Manchester: Manchester University Press, 1984).

20. Saul Bellow, *The Dean's December* (New York: Simon and Schuster, 1982), p. 346.

21. Cf. Michel Foucault on "enunciation" in *The Archaeology of Knowledge*, pp. 50–55; 88–105.

22. Pêcheux, pp. 155–60.

10. The Fictions of Political Discourse and the Politics of Reading

1. Michel Foucault, *Power, Truth, Strategy*, ed. Meaghan Morris and Paul Patton (Sydney: Feral Publications, 1979), p. 72.

2. For discussions of the principles of the politics of reading, see *The Politics of Interpretation* ed. W. J. T. Mitchell (Chicago: University of Chicago Press, 1983).

3. J. P. Stern, *Hitler: The Führer and the People* (London: Fontana and Collins, 1975), pp. 9–15.

4. Colin S. Gray and Keith Payne, "Under the Nuclear Gun (1): Victory is Possible," *Foreign Policy* 39 (1980): 14–27; 1, 21.

5. Terry Eagleton, *Literary Theory: An Introduction* (Oxford: Basil Blackwell, 1983), pp. 194–217; Martin Heidegger, *Being and Time*, trans. John Macquarie and Edward Robinson (London: SCM Press, 1962), pp. 200; 195.

6. Frederic Jameson, *The Political Unconscious: Narrative as a Socially Symbolic Act* (Ithaca: Cornell University Press, 1982), pp. 10–21.

7. Michel Pêcheux, *Language, Semantics and Ideology*, trans. H. Nagpal, (London: Macmillan, 1986), p. 81f.

8. Ibid., p. 47.

9. Ibid., p. 160.

10. Ibid., p. 26.

11. Ibid., p. 30.

12. Ibid., p. 47.

13. Ibid., pp. 86f.

14. Ibid., p. 108.

15. Ibid., p. 14 and n. 11

16. Ibid., pp. 11f.

17. Ibid., pp. 121f.

18. Ibid., p. 182.

19. Ibid., p. 181.

20. Ibid., p. 24.

21. Jürgen Habermas, "A Reply to My Critics," in *Habermas: Critical Debates*, ed. John B. Thompson and David Held (Cambridge, Mass.: MIT Press, 1982), pp. 219–83.

22. Pêcheux, p. 123.

23. Ibid., p. 113.

24. Ibid., p. 196.

25. Ibid., esp. pp. 31–34.

26. John Frow, *Marxism and Literary History* (Oxford: Basil Blackwell, 1986), pp. 4f.; 6; 17.

27. Ibid., pp. 50f.

28. Ibid., pp. 57; 72; 58; 83; 81.

29. Ibid., pp. 82f.; 85.

30. Ibid., pp. 102; 105.

31. Ibid., pp. 125; 169; 206.

32. Ibid., pp. 207; 209f.; 214f.

33. Ibid., pp. 221; 231f.

34. Ibid., pp. 233ff.

35. Jürgen Habermas, *The Philosophical Discourse of Modernity* (London: Polity Press, 1987), pp. 294–326; 315; 312f. Cf. Lyotard's critique of Habermas's ideal of consensus in

The Postmodern Condition. But also note that toward the end of this book Lyotard concedes his repressed goal of "justice."

36. Habermas, *The Philosophical Discourse of Modernity*, pp. 171f.; Jacques Derrida, *Speech and Phenomena* (Evanston: Northwestern University Press, 1973), p. 52.

37. Habermas, *The Philosophical Discourse of Modernity*, pp. 178f., 183.

38. Rita Felski, *Beyond Feminist Aesthetics: Feminist Literature and Social Change* (Cambridge, Mass.: Harvard University Press, 1989), p. 154.

39. Ibid., p. 161.

40. Ibid., p. 164.

41. Ibid., p. 167.

42. Ibid., p. 182.

43. Jürgen Habermas, "What Is Universal Pragmatics?" in *Communication and the Evolution of Society* (London: Heinemann, 1979), pp. 1–68.

44. Felski, esp. pp. 40ff., 62ff.

45. See Julia Kristeva, *Desire in Language: A Semiotic Approach to Literature and Art*, trans. Thomas Gora, Alice Jardin, and Leon S. Roudiez (Oxford: Basil Blackwell, 1980), and *Revolution in Poetic Language*, trans. Margaret Waller (New York: Columbia University Press, 1984). Also Luce Irigaray, *This Sex Which Is Not One*, trans. Catherine Porter (Ithaca: Cornell University Press, 1985).

Conclusion

1. Michael Riordan, *The Hunting of the Quark* (New York: Simon and Schuster, 1987).

2. Ilya Prigogine and Isabella Stengers, *Order out of Chaos: Man's New Dialogue with Nature* (London: Fontana, 1988).

3. Cf. the Nobel Prize winning research by Sidney Altman and Thomas Chech.

4. Steven W. Hawking, *A Brief History of Time: From the Big Bang to Black Holes* (London: Bantam, 1989); P. C. W. Davies, "Why Is the Universe Knowable?," in *Science and Mathematics*, ed. Ronald Mickens (London: World Scientific Publishing, 1990), pp. 14–33.

5. Saul Kripke, *Naming and Necessity* (Cambridge, Mass.: Harvard University Press, 1980), p. 136.

6. Charles Taylor, "Theory of Meaning," *Man and World* 13 (1980): 281–302; 286.

7. C. I. Lewis, "The Modes of Meaning," in *Semantics and the Philosophy of Language*, ed. Leonard Linsky (Urbana: The University of Illinois Press, 1964), pp. 50–63; 61. Cf. also Nietzsche: "the *picturing* of identical cases, of the *seemingness* of identity, is more primeval than the cognition of identity," *The Will to Power*, vol. 2, (London: George Allen and Unwin, 1924), p. 544.

8. P. F. Strawson, "On Referring," *Mind* 59 (1950): 320–44; 321ff.

9. Julia Kristeva, "The System and the Speaking Subject," in *The Tell-Tale Sign*, ed. T. A. Sebeok (Lisse, The Netherlands: Peter de Ridder, 1975), pp. 47–55.

10. Alfred Schutz, "But where is the origin or foundation of his [Husserl's] intersubjective or transsubjective validity?" "Type and Eidos in Husserl's Late Philosophy," *Philosophy and Phenomenological Research* 20 (1959): 147–65; 163. Schutz's work as a whole is a provisional answer to this question.

11. Bertrand Russell, *An Inquiry into Meaning and Truth* (London: George Allen and Unwin, 1961), pp. 108–115.

12. Jacques Lacan, *The Four Fundamental Concepts of Psychoanalysis*, trans. Alan Sheridan (New York: W. W. Norton, 1978), pp. 203–243; 281. Cf. also *Ecrits: A Selection*, trans. Alan Sheridan (New York: W. W. Norton, 1977), pp. 192–235; 164ff.

13. Wolfgang Iser, *The Implied Reader* (Baltimore: The Johns Hopkins University Press, 1975). Cf. also his *The Act of Reading* (London: Routledge and Kegan Paul, 1978), esp. pp. 30ff.

14. John Frow, "The Subject of Law," in *Social Theory and Legal Politics*, ed. Gary Wickham (Sydney: Local Consumption, 1987), pp. 68–74.

15. Jean-François Lyotard, *The Postmodern Condition: A Report on Knowledge* (Manchester: Manchester University Press, 1984), pp. 15–17; 30f.

16. Michel Foucault, *The Archaeology of Knowledge* (London: Tavistock, 1973), e.g., pp. 72f., 115f.

17. Kaja Silverman, "The Subject," in *The Subject of Semiotics* (New York: Oxford University Press, 1983), pp. 126–93; Michel Pêcheux, *Language, Semantics, Ideology*, (London: Macmillan, 1986), p. 187.

18. John Frow, *Marxist Literary Theory: System and History*, (Cambridge, Mass.: Harvard University Press, 1986), p. 151.

19. Wilhelm von Humboldt, *Werke*, ed. A. Leitzmann, vol. 7, (Berlin: Walter de Gruyter, 1968), pp. 46f.

20. Nietzsche, *The Will to Power*, esp. pp. 43ff.

21. Alfred Schutz, "Type and Eidos in Husserl's Late Philosophy," 161.

22. Charles Sanders Peirce, "What Pragmatism Is," in *Collected Papers of Charles Sanders Peirce*, vol. 5, ed. Charles Hartshorne and Paul Weiss (Cambridge, Mass.: Harvard University Press, 1974), pp. 272–92; 284.

23. J. L. Austin, *How to Do Things with Words* (Oxford: Clarendon Press, 1962).

24. Jacques Derrida, "*La forme et la vouloir-dire*," *Revue International de Philosophie* 21 (1967): 277–99. Cf. also Peter A. Facione, "Meaning and Intending," *American Philosophical Quarterly* 10 (1973): 277–87.

25. Ludwig Wittgenstein, *Philosophical Investigations*, trans. G. E. M. Anscombe (New York: Macmillan, 1953), esp. 23 and 25.

26. Foucault, pp. 52, 22.

27. Jean-François Lyotard, "The Differend, the Referend, and the Proper Name," *Diacritics* (1984): 4–14; 7.

28. Alfred Schutz, "Type and Eidos in Husserl's Late Philosophy," 152.

29. Ragner Rommeveit, *Words, Meanings and Messages, Theory and Experiments in Psycholinguistics* (New York: Academic Press, 1968), p. 185.

30. Jürgen Habermas, e.g., in "Modernity versus Postmodernity," *New German Critique* 22 (1981): 3–14; and Jean-François Lyotard, *The Postmodern Condition, passim*.

31. Cf. Derek Phillips, *Wittgenstein and Scientific Knowledge: A Sociological Perspective* (London: Macmillan, 1977).

32. Alfred Schutz, "Type and Eidos," p. 153.

33. Michael Bottner and Arnold Gunter, "An Analytical Outline of A. Schutz's Semiotics," *Semiotica* 38 (1982): 77–89; 88. Cf. also Husserl's *Cartesian Meditations* on "ego," "alter-ego," and "appresentation," Fifth Meditation.

34. Kristeva, p. 51.

35. Don Ihde, "Interpreting Hermeneutics: Origins, Developments and Prospects," *Man and World* 13 (1980): 325–43; 337.

36. Saul Kripke, *Naming and Necessity* (Cambridge, Mass.: Harvard University Press, 1980), p. 136.

37. J. N. Mohanty, *Edmund Husserl's Theory of Meaning* (The Hague: Martinus Nijhoff, 1964), p. 136.

38. John R. Searle, *Expression and Meaning: Studies in the Theories of Speech Acts* (Cambridge: Cambridge University Press, 1979), pp. 117–36. Cf. also Victor Raskin, "Literal Meaning and Speech Acts," *Theoretical Linguistics* 4 (1977): 209–225; Archibald A. Hill, "Literary Meanings—Complex or Simple," in *Studies in Descriptive and Historical Linguistics*, ed. P. J. Hopper (Amsterdam: John Benjamins, 1977), pp. 109–124; and Thomas R. Hofmann, "Varieties of Meaning," *Language Sciences* 39 (1976): 6–18.

39. Harold Bloom, "The Breaking of Form," in *Deconstruction and Criticism* (New York: Continuum, 1979), p. 9.

40. Geoffrey Hartman, *Criticism in the Wilderness: The Study of Literature Today* (New Haven: Yale University Press, 1980), p. 203.

41. Michel Foucault, *History of Sexuality* (New York: Pantheon Books, 1978), p. 100.

42. Thomas S. Kuhn, "Reflections on My Critics," in *Criticism and the Growth of Knowledge*, ed. Imre Lakatos and Alan Musgrave (Cambridge: Cambridge University Press, 1970), p. 254.

43. Frank Lentricchia, *After the New Criticism* (Chicago: The University of Chicago Press, 1980), p. 351.

44. Frederic Jameson, *The Political Unconscious* (Ithaca, N.Y.: Cornell University Press, 1981), p. 13. Cf. also Harold Bloom, "The Breaking of Form": "a strong reading is the only text, the only lie against time that endures," p. 7.

45. Martin Heidegger, "The Principle of Identity," in *Identity and Difference*, trans. Joan Stambaugh (New York: Harper and Row, 1974), pp. 23–41; 41.

46. Jean-François Lyotard, *The Postmodern Condition*, p. 11.

47. Klaus Hartmann, "Thought, Word and Picture," *Journal of the British Society for Phenomenology* 12 (1981): 14–28; 19.

48. Maurice Merleau-Ponty, *Signs*, trans. Richard C. McCleary (Evanston: Northwestern University Press, 1964), p. 85.

49. Walter Benjamin, *Illuminations* (New York: Harcourt, Brace and World, 1968), p. 149.

50. Jameson, p. 9.

51. Cf. Willard van Orman Quine, "Ontological Relativity," in *Ontological Relativity and Other Essays* (New York: Columbia University Press, 1969), pp. 26–68.

52. Rosalind Coward and John Ellis, *Language and Materialism* (London: Routledge and Kegan Paul, 1980), pp. 144f.

53. R. G. Piotrovski, *Text-Computer-Mensch*, Quantitative Linguistics, vol. 24 (Bochum: Brockmeyer, 1984), pp. 41ff.

54. Entirely without warning or reason do Richard A. Lanham and David Porush defer in their otherwise enlightening articles on the digital and cybernetics to "the heart of the Western self" in "The Electronic Word: Literary Study and the Digital Revolution," *New Literary History* 20, 2 (1989): 265–90; 288, and to the hope that "humans will preserve humaneness by way of a postmodern 'counternarrative'," in "Cybernetic Fiction and Postmodern Science," Ibid., pp. 373–396; 379.

55. Charles Sanders Peirce, *Collected Papers*, vol. 4, ed. Charles Hartshorne and Paul Weiss (Cambridge, Mass.: The Belknap Press, 1974), 4.536; 4.551. Cf. also his unpublished Harvard ms. 283:111, 117, 130.

56. For a recent discussion cf. Roger Penrose, *The Emperor's New Mind: Concerning Computers, Minds, and the Laws of Physics* (Oxford: Oxford University Press, 1990).

57. Humberto Maturana and Francisco Varela, *The Tree of Knowledge: The Biological Roots of Human Understanding* (Boston: Shambala Publications, 1989).

BIBLIOGRAPHY

Abraham, M. H. "How To Do Things with Texts." *Partisan Review* 44 (1978), 566–88.

Altieri, Charles. "Wittgenstein on Consciousness and Language: A Challenge to Derridean Theory." *Modern Language Notes* 91, 6 (1976), 1397–1423.

———. "The Hermeneutics of Literary Indeterminacy: A Dissent from the New Orthodoxy." *New Literary History* 10 (1978), 71–99.

Apel, Karl-Otto. *Analytic Philosophy of Language and the Geisteswissenschaften*. Dordrecht: Reidel, 1967.

Aristotle. *Poetics*, trans. G. F. Else. Ann Arbor: University of Michigan Press, 1973.

Audra, E., and Audrey Williams, eds. *The Poems of Alexander Pope*, vol. I., *Pastoral Poetry*. London: Methuen, 1961.

Austin, J. L. *How To Do Things with Words*. Oxford: Clarendon Press, 1962.

Ayer, A. J. *Language, Truth and Logic*. London: Gollancz, 1946.

Bar-Hillel, Y. "Husserl's Conception of a Purely Logical Grammar," in *Readings on Edmund Husserl's 'Logical Investigations'*, ed. J. N. Mohanty. The Hague: Martinus Nijhoff, 1977, pp. 128–36.

Barrett, Robert B., and Roger F. Gibson, eds. *Perspectives on Quine*. Oxford: Basil Blackwell, 1990.

Barthes, Roland. *S/Z*, trans. Richard Miller. New York: Hill and Wang, 1974.

Bayer, Roberta M. *Voyage into Creativity: A Comparative Study of the Development of the Artist*. Ph.D. Dissertation, New York University. Ann Arbor: University Microfilms, 1975.

Bellow, Saul. *The Dean's December*. New York: Simon and Schuster, 1982.

Bengsten, Gunilla. *Thomas Mann's Doctor Faustus: The Sources and the Structure of the Novel*, trans. Krishna Winston. Chicago: University of Chicago Press, 1969.

Benjamin, Walter. *Illuminations*. New York: Harcourt, Brace and World, 1968.

Bennett, C. E., ed. *Horace, The Odes and Epodes*, trans. C. E. Bennett. Cambridge, Mass.: Harvard University Press, 1968.

Bennington, Geoffrey. *Lyotard: Writing the Event*. Manchester: Manchester University Press, 1988.

Bersani, Leo. *Marcel Proust: The Fictions of Life and Art*. London: Oxford University Press, 1975.

Birch, David. *Language, Literature and Critical Practice: Ways of Analysing Text*. London: Routledge, 1989.

Black, Max. "Meaning and Intention: An Examination of Grice's Views." *New Literary History* 4 (1973), 257–79.

———. "How Metaphors Work: A Reply to Donald Davidson," in *On Metaphor*, ed. Sheldon Sacks. Chicago: University of Chicago Press, 1979, pp. 190–92.

———. "More About Metaphor," in *Metaphor and Thought*, ed. Andrew Ortony. Cambridge: Cambridge University Press, 1979, pp. 21–41.

———. "Metaphor," in *Philosophical Perspectives on Metaphor*, ed. Mark Johnson. Minneapolis: University of Minnesota Press, 1981, pp. 63–82.

Bloom, Harold. "The Ode to Autumn," in *Twentieth Century Interpretations of Keats's Odes: A Collection of Critical Essays*, ed. Jack Stillinger. Englewood Cliffs, N.J.: Prentice Hall, 1968.

———. *Poetry and Repression*. New Haven: Yale University Press, 1976.

———. "The Breaking of Form," in *Deconstruction and Criticism*. New York: Continuum, 1979.

————. *The Breaking of the Vessel*. Chicago: University of Chicago Press, 1982.

Booth, Stephen, ed. *Shakespeare's Sonnets*. New Haven: Yale University Press, 1977.

Borgmann, Albert. *The Philosophy of Language: Historical Foundations and Contemporary Issues*. The Hague: Martinus Nijhoff, 1974.

Bottcher, Michael, and Arnold Gunther. "An Analytical Outline of A. Schutz's Semiotics." *Semiotica* 38 (1982), 77–89.

Brady, Veronica. "Patrick White, *Flaws in the Glass: A Self-Portrait*." *Westerly* 27, 1 (1982), 102–109.

Bragg, Gordon M. *Principles of Experimentation and Measurement*. Englewood Cliffs, N.J.: Prentice-Hall, 1974.

Braudy, Leo. *Narrative Form in History and Fiction: Hume, Fielding and Gibbon*. Princeton: Princeton University Press, 1970.

Brock, Jarrett. "Principal Themes in Peirce's Logic of Vagueness." *Peirce Studies* 1 (1979), 41–50.

Bruss, Elizabeth W. *Autobiographical Acts: The Changing Situation of a Literary Genre*. Baltimore: The Johns Hopkins University Press, 1976.

Bullett, Gerald, ed. *John Keats's Poems*. London: Dent, 1961.

Cairns, Dorion. "The Ideality of Verbal Expressions." *Philosophy and Phenomenological Research* 1 (1941), 435–56.

Carnap, R. *Meaning and Necessity*. Chicago: Chicago University Press, 1956.

Carnegy, Patrick. *Faust as Musician: A Study of Thomas Mann's Novel Doctor Faustus*. London: Chatto and Windus, 1973.

Carroll, David. *Paraesthetics: Foucault, Lyotard, Derrida*. New York: Methuen, 1987.

Cassidy, Brendan. "Whose Law, Which Discourse?," in *Social Theory and Legal Politics*, ed. Gary Wickham. Sydney: Local Consumption, 1987, pp. 24–39.

Clack, Robert J. *Bertrand Russell's Philosophy of Language*. The Hague: Martinus Nijhoff, 1969.

Coetzee, J. M. "Newton and the Ideal of a Transparent Scientific Language." *Journal of Literary Semantics* 11 (1982), 3–13.

Cohen, Jonathan L. "Spoken and Unspoken Meanings," in *The Tell-Tale Sign: A Survey of Semiotics*, ed. T. A. Sebeok. Lisse, The Netherlands: Peter de Ridder, 1975.

Cooper, David E. *Philosophy and the Nature of Language*. London: Longman, 1973.

Coward, Rosalind, and John Ellis. *Language and Materialism*. London: Routledge and Kegan Paul, 1980.

Culler, Jonathan. *Structuralist Poetics*. London: Routledge and Kegan Paul, 1975.

————. *On Deconstruction*. London: Routledge and Kegan Paul, 1981.

————. *The Pursuit of Signs*. London: Routledge and Kegan Paul, 1981.

————. *Framing the Sign: Criticism and Its Institutions*. Oxford: Basil Blackwell, 1988.

Dasenbrock, Reed Way. *Redrawing the Lines: Analytic Philosophy, Deconstruction, and Literary Theory*. Minneapolis: University of Minnesota Press, 1989.

Davidson, Donald, "Truth and Meaning." *Synthese* 17 (1967), 304–323, and in *Inquiries into Truth and Interpretation*, pp. 17–36.

————. "Radical Interpretation." *Dialectica* 27 (1973), pp. 313–27, and in *Inquiries into Truth and Interpretation*, pp. 125–39.

————. "Belief and the Basis of Meaning." *Synthese* 27 (1974), pp. 309–323, and in *Inquiries into Truth and Interpretation*, pp. 141–54.

————. "Thought and Talk," in *Mind and Language*, ed. Samuel Guttenplan. London: Oxford University Press, 1975, and in *Inquiries into Truth and Interpretation*, pp. 155–70.

————. "Moods and Performances," in *Meaning and Use*, ed. A. Margalit. Dordrecht: Reidel, 1979, pp. 9–20, and in *Inquiries into Truth and Interpretation*, pp. 109–121.

————. "Toward a Unified Theory of Meaning and Action." *Grazer Philosophische Schriften* 2 (1980), 1–12; 7.

————. "What Metaphors Mean," in *On Metaphor*, ed. Sheldon Sacks. Chicago: Chicago University Press, 1981, pp. 29–45, and in *Inquiries into Truth and Interpretation*, pp. 245–64.

————. *Inquiries into Truth and Interpretation*. Oxford: Clarendon Press, 1984.

Davies, P. C. W. "Why Is the Universe Knowable?," in *Science and Mathematics*, ed. Ronald Mickens. London: World Scientific Publishing, 1990, pp. 14–33.

Davies, Stephen. "Truth-Values and Metaphors." *Journal of Aesthetics and Art Criticism* 42 (1984), pp. 291–302.

Deleuze, Gilles. *Nietzsche et la philosophie*. Paris: PUF, 1973.

————. *Proust and Signs*, trans. Richard Howard. London: The Penguin Press, 1973.

de Man, Paul. *Blindness and Insight*. New York: Oxford University Press, 1971.

————. "The Epistemology of Metaphor." *Critical Inquiry* 5 (1978), pp. 13–20.

————. *Allegories of Reading*. New Haven: Yale University Press, 1979.

————. "Autobiography as Defacement." *Modern Language Notes* 94 (1979), pp. 918–30.

Derrida, Jacques. "La forme et la vouloir-dire." *Revue Internationale de Philosophie* 21 (1967), 277–99.

————. *Speech and Phenomena*, trans. David B. Allison. Evanston: Northwestern University Press, 1973.

————. *Of Grammatology*, trans. Gayatri Chakravorty Spivak. Baltimore: The Johns Hopkins University Press, 1974.

————. "Limited Inc abc . . . ," in *Glyph: Johns Hopkins Textual Studies*. Baltimore: The Johns Hopkins University Press, 1977, pp. 162–254.

————. "The *Retrait* of Metaphor." *Enclitic*, 2, 2 (1978), 5–33.

————. *Writing and Difference*, trans. Alan Bass. London: Routledge and Kegan Paul, 1978.

————. *Positions*, trans. Alan Bass. Chicago: University of Chicago Press, 1981.

————. *Margins of Philosophy*, trans. Alan Bass. Chicago: University of Chicago Press, 1982.

————. "Signsponge 1," and "Signsponge 2." *Oxford Literary Review* 5 (1982), 97–112.

de Saussure, Ferdinand. *Course in General Linguistics*, trans. Wade Baskin. London: Fontana, 1974.

Devitt, Michael. "Dummett's Anti-Realism." *Journal of Philosophy* 80 (1983), 73–99; 76.

Devitt, Michael, and Kim Sterelny. *Language and Reality: An Introduction to the Philosophy of Language*. Cambridge, Mass.: MIT Press, 1987.

Dewey, John. "Peirce's Theory of Linguistic Signs, Thought, and Meaning." *Journal of Philosophy* 43 (1946), pp. 85–95.

Douglas, Ian. *Film and Meaning*, ed. Horst Ruthrof. Perth: Continuum, 1989.

Dummett, Michael. *Truth and Other Enigmas*. Cambridge, Mass.: Harvard University Press, 1978.

————. *The Interpretation of Frege's Philosophy*. Cambridge, Mass.: Harvard University Press, 1981.

Duncan, Ann J. "Imaginary Artists in 'A la recherche du temps perdu'." *The Modern Language Review* 64 (1969), 555–64.

Dunstan, Keith. *Ratbags*. Sydney: Golden Press, 1979.

Dworkin, Ronald. "Law as Interpretation." *Critical Inquiry*, 9 (1982/3), 179–200.

Eagleton, Terry. *Criticism and Ideology*. London: New Left Books, 1976.

————. *The Rape of Clarissa*. Oxford: Basil Blackwell, 1982.

————. *Literary Theory: An Introduction*. Oxford: Basil Blackwell, 1983.

Eaton, Trevor. "Literary Semantics: Modality and Style." *Journal of Literary Semantics* 7 (1978), 5–28.

Eco, Umberto. *The Role of the Reader: Explorations in the Semiotics of Texts*. Bloomington: Indiana University Press, 1979.

————. *A Theory of Semiotics*. Bloomington: Indiana University Press, 1979.

————. *Semiotics and the Philosophy of Language*. London: Macmillan, 1984.

Edie, James M. *Speaking and Meaning: The Phenomenology of Language*, Bloomington: Indiana University Press, 1976.

Elliott, Brian. *The Landscape of Australian Poetry*. Melbourne: Cheshire, 1967.

Ellmann, Richard. *The Consciousness of Joyce*. London: Faber and Faber, 1977.

Erdman, David, ed. *The Complete Poetry and Prose of William Blake*. Berkeley: University of California Press, 1982.

Evans, Gareth. *The Varieties of Reference*, ed. John McDowell. Oxford: Clarendon Press, 1982.

Evans, J. L. "On Meaning and Verification." *Mind* 62 (1953), 1–19.

Facione, Peter A. "Meaning and Intending." *American Philosophical Quarterly* 10 (1973), 277–87.

Fawcett, Robin P., and M. A. K. Halliday, *et al*. eds. *The Semiotics of Culture and Language*, vol. 2, Language and Other Semiotic Systems of Culture. London: Frances Pinter, 1984.

Felperin, Howard. *Beyond Deconstruction: The Uses and Abuses of Literary Theory*. Oxford: Clarendon Press, 1985.

Felski, Rita. *Beyond Feminist Aesthetics: Feminist Literature and Social Change*. Cambridge, Mass.: Harvard University Press, 1989.

Feyerabend, Paul. *Against Method*. London: New Left Books, 1975.

————. *Science in a Free Society*. London: New Left Books, 1978.

————. *Farewell to Reason*. London: Verso, 1987.

Feynman, Richard. *The Character of Physical Law*. Cambridge, Mass.: MIT Press, 1967.

Finch, Peter. "*Im Anfang war die Tat*," in *Perspectives on the Philosophy of Wittgenstein*, ed. Irving Block. Oxford: Basil Blackwell, 1981, pp. 159–78.

Fish, Stanley. "Working on the Chain Gang: Interpretation in the Law and in Literary Criticism," in *The Politics of Interpretation*, ed. W. J. T. Mitchell. Chicago: University of Chicago Press, 1983, pp. 271–86.

Fisher, Ronald A. *The Design of Experiments*. New York: Hafner, 1960.

Føllesdal, Dagfinn. "Husserl's Notion of Noema." *Journal of Philosophy* 66 (1969), pp. 680–87.

Foucault, Michel. *The Archaeology of Knowledge*, trans. Sheridan Smith. London: Tavistock, 1978.

————. *The History of Sexuality*, trans. Robert Hurley. New York: Pantheon, 1978.

————. "My Body, This Paper, This Fire." *Oxford Literary Review* 4 (1979), 9–28.

————. *Power, Truth, Strategy*, ed. Meagan Morris and Paul Patton. Sydney: Ferral, 1979.

————. "What Is an Author?," in *Textual Strategies*, ed. J. V. Harari. London: Methuen, 1979, pp. 141–60.

Franklin, Miles. *My Career Goes Bung*. Melbourne: Georgian House, 1946.

————. *My Brilliant Career*. Sydney: Angus and Robertson, 1974.

Frege, Gottlob. "Function and Concept," in *Translations from the Philosophical Writings of Gottlob Frege*, ed. Peter Geach and Max Black. Oxford: Basil Blackwell, 1966, pp. 21–41.

————. "On Concept and Object," in *Translations from the Philosophical Writings of Gottlob Frege*, pp. 42–55.

————. "On Sense and Reference," in *Translations from the Philosophical Writings of Gottlob Frege*, pp. 56–78.

————. "Review of Dr E. Husserl's Philosophy of Arithmetic," in *Readings on Edmund Husserl's 'Logical Investigations,'* ed. J. N. Mohanty. The Hague: Martinus Nijhoff, 1977, pp. 6–21.

Frow, John. "Discourse Genres." *Journal of Literary Semantics* 9 (1980), 73–81.

————. "The Literary Frame." *Journal of Aesthetic Education* 16 (1982), 25–30.

————. *Marxism and Literary History*. Cambridge, Mass.: Harvard University Press, 1986.

————. "The Subject of Law," in *Social Theory and Legal Politics*, ed. Gary Wickham. Sydney: Local Consumption, 1987, pp. 68–74.

Gadamer, Hans-Georg. *Truth and Method*, trans. William Glen-Doepel, ed. John Cumming and Garrett Barden. New York: Seabury Press, 1975.

Gardner, W. H., and N. H. McKenzie, eds. *The Poems of Gerard Manly Hopkins*. London: Oxford University Press, 1967.

Gasché, Rodolphe. *The Tain of the Mirror: Derrida and the Philosophy of Reflection*. Cambridge, Mass.: Harvard University Press, 1986.

Geach, P., and M. Black, eds. *Translations from the Philosophical Writings of Gottlob Frege*. Oxford: Basil Blackwell, 1966.

Gibbon, Edward. *The History of the Decline and Fall of the Roman Empire* vol. 4, ed. J. B. Bury. London: Methuen, 1925.

Gödel, Kurt. *"Über eine bisher noch nicht benützte Erweiterung des finiten Standpunktes."* *Dialectica* 12 (1958), 280–87.

————. "What Is Cantor's Continuum Problem?," in *Philosophy of Mathematics*, ed. P. Benacerraf and Hilary Putnam. Cambridge: Cambridge University Press, 1982, pp. 470–85.

————. *On Formally Undecidable Propositions of Principia Mathematica and Related Systems I*, ed. B. Meltzer, intr. R. B. Braithwaite. London: Oliver & Boyd, 1962.

Godzich, Wlad. "The Semiotics of Semiotics." *Australian Journal of Cultural Studies* 2 (1984), 3–22.

Goodman, Nelson. *Ways of Worldmaking*. Indianapolis: Hackett Publishing, 1978.

Goold, P., ed. *Ovid Metamorphoses*, vol. I., trans. Frank Justus Miller. Cambridge, Mass.: Harvard University Press, 1977.

Gray, Colin S., and Keith Payne. "Under the Nuclear Gun (1): Victory is Possible." *Foreign Policy* 39 (1980), 14–27.

Greimas, A. J., and J. Courtés. *Semiotics and Language: An Analytical Dictionary*, trans. Larry Crist, Daniel Patte, *et al*. Bloomington: Indiana University Press, 1982.

Gribbin, John. *In Search of Schrödinger's Cat: Quantum Physics and Reality*. New York: Bantam, 1984.

Grice, H. P. "Meaning." *The Philosophical Review* 66 (1957), 377–88.

————. "Utterer's Meaning and Intentions." *The Philosophical Review* 78 (1969), 147–77.

————. "Logic and Conversation," in *Syntax and Semantics, 3: Speech Acts*, ed. P. Cole and J. L. Morgan. New York: Academic Press, 1975, pp. 41–58.

————. "Presupposition and Conversational Implicature," in *Radical Pragmatics*, ed. P. Cole. New York: Academic Press, 1981, pp. 183–98.

————. "Meaning Revisited," in *Mutual Knowledge*, ed. N. Smith. London: Academic Press, 1982, pp. 223–43.

Habermas, Jürgen. *Toward a Rational Society: Student Protest, Science and Politics*, trans. J. J. Shapiro. London: Heinemann, 1971.

————. *Communication and the Evolution of Society*. London: Heinemann, 1979.

————. "Modernity versus Postmodernity." *New German Critique* 22 (1981), 3–14.

————. "A Reply to My Critics," in *Habermas: Critical Debates*, ed. John B. Thompson and David Held. Cambridge, Mass: MIT Press, 1982, pp. 219–83.

————. *The Philosophical Discourse of Modernity*. London: Polity Press, 1987.

Hacking, Ian. *Why Does Language Matter to Philosophy?* Cambridge: Cambridge University Press, 1975.

Hallett, Garth. *Wittgenstein's Definition of Meaning as Use*. New York: Fordham University Press, 1967.

Halliday, M. A. K. *Language as Social Semiotic*. London: Edward Arnold, 1978.

————. *An Introduction to Functional Grammar*. London: Edward Arnold, 1985.

————. "Language and the Order of Nature," in *The Linguistics of Writing: Arguments between Language and Literature*, ed. Nigel Fabb, Derek Attridge *et al.* Manchester: Manchester University Press, 1987, pp. 135–54.

———. "On the Ineffability of Grammatical Categories," in *Linguistics in a Systemic Perspective*, ed. James D. Benson, Michael J. Cummings, and William S. Greaves. Amsterdam: John Benjamin, 1988, pp. 27–51.

Hamann, A., and L. E. Upcott. *Lessing's Laokoon*. Oxford: Clarendon Press, 1892.

Hanson, N. R. *Patterns of Discovery*. Cambridge: Cambridge University Press, 1958.

Hart, L. A. *Essays in Jurisprudence and Philosophy*. Oxford: Clarendon Press, 1983.

Hartman, Geoffrey. *Criticism in the Wilderness: The Study of Literature Today*. New Haven: Yale University Press, 1980.

———. *Saving the Text: Literature, Derrida, Philosophy*. Baltimore: The Johns Hopkins University Press, 1981.

Hartmann, Klaus. "Thought, Word, Picture." *Journal of the British Society for Phenomenology* 12 (1981), 14–28.

Hawking, Steven W. *A Brief History of Time: From the Big Bang to Black Holes*. London: Bantam, 1989.

Heidegger, Martin. *Nietzsche*, vol. 1, Pfullingen: Neske, 1961.

———. *Being and Time*, trans. John Macquarrie and Edward Robinson. London: SCM Press, 1962.

———. "The Problem of Reason," in *The Essence of Reason*, trans. Terrence Malick. Evanston: Northwestern University Press, 1969, pp. 11–33.

———. "Language in the Poem," in *On the Way to Language*, pp. 159–98.

———. "The Way to Language," in *On the Way to Language*, trans. Peter D. Hertz. New York: Harper and Row, 1971, pp. 111–36.

———. *The Question Concerning Technology and Other Essays*. New York: Garland, 1977.

———. "The Principle of Identity," in *Identity and Difference*, trans. Joan Stambaugh. New York: Harper and Row, 1974, pp. 23–41.

———. "Language," in *Poetry, Language, Thought*, pp. 189–210.

———. "The Origin of the Work of Art," in *Poetry, Language, Thought*, ed. and trans. Albert Hofstadter. New York: Harper and Row, 1975, pp. 15–87.

Hill, Archibald A. "Literary Meanings—Complex or Simple," in *Studies in Descriptive and Historical Linguistics*, ed. J. P. Hopper. Amsterdam: John Benjamins, 1977, pp. 109–124.

Hirsch, E. D. *Validity in Interpretation*. New Haven: Yale University Press, 1971.

———. *The Aims of Interpretation*. Chicago: University of Chicago Press, 1976.

———. *The Philosophy of Composition*. Chicago: University of Chicago Press, 1977.

Hjelmslev, Louis. *Language: An Introduction*, trans. Francis J. Whitfield. Madison: University of Wisconsin Press, 1970.

Hodge, Robert, and Gunther Kress. *Language as Ideology*. London: Routledge and Kegan Paul, 1979.

———. *Social Semiotics*. London: Polity Press, 1988.

Hofmann, Thomas R. "Varieties of Meaning." *Language Sciences* 39 (1976), 6–18.

Hollis, Martin, and Steven Lukes, eds. *Rationality and Relativism*. Oxford: Basil Blackwell, 1982.

Hope, A. D. *Collected Poems*. Sydney: Angus and Robertson, 1977.

Hughes, G. E., and M. J. Cresswell. *An Introduction to Modal Logic*. London: Methuen, 1968.

Husserl, Edmund. *Logische Untersuchungen*, 2 vols. Halle: Max Niemeyer, 1922.

———. *Erfahrung und Urteil: Untersuchungen zur Genealogie der Logik*, ed. Ludwig Landgrebe. Hamburg: Claasen, 1964.

———. *Formal and Transcendental Logic*, trans. Dorion Cairns. The Hague: Martinus Nijhoff, 1969.

———. *Ideas, General Introduction to Pure Phenomenology*, trans. W. R. Boyce Gibson. London: Collier-Macmillan, 1969.

———. *Logical Investigations*, vol. 1, trans. J. N. Finlay. London: Routledge and Kegan Paul, 1970.

———. "Zur Logik der Zeichen (Semiotik)," in *Gesammelte Werke* vol. 12, ed. Lothar Eley, in *Husserliana*, vol. 12. The Hague: Martinus Nijhoff, 1970, pp. 340–73.

———. *Cartesian Meditations: An Introduction to Phenomenology*, trans. Dorion Cairns. The Hague: Martinus Nijhoff, 1973.

———. *Experience and Judgment: Investigations in a Genealogy of Logic*, rev. and ed. Ludwig Landgrebe, trans. James S. Churchill and Karl Ameriks. London: Routledge and Kegan Paul, 1973.

Ihde, Don. *Hermeneutic Phenomenology: The Philosophy of Paul Ricoeur*. Evanston: Northwestern University Press, 1971.

———. "Interpreting Hermeneutics: Origins, Developments and Prospects." *Man and World* 13 (1980), 325–43.

Ihde, Don, ed. *Interdisciplinary Phenomenology*. The Hague: Martinus Nijhoff, 1977.

Ihde, Don and Richard M. Zaner, eds. *Dialogues in Phenomenology*. The Hague: Martinus Nijhoff, 1975.

Ingarden, Roman. *The Cognition of the Literary Work of Art*. Evanston: Northwestern University Press, 1973.

———. *The Literary Work of Art*. Evanston: Northwestern University Press, 1973.

Innis, Robert E. *Semiotics: An Introductory Reader*. London: Hutchinson, 1986.

Irigaray, Luce. *This Sex Which Is Not One*, trans. Catherine Porter. Ithaca: Cornell University Press, 1985.

Iser, Wolfgang. *The Implied Reader*. Baltimore: The Johns Hopkins University Press, 1975.

———. *The Act of Reading*. London: Routledge and Kegan Paul, 1979.

Jakobson, Roman. *Language in Literature*, ed. Krystyna Pomorska and Stephen Rudy. Cambridge, Mass.: Belknap Press, 1987.

Jameson, Frederic. *The Political Unconscious*. Ithaca: Cornell University Press, 1981.

Jauss, Hans Robert. *Question and Answer: Forms of Dialogic Understanding*, trans. Michael Hays. Minneapolis: University of Minnesota Press, 1989.

Johnson, Colin (Mudrooroo Narogin). *Wild Cat Falling*. Sydney: Angus and Robertson, 1965.

———. *Long Live Sandawara*. Melbourne: Quartet Books, 1979.

———. *Doctor Wooreddy's Prescription for Enduring the Ending of the World*. Melbourne: Hyland House, 1983.

———. "White Forms, Aboriginal Content," in *Aboriginal Writing Today*, ed. Bob Hodge. Canberra: Australian Institute of Aboriginal Studies, 1985.

———. "Guerilla Poetry: Lionel Fogarty's Response to Language Genocide," in *Long Water: Aboriginal Art and Literature*. Bathurst: Robert Brown, 1986.

———. "Sunlight Spreadeagles Perth in Blackness: A Bicentennial Gift Poem." [abbreviated] *New Literatures Review* 17 (1989), 50–68.

———. *Writing the Fringe: A Study of Aboriginal Literature in Australia*. Melbourne: Hyland House, 1990.

Kahler, Erich. *The Orbit of Thomas Mann*. Princeton: Princeton University Press, 1969.

Kalaga, Wojciech. "Indeterminacy in the Literary Work." *Les Problèmes des Genres Littéraires* 26 (1985), 59–75.

———. "The Concept of Interpretant in Literary Semiotics." *Transactions of the Charles S. Peirce Society* 22, 1 (1986), 43–59.

Kant, Immanuel. *Critique of Pure Reason*, trans. Norman Kemp Smith. London: Macmillan, 1973.

Kendon, Adam, ed. *Nonverbal Communication, Interaction, and Gesture: Selections from Semiotica*. The Hague: Mouton, 1981.

King, David. *From Gödel to Derrida: Undecidability, Indeterminacy, and Infinity*. Ph.D. Dissertation, Murdoch University (in preparation).

Koneya, Mele. "Unresolved Issues in Non-verbal Communication." *Semiotics* 37 (1981), 1–13.

Kripke, Saul. "Naming and Necessity," in *Semantics of Natural Language*, ed. G. Harman and D. Davidson. Dordrecht: Reidel, 1972, pp. 253–355.

———. *Naming and Necessity*. Cambridge, Mass.: Harvard University Press, 1980.

Kristeva, Julia. "The System and the Speaking Subject," in *The Tell-Tale Sign: A Survey of Semiotics*, ed. T. A. Sebeok. Lisse, the Netherlands: Peter de Ridder, 1975, pp. 47–55.

———. *Desire in Language: A Semiotic Approach to Literature and Art*, trans. Thomas Gora, Alice Jardin, and Leon S. Roudiez. Oxford: Basil Blackwell, 1980.

———. *Revolution in Poetic Language*, trans. Margaret Waller. New York: Columbia University Press, 1984.

Kuhn, Thomas S. "Reflections on My Critics," in *Criticism and the Growth of Knowledge*, ed. Imre Lakatos and Alan Musgrave. Cambridge: Cambridge University Press, 1970.

Küng, Guido. "The World as Noema and as Referent." *The Journal of the British Society for Phenomenology* 3 (1972), 15–26

Kupperman, Joel, and Arthur S. McGrade. *Fundamentals of Logic*. New York: Doubleday, 1966.

LaCapra, Dominick. *History and Criticism*. Ithaca: Cornell University Press, 1985.

Lakoff, George, and Mark Johnson. "Conceptual Metaphor in Everyday Language." *The Journal of Philosophy* 77 (1980), 453–86.

Landesman, Charles. *Discourse and its Presuppositions*. New Haven: Yale University Press, 1972.

Lanham, Richard A. "The Electronic Word: Literary Study and the Digital Revolution." *New Literary History* 20, 2 (1989), 265–90.

Leibniz, Gottfried Wilhelm. "The Monadology," in *Leibniz: Philosophical Writings*, trans. Mary Morris and G. H. R. Parkinson. London: Dent, 1934, pp. 179–94.

Lentricchia, Frank. *After the New Criticism*. Chicago: University of Chicago Press, 1980.

Lévi-Strauss, Claude. *L'Homme Nu*. Paris: Plon, 1971.

———. "The Structural Study of Myth," in *Structural Anthropology*. Harmondsworth: Penguin, 1977, pp. 206–231.

———. *Myth and Meaning*. New York: Schocken Books, 1979.

Lewis, C. I. "The Modes of Meaning," in *Semantics and the Philosophy of Language*, ed. Leonard Linsky. Urbana: University of Illinois Press, 1964, pp. 50–63.

Liszka, James Jakob. "Peirce's Interpretant." *Transactions of the Charles S. Peirce Society* 26, 1 (1990), 17–62.

Lucid, Daniel P., ed. *Soviet Semiotics*. Baltimore: The Johns Hopkins University Press, 1977.

Lukács, Georg. *Essays on Thomas Mann*, trans. Stanley Mitchell. London: Merlin Press, 1964.

Lyons, J. *Semantics*, 2 vols. London: Cambridge University Press, 1977.

———. *Language and Linguistics: An Introduction*. Cambridge: Cambridge University Press, 1981.

———. *Language, Meaning and Context*. London: Fontana, 1981.

Lyotard, Jean-François. *Discours, Figure*. Paris: Klincksieck, 1978.

———. *Just Gaming*. Minneapolis: University of Minnesota Press, 1985.

———. "The Differend, the Referent, and the Proper Name." *Diacritics* (1984), 4–14.

———. *The Postmodern Condition: A Report on Knowledge* vol. 10, Theory and History of Literature, ed. Wlad Godzich and Jochen Schulte-Sasse. Manchester: Manchester University Press, 1984.

———. *The Differend: Phrases in Dispute*. Manchester: Manchester University Press, 1988.

McGinn, Colin. *Wittgenstein on Meaning*. Oxford: Basil Blackwell, 1984.

Mach, Ernst. "The Economical Nature of Physical Inquiry," in *Popular Scientific Lectures*. Chicago: Open Court Publishing Company 1895, pp. 197–98.

MacKay, Alfred F. "Professor Grice's Theory of Meaning." *Mind* 81 (1972), 57–66.

Maclean, Marie. *Narrative as Performance: The Baudelairean Experiment*. London: Routledge, 1988.

Malpas, J. E. "Shanks, King-Farlow, and the Refutation of Davidson." *Idealistic Studies* 18 (1988), 20–31.

Malpas, J. E. *Agreement and Interpretation*. Ph.D. Dissertation, Australian National University, 1986.

Mann, Thomas. *The Genesis of a Novel*, trans. Richard and Clara Winston. London: Secker and Warburg, 1961.

———. *Doctor Faustus*. Harmondsworth: Penguin, 1968.

Margolis, Joseph. "Robust Relativism." *The Journal of Aesthetics and Art Criticism* 35 (1976), 37–46.

Marler, Peter. "Visual Systems," in *Animal Communication: Techniques of Study and Results of Research*, ed. Thomas A. Sebeok. Bloomington: Indiana University Press, 1968, pp. 103–126.

Maturana, Humberto, and Francisco Varela. *The Tree of Knowledge: The Biological Roots of Human Understanding*. Boston: Shambala Publications, 1989.

McHoul, A. W. *Telling How Texts Talk: Essays on Reading and Ethnomethodology*. London: Routledge and Kegan Paul, 1982.

McHoul, A. W., and David Wills. *Writing Pynchon: Strategies in Fictional Analysis*. Basingstoke: Macmillan, 1990.

Merleau-Ponty, Maurice. *Signs*, trans. Richard C. McCleary. Evanston: Northwestern University Press, 1964.

Meyers, C. M. "The Determinate and Determinable Modes of Appearing." *Mind* 67 (1958), 32–49.

Miall, David S., ed. *Metaphor: Problems and Perspectives*. Sussex: Harvester Press, 1982.

Michalos, Alex C. *Principles of Logic*. Englewood Cliffs, N.J.: Prentice-Hall, 1969.

Miller, J. Hillis. *Fiction and Repetition: Seven English Novels*. Cambridge, Mass.: Harvard University Press, 1982.

Mitchell, Adrian. "Eventually, White's Language: Words, and More Than Words," in *Patrick White: A Critical Symposium*, ed. R. Shepherd and K. Singh. Adelaide: CRNLE, 1978, pp. 5–16.

Mitchell, W. J. T. *The Politics of Interpretation*. Chicago: University of Chicago Press, 1983.

Mohanty, J. N. *Edmund Husserl's Theory of Meaning*. The Hague: Martinus Nijhoff, 1964.

———. "Intentionality and Noema." *Journal of Philosophy* 78, 11 (1981), 706–717.

Moore, F. T. C. "On Taking Metaphors Literally," in *Metaphor: Problems and Perspectives*, ed. David S. Miall. Sussex: Harvester Press, 1982, pp. 1–13.

Morley, Patricia A. *The Mystery of Unity*. Toronto: Bryant Press, 1972.

Muller, Marcel. *Les voix narratives dans la "Recherche du temps perdu"*. Geneva: Droz, 1965.

Mulligan, Kevin. "Inscriptions and Speaking's Place: Derrida and Wittgenstein." *The Oxford Literary Review* 8 (1978), 62–67.

Nagel, Thomas. *The View from Nowhere*. Oxford: Clarendon Press, 1986, p. 91.

Natanson, Maurice. *Edmund Husserl*. Evanston: Northwestern University Press, 1973.

———. "Erwin Straus and Alfred Schutz." *Philosophy and Phenomenological Research* 42 (1982), 335–42.

Newton-Smith, W. "Relativism and the Possibility of Interpretation," in *Rationality and Relativism*, ed. Martin Hollis and Steven Lukes. Oxford: Basil Blackwell, 1982, pp. 106–122; 119.

Nietzsche, Friedrich. *The Will to Power: An Attempted Transvaluation of All Values*, trans. Anthoni M. Ludovici, vol. 2, London: George Allen and Unwin, 1924.

———. "On Truth and Falsity in Their Ultramoral Sense," in *The Complete Works of*

Friedrich Nietzsche, vol. 2, ed. Oscar Levy, trans. M. A. Mügge. London: Allen and Unwin, 1911, pp. 171–92.

Norris, Christopher. *The Contest of Faculties: Philosophy and Theory after Deconstruction*. London: Methuen, 1985.

Novitz, David. *Knowledge, Fiction and Imagination*. Philadelphia: Temple University Press, 1987.

O'Brien, Darcy. *The Conscience of James Joyce*. Princeton: Princeton University Press, 1968.

O'Toole, Michael. "Semiotic Systems in Painting and Poetry," in *A Festschrift for Dennis Ward*, ed. M. Falchhikov, C. Pike, and R. Russell. Nottingham: Astra Press, 1989.

———. "A Systematic Semiotics of Art," in *Discourse in Society: Functional Perspectives*, ed. P. Fries and M. Gregory. Norwood, N.J.: Ablex, 1991.

———. "A Functional Semiotics of the Visual Arts," in *Essays in Cultural Studies*, ed. J. Andrew and C. Pike (in press).

———. *A Semiotics of Art* (forthcoming).

———. "A Semiotics of Painting and Architecture." *Semiotica* (in press).

Paris, Jeff, and Harrington, Leo. "A Mathematical Incompleteness In Peano Arithmetic," in *Handbook of Mathematical Logic*, ed. Jon Barwise. Amsterdam: North-Holland, 1977, pp. 1134–42.

Patterson, Charles I. *The Daemonic in the Poetry of John Keats*. Urbana: University of Illinois Press, 1970.

Pavel, Thomas G. *Fictional Worlds*. Cambridge, Mass.: Harvard University Press, 1986.

Pêcheux, Michel. *Language, Semantics and Ideology*. London: Macmillan, 1986.

Peirce, Charles Sanders. *Collected Papers*, vols. 7 and 8, Science and Philosophy, ed. Arthur W. Burks. Cambridge, Mass.: Harvard University Press, 1958.

———. *Collected Papers*, vols 1 to 6, ed. Charles Hartshorne and Paul Weiss. Cambridge, Mass.: Harvard University Press, 1974.

———. *Unpublished Manuscript*, Harvard University.

Penrose, Roger. *The Emperor's New Mind*. Oxford: Oxford University Press, 1990.

Phillips, Derek L. *Wittgenstein and Scientific Knowledge: A Sociological Perspective*. London: Macmillan, 1977.

Pilling, John. *Autobiography and Imagination: Studies in Self-Scrutiny*. London: Routledge and Kegan Paul, 1981.

Plato. *The Last Days of Socrates*. Harmondsworth: Penguin, 1984.

Platts, Mark. *Ways of Meaning*. London: Routledge and Kegan Paul, 1979.

Popper, Karl. "Epistemology without a Knowing Subject," in *Objective Knowledge: An Evolutionary Approach*. Oxford: Oxford University Press, 1972.

———. *The Logic of Scientific Discovery* (1934). London: Hutchinson, 1975.

Porush, David. "Cybernetic Fiction and Postmodern Science." *New Literary History* 20, 2 (1989), 373–96.

Poyates, Fernando. *New Perspectives in Nonverbal Communication*. New York: Pergamon Press, 1982.

Pratt, Louise. "Ideology and Speech-Act Theory." *Poetics Today* 7, 1 (1986), 59–71.

Prigogine, Ilya, and Isabella Stengers. *Order out of Chaos: Man's New Dialogue with Nature*. London: Fontana, 1988.

Proust, Marcel. *A la recherche du temps perdu, v. III. Les temps retrouvé*, trans. Scott Moncrieff and Terence Kilmartin. London: Chatto and Windus, 1981.

Putnam, Hilary. *Reason, Truth and History*. Cambridge: Cambridge University Press, 1983.

Quine, Willard van Orman. *Word and Object*. Cambridge, Mass.: MIT Press, 1964.

———. "Ontological Relativity," in *Ontological Relativity and Other Essays*. New York: Columbia University Press, 1969, pp. 26–68.

Quine, Willard van Orman, and J. S. Ullian. *The Web of Belief*. New York: Random House, 1970.

Ray, William. *Literary Meaning: From Phenomenology to Deconstruction*. Oxford: Basil Blackwell, 1984.

Redford, Grant H. "The Role of Structure in Joyce's 'Portrait'." *Modern Fiction Studies* 4 (1958), 21–30.

Reed, T. J. *Thomas Mann: The Uses of Tradition*. Oxford: Clarendon Press, 1966.

Ricoeur, Paul. *The Rule of Metaphor*, trans. Robert Cerny. London: Routledge and Kegan Paul, 1978.

———. *Hermeneutics and the Human Sciences*. Cambridge: Cambridge University Press, 1981.

Riordan, Richard. *The Hunting of the Quark*. New York: Simon and Schuster, 1987.

Rommnetveit, Ragnar. *Words, Meanings and Messages: Theory and Experiments in Psycholinguistics*. New York: Academic Press, 1968.

Rorty, Richard, "The World Well Lost." *Journal of Philosophy* 69 (1972), 649–65.

———. *Philosophy and the Mirror of Nature*. Oxford: Basil Blackwell, 1980.

———. *Consequences of Pragmatism*. Minneapolis: University of Minnesota Press, 1982.

Russell, Bertrand. *The Analysis of Mind*. London: George Allen and Unwin, 1921.

———. "Vagueness." *The Australian Journal of Psychology and Philosophy* 1 (June 1923), 84–92.

———. *Human Knowledge: Its Scope and Limits*. New York: Simon and Schuster, 1948.

———. "Logical Positivism." *Revue internationale de philosophie* 4 (1950), 3–19.

———. "Mr. Strawson on Referring." *Mind* 66 (1957), 385–89.

———. *An Inquiry into Meaning and Truth*. London: George Allen and Unwin, 1961.

———. *The Problems of Philosophy*. Oxford: Oxford University Press, 1912.

———. "On Denoting," in *Essays in Analysis*, ed. Douglas Lackey. New York: George Braziller, 1973, 103–119.

———. *Essays on Language, Mind and Matter*, ed. John G. Slater. London: Unwin Hyman, 1988.

Russell, Bertrand, and Alfred North Whitehead. *Principia Mathematica*, vol. 1., Cambridge: Attlee University Press, 1963.

Ruthrof, Horst. *The Reader's Constructions of Narrative*. London: Routledge and Kegan Paul, 1981.

———. "Text and the Construction of Meaning: A Phenomenological Approach." *Southern Review* 16 (1983), 110–20.

———. "The Problem of Inferred Modality in Narrative." *Journal of Literary Semantics* 13 (1984), 97–108.

———. "Literature and the Ladder of Discourse." *Analecta Husserliana* 19 (1985), 413–31.

———. "The Infrastructures of Deconstruction: Gasché's *The Tain of the Mirror*." *Southern Review* 21 (1988), 203–210.

———. "Identity and Differance." *Poetics* 17 (1988), 99–112.

———. "Narrative and the Digital: On the Syntax of the Postmodern." *Narrative Issues*, Special issue of the AUMLA (1990), 185–200.

———. "The Two Paradigms: Is a Dialogue Possible?" in *On Literary Theory and Philosophy: A Cross-Disciplinary Encounter*, ed. Richard Freadman and Lloyd Reinhardt. London: Macmillan, 1991, pp. 213–34.

———. "Towards an Intersemiotic Theory of Meaning" (forthcoming).

Ryle, Gilbert. "The Theory of Meaning," in *British Philosophy in the Mid-Century*, ed. C. A. Mace. London: George Allen and Unwin Limited, 1957, pp. 239–64.

———. "Rudolf Carnap: *Meaning and Necessity*." *Philosophy* 24 (1949), 69–76.

Sacks, Sheldon, ed. *On Metaphor*. Chicago: University of Chicago Press, 1981.

Said, Edward. "The Problem of Textuality: Two Exemplary Positions." *Critical Inquiry* 4 (1978), 673–714.

Schatzki, Theodor R. "The Prescription Is Description: Wittgenstein's View of the Human

Sciences," in *The Need for Interpretation*, ed. S. Mitchell and Michael Rosen. London: Athlone Press, 1983, pp. 118–40.

Schiffer, Stephen R. *Meaning*. Oxford: Clarendon Press, 1972.

Schlick, Moritz. "Meaning and Verification." *Philosophical Review* 45 (1936), 339–69.

Schutz, Alfred. "Type and Eidos in Husserl's Late Philosophy." *Philosophy and Phenomenological Research* 20 (1959), 147–65.

——. *The Phenomenology of the Social World*, trans. George Welsh and Frederick Lehnert. Evanston: Northwestern University Press, 1967.

——. *Reflections on the Problem of Relevance*. New Haven: Yale University Press, 1970.

Schutz, Alfred, and Thomas Luckmann. *The Structures of the Life-World*, trans. Richard A. Zaner and H. Tristram Engelhardt, Jr.. Evanston: Northwestern University Press, 1973.

Searle, John R. "The Logical Status of Fictional Discourse." *New Literary History* 6 (1975), 319–32.

——. "A Classification of Illocutionary Acts." *Language in Society* 5 (1976), 1–23.

——. *Speech Acts: An Essay in the Philosophy of Language*. London: Cambridge University Press, 1977.

——. *Expression and Meaning: Studies in the Theories of Speech Acts*. Cambridge: Cambridge University Press, 1979.

——. "The Background of Meaning," in *Speech Act Theory and Pragmatics*, ed. John R. Searle, Ferenc Kiefer, and Manfred Bierwisch. Dordrecht: Reidel, 1980, pp. 221–32.

——. *Intentionality: An Essay in the Philosophy of Mind*. Cambridge: Cambridge University Press, 1983.

Sebeok, Thomas A. "Zoosemiotic Components of Human Communication," in *Semiotics: An Introductory Reader*, ed. Robert E. Innis. London: Hutchison, 1986, pp. 294–324.

Sebeok, Thomas A., ed. *Animal Communication: Techniques of Study and Results of Research*. Bloomington: Indiana University Press, 1968.

——. *The Tell-Tale Sign*. Lisse, the Netherlands: Paul de Ridder, 1975.

——. *A Perfusion of Signs*. Bloomington: Indiana University Press, 1977.

Shakespeare, William. *Measure for Measure*, ed. R. E. C. Houghton. Oxford: Clarendon Press, 1970.

Shirer, William L. *The Rise and Fall of the Third Reich: A History of Nazi Germany*. New York: Simon and Schuster, 1960.

Shukman, Ann. *Literature and Semiotics: A Study of the Writings of Yu. M. Lotman*. Amsterdam: North-Holland, 1977.

Silverman, Kaja. "The Subject," in *The Subject of Semiotics*. New York: Oxford University Press, 1983.

Spenser, Edmund. *The Faerie Queene*, ed. Thomas P. Roche. Harmondsworth: Penguin, 1983.

Splitter, Randolph. *Proust's "Recherche": A Psychoanalytic Interpretation*. Boston: Routledge and Kegan Paul, 1981.

Stambolian, George. *Marcel Proust and the Creative Encounter*. Chicago: University of Chicago Press, 1972.

Stampe, Dennis W. "Toward a Grammar of Meaning." *Philosophical Review* 77 (1968), 137–74.

Stanzel, Franz. *Narrative Situations in the Novel*. Bloomington: Indiana University Press, 1971.

Staten, Henry. *Wittgenstein and Derrida*. Oxford: Basil Blackwell, 1985.

Stern, J. P. *Hitler: The Führer and the People*. London: Fontana, 1975.

Strawson, P. F. "On Referring." *Mind* 59 (1950), 320–44.

——. "Intention and Convention in Speech Acts." *The Philosophical Review* 73 (1964), 439–60.

———. *Logico-Linguistic Papers*. London: Methuen, 1971.

———. *Individuals*. London: Methuen, 1987.

Tarski, A. *Logic, Semantics, Metamathematics*, trans. J. H. Woodger. Oxford: Clarendon Press, 1956.

Taylor, Charles. "Theories of Meaning." *Man and World* 13 (1980), 281–302.

Thiel, Christian. *Sense and Reference in Frege's Logic*. Dordrecht: Reidel, 1968.

Turnell, Martin. *Baudelaire: A Study of His Poetry*. New York: New Directions, 1953.

van Humboldt, Wilhelm. *Werke*, ed. A. Flitner and K. Giel. Stuttgart: Cotta, 1963.

Virgil. *Georgics*, trans. Smith Palmer Bovie. Chicago: University of Chicago Press, 1956.

Voloshinov, V. N. *Marxism and the Philosophy of Language*. New York: Seminar Press, 1973.

———. *Freudianism: A Marxist Critique*. New York: Academic Press, 1976.

Wandruszka, Mario. *Interlinguistik: Umrisse einer neuen Sprachwissenschaft*. Munich: Piper, 1971.

Ward, Aileen. *John Keats: The Making of a Poet*. New York: The Viking Press, 1963.

Watson-Williams, Helen. "Land into Literature: The Western Australian Bush Seen by Some Early Writers and D. H. Lawrence." *Westerly* 25 (1980), 59–72.

Welsh-Ovcharov, Boogomila, ed. *Van Gogh in Perspective*. Englewood Cliffs, N.J.: Prentice-Hall, 1974.

White, Hayden V. *Metahistory*. Baltimore: The Johns Hopkins University Press, 1973.

———. *Tropics of Discourse*. Baltimore: The Johns Hopkins University Press, 1978.

White, Patrick. *The Vivisector*. Harmondsworth: Penguin, 1977.

———. *Flaws in the Glass: A Self-Portrait*. London: Jonathan Cape, 1981.

Whitehead, Alfred North. *Adventures of Ideas*. New York: Macmillan, 1943.

———. *Science and the Modern World*. New York: The Free Press, 1967.

———. *Process and Reality: An Essay in Cosmology*. New York: The Free Press, 1969.

Wickham, Gary, ed. *Social Theory and Legal Politics*. Sydney: Local Consumption, 1987.

Wienpahl, P. D. "Frege's Sinn und Bedeutung." *Mind* 59 (1950), 483–94.

Wittgenstein, Ludwig. *Philosophical Investigations*, trans. G. E. M. Anscombe. New York: Macmillan, 1953.

———. *The Blue and Brown Books*. Oxford: Basil Blackwell, 1960.

———. *Tractatus Logico-Philosophicus*, trans. D. F. Pears and B. F. McGuiness, intr. Bertrand Russell. London: Routledge and Kegan Paul, 1963.

———. *Zettel*, ed. G. E. M. Anscombe and G. H. von Wright. Oxford: Basil Blackwell, 1967.

———. *On Certainty*, ed. G. E. M. Anscombe and H. G. von Wright, trans. Denis Paul and G. E. M. Anscombe. Oxford: Basil Blackwell, 1969.

———. "Cause and Effect in Intuitive Awareness," ed. and trans. Peter Winch. *Philosophia* 6, 3–4 (Sept.–Dec. 1976).

———. *Lectures on the Foundations of Mathematics* (Cambridge, 1939). Hassocks, Sussex: Harvester Press, 1976.

———. *Vermischte Bemerkungen*, ed. George Henrick von Wright and Heikki Nyman. Oxford: Basil Blackwell, 1977.

———. *Remarks on Frazer's Golden Bough*, ed. Rush Rhees. Retford: Brynbwill Press, 1979.

Yeats, W. B. *Collected Poems*. London: Macmillan, 1969.

Young, Hugh D. *Statistical Treatment of Experimental Data*. New York: McGraw-Hill, 1962.

Zadeh, Lofti Asker. "Quantitative Fuzzy Semantics." *Information Sciences* 3, 2 (1971), 159–76.

Zeman, J. Jay. "Peirce's Theory of Signs," in *A Perfusion of Signs*, ed. Thomas A. Sebeok, pp. 22–39.

———. "The Esthetic Sign in Peirce's Semiotic." *Semiotica* 19 (1970), 241–58.

Ziff, Paul. "On H. P. Grice's Account of Meaning." *Analysis* 28 (1967), 1–8.

INDEX

HORST RUTHROF teaches English and comparative literature at Murdoch University in Perth, Western Australia. He has published in literary, linguistic and philosophical journals, edited two books, and is the author of *The Reader's Construction of Narrative*.